Communications
in Computer and Information Science   1322

More information about this series at http://www.springer.com/series/7899

Chawki Djeddi · Yousri Kessentini ·
Imran Siddiqi · Mohamed Jmaiel (Eds.)

Pattern Recognition and Artificial Intelligence

4th Mediterranean Conference, MedPRAI 2020
Hammamet, Tunisia, December 20–22, 2020
Proceedings

Springer

Editors
Chawki Djeddi (iD)
Larbi Tebessi University
Tebessa, Algeria

Yousri Kessentini (iD)
Digital Research Center of Sfax
Sfax, Tunisia

Imran Siddiqi
Bahria University
Islamabad, Pakistan

Mohamed Jmaiel
Digital Research Centre of Sfax
Sfax, Tunisia

ISSN 1865-0929   ISSN 1865-0937 (electronic)
Communications in Computer and Information Science
ISBN 978-3-030-71803-9   ISBN 978-3-030-71804-6 (eBook)
https://doi.org/10.1007/978-3-030-71804-6

This Springer imprint is published by the registered company Springer Nature Switzerland AG
The registered company address is: Gewerbestrasse 11, 6330 Cham, Switzerland

Preface

It gives us immense pleasure to introduce this volume of proceedings for the 4th Mediterranean Conference on Pattern Recognition and Artificial Intelligence (Med-PRAI 2020). The conference was organized by the Digital Research Center of Sfax (CRNS), Sfax, Tunisia, on December 20–22, 2020. The conference aimed to provide researchers and practitioners from academia and industry with a forum on the latest developments in pattern recognition and artificial intelligence.

We are pleased to share that the response to the Call for Papers for MedPRAI 2020 was very encouraging. A total of 72 papers covering different themes in pattern recognition and artificial intelligence were submitted to the conference. These papers were reviewed by renowned researchers in the respective fields from all over the world. After a thorough and competitive paper review and selection process, 27 high-quality papers were accepted for presentation at the conference, yielding an acceptance rate of 37%. This volume comprises 24 papers which eventually qualified for presentation in the conference.

We would like to take this opportunity to thank the reviewers for their time and efforts in reviewing the papers and providing constructive feedback to the authors. We are also thankful to the keynote speakers, the authors and the participants of the conference. We would also like to extend our cordial appreciation to all members of the organizing committees for their untiring efforts in making this event a success.

We thank all the attendees for participation in the conference and hope that the event provided valuable knowledge-sharing and networking opportunities.

December 2020

Chawki Djeddi
Yousri Kessentini
Imran Siddiqi
Mohamed Jmaiel

The original version of the book was revised: The affiliations of the first two volume editors were corrected. The correction to the book is available at
https://doi.org/10.1007/978-3-030-71804-6_25

Organization

General Chairs

Chawki Djeddi	Larbi Tebessi University, Algeria
Mohamed Jmaiel	Digital Research Center of Sfax, Tunisia

Program Committee Chairs

Yousri Kessentini	Digital Research Center of Sfax, Tunisia
Imran Siddiqi	Bahria University, Pakistan

Steering Committee

Javad Sadri	Concordia University, Canada
Akhtar Jamil	Istanbul Sabahattin Zaim University, Turkey
Abdel Ennaji	University of Rouen, France
Ameur Bensefia	Higher Colleges of Technology, Abu Dhabi, UAE
Haikal El Abed	TTC, German International Cooperation, Lebanon
M. El Youssfi El Kettani	Ibn Tofail University, Morocco

International Liaison Chairs

Hamid Laga	Murdoch University, Australia
Benjamin Rosman	University of the Witwatersrand, South Africa
Bernd Freisleben	University of Marburg, Germany
Alicia Fornés	Computer Vision Center, Spain
Rostom Kachouri	ESIEE Paris, France
Mohamed Abid	ENIS Sfax, Tunisia

Local Arrangements Committee

Sourour Ammar	Digital Research Center of Sfax, Tunisia
Ahmed Cheikh Rouhou	Digital Research Center of Sfax, Tunisia
Tayeb Benzenati	Digital Research Center of Sfax, Tunisia
Mahmoud Ghorbel	Digital Research Center of Sfax, Tunisia
Marwa Dhief	Digital Research Center of Sfax, Tunisia
Ines Feki	Digital Research Center of Sfax, Tunisia
Ilef Ben Slima	Digital Research Center of Sfax, Tunisia
Sana Khamekhem Jemni	University of Sfax, Tunisia

Publicity Committee

Benjamin Rosman	University of the Witwatersrand, South Africa
Moises Diaz	Universidad de Las Palmas de Gran Canaria, Spain
Jawad Rasheed	Istanbul Sabahattin Zaim University, Turkey
Akhtar Jamil	Istanbul Sabahattin Zaim University, Turkey
Sobhan Sarkar	University of Edinburgh, UK

Program Committee

Abdallah Meraoumia	Larbi Tebessi University, Algeria
Sergey Ablameyko	Belarusian State University, Belarus
Hammad Afzal	NUST, Pakistan
Somaya Al-maadeed	Qatar University, Qatar
Marco Anisetti	Università degli Studi di Milano, Italy
Paulo Batista	University of Évora, Portugal
Ameur Bensefia	Higher Colleges of Technology, Abu Dhabi, UAE
Jocelyn Chanussot	Grenoble Institute of Technology, France
Abbas Cheddad	Blekinge Institute of Technology, Sweden
Youcef Chibani	USTHB, Algeria
Vincent Christlein	University of Erlangen-Nuremberg, Germany
Youssef El merabet	Ibn Tofail University, Morocco
Christian Esposito	University of Naples Federico II, Italy
Najoua Ben Amara	University of Sousse, Tunisia
Lincoln Faria da Silva	Universidade Federal Fluminense, Brazil
Francesco Fontanella	University of Cassino and Southern Lazio, Italy
Abdeljalil Gattal	Larbi Tebessi University, Algeria
Murat Gezer	Istanbul University, Turkey
Said Ghoul	Philadelphia University, Jordan
Chayan Halder	West Bengal State University, India
Yaâcoub Hannad	NISAE, Morocco
Abdelhakim Hannousse	Guelma University, Algeria
Rachid Hedjam	Sultan Qaboos University, Oman
Renjie Hu	University of Iowa, USA
Khurram Khurshid	Institute of Space Technology, Pakistan
Pınar Kırcı	Uludag University, Turkey
Laimeche Lakhdar	Larbi Tebessi University, Algeria
Simon Liao	University of Winnipeg, Canada
Josep Lladós	Universitat Autònoma de Barcelona, Spain
Georgios Louloudis	NCSR "Demokritos", Greece
Ana Mendonça	University of Porto, Potugal
Serge Miguet	Université Lumière Lyon 2, France
Momina Moetesum	Bahria University, Pakistan
Volker Märgner	Technische Universität Braunschweig, Germany
Hassiba Nemmour	USTHB, Algeria
Jean-Marc Ogier	University of la Rochelle, France

Sankar Kumar Pal	Indian Statistical Institute, India
Rafik Menassel	Larbi Tebessi University, Algeria
Javad Sadri	Concordia University, Canada
Toufik Sari	Badji Mokhtar-Annaba University, Algeria
Sibel Senan	Istanbul University, Turkey
Faisal Shafait	NUST, Pakistan
Nabin Sharma	University of Technology Sydney, Australia
Imran Siddiqi	Bahria University, Pakistan
Nicolas Sidère	University of La Rochelle, France
Humberto Sossa	Instituto Politécnico Nacional, Mexico
Nikolaos Stamatopoulos	NCSR "Demokritos", Greece
Nicole Vincent	University of Paris, France
Hong Wei	University of Reading, UK
Hedi Tabia	University of Paris-Saclay, France
Cemal Okan Şakar	Bahçeşehir University, Turkey
Lotfi Chaari	University of Toulouse, France
Alicia Fornés	Computer Vision Center, Spain
Thierry Paquet	University of Rouen, France
Hamid Laga	Murdoch University, Australia
Muhammed Cinsdikici	Manisa Celal Bayar University, Turkey
Rostom Kachouri	ESIEE Paris, France
Boubakeur Boufama	University of Windsor, Canada
Bernd Freisleben	University of Marburg, Germany
Tolga Berber	Karadeniz Technical University, Turkey
Vijayan Asari	University of Dayton, USA
Bart Lamiroy	University of Reims Champagne-Ardenne, France
Sobhan Sarkar	University of Edinburgh, UK
Tayeb Benzenati	Digital Research Center of Sfax, Tunisia
Muhammad Khan	Sejong University, Republic of Korea

Additional Reviewers

Muhammad Asad Ali	Payel Rakshit
Maham Jahangir	Ayesha Sarwar

Contents

Computer Vision and Image Processing

Document and Media Analysis

Artificial Intelligence and Intelligent Systems

Computer Vision and Image Processing

Fine-Tuning a Pre-trained CAE for Deep One Class Anomaly Detection in Video Footage

Slim Hamdi[1,2]([✉]), Hichem Snoussi[1], and Mohamed Abid[2]

[1] LM2S University of Technology of Troyes,
12, rue Marie Curie - CS 42060, 10004 Troyes Cedex, France
`slim.hamdi@utt.fr`
[2] CES Laboratory ENIS National Engineering School University of Sfax,
B.P. 3038, Sfax, Tunisia

Abstract. In recent years, abnormal event detection in video surveillance has become a very important task mainly treated by deep learning methods taken into account many challenges. However, these methods still not trained on an anomaly detection based objective which proves their ineffectiveness in such a problem. In this paper, we propose an unsupervised method based on a new architecture for deep one class of convolutional auto-encoders (CAEs) for representing a compact Spatio-temporal feature for anomaly detection. Our CAEs are constructed by added deconvolutions layers to the CNN VGG 16. Then, we train our CAEs for a one-class training objective by fine-tuning our model to properly exploit the richness of the dataset with which CNN was trained. The first CAE is trained on the original frames to extract a good descriptor of shapes and the second CAE is learned using optical flow representations to provide a strength description of motion between frames. For this purpose, we define two loss functions, compactness loss and representativeness loss for training our CAEs architectures not only to maximize the inter-classes distance and to minimize the intra-class distance but also to ensure the tightness and the representativeness of features of normal images. We reduce features dimensions by applying a PCA (Principal Component Analyser) to combine our two descriptors with a Gaussian classifier for abnormal Spatio-temporal events detection. Our method has a high performance in terms of reliability and accuracy. It achieved abnormal event detection with good efficiency in challenging datasets compared to state-of-the-art methods.

Keywords: Deep Learning · Anomaly detection · Convolutional Auto-Encoder

1 Introduction

Security is a founding value of any modern society, it contributes strongly to creating a climate of peace necessary for good social development. Currently,

© Springer Nature Switzerland AG 2021
C. Djeddi et al. (Eds.): MedPRAI 2020, CCIS 1322, pp. 3–17, 2021.
https://doi.org/10.1007/978-3-030-71804-6_1

the conditions and the various mechanisms for its implementation are major concerns, whether at the individual or collective level. In recent decades, cameras are used everywhere in public space for security purposes. Video surveillance is a system composed of cameras and signal transmission equipment. The use of video surveillance is an essential tool for fighting crime and strengthening security. It allows controlling the necessary conditions for security and the identification of the risked elements in the scene. In the current context, one operator is in charge of several scenes at the same time and may on the same screen. In [1], the author proves that an operator can miss 60% of target events when it is in charge of viewing 9 or more video streams. A possible solution to this problem would be the use of intelligent video surveillance systems. Theses systems will have to be able to learn the normal behavior of a monitored scene and detect any abnormal behavior that may represent a safety risk.

The AE auto-encoder is a fully connected and neural network widely used in unsupervised learning. It consists of an input layer, an output layer, and one or more hidden layers. The hidden layers are distributed between the encoder and the decoder, the encoder is used to encode the input data into a more compact representation, the decoder is used to reconstruct the data according to the representation generated by the encoder. To exploit its unsupervised learning capacity, the AE has been widely explored in the detection of abnormal events. The author in [2] proposes AMDN (Appearance and Motion DeepNet) a network consisting of three SDAEs (stacked denoising auto-encoders) a first trained to reconstruct patches extracted from normal images, a second trained with the optical flow representations corresponding to the patches and a third trained with the concatenation of the patches and their optical flow representations. Moreover, based on CAEs the author in [3] proposes to train a CAE for the reconstruction of 3D input volumes and the optical flux extracted from the image and the previous image. In, [4] compared two methods also based on CAEs. The first method suggests that a CAE should be trained to reconstruct low-level characteristics (HOG and HOF) extracted from samples in the normal class. In the second method, the authors propose to use a Spatio-temporal CAE trained on video volumes. In effect, in both approaches, the anomalies are captured using a regularity score calculated with the error of reconstruction. In recent years, many works exploit the progress that has been made in both areas of Deep Learning (DL) and Computer Vision (CV) to automate surveillance for abnormal events detection. Deep Learning automatizes the feature extraction from raw data to realize many purposes such as image classification [5], facial recognition [6], automatic generation of computer code [7], automatic natural language processing [8] and automatic speech recognition [9]. Unsupervised Deep Learning is often used in the field of anomaly detection not only due to the subjective aspect of the anomaly but also usually only normal data are available for training. The development of learning methods that do not require a labeled database has always been a primary objective in the field of automatic learning. In this perspective, many recent works have aspired to the development of deep one-class networks has have been proposed [35]. However, these methods proposed to use an extra data set to ensure the compactness of normal features with a deep CNN. To remedy those drawbacks we propose in this paper, a new deep architecture for abnormal event detection. It consists of two convolutional auto-encodes, one formed on images and other on optical flow representations to obtain compact and descriptiveness features. This combination allows extracting high-level compact representation able to describe complex behaviors and dissociate between normal and abnormal events. In this paper, we propose new method based on a combination between auto-encoders to extract deep features contain both information about motion and shapes. The aim of this combination is to extract tight and representative spatio-temporal features of normal frames, and subsequently, these features are more easy to isolate it from abnormal frames. The originality of this work is to extract a deep spatio-temporal features of deep one class without using any external database.

2 Related

Anomaly detection in video footage is very import task in computer vision. Usually, state-of-the-art methods try to train a model to represent the normal events and labelled any new event at the testing phase that has small occurrence during the training as abnormal events. The earlier methods were proposed to extract low-level features to train a model, for example in [10], the author used the Histogram of Oriented Social Force (HOSF) to represent the events and in [11], the authors propose multiples features extraction such as size, color, and edges on small regions at any frame of input video obtained by foreground segmentation technique. Multiple classifier for each feature are exploited to decide if that region is contain anomaly or not. [12], use Histograms of Optical Flow (HOF) to represent the motion information of each frame enhanced by one class Support Vector Machine (SVM) classifier to pick up abnormal motion. In [13], the author propose to train a model from the available frames at the training using sparse coding and based on the assumption: "Usual events in a video footage are more reconstructible from a normal event dictionary compared to unusual events". The dictionary is obtain a model capable of computing normality score at each new event in order to dissociate normal and abnormal events. Moreover, other trajectory-based methods have been applied in order to recognize unusual trajectories in monitored scene. [14] propose to represent trajectories by Kanade Lucas-Tomasi Feature Tracker (KLT) and use Multi-Observation Hidden Markov Model (MOHMM) to determine if trajectory are normal or abnormal. [15] propose to train One-Class Support Vector Machine model to recognize the normal trajectories and pick up any abnormal events may occur. [16] combine two models; a vector quantization and a neural networks to extract robust representation. In last few years, several researchers based their works on deep learning. They have obtained greats results on various applications such as object detection [17], action recognition [18], face recognition [19]. This success come from to their capability to learn non-linear and complex representations from raw images, which is important because the real-world application contain many non-linear relationships. These methods also have a good property of generalization: they can be applied on data unused during the learning process. The author of [20] propose to apply optical flow to extract spatial–temporal volumes of interest (SVOI) and use them to train a 3D - CNN to classify events into normal and abnormal. [21] combine pre-trained CNN completed with Binary Quantization Layer (BQL) and optical flow to detect local anomalies. [22] propose a method called AVID (Adversarial Visual Irregularity Detection) to detect and locate abnormalities in videos footage. A GAN composed of a generator trained to remove abnormalities in the input images and replace them with the dominant patterns of the same images and a discriminator in the form of an FCN that predicts the probability that the different regions (patches) of the input images will be abnormal. The two networks are trained in an adversarial manner and the abnormalities are simulated using Gaussian noise. After the training, each of the two networks is capable to detect abnormalities.

3   Proposed Method

3.1   Architecture

One-class classification is a machine learning problem that has received important attention by many researchers in different fields such as novelty detection, anomaly detection, and medical imaging. Nevertheless, the lack of data in the training phase reduces the depth of network architecture which in turn reduces the representativeness of features. To solve this weakness we propose to fine-tuning a pre-trained CAE for a one-class training objective constructed from VGG 16 CNN which is achieved 92.7% top-5 test accuracy. The database used to train VGG 16 CNN is ImageNet which is a dataset of over 14 million high-resolution images belonging to 1000 classes. The images were collected from the web and labeled by humans using Amazon's Mechanical Turk crowd-sourcing tool. We freeze the first layers of convolutions to properly exploit the richness of the database with which the CNN was trained (Fig. 1). The objective of the convolution operation is to extract the high-level features from the input image. Our architecture need not be limited to only one convolution layer. Conventionally, the first convolution layer is responsible for capturing the Low-Level features such as edges, color, gradient orientation, etc. With added layers, the architecture adapts to the High-Level features as well, giving us a network that has the wholesome understanding of images in the dataset, similar to how we would. So, we construct the encoder part of our CAE architecture based on convolutions layers of pre-trained CNN VGG16. We freeze the first convolutional block of VGG 16 and we keep the others convolutional blocks trainable (Fig. 2). In the hand, the decoder part is a plane network made up of four 2D-deconvolution layers to be able to reconstruct the original frames, Its hyper-parameters is given in (Table 1).

Similar to the traditional auto-encoder, the CAE is composed of two parts. The encoder part which is a sequence of convolutional layers aims to extract compressed data of input image at the bottleneck layer and the decoder part

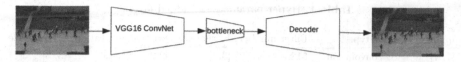

Fig. 1. 2D-CAE based on pre-trained CNN VGG16 ConvNet

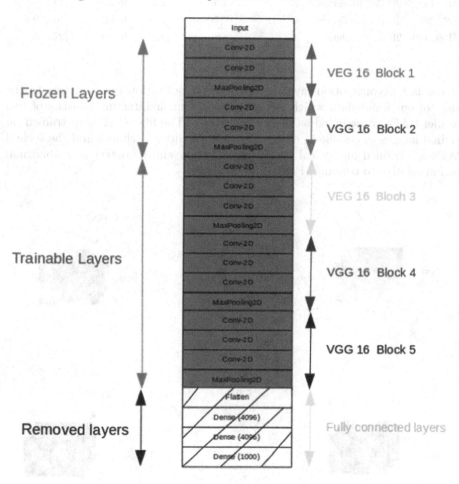

Fig. 2. VGG 16 architecture used for fine-tuning one class objective

which is successive of deconvolutional layers aims to reconstruct the input data from compressed data at bottleneck layer. The CAE can reconstruct better the data with was trained than the data that have ever seen, so the bottleneck layer must be reduced and representative as possible which in reality presents a compromise, many tests are done to select properly the bottleneck dimension (Table 1). A non-linear activation function is used at the convolutional and deconvolutional layers to obtain more useful and robust representations, except

Table 1. Hyper parameter of added layers

Input size	Layer type	Filter number	Kernel size	Strides	Activation	Output size
[7, 7]	2D-convolution	512	[3,3]	[2,2]	Relu	[3, 3]
[3, 3]	2D-deconvolution	256	[5,5]	[3,3]	Relu	[11,11]
[11, 11]	2D-deconvolution	128	[5,5]	[2,2]	Relu	[35,35]
[35, 35]	2D-deconvolution	96	[7,7]	[2,2]	Relu	[109,109]
[109, 109]	2D-deconvolution	1	[8,8]	[2,2]	linear	[224, 224]

for the last deconvolution layer we used linear activation function due to the range of our input data which is [−255, 255]. Our architecture consists of two parallel CAEs constructed as mentioned above. The first CAEs are trained on original images to be able to detect any abnormalities in shapes and the second CAEs are trained on optical flow representation aim to detect any abnormal motion relative to training (Fig. 3).

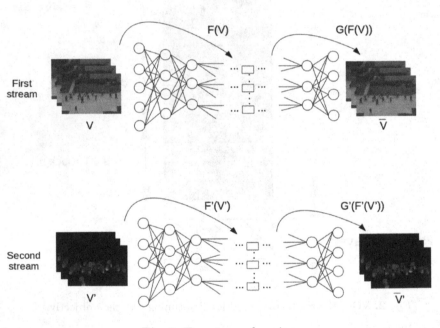

Fig. 3. Two stream learning

3.2   Training

The training phase aims to obtain a model capable to get representative and compact features of normal images for easy classification. We can ensure that in two methods; the first method (Fig. 4) is to do training in cascade objectives by training only at the beginning with the reconstruction objective and after a few epochs we extract a representative point denoted "c" of features of the dataset which with our model is training at bottleneck layer as the mean of features. Then, we do training only with the compactness objective and we fix the point c as the target of our new features. The disadvantage of this training method is that the representativeness of the images is not robust but it gives very compacted features. To remedy this flaw, a second training method is proposed with pseudo-parallel objectives (Fig. 3), we start the training with only reconstruction objective then as we have done at the first method we extract a fixed point "c" as the target of features then we continue the training with both compactness and reconstruction objectives to get robust model.

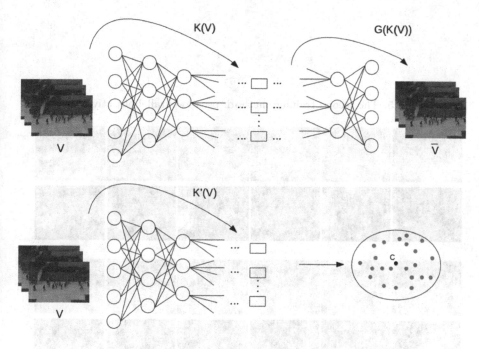

Fig. 4. The first training method: Cascade objectives

During the training phase (Fig. 5), both 2D-CAE are trained, one is trained with a stream of a sequence of original images and the other is trained with a stream of a sequence of optical flow representation. The optical flow is the pattern of apparent motion of image objects between two consecutive frames caused by the movements of the object. We have used a color code for better visualization. (Figure 6) shows some samples of images and optical flow images.

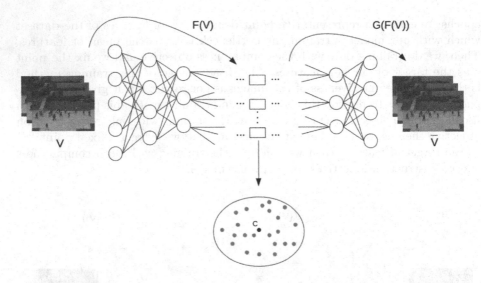

Fig. 5. The second training method: pseudo-parallel objectives

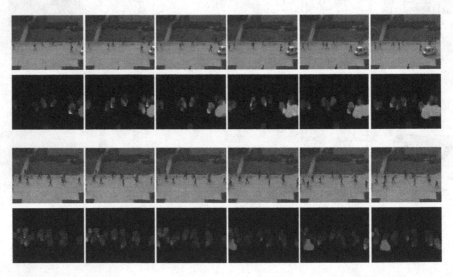

Fig. 6. Examples of optical flow representations and original images

Representativeness Loss: L_r The aim of representativeness loss is to evaluate the capacity of the learned feature to generalize normal class. The representativeness loss increases the capacity of our model to raise the distance inter-classes.

$$L_r = \frac{1}{n} \sum_{i=1}^{n} (V - \hat{V}) \tag{1}$$

Compactness Loss: L_c The objective of compactness loss is to tight all the features used during the training phase belonging to the normal class. Compactness loss evaluates the similarity between each feature vector and the fixed point 'C'. It is used to decrease the intra-class variance of the normal class.

$$L_c = \frac{1}{n} \sum_{i=1}^{n} (F(V) - M) \tag{2}$$

To perform back-propagation using this loss, it is necessary to assess the contribution each element of the input has on the final loss. For each ith sample $F(V) = \{Fv_{i1}, Fv_{i2}, ... Fv_{ik}\} \in R^k$ and the fixed point as $m_i = \{m_{i1}, m_{i2}, ... m_{ik}\}$, we define the gradient l_c with respect to the input Fv_{ij} is given as,

$$\frac{\partial L_c}{\partial Fv_{ij}} = \frac{2}{(n-1)n_k} [n \times (Fv_{ij}) - \sum_{k=1}^{n} (Fv_{ik} - m_{ik})] \tag{3}$$

3.3   Testing

The proposed testing procedure aims to classify features of testing images as normal or abnormal based on the Mahalanobis distance threshold. Both motion and shapes features vectors noted respectively $F(v) = \{Fv_{i1}, Fv_{i2}, ... Fv_{ik}\} \in R^k$ and $F'(v') = \{F'v'_{i1}, F'v'_{i2}, ... F'v'_{ik}\} \in R^k$ are extracted from trained encoders parts to be concatenated into one vector. Then we apply PCA to this vector to reduce dimension and to extract important information noted $X = \text{PCA}([F(V); F'(V')] = \{X_{i1}, X_{i2}, ... X_{ik}, X_{i1}\} \in R^p$ when $p < 2 \times k$ (Fig. 7). Using PCA is made the calculation of the covariance matrix Q faster and not complicate.

For each new feature vector X_{test} we calculate a Mahalanobis distance between each feature vector and $\bar{X}$ as given:

$$d = (X_{test} - \bar{X}) \times Q^{-1} \times (X_{test} - \bar{X})^t \tag{4}$$

When $\bar{X}$ as the mean of $X \in R^p$ and $Q \in R^{p \times p}$ as its covariance.

The classification process is carried out according to the following process: In the first step, we extract feature vectors $X = \{x_i\}, x_i \in R^{512}$ from the normal training examples, the mean M and the inverse of the covariance matrix Q of X are then calculated. In the second step, we evaluate each feature vector x_j of the testing frames with Mahalanobis distance d_j using M and Q. This is represented in the following equation:

$$d\_j = (x\_j - M) * Q * (x\_j - M)' \tag{5}$$

The outlier vectors, which actually represents abnormal frames, are then picked by thresholding the distance. If the distance exceeds a threshold α, the vector x_j is considered as outlier and the frame p_j is labeled as abnormal, Eq. (6).

$$p_j : \begin{cases} Normal & if \quad d_j \leq \alpha \\ Abnormal & if \quad d_j > \alpha \end{cases} \tag{6}$$

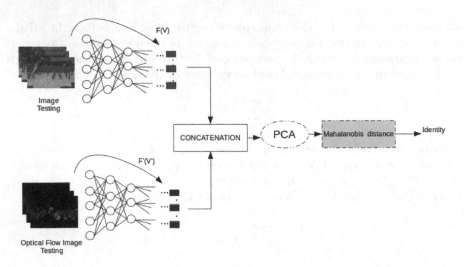

Fig. 7. Classification flowcharts

4   Experimental Results

UCSD Peds2 and UMN are challenging anomaly detection datasets. Both of them contain normal events like people are walking and abnormal events like the walking movement of bikers, skaters, cyclists, and small carts in the case of Ped2, and people are running in the case of UMN. Ped2 contains 16 training and 12 testing video samples and provides frame-level ground truth to evaluate the detection performance by comparing our method with others stat- of-the-art anomaly detection methods. In the other hand, The UMN dataset has consisted of 3 scenes: lawn (1450 frames), indoor (4415 frames) and plaza (2145 frames) and the ground truth is provided in the video frames that need to be extracted to evaluate the performance.

We evaluate our different methods using (Error Equal Rate) EER and (Area Under Curve ROC) AUC as evaluation criteria. A smaller EER corresponds with better performance. As for the AUC, a bigger value corresponds with better performance.

Our two methods have the same results nearly, with a little advantage for the pseudo-parallel objectives method.

It proves the robustness to occlusion and high performance in anomaly detection compared with state-of-the-art methods. To visualize the important effect of the compactness loss function we extract from each feature extracted by our architecture two components by applying the PCA. These components are named later features for visualization. Figure 8 illustrates the results, just to better understand its effects, we will categorize our database into three classes.

– Normal images contains only normal events as mentioned in ground truth, this class represented by green points in Fig. 8.

– Confused images when a portion of anomaly start to appear and not a whole of the anomaly enter in the scene, this class is presented by blue points in Fig. 8.
– Abnormal images when a more of the half of anomaly enter in the scene, this class represented by red points in Fig. 8.

The Fig. 8 1.a represents features for visualisations of our architecture trained with only representativeness loss, as we can see in this figures each of three classes reserved a region of space. Which is mean representativeness loss has increased the inter-classes distance between the three classes in an unsupervised way and using only the class of normal images (Class one). In order to decrease the intra-class distance for normal image we have used compactness loss. The Fig. 2 1.b represents features for visualisations of our architecture trained with both representativeness loss and compactness loss. In this case, the normal images not only are reserved region in space but also are very tight and easy to separate from abnormal images.

Combining the two CAEs have decreased the EER from 17% to 11% which make the importance of using of optical flow image to represent the motion in each frames. The Table 2 shows our results on Ped2 dataset and proves the robustness of our method compared to others state of the art methods.

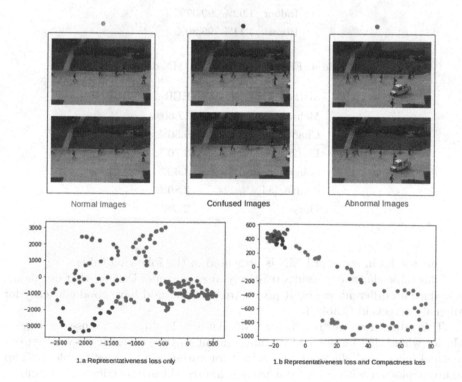

Fig. 8. Compactness loss importance

Table 2. EER comparison of UCSD Peds2

Method	EER
Mehran. [23]	42.00%
Kim (MPCCA). [24]	30.00%
Bertini. [25]	30.00%
Zhou. [26]	24.40%
Bouindour. [27]	24.20%
Hamdi. [28]	14.5%
Li. [29]	18.50%
Chong. [30]	12.00%
Tan Xiao. [31]	10.00%
Ours (Cascade)	**12%**
Ours (pseudo parallel)	**11%**

Table 3. Results in UMN dataset

Scene	EER	AUC
Lawn	3.17%	99.23%
Indoor	1.92%	99.37%
Plaza	1.11%	99.80%

Table 4. ERR comparison of UMN dataset

Method	EER
Mehran. [23]	12.60%
Chaotic invariants [32]	5.30%
Li. [29]	3.70%
Saligrama et al. [33]	3.40%
Sparse. [34]	2.80%
Ours	**2.28%**

Our results in scene of UMN is presented in the following table:

This table shows our results relatively at each scene. Despite that our model is trained on different scenes. It proves that our method have good efficiency for anomaly detection (Table 3).

This table shows our results for UMN dataset, in this case we use one threshold for whole the dataset and its independent to the scenes. It proves that our method have good efficiency and robust for variation of scenes (Table 4). This figure is plotted with tools from python library sklearn.metrics and roc_curve. It proves that our architecture achieve more then 99% of AUC.

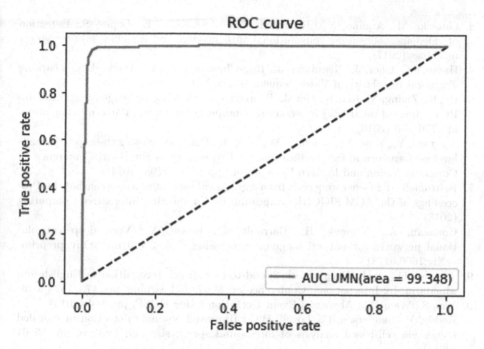

Fig. 9. ROC Curve of UMN dataset

5   Conclusion

In this paper, a new unsupervised methods were proposed to train CAEs for the Deep One-Class objective. We used these methods to learn a new architecture composed of two CAEs, one trained on video volumes and the second on optical flow representations. Our two networks allow extracting high-level Spatio-temporal features taking into account the movements and shapes present in each small region of the video. This robust representation makes possible, with a simple classifier, to differentiate between normal and abnormal events. We have tested our network on challenging datasets, containing crowded scenes (USCD Ped2 and UMN) Our method obtained high results competing with the best state-of-the-art methods in the detection of abnormal events (Fig. 9).
Our future works will investigate the strengthening of our learning process and apply our model on drone video for anomaly detection.

References

1. Beltramelli, T.: Generating code from a graphical user interface screenshot. In: Proceedings of the ACM SIGCHI Symposium on Engineering Interactive Computing Systems, pp. 329–343 (2018)
2. Xu, D., Ricci, E., Yan, Y., Song, J., Sebe, N.: Learning deep representations of appearance and motion for anomalous event detection (2015)

3. Gutoski, M., Aquino, N.M.R., Ribeiro, M., Lazzaretti, E., Lopes, S.: Detection of video anomalies using convolutional autoencoders and one-class support vector machines (2017)
4. Hasan, M., Choi, J., Neumann, J., Roy-Chowdhury, A.K., Davis, L.S.: Learning Temporal Regularity in Video Sequences, pp. 733–742 (2016)
5. He, K., Zhang, X., Ren, S., Sun, J.: Deep residual learning for image recognition. In: Proceedings of the IEEE Conference on Computer Vision and Pattern Recognition, pp. 770–778 (2016)
6. Taigman, Y., Yang, M., Ranzato, M., Wolf, L.: Deepface: closing the gap to human-level performance in face verification. In: Proceedings of the IEEE Conference on Computer Vision and Pattern Recognition, pp. 1701–1708 (2014)
7. Beltramelli, T.: Generating code from a graphical user interface screenshot. In: Proceedings of the ACM SIGCHI Symposium on Engineering Interactive Computing (2018)
8. Conneau, A., Schwenk, H., Barrault, L., Lecun, Y.: Very deep convolutional networks for natural language processing, vol. 2 (2016). arXiv preprint. arXiv:1606.01781
9. Amodei, D., et al.: Deep speech 2: end-to-end speech recognition in English and Mandarin. In: International Conference on Machine Learning, pp. 173–182 (2016)
10. Yen, S., Wang, C.: Abnormal Event Detection Using HOSF, pp. 1–4 (2013)
11. Reddy, V., Sanderson, C., Lovell, B.C.: Improved anomaly detection in crowded scenes via cell-based analysis of foreground speed, size and texture, pp. 55–61 (2011)
12. Wang, T., Snoussi, H.: Detection of abnormal visual events via global optical flow orientation histogram. IEEE Trans. Inf. Forensics Secur. 9(6), 988–998 (2014)
13. Zhao, B., Fei-Fei, L., Xing, E.P.: Online detection of unusual events in videos via dynamic sparse coding. In: CVPR 2011, pp. 3313–3320 (2011)
14. Zhou, S., Shen, W., Zeng, D., Zhang, Z.: Unusual event detection in crowded scenes by trajectory analysis. In: 2015 IEEE International Conference on Acoustics Speech and Signal Processing (ICASSP), pp. 1300–1304 (2015)
15. Piciarelli, C., Micheloni, C., Foresti, G.L.: Trajectory-based anomalous event detection. IEEE Trans. Circuits Syst. Video Technol. 18, 1544–1554
16. Johnson, N., Hogg, D.: Learning the distribution of object trajectories for event recognition. Image Vis. Comput. 14(8), 609–615 (1996). ISSN 0262–8856. https://doi.org/10.1016/0262-8856(96)01101-8
17. Redmon, J., Farhadi, A.: YOLOv3: An Incremental Improvement (2018)
18. Tran, D., Bourdev, L., Fergus, R., Torresani, L., Paluri, M.: Learning spatiotemporal features with 3D convolutional networks. In: The IEEE International Conference on Computer Vision (ICCV) (2015)
19. Schroff, F., Kalenichenko, D., Philbin, J.: FaceNet: a unified embedding for face recognition and clustering. In: The IEEE Conference on Computer Vision and Pattern Recognition (CVPR) (2015)
20. Zhou, S., Shen, W., Zeng, D., Fang, M., Wei, Y., Zhang, Z.: Spatial-temporal convolutional neural networks for anomaly detection and localization in crowded scenes. Sig. Process. Image Commun. 47, 358–368 (2016)
21. Ravanbakhsh, M., Nabi, M., Mousavi, H., Sangineto, E., Sebe, N.: Plug-and-Play CNN for crowd motion analysis: an application in abnormal event detection. In: 2018 IEEE Winter Conference on Applications of Computer Vision (WACV) (2018)
22. Sabokrou, M., et al.: Avid: adversarial visual irregularity detection. arXiv preprint arXiv:1805.09521 (2018)

23. Mehran, R., Oyama, A., Shah, M.: Abnormal crowd behavior detection using social force model. In: Computer Vision and Pattern Recognition, pp. 935–942 (2009)
24. Kim, J., Grauma, K.: Observe locally, infer globally: a space-time MRF for detecting abnormal activities with incremental updates. In: Computer Vision and Pattern Recognition, pp. 2921–2928 (2009)
25. Bertini, M., Del Bimbo, A., Seidenari, L.: Multi-scale and real-time non-parametric approach for anomaly detection and localization. Computer Vis. Image Underst. 116(3), 320–329 (2012)
26. Zhou, S., Shen, W., Zeng, D., Fang, M., Wei, Y., Zhang, Z.: Spatial-temporal convolutional neural networks for anomaly detection and localization in crowded scenes. Signal Process. Image Commun. 47, 358–368 (2016)
27. Bouindour, S., Hittawe, M.M., Mahfouz, S., Snoussi, H.: Abnormal event detection using convolutional neural networks and 1-class SVM classifier. In: 8th International Conference on Imaging for Crime Detection and Prevention (ICDP 2017) (2017)
28. Hamdi, S., Bouindour, S., Loukil, K., Snoussi, H., Abid, M.: Hybrid deep learning and HOF for Anomaly Detection. In: 2019 6th International Conference on Control, Decision and Information Technologies (CoDIT), pp. 575–580 (2019)
29. Li, W., Mahadevan, V., Vasconcelos, N.: Anomaly detection and localization in crowded scenes. IEEE Trans. Pattern Anal. Mach. Intell. 36(1), 18–32 (2014)
30. Chong, Y.S., Tay, Y.H.: Abnormal event detection in videos using spatiotemporal autoencoder. In: Proceedings CVPRR in International Symposium on Neural Networks, pp. 189–196 (2017)
31. Xiao, T., Zhang, C., Zha, H.: Learning to detect anomalies in surveillance video. IEEE Sig. Process. Lett. I 22(9), 1477–1481 (2015)
32. Wu, S., et al.: Chaotic invariants of Lagrangian particle trajectories for anomaly detection in crowded scenes. In: IEEE Conference on Computer Vision Pattern Recognition, pp. 2054–2060 (2010)
33. Saligrama, V., Chen, Z.: Chaotic invariants based on local statistical aggregates. J. IEEE Conf. Comput. Vis. Pattern Recogn. 2112–2119 (2012)
34. Cong, Y., et al.: Sparse reconstruction cost for abnormal event detection. In: IEEE Conference on Computer Vision Pattern Recognition, pp. 3449–3456 (2011)
35. Perera, P., Patel, V.M.: Learning deep features for one-class classification. In: IEEE Conference on Computer Vision Pattern Recognition, pp. 3449–3456 (2011)

Plant Disease Recognition Using Optimized Deep Convolutional Neural Networks

Ali Ghofrani[1], Rahil Mahdian Toroghi[1(✉)], and Hamid Behnegar[2]

[1] Iran Broadcasting University (IRIBU), Tehran, Iran
{alighofrani,mahdian}@iribu.ac.ir
[2] Department of Computer Engineering, Khatam University, Tehran, Iran
h.behnegar@khatam.ac.ir

Abstract. In this paper, the problem of recognizing the plant's diseases and pests using deep learning methods has been addressed. This work can be implemented on a client-side or integrated with IoT concept, in order to be employed efficiently in smart farms. Nearly 40% of global crop yields each year are lost due to pests. By considering the global population growth, the agricultural food will run out of its resources very soon and this will endanger the lives of many people. A pretrained EfficientNet deep neural network architecture with student noise has been optimized, both in volume and the parameter number, and has been involved in this setup. Two different approaches have been adopted. First, achieving the highest accuracy of recognition using the optimum algorithms in development step. Second, preparation of the system as a microservice model in order to be integrated with other services in a smart agriculture deployment. Using an efficient number of parameters and inference time, it has become doable to implement this system as a service in a real world scenario. The dataset used in the training step is the plant village data. By implementing the model on this dataset, we could achieve the accuracy of 99.69% on test data, 99.85% on validation data, and 99.78% on training data, which is remarkably competitive with the state-of-the-art.

Keywords: Plant disease recognition · Convolutional neural network · EfficientNet · Smart farm

1 Introduction

The ever-increasing growth of the population of our planet, necessitates the food supplier organizations concern this critical problem for a sustainable future of the world due to the limited resources. On the other hand, the agricultural productivity will be decreased by growing the plant diseases and pests.

One development strategy would be migrating toward smart farms in order to improve the productivity through incorporating the smart irrigation, planting

© Springer Nature Switzerland AG 2021
C. Djeddi et al. (Eds.): MedPRAI 2020, CCIS 1322, pp. 18–30, 2021.
https://doi.org/10.1007/978-3-030-71804-6_2

and other agricultural procedures. This will diminish the environmental damages, as well as the productivity losses which is normal in conventional farming techniques.

A crucial issue for treating a plant is to diagnose the disease early enough. One challenging point for large countries (e.g. Iran) is vastness of the lands and non-uniform distribution of herbalists in different provinces of the country. This causes a long delay and the golden time for treatment of the plant that suffers from a disease will be running late. Thus, irrecoverable damages would happen to the plants.

In recent years, owing to the rapid advancements in computer vision and artificial intelligence, it has become possible to integrate different engineering fields in order to be able to deal with a broader category of multi-disciplinary applications.

In this research work, our effort has been dedicated to develop an intelligent plant disease diagnosis system using the modern deep neural network architectures. This server-based system is able to get the image of the sick plant even on the farm, diagnose the disease and using the pretrained system which has been already used the knowledge of the herbalists for a wide range of diseases, determine a proper remedy for it. Thus, the whole integrated smart setup helps us diagnose and perform the plant treating during the golden time, without the presence of a herbalist.

2   Related Works

A handful of techniques have been proposed so far, in order to tackle the problem of plant's disease detection. Some approaches leverage image processing techniques and extracting features, such as LBP (Local Binary Pattern) and HBBP (Brightness Bi-Histogram Equalization) [17]. Other methods, extract features using HoG (Histogram of Gradients) followed by SVM classifiers [9,18]. The state-of-the-art of these methods has been achieved, through using the Otsu's classifier [13,19].

In recent years, by advancement of the computer vision field through leveraging the deep learning techniques, methods based on deep convolutional neural networks have been widely proposed for both plant's disease diagnosis, as well as classification of the healthy and infected plants [3,7].

3   The Proposed Framework

3.1   Dataset

Despite the potential capabilities of deep neural networks, one drawback of these systems is that they need a huge amount of data in order to train their few million network parameters. Providing such amount of data in many problems is practically a big challenge, by itself. In this work, we elaborate presenting different models in order to deal with various types of applications (Fig. 1).

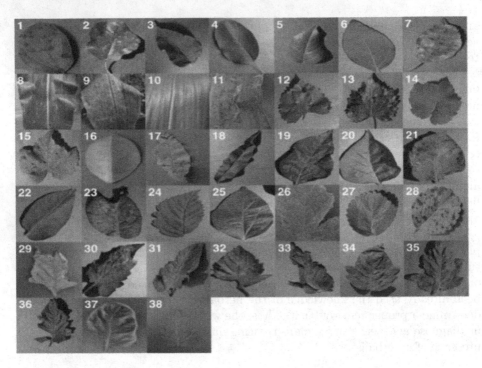

Fig. 1. Example of leaf images from the PlantVillage dataset, representing every crop-disease pair used. 1) Apple Scab, Venturia inaequalis 2) Apple Black Rot, Botryosphaeria obtusa 3) Apple Cedar Rust, Gymnosporangium juniperi-virginianae 4) Apple healthy 5) Blueberry healthy 6) Cherry healthy 7) Cherry Powdery Mildew, Podosphaera spp. 8) Corn Gray Leaf Spot, Cercospora zeae-maydis 9) Corn Common Rust, Puccinia sorghi 10) Corn healthy 11) Corn Northern Leaf Blight, Exserohilum turcicum 12) Grape Black Rot, Guignardia bidwellii, 13) Grape Black Measles (Esca), Phaeomoniella aleophilum, Phaeomoniella chlamydospora 14) Grape Healthy 15) Grape Leaf Blight, Pseudocercospora vitis 16) Orange Huanglongbing (Citrus Greening), Candidatus Liberibacter spp. 17) Peach Bacterial Spot, Xanthomonas campestris 18) Peach healthy 19) Bell Pepper Bacterial Spot, Xanthomonas campestris 20) Bell Pepper healthy 21) Potato Early Blight, Alternaria solani 22) Potato healthy 23) Potato Late Blight, Phytophthora infestans 24) Raspberry healthy 25) Soybean healthy 26) Squash Powdery Mildew, Erysiphe cichoracearum, Sphaerotheca fuliginea 27) Strawberry Healthy 28) Strawberry Leaf Scorch, Diplocarpon earlianum 29) Tomato Bacterial Spot, Xanthomonas campestris pv. vesicatoria 30) Tomato Early Blight, Alternaria solani 31) Tomato Late Blight, Phytophthora infestans 32) Tomato Leaf Mold, Fulvia fulva 33) Tomato Septoria Leaf Spot, Septoria lycopersici 34) Tomato Two Spotted Spider Mite, Tetranychus urticae 35) Tomato Target Spot, Corynespora cassiicola 36) Tomato Mosaic Virus 37) Tomato Yellow Leaf Curl Virus 38) Tomato healthy.

One useful dataset to deal with the plant's disease problem is called **Plant Village** [10]. This dataset has been publicly available and contains 54, 306 images of the plants, including the healthy ones, as well as the sick plants and have been classified into 38 classes with 14 different plant species and 26 different types of plant's diseases.

In paper [10], the AlexNet and GoogleNet architectures have been used and the accuracy of 99.35% on disease diagnosis have been achieved.

Another dataset, namely **PlantDoc** [16], has been released on 2019 which contains 2, 598 images on 13 different plant species and 27 classes (10 healthy and 17 diseased classes). The main difference between this dataset and the Plant Village is that the images of the new dataset have been gathered in real life, whereas the old one has collected the images in a lab-controlled fashion.

3.2   The Proposed Method

In PlantVillage paper [10], AlexNet and GoogleNet architectures have been used in order to perform the classification task. However, both these architectures are so large and not efficient and unlike to be implementable on the client side.

In this paper, we have proposed two different models. First, we propose a model based on EfficientNet architecture to achieve a high accuracy and implementability on the client side as an internet-based service [20]. Second, we propose a model based on tiny MobileNet V2 [12], and the separable CNN logic which has been presented in *Xception* architecture [1]. This model yields a reasonably small number of controllable parameters in a light model and makes it suitable as an end system on the client's mobile handset (Fig. 2).

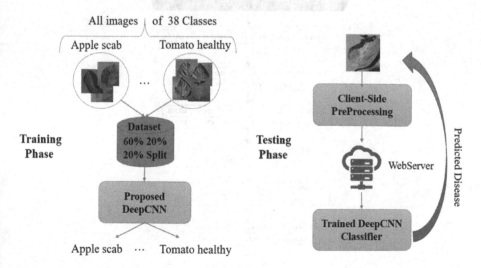

Fig. 2. Process flowgraph of the entire proposed architecture for: (left) training and (right) testing phases.

Our proposed architectures have been trained by Plant Village dataset, with 60% − 20% − 20% chunks for training, validation, and test steps, respectively.

Overall saying, the model is first trained using the Plant Village dataset. However, in a server-based implementation the input image being taken by the user is to be preprocessed to get suitable dimensions corresponding to the network input resolution and then sent to the server. In addition, as the second method an architecture with a relatively small number of parameters has been proposed that could be implemented on all kinds of smart mobile handsets directly with a slightly worse, yet acceptable accuracy.

3.3 EfficientNet Architecture

EfficientNet B0 is a CNN architecture being employed in our first proposed model [20], as depicted in Fig. 3.

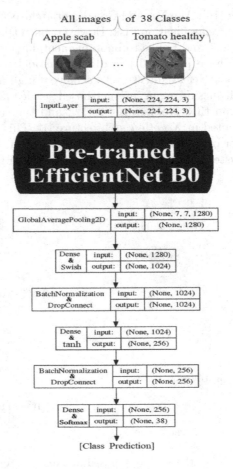

Fig. 3. The first proposed architecture based on EfficientNet B0. Transfer learning has been involved regarding the weights of the network.

This network has been already trained on ImageNet [2], with input dimensions of $224 \times 224 \times 3$ for 1000 different classes of images and could be employed in similar applications using transfer learning, since it can seriously expedite the training process of the networks being involved. Figure 4, visualizes the final dense layer perception of EfficientNet B0 on ImageNet data. This figure implicates that the pretrained model on the ImageNet data could be logically justified as a suitable model to be transferred for learning the plant disease problem. This can be realized from the fact that visualizing the final model layers before clipping them for the training phase has strong similarities with the classes that are included in our problem. This helps our pretrained model using its original weights be converged quite faster than the model being initialized by the random noise weights.

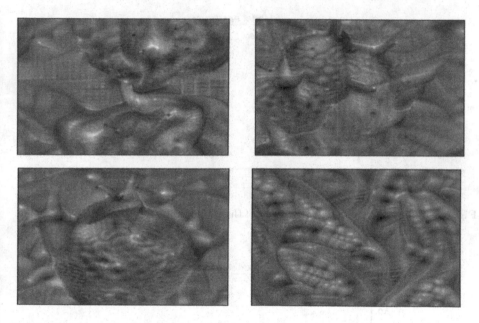

Fig. 4. Visualized final layer of the trained EfficientNet model on ImageNet. (Top-Left) 945: Bell pepper, (Top-right) 949: strawberry, (Bottom-left) 950: orange, (Bottom-right) 987: corn

Next step would be modifying the architecture appropriately to meet the requirements of our problem. After dropping off the FC (Fully Connected) layer of ImageNet classifier, we add our determined stack of layers to the model. This stack includes a CNN connected to a dense layer with 1024 neurons that are initiated with *Swish* activation functions [11], due to a better performance compared with the Leaky ReLU, and it would be connected to the next hidden layer. In order to avoid overfitting the dropconnect technique has been incorporated with 0.5 deactivation coefficient [21]. The batch-normalization has been also employed [8], and the layer is then connected to another fully-connected layer. Then, the dimension has been reduced to 256 and *Tanh* activation function has been used. This stack of batch-normalization and dropconnect, has been repeated until it boils down to 38 neurons with *Softmax* activation function in the output in order to perform a probabilistic multi-class classification. This stack has been pretrained and the model parameters have been weighted using *Xavier* Normal technique in order to make the model converge rapidly [6]. Then, the entire model has been trained on the Plant Village dataset using these pretrained weights.

Since a multi-class classification is to be performed, the categorical cross entropy has been used as the loss function and the proposed model is monitored through maximizing the accuracy over the validation data at each epoch.

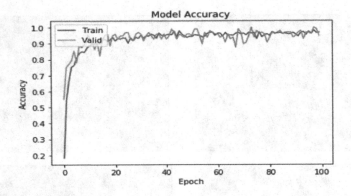

Fig. 5. Training and validation **accuracy** of the proposed model, based on EfficientNet.

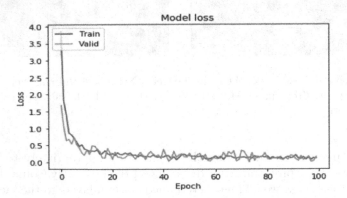

Fig. 6. Training and validation **loss** of the proposed model, based on EfficientNet.

As it is obvious from Fig. 5 and 6, the validation accuracy and loss are slightly better than that of training accuracy and loss, respectively. That is due to using dropconnect during the training phase which prevents our model from overfitting.

The final proposed architecture contains 5,988,002 parameters which are to be trained. Moreover, the final model needs about 68 MBytes to be saved.

The proposed model outperforms both the GoogleNet and AlexNet-based models being tested on Plant Village dataset from both the accuracy aspect and having the smaller size. This highlights the idea of leveraging the proposed model and implementing it as a web service. The results of the average training, validation and test accuracy and loss for the proposed model is shown in Table 1.

Table 1. Accuracy and Loss of Training, Validation and testing of the model.

	Training	Validation	Testing
Accuracy	99.78	99.85	99.69
Loss	0.0363	0.0089	0.0403

3.4   MobileNet V2 - Lite Version

In addition to the previously proposed architecture that could be implemented as a web service, we further elaborated a low weight model which could be deployed and executed on mobile device processors, to the cost of a slight degradation on the accuracy level as a trade-off with the model size.

In order to implement this model the separable CNN logic (i.e., the Point-wise, Depth-wise blocks [4]) has been leveraged which has already been employed in Xception architecture [1], and the MobileNet V2 has been optimized to meet the requirements of our problem. To achieve that, we have omitted the dense layer with 1000 neurons and connected our stack of blocks to the final CNN layer. Similar to the previously proposed architecture, we have used the Ima-geNet pretrained model for CNN as the initial weights and the Xavier Normal technique has been employed for training the weights on the remaining parts of the architecture [5].

The input resolution size has been resized to 96×96 and the kernel numbers have been reduced to one third, as well. Instead of using Swish activation function which entails a heavy burden for the processor, the *Leaky ReLU* has been used. furthermore, dropconnect technique has been involved in place of dropout to be more efficient [21], and the batch size has been increased form 48 to 512. Hence, a group-normalizer has been used instead of batch-normalization [22]. Finally, similar to the previously proposed model the stack of fully connected layers has been attached to the CNN final layer. The entire model has been depicted in Fig. 7.

The total number of parameters for the proposed model has been reduced to 279,169 and the model size has become 3,92 MBytes, as well. Needless to say that after performing the postprocessing methods such as quantization and pruning the model size will boil down to about 270 KBytes.

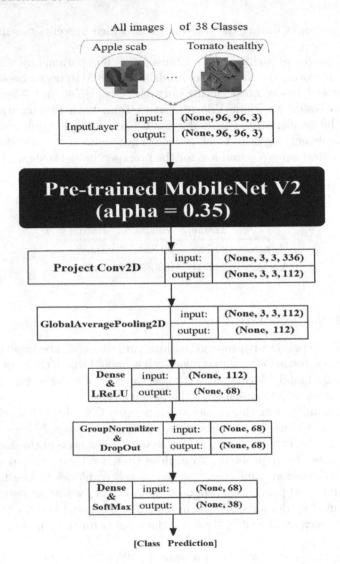

Fig. 7. Our proposed architecture based on lite mobileNet V2. Transfer learning has been involved for the weights of the network.

Despite the simplifications imposed to the model architecture, the model could still achieve the reasonable accuracy of 95, 64% on the test dataset. The accuracy and loss of the model on training and validation datasets have been depicted in Fig. 8 and Fig. 9. Moreover, the results of the average training, validation and test accuracy and loss for the simplified proposed model is shown in Table 2.

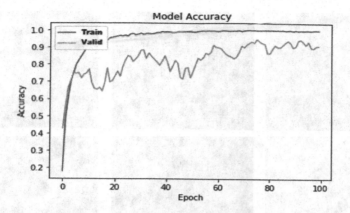

Fig. 8. Training and validation accuracy results for the proposed architecture based on lite-mobilenetV2

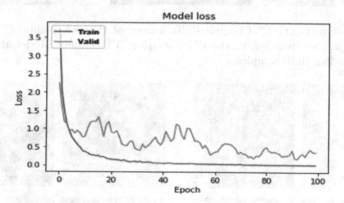

Fig. 9. Training and validation losses for the proposed architecture based on lite-mobilenetV2

Table 2. Accuracy and Loss of Training, Validation and testing of the simplified model.

	Training	Validation	Testing
Accuracy	99.62	95.82	95.46
Loss	0.0363	0.0089	0.2234

In a practical implementation of the tiny MobileNet version (with 270 KBytes) two samples of the test data have been given to the model. Figure 10 illustrates the sample infected leaves along with their saliency maps [15], as well as their corresponding heat-maps [14]. As it is depicted in Fig. 10 the model attention has been correctly placed on the infected parts of the leaves, as expected by a human expert [14].

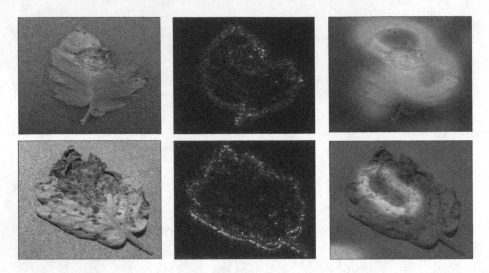

Fig. 10. (Left to right) 1st Column: RGB images of the sick plants, 2nd column: Saliency maps corresponding to the RGB samples, 3rd column: Model attention of the corresponding RGB samples

Fig. 11. (Top row: Left to right) Corn maize healthy, Corn maize with Cercospora leaf spot disease, Apple healthy, Apple Scab. (Bottom row: Left to right) Visualization of the corresponding dense layer of "Corn maize healthy", Visualization of the corresponding dense layer of "Corn maize with Cercospora leaf spot disease", Visualization of the corresponding dense layer of "Apple healthy", Visualization of the corresponding dense layer of "Apple scab", all for lite MobileNet V2.

Furthermore, as depicted in Fig. 11 the discrepancies between the visualized outputs of the neurons corresponding to the sample images has been clearly illustrated. The visualized outputs belong to the dense layers corresponding to the input class of images.

4   Conclusion

The gist of this paper has been to recognize the plant's disease using deep learning techniques. To achieve this, we have proposed two models based on convolutional neural networks. The first proposed model uses an EfficientNet B0 CNN as a core block which has been customized to meet the requirements of our problem and has been optimized to be properly usable as a server-based application. The second model involves MobileNet V2 as a core block and simplifies it to be deployable on a mobile device. The first model outperforms the state-of-the-art in the accuracy sense, and the second model in spite of simplicity performs reseanably well for diagnosing the plant's diseases and pests on Plant Village test data samples. Specifications of the proposed systems qualifies them for being employed as a microservice model in an integration with other required services in a smart farm and other agricultural activities.

Acknowledgement. This work is heavily owing to Sarvban startup company in agricultures and specifically expresses the deepest thanks to Erfan MirTalebi and Aref Samadi for their friendly cooperation and cordially sharing their knowledge with us.

References

1. Chollet, F.: Xception: deep learning with depthwise separable convolutions. In: Proceedings of the IEEE Conference on Computer Vision and Pattern Recognition, pp. 1251–1258 (2017)
2. Deng, J., Dong, W., Socher, R., Li, L.J., Li, K., Fei-Fei, L.: Imagenet: a large-scale hierarchical image database. In: 2009 IEEE Conference on Computer Vision and Pattern Recognition, pp. 248–255. IEEE (2009)
3. Ferentinos, K.P.: Deep learning models for plant disease detection and diagnosis. Comput. Electron. Agric. **145**, 311–318 (2018)
4. Ghofrani, A., Toroghi, R.M., Ghanbari, S.: Realtime face-detection and emotion recognition using MTCNN and minishufflenet v2. In: 2019 5th Conference on Knowledge Based Engineering and Innovation (KBEI), pp. 817–821. IEEE (2019)
5. Ghofrani, A., Toroghi, R.M., Tabatabaie, S.M.: Attention-based face antispoofing of RGB camera using a minimal end-2-end neural network. In: 2020 International Conference on Machine Vision and Image Processing (MVIP), pp. 1–6. IEEE (2020)
6. Glorot, X., Bengio, Y.: Understanding the difficulty of training deep feedforward neural networks. In: Proceedings of the Thirteenth International Conference on Artificial Intelligence and Statistics, pp. 249–256 (2010)
7. Hanson, A., Joel, M., Joy, A., Francis, J.: Plant leaf disease detection using deep learning and convolutional neural network. Int. J. Eng. Sci. **5324** (2017)
8. Ioffe, S., Szegedy, C.: Batch normalization: accelerating deep network training by reducing internal covariate shift. arXiv preprint arXiv:1502.03167 (2015)

9. Islam, M.A., Yousuf, M.S.I., Billah, M.: Automatic plant detection using hog and LBP features with SVM. Int. J. Comput. (IJC) **33**(1), 26–38 (2019)
10. Mohanty, S.P., Hughes, D.P., Salathé, M.: Using deep learning for image-based plant disease detection. Frontiers Plant Sci. **7**, 1419 (2016)
11. Ramachandran, P., Zoph, B., Le, Q.V.: Swish: a self-gated activation function, vol. 7. arXiv preprint arXiv:1710.05941 (2017)
12. Sandler, M., Howard, A., Zhu, M., Zhmoginov, A., Chen, L.C.: Mobilenetv 2: inverted residuals and linear bottlenecks. In: Proceedings of the IEEE Conference on Computer Vision and Pattern Recognition, pp. 4510–4520 (2018)
13. Saradhambal, G., Dhivya, R., Latha, S., Rajesh, R.: Plant disease detection and its solution using image classification. Int. J. Pure Appl. Math. **119**(14), 879–884 (2018)
14. Selvaraju, R.R., Cogswell, M., Das, A., Vedantam, R., Parikh, D., Batra, D.: Grad-cam: visual explanations from deep networks via gradient-based localization. In: Proceedings of the IEEE International Conference on Computer Vision, pp. 618–626 (2017)
15. Simonyan, K., Vedaldi, A., Zisserman, A.: Deep inside convolutional networks: visualising image classification models and saliency maps. arXiv preprint arXiv:1312.6034 (2013)
16. Singh, D., Jain, N., Jain, P., Kayal, P., Kumawat, S., Batra, N.: Plantdoc: a dataset for visual plant disease detection. In: Proceedings of the 7th ACM IKDD CoDS and 25th COMAD, pp. 249–253 (2020)
17. Singh, K., Kumar, S., Kaur, P.: Automatic detection of rust disease of lentil by machine learning system using microscopic images. Int. J. Electr. Comput. Eng. **9**(1), 660 (2019)
18. Sullca, C., Molina, C., Rodríguez, C., Fernández, T.: Diseases detection in blueberry leaves using computer vision and machine learning techniques. Int. J. Mach. Learn. Comput. **9**(5) (2019)
19. Sun, G., Jia, X., Geng, T.: Plant diseases recognition based on image processing technology. J. Electr. Comput. Eng. **2018** (2018)
20. Tan, M., Le, Q.V.: Efficientnet: rethinking model scaling for convolutional neural networks. arXiv preprint arXiv:1905.11946 (2019)
21. Wan, L., Zeiler, M., Zhang, S., Le Cun, Y., Fergus, R.: Regularization of neural networks using dropconnect. In: International Conference on Machine Learning, pp. 1058–1066 (2013)
22. Wu, Y., He, K.: Group normalization. In: Proceedings of the European Conference on Computer Vision (ECCV), pp. 3–19 (2018)

APS: A Large-Scale Multi-modal Indoor Camera Positioning System

Ali Ghofrani[1,3], Rahil Mahdian Toroghi[1(✉)], and Seyed Mojtaba Tabatabaie[2]

[1] Iran Broadcasting University (IRIBU), Tehran, Iran
mahdian@iribu.ac.ir
[2] CEO/CTO at Alpha Reality, AR/VR Solution Company, Tehran, Iran
smtabatabaie@alphareality.io
[3] VP of Artificial Intelligence at Alpha Reality, Tehran, Iran
a.ghofrani@alphareality.io

Abstract. Navigation inside a closed area with no GPS-signal accessibility is a highly challenging task. In order to tackle this problem, recently the imaging-based methods have grabbed the attention of many researchers. These methods either extract the features (e.g. using SIFT, or SOSNet) and map the descriptive ones to the camera position and rotation information, or deploy an end-to-end system that directly estimates this information out of RGB images, similar to PoseNet. While the former methods suffer from heavy computational burden during the test process, the latter suffers from lack of accuracy and robustness against environmental changes and object movements. However, end-to-end systems are quite fast during the test and inference and are pretty qualified for real-world applications, even though their training phase could be longer than the former ones. In this paper, a novel multi-modal end-to-end system for large-scale indoor positioning has been proposed, namely APS (Alpha Positioning System), which integrates a Pix2Pix GAN network to reconstruct the point cloud pair of the input query image, with a deep CNN network in order to robustly estimate the position and rotation information of the camera. For this integration, the existing datasets have the shortcoming of paired RGB/point cloud images for indoor environments. Therefore, we created a new dataset to handle this situation. By implementing the proposed APS system, we could achieve a highly accurate camera positioning with a precision level of less than a centimeter.

Keywords: Indoor camera positioning · Point-cloud data · Convlutional Neural Network · Pix2Pix GAN

1 Introduction

Throughout the development of navigation systems, there are lots of challenges along the way, which have been mainly solved by development of GPS systems. However, the indoor navigation, due to the lack of GPS data, has remained

© Springer Nature Switzerland AG 2021
C. Djeddi et al. (Eds.): MedPRAI 2020, CCIS 1322, pp. 31–46, 2021.
https://doi.org/10.1007/978-3-030-71804-6_3

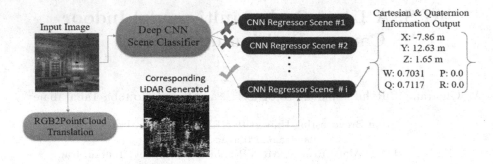

Fig. 1. The entire proposed APS process flowgraph, pictorially demonstrated.

unsolved, yet. Inside malls, airports, large towers, warehouses, and many other places the position can easily get lost, when the GPS data is hardly available.

One solution has been to place very small bluetooth broadcasting devices all over the area, so that they can detect the target and based on their distribution topology predict the position. However, that could have several disadvantages [5,11,13,25]. For example, extra devices become necessary which entails periodic monitoring and maintenance, as well as calibrations. Moreover, the battery lifetime of the bluetooth devices would be a critical issue and the target could be easily lost when the battery goes off. In addition, only a rough estimation of the position could be achieved and this may hardly work in a crowded and winding corridor. With a same logic, using WiFi signals have also been leveraged [2,34,41], yet the position precision has not been highly improved and the installation of extra devices would still be a need [21,24,26]. The latest Apple localization system using WiFi signals, have achieved the accuracy of 3 to 5 m [23,44]. Although, this precision might be acceptable for outdoor navigations, it may not work for indoor scenarios, such as autonomous driving, or augmented reality applications in which the digital overlays require a centimeter precision scale [7,29,35,36].

A different solution has been through geometry-aware systems, which incorporate perceptual and temporal features of camera imaging in order to extract the position and quaternion information. This is pretty similar to the human way of memorizing a location and navigating by using visual and temporal features. Some conventional methods in this regard, either use RGB images along with a depth-assisted camera [3,10,18,40,42,43], or they employ SIFT-based algorithms [19,32,38]. In many realistic scenarios however, the depth-based camera or bluetooth or WiFi signals are not available [4,22,33], at all.

In this paper, following the works of [6,7] we present an end-to-end deep neural network system that involves the RGB data of a particular scene in one hand and the point-cloud data corresponding to it on the other hand; then integrates them and provides the camera position and quaternion estimates with a high accuracy. Furthermore, the proposed system is proved to be robust against environmental variations including partially masking of the images, light changes, etc. in contrast to ICPS-net work [7].

The outline goes, as follows. First, the related works are explained. Then, a big-picture of the proposed end-to-end system along with its building blocks is introduced. Next, the training and evaluation processes of the architecture are explained. In addition, a dataset has been created for this purpose, and the way to employ it for the training processes is mentioned. Alongside, the experiments and the evaluation measures are introduced. The paper is finally terminated by the results, conclusion, and the references being cited within the contained sections.

2 Related Works

A pioneering work for outdoor positioning using deep neural networks proposed in [15], as PoseNet. This system employs a convolutional neural network for a real-time 6 degree-of-freedom camera relocalization. MapNet is another deep network based system, which uses geometrical information of the images for the camera localization [9]. Both of these methods, were presented to address the outdoor positioning problem.

For outdoor places, the positioning is possible due to using image processing methods and the existence of indicative objects in the environment as the markers. However, for indoor places, due to limited scales and conditions, there would be many identical patterns which hinder the SIFT or SURF-based methods to work well in practice [1,8,20,31,38]. Moreover, inside buildings the configurations are usually subject to changes such as object replacements or movements, which in turn modify the status of the patterns over the course of the imaging period.

In order to pave the way for indoor positioning, a deep conventional neural network system, namely ICPS-net [7] was proposed, primarily. In this work, a photogrammetry was performed on selected scenes in the area of interest. An EfficientNet CNN network [37], is then employed which has been already trained on the sequence of images associated to each specific scene inside the interested area. This CNN network, then takes in the user image and classifies it as one of the previously trained scenes. When the scene associated to the user input image is identified, another MobileNet-V2 CNN is employed [30], which has been already trained to perform the regression over the camera Cartesian positions, as well as the quaternion information. While these tandem connected networks as a system is able to achieve a high position accuracy, it suffers from the lack of robustness due to environmental changes that could easily confuse the system. Another problem with this system is that creating data for the model requires excruciating efforts. Later, a LiDAR ICPS-net [6] was proposed which involves the point cloud data being extracted through a LiDAR system to make the model sufficiently robust against the environmental changes. The disadvantage of this model was that it could get stuck in the model convergence problem, and the training phase could be extremely prolonged. In addition, the accuracy was deteriorated significantly with respect to the ICPS-net system with RGB data.

In the current work, we are integrating the prominent properties of the ancestral ICPS-net based systems and we integrate them so that the final architecture performs a higher precision estimates while the entire data preparation and model convergence, as well as the estimation precision are all significantly improved. Briefly speaking, a place is initially introduced to our system for indoor navigation. We divide it into different scenes, and we show all the possible views of the scenes through camera moving strategies. Then, we train our model based on these obtained images for the purpose of scene classification and final navigation step.

3   The Proposed Architecture

As depicted in the system architecture in Fig. 1, there is a convolutional neural network (CNN), which is trained in order to identify the specified scene out of divided segments form the interested area based on the user input RGB image taken by the mobile phone, for instance. The input image size is changed to become compatible with the employed CNN structure (here, an EfficientNet B0 network [32], as in Fig. 2). The point-cloud data associated to the RGB images of the interested area have to be already extracted using a LiDAR system. The entire process has been explained in [6].

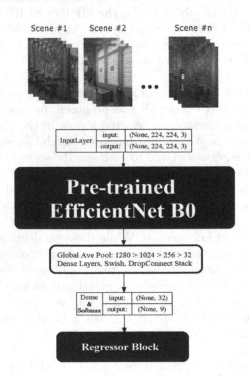

Fig. 2. Scene classifier based on EfficientNet-B0 CNN. **Input**: RGB data; **Output**: Associated scene number

During training of the system, the imagery RGB data is given to a UNET-based network (as in Fig. 6) to reconstruct the point-cloud image associated to the RGB image [28]. This network is a Pix2Pix GAN (*Generative Adversarial Network*), which produces these corresponding pairs of (RGB, Point-cloud) images [12]. The input RGB images are augmented for the Pix2Pix GAN network, using different contrast and brightness levels as well as masking objects as depicted in Fig. 8, in order to make the reconstruction of pointcloud images of the network sufficiently robust. Then, two CNN models are trained, simultaneously on the RGB images, as well as the LiDAR reconstructed point-cloud images, respectively. These CNNs are trained in a parallel regime, to perform as the regression models for the position estimates. The complete data (including RGB, Point-cloud and augmented ones) with more than one million samples will be released for further research works. The process is explained in the sequel.

3.1 Created Dataset

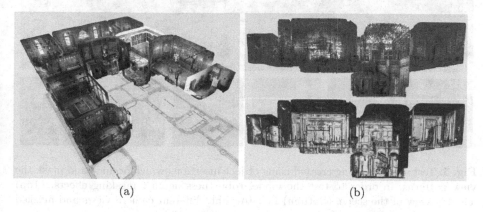

(a)   (b)

Fig. 3. (a) 3D model of the Hallwyl museum; (b) Top: Model vertices to produce Lidar-like dataset, Bottom: Material Capture including lighting and reflections

The dataset is created in the following procedure. First, 3D scanned images of the Hallwyl museum in Stockholm[1], has been sampled using the Unity software, and the normalized outputs are saved. This museum, as in Fig. 3a, has been divided into 9 scenes. More than one Million pure data samples[2] has been generated from all scenes using different regimes for the camera, as depicted in Fig. 4. The equivalent pointcloud data for each of the samples are created as depicted in Fig. 3b. The complete procedure has been explained in [6,7]. The augmentation process over the images through brightness variations and mask

---

[1] https://sketchfab.com/TheHallwylMuseum.
[2] http://opensource.alphareality.io.

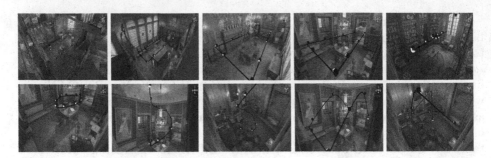

Fig. 4. Camera movement trajectory regimes inside different scenes to produce the RGB training images. Styles are: rectangular, spiral, circular, semicircular, and random with forward and backward viewpoints.

Fig. 5. Test samples being created using object insertions which occlude and mask the view patterns, in order to test the model robustness against masking effects. (Top) The big view of the scene, (Bottom) Left-to-right: different camera views and masked patterns due to object occlusions

insertions are performed and the outputs are added to both the RGB and point-cloud datasets. In order to evaluate the masking effect on the position regression network, we have created test samples in which some unseen objects are inserted to the scenes, a sample of which is depicted in Fig. 5.

3.2 Training of the Model

The complete procedure of the model training is shown in Algorithm 1. The RGB images created from the segmented scenes, and their corresponding pointcloud (P.C.) images, are the two datasets being available, as discussed in the previous section. During the test phase, we have no pointcloud data. Therefore, we train a generative neural network based on the UNET architecture [28] to estimate the pointcloud equivalent to the input user RGB image. This GAN has a Pix2Pix

Algorithm 1. Training phase of the Model components

Dataset 1: RGB images of the scenes.
Dataset 2: Point cloud (P.C.) images of the same scenes.
CNN 1: Scene classifier (**EfficientNet B0**)
 input: Dataset 1
 Output: Scene No.
GAN: RGB-2-Point Cloud Translator (**Pix2Pix GAN**)
 input 1: Dataset 1
 input 2: Dataset 2
 Output: Reconstructed P.C. image $\equiv$ Dataset 3.
CNN 2: Multi-Modal Regressor (**2 EfficientNet CNNs**)
 input 1: Dataset 3
 input 2: Dataset 1
 Output: Location.

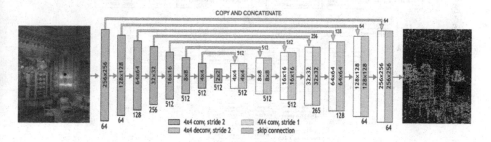

Fig. 6. RGB-to-Pointcloud translation, using Pix2Pix GAN

architecture, as in [12], and has been made robust using augmented data with brightness variations that is depicted in Fig. 6.

A CNN based on EfficientNet-B0 architecture [37], is trained as the scene classifier that gets the input RGB image of a specified scene inside the area of interest and outputs the scene number. The output layers of the standard EfficientNet-B0 is modified according to the problem requirements. Therefore, the stack of MLPs has been converted to $1024 \times 256 \times 32$, and the *Swish* activation function has being involved [27]. In addition, the batch normalization, and dropconnect [39], have also been employed in order to avoid model overfitting.

Localizing the user image is a task to be performed by a multi-modal CNN structure, as depicted in Fig. 7. In this innovative architecture, two individual CNNs are trained, separately. The CNN on the right-hand side of Fig. 7 gets the RGB images and their associated location information as the input-output pairs of samples, according to ICPS-net architecture [7]. The left-hand side CNN, takes the reconstructed pointcloud images obtained from the GAN (as the equivalent pointcloud images of the user RGB images) and the corresponding location information, as pairs. However, these two structures are both clipped from a middle layer (i.e. the stack of MLP layers) and concatenated, as in Fig. 7, to inherit the prominent properties of their ancestors. The trained models of each individ-

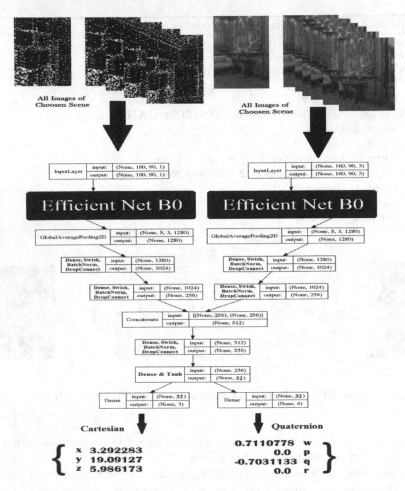

Fig. 7. A novel multi-modal regressor CNNs. Left path is only trained on the pointcloud data obtained from the GAN output; Right path only on RGB data.

ual path has been pretrained for 40 epochs [17], and after concatenation, the architecture has been again trained completely from the scratch for 90 epochs.

There are two critical problems for this multimodal regressor. First, each CNN branch contains more than 3 million parameters to be trained. This will lead to model overfitting. We do data augmentation to avoid it. However, the images which are augmented through zooming, sheering, or rotating, can modify the associated position outputs drastically and corrupt the model performance. On the other hand, for indoor areas there are not sufficient indicatives and stationary objects which can perform as the markers of the environment. As a result, moving of the objects may cause serious mismatches between training and test conditions, hence leading to contradictions between what model has been trained with, and what the user feeds to the model. In order to solve both

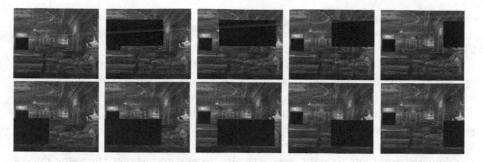

Fig. 8. Data augmenting by mask insertion and sliding completely over the reference image, on the top-left corner.

problems simultaneously, we used a dark mask window which slides over all images of the input datasets and generates the augmented data for the model, as depicted in Fig. 8. These masked images correspond to the same output, as the original ones. However, by doing that we can make the model robust against trivial environmental changes. This augmentation is performed in addition to the brightness variations, mentioned earlier. The masking augmentation has been applied to the input data including the RGB and associated pointcloud images,

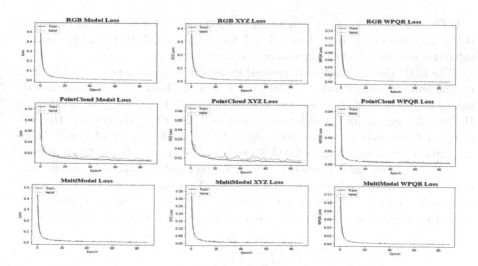

Fig. 9. Train vs validation losses of the regressor (Individual CNNs (top 2 rows) vs multi-modal CNN (last row)): (1st row)-left to right: Train vs validation losses of, 1) RGB CNN, 2) Cartesian position est. of the RGB-CNN, 3) quaternion est. of the RGB-CNN;(2nd row)-left to right: Train vs validation losses of, 1) Pointcloud CNN, 2) pointcloud Cartesian est., 3) point-cloud CNN quaternion est., (3rd row)-left to right: Train vs validation losses of, 1) multi-modal CNN, 2) multi-modal Cartesian position est., 3) multi-modal CNN quaternion estimates.

as in Fig. 8. As explained during the model training, the effect of these augmented data would be two-fold: 1) To make the regressors robust against input changes, 2) to avoid the model overfitting.

The accuracy and loss curves related to the training of the regressor (based on Algorithm 1) has been depicted in Fig. 9. This figure illustrates the train and validation losses of the regressor, which is a bundle of two CNN architectures. The first row images, show the training and validation losses of the right-hand side of the regressor structure of Fig. 7, which belongs to the RGB images. Model loss, training loss of location information and validation loss of these information are depicted from left-to-right, respectively. Second row shows the same curves for the pointcloud based CNN regressor (left branch of the Fig. 7). Third row, further illustrates the aforementioned curves for the integrated regressor model of CNNs. As clearly shown in Fig. 9, the training and validation losses of the RGB model are pretty well converged. For the pointcloud CNN regressor the convergence is not so good and validation curve is nasty. However, for the combined model, decaying curves mostly follow the RGB model, but the error of training and validation is slightly worse than the RGB-CNN model. Therefore, the premium features of each of the CNN models are inherited in the combined model.

4   Experimental Analysis and Results

A GTX 1080 NVIDIA GPU, on an Intel 7700 core-i7 CPU, with 32 GBytes of RAM have been employed. Tensorflow 1.13.1 with CUDA 10.1, and Keras 2.2.4 softwares are also used to implement the algorithms.

The RGB sample images are created using a moving camera with an imaging regime and movement styles, as depicted in Fig. 4. However, the number of the scenes assigned to each interested area is optional. Here, we have divided the Hallwyl 3D graph into 9 different scenes and the RGB images are the ones sampled from each scene, individually. The point-cloud pair of these images are further extracted using a LiDAR system. The created datasets are divided into 60% training, 20% validation, and 20% test data samples. The regression results are further evaluated on the unseen 20% of data samples. The output positioning data has also been normalized to the values between 1, and −1, in order to expedite the convergence process. The normalization is performed as,

$$P = 2\frac{P - P_{Min}}{P_{Max} - P_{Min}} - 1 \tag{1}$$

where P is the position, and P_{Max} and P_{Min} are the maximum and minimum samples of each class, respectively.

4.1   Testing of the Model

The complete test procedure is depicted in the Algorithm 2. The user RGB image is resized to match the input of the classifier CNN. The EfficientNet B0 classifier

Algorithm 2. Testing phase of the system

Input: User RGB image ≡ **inData**.
CNN 1: Scene classifier (**EfficientNet B0**)
    input: **inData**.
    Output: Scene No.
    pre-process: Map the user image to the model image size.
GAN: RGB-2-Point Cloud Translator (**Pix2Pix GAN**)
    input 1: **inData**
    Output: Reconstructed P.C. image of **inData**.
CNN 2: Multi-Modal Regressors (**2 EfficientNet CNNs**)
    input 1: Reconstructed P.C. image of **inData**.
    input 2: **inData**
    Output: Location.

Table 1. Classifier errors and accuracy values.

	Training	Validation	Test
Loss	0.06415	0.021851	0.063899
Accuracy	%98.514	%100	%98.099

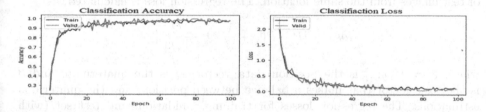

Fig. 10. Classification accuracy (left), and Classification loss (right) based on the categorical cross-entropy.

CNN, could be easily replaced by the MobileNet V2, and the activation function could be replaced by ReLU in order to reduce the computational burden, to the cost of a trivial growth of the estimation error.

Loss function of the classification CNN is the categorical cross-entropy, and the model is optimized for maximizing the validation accuracy. The scene classification accuracy and loss over the training and test data have been depicted in Fig. 10, and further shown in Table 1. Using strategies to avoid overfitting such as dropout and dropconnect during training causes the training error exceed the validation error.

As the confusion matrix in Fig. 11 clarifies the classification has been performed almost perfectly. The worst misclassification belongs to the *Armoury*, and *SmallDrowing* rooms. This is due to the similar patterns which are generated from rectangular trajectory X-Y, in which the camera is close to the wall and the observed patterns get quite similar. This would be completely solved

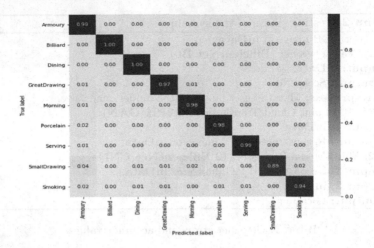

Fig. 11. The confusion matrix for scene classifier using EfficientNet B0 model.

through taking a sequence of panorama-capturing images which create a batch of test images from the same location. The regression loss is calculated, as

$$loss = ||P - \hat{P}||_2 + \frac{1}{\beta}||\hat{Q} - \frac{Q}{||Q||}||_2 \tag{2}$$

where $P = [x; y; z]$ is the position data vector, Q is the quaternion, and β is the scale factor that makes a balance between position, and the quaternion estimations. The regression losses for training, validation, and test set (with 60,20,20 partitioning rates, respectively) are shown in Table 2. The comparison among the proposed **APS** model and the previous models show that the APS model is highly accurate, however it does not carry the problems of the ICPS-net model. The regression loss is chosen based on [14, 16].

In addition, the average errors of the position and quaternion estimates in the output of the proposed model and the competitors are shown in Table 3. The average disruption loss, over the entire test set in a comparison with the other methods is further shown in Table 4, which indicates the superiority of the proposed model.

Table 2. Training, validation, and test losses of the models

Method vs Loss	Training	Validation	Test
RGB (ICPS-net)	0.00781	0.00688	0.00938
P.Cloud (LiDAR ICPS-net)	0.01286	0.01334	0.02964
APS	0.00813	0.00712	0.00972

Table 3. Average errors of the methods on the position (X,Y,Z) estimates (millimeter), and the Quaternion (degree)

Method vs AvgErr	x	Y	Z	Quaternion
RGB (ICPS-net)	2.6	3.4	1	0.0086
(LiDAR ICPS-net)	19	27	7.3	0.0096
APS	3.1	3.9	1.3	0.0097

Table 4. Average disruption error values of the models

Method	Disruption test loss
RGB (ICPS-net)	0.0219
P.Cloud (LiDAR ICPS-net)	0.0365
APS	0.0167

5   Conclusion

In this paper an end-to-end system has been proposed to address the indoor positioning problem. This work improves the previously proposed systems, namely ICPS-net, and LiDAR ICPS-net. The ICPS-net has become robust against environmental changes due to objects with dynamicity in the background. The LiDAR ICPS-net had the advantage of easier data generation and more robustness against input variations. However, it suffered from lack of precision. Another novelty has been through using the Pix2Pix GAN to generate the point-cloud data which could help data augmentation by generating the images with a distribution close to the dataset. While new data prevents model overfitting, it helps providing robust point-cloud data when input RGB images are masked and occluded. The third novelty has been a multi-modal CNN which merges two individual CNN models and outperforms them for both the regression precision, and the convergence ability. The Cartesian position and quaternion estimates, have been remarkably improved with respect to the SOTA. The novelties of the proposed model simplifies leveraging of the system in various applications, such as large buildings, malls, tunnels, and AR/VR applications.

References

1. Brahmbhatt, S., Gu, J., Kim, K., Hays, J., Kautz, J.: Geometry-aware learning of maps for camera localization. In: Proceedings of the IEEE Conference on Computer Vision and Pattern Recognition, pp. 2616–2625 (2018)
2. Caso, G., De Nardis, L., Lemic, F., Handziski, V., Wolisz, A., Di Benedetto, M.G.: Vifi: virtual fingerprinting wifi-based indoor positioning via multi-wall multi-floor propagation model. IEEE Trans. Mobile Comput. (2019)
3. Duque Domingo, J., Cerrada, C., Valero, E., Cerrada, J.: An improved indoor positioning system using RGB-D cameras and wireless networks for use in complex environments. Sensors **17**(10), 2391 (2017)

4. Duque Domingo, J., Cerrada, C., Valero, E., Cerrada, J.A.: Indoor positioning system using depth maps and wireless networks. J. Sens. **2016** (2016)
5. Faragher, R., Harle, R.: An analysis of the accuracy of bluetooth low energy for indoor positioning applications. In: Proceedings of the 27th International Technical Meeting of The Satellite Division of the Institute of Navigation (ION GNSS + 2014), vol. 812, pp. 201–210 (2014)
6. Ghofrani, A., Mahdian, R., Tabatabaie, S.M., Tabasi, S.M.: L-icpsnet: Lidar indoor camera positioning system for RGB to point cloud translation using end2end generative network. In: 2020 8th Iranian Joint Congress on Fuzzy and intelligent Systems (CFIS), pp. 110–115. IEEE (2020)
7. Ghofrani, A., Toroghi, R.M., Tabatabaie, S.M.: Icps-net: An end-to-end RGB-based indoor camera positioning system using deep convolutional neural networks. arXiv preprint arXiv:1910.06219 (2019)
8. Guan, K., Ma, L., Tan, X., Guo, S.: Vision-based indoor localization approach based on surf and landmark. In: 2016 International Wireless Communications and Mobile Computing Conference (IWCMC), pp. 655–659. IEEE (2016)
9. Henriques, J.F., Vedaldi, A.: Mapnet: An allocentric spatial memory for mapping environments. In: Proceedings of the IEEE Conference on Computer Vision and Pattern Recognition, pp. 8476–8484 (2018)
10. Henry, P., Krainin, M., Herbst, E., Ren, X., Fox, D.: RGB-D mapping: using depth cameras for dense 3D modeling of indoor environments. In: Khatib, O., Kumar, V., Sukhatme, G. (eds.) Experimental Robotics. STAR, vol. 79, pp. 477–491. Springer, Heidelberg (2014). https://doi.org/10.1007/978-3-642-28572-1_33
11. Huang, K., He, K., Du, X.: A hybrid method to improve the BLE-based indoor positioning in a dense bluetooth environment. Sensors **19**(2), 424 (2019)
12. Isola, P., Zhu, J.Y., Zhou, T., Efros, A.A.: Image-to-image translation with conditional adversarial networks. In: Proceedings of the IEEE Conference on Computer Vision and Pattern Recognition, pp. 1125–1134 (2017)
13. Jianyong, Z., Haiyong, L., Zili, C., Zhaohui, L.: RSSI based bluetooth low energy indoor positioning. In: 2014 International Conference on Indoor Positioning and Indoor Navigation (IPIN), pp. 526–533. IEEE (2014)
14. Kendall, A., Cipolla, R.: Geometric loss functions for camera pose regression with deep learning. In: Proceedings of the IEEE Conference on Computer Vision and Pattern Recognition, pp. 5974–5983 (2017)
15. Kendall, A., Grimes, M., Cipolla, R.: Posenet: a convolutional network for real-time 6-dof camera relocalization. In: Proceedings of the IEEE International Conference on Computer Vision, pp. 2938–2946 (2015)
16. Kingma, D.P., Ba, J.: Adam: a method for stochastic optimization. arXiv preprint arXiv:1412.6980 (2014)
17. Kumar, S.K.: On weight initialization in deep neural networks. arXiv preprint arXiv:1704.08863 (2017)
18. Lai, C.C., Su, K.L.: Development of an intelligent mobile robot localization system using kinect RGB-D mapping and neural network. Comput. Electr. Eng. **67**, 620–628 (2018)
19. Liang, J.Z., Corso, N., Turner, E., Zakhor, A.: Image based localization in indoor environments. In: 2013 Fourth International Conference on Computing for Geospatial Research and Application, pp. 70–75. IEEE (2013)
20. Liang, J.Z., Corso, N., Turner, E., Zakhor, A.: Image-based positioning of mobile devices in indoor environments. In: Choi, J., Friedland, G. (eds.) Multimodal Location Estimation of Videos and Images, pp. 85–99. Springer, Cham (2015). https://doi.org/10.1007/978-3-319-09861-6_5

21. Lin, X.Y., Ho, T.W., Fang, C.C., Yen, Z.S., Yang, B.J., Lai, F.: A mobile indoor positioning system based on ibeacon technology. In: 2015 37th Annual International Conference of the IEEE Engineering in Medicine and Biology Society (EMBC), pp. 4970–4973. IEEE (2015)

22. Liu, T., Zhang, X., Li, Q., Fang, Z., Tahir, N.: An accurate visual-inertial integrated geo-tagging method for crowdsourcing-based indoor localization. Remote Sens. **11**(16), 1912 (2019)

23. Ma, Z., Wu, B., Poslad, S.: A wifi RSSI ranking fingerprint positioning system and its application to indoor activities of daily living recognition. Int. J. Distrib. Sensor Networks **15**(4), 1550147719837916 (2019)

24. Mekki, K., Bajic, E., Meyer, F.: Indoor positioning system for IoT device based on BLE technology and MQTT protocol. In: 2019 IEEE 5th World Forum on Internet of Things (WF-IoT), pp. 787–792. IEEE (2019)

25. Mendoza-Silva, G.M., Torres-Sospedra, J., Huerta, J.: A meta-review of indoor positioning systems. Sensors **19**(20), 4507 (2019)

26. Morgado, F., Martins, P., Caldeira, F.: Beacons positioning detection, a novel approach. In: The 10th International Conference on Ambient Systems, Networks and Technologies (ANT 2019), vol. 151, pp. 23–30 (2019)

27. Ramachandran, P., Zoph, B., Le, Q.V.: Swish: a self-gated activation function, vol. 7. arXiv preprint arXiv:1710.05941 (2017)

28. Ronneberger, O., Fischer, P., Brox, T.: U-Net: convolutional networks for biomedical image segmentation. In: Navab, N., Hornegger, J., Wells, W.M., Frangi, A.F. (eds.) MICCAI 2015. LNCS, vol. 9351, pp. 234–241. Springer, Cham (2015). https://doi.org/10.1007/978-3-319-24574-4_28

29. Russ, M., et al.: Augmented reality systems and methods for providing player action recommendations in real time, 14 February 2019. US Patent App. 15/852, 088

30. Sandler, M., Howard, A., Zhu, M., Zhmoginov, A., Chen, L.C.: Mobilenetv 2: inverted residuals and linear bottlenecks. In: Proceedings of the IEEE Conference on Computer Vision and Pattern Recognition, pp. 4510–4520 (2018)

31. Sattler, T., Leibe, B., Kobbelt, L.: Improving image-based localization by active correspondence search. In: Fitzgibbon, A., Lazebnik, S., Perona, P., Sato, Y., Schmid, C. (eds.) ECCV 2012. LNCS, vol. 7572, pp. 752–765. Springer, Heidelberg (2012). https://doi.org/10.1007/978-3-642-33718-5_54

32. Sattler, T., Leibe, B., Kobbelt, L.: Efficient and effective prioritized matching for large-scale image-based localization. IEEE Trans. Pattern Anal. Mach. Intell. **39**(9), 1744–1756 (2016)

33. Shao, S., Shuo, N., Kubota, N.: An ibeacon indoor positioning system based on multi-sensor fusion. In: 2018 Joint 10th International Conference on Soft Computing and Intelligent Systems (SCIS) and 19th International Symposium on Advanced Intelligent Systems (ISIS), pp. 1115–1120. IEEE (2018)

34. Sharp, I., Yu, K.: Indoor WiFi positioning. Wireless Positioning: Principles and Practice. NST, pp. 219–240. Springer, Singapore (2019). https://doi.org/10.1007/978-981-10-8791-2_8

35. Shen, Z., Liu, J., Zheng, Y., Cao, L.: A low-cost mobile VR walkthrough system for displaying multimedia works based on unity3d. In: 2019 14th International Conference on Computer Science and Education (ICCSE), pp. 415–419. IEEE (2019)

36. Sieberth, T., Dobay, A., Affolter, R., Ebert, L.C.: Applying virtual reality in forensics-a virtual scene walkthrough. Forensic Sci. Med. Pathol. **15**(1), 41–47 (2019)

37. Tan, M., Le, Q.V.: Efficientnet: rethinking model scaling for convolutional neural networks. arXiv preprint arXiv:1905.11946 (2019)
38. Valgren, C., Lilienthal, A.J.: Sift, surf and seasons: appearance-based long-term localization in outdoor environments. Robot. Auton. Syst. **58**(2), 149–156 (2010)
39. Wan, L., Zeiler, M., Zhang, S., Le Cun, Y., Fergus, R.: Regularization of neural networks using dropconnect. In: International Conference on Machine Learning, pp. 1058–1066 (2013)
40. Wang, R., Wan, W., Di, K., Chen, R., Feng, X.: A high-accuracy indoor-positioning method with automated RGB-D image database construction. Remote Sens. **11**(21), 2572 (2019)
41. Yang, C., Shao, H.R.: Wifi-based indoor positioning. IEEE Commun. Mag. **53**(3), 150–157 (2015)
42. Yuan, W., Li, Z., Su, C.Y.: RGB-D sensor-based visual slam for localization and navigation of indoor mobile robot. In: 2016 International Conference on Advanced Robotics and Mechatronics (ICARM), pp. 82–87. IEEE (2016)
43. Zhang, F., et al.: Real-time calibration and registration method for indoor scene with joint depth and color camera. Int. J. Pattern Recogn. Artif. Intell. **32**(07), 1854021 (2018)
44. Zuo, Z., Liu, L., Zhang, L., Fang, Y.: Indoor positioning based on bluetooth low-energy beacons adopting graph optimization. Sensors **18**(11), 3736 (2018)

Improved Bilinear Model for Facial Expression Recognition

M. Amine Mahmoudi[1,3](✉), Aladine Chetouani[2], Fatma Boufera[1],
and Hedi Tabia[3]

[1] Mustapha Stambouli University of Mascara, Mascara, Algeria
mohamed.mahmoudi@univ-mascara.dz
[2] PRISME Laboratory, University of Orleans, Orleans, France
[3] Université Paris Saclay, IBISC, Univ Evry, Evry, France

Abstract. Facial Expression Recognition (FER) systems aims to classify human emotions through facial expression as one of seven basic emotions: happiness, sadness, fear, disgust, anger, surprise and neutral. FER is a very challenging problem due to the subtle differences that exist between its categories. Even though convolutional neural networks (CNN) achieved impressive results in several computer vision tasks, they still do not perform as well in FER. Many techniques, like bilinear pooling and improved bilinear pooling, have been proposed to improve the CNN performance on similar problems. The accuracy enhancement they brought in multiple visual tasks, shows that their is still room for improvement for CNNs on FER. In this paper, we propose to use bilinear and improved bilinear pooling with CNNs for FER. This framework has been evaluated on three well known datasets, namely ExpW, FER2013 and RAF-DB. It has shown that the use of bilinear and improved bilinear pooling with CNNs can enhance the overall accuracy to nearly 3% for FER and achieve state-of-the-art results.

Keywords: Facial expression recognition · Bilinear pooling · Improved bilinear pooling

1 Introduction

Facial expression recognition is a research area which consists of classifying the human emotions through the expressions on their faces as one of seven basic emotions: happiness, sadness, fear, disgust, anger, surprise and neutral. FER finds applications in different fields including security, intelligent human-computer interaction, robotics, and clinical medicine for autism, depression, pain and mental health problems.

With the resurgence of deep learning techniques, the computer vision community has witnessed an era of blossoming result thanks to the use of very large training databases. Big data is crucial to avoid the model being prone to overfitting. This was a very limiting factor for the use of deep learning for FER

© Springer Nature Switzerland AG 2021
C. Djeddi et al. (Eds.): MedPRAI 2020, CCIS 1322, pp. 47–59, 2021.
https://doi.org/10.1007/978-3-030-71804-6_4

at the beginning, due to the limited size of facial expression datasets. This is not the case anymore with the emergence of very large in-the-wild datasets of facial expressions (e.g. FER2013 [7], ExpW [25], AffectNet [20], etc.). Yet, these datasets are more challenging because facial expressions are more affected by the in-the-wild conditions than other.

Bilinear CNN model is a combination of two CNNs A and B that takes as input the same image and output two feature maps. These feature maps are then multiplied at each location using tensor product. The result is pooled to obtain a global image descriptor of the image. The latter is passed to a classifier throughout make a prediction. Compared to single CNNs, bilinear CNN models have shown to achieve very good results on various visual tasks. For instance, semantic segmentation, visual questions answering and fine-grained recognition.

Fine-grained recognition is a research area that is interested in developing algorithms for automatically discriminating categories with only small subtle visual differences. Given that FER datasets contain very few categories that are nearly identical, we believe that any solution which is efficient for fine-grained recognition, like bilinear CNNs, may perform as well for FER.

In this paper, in addition of using bilinear CNN models, we propose to use an improved bilinear pooling with CNNs models for FER. In this framework, various ways of normalization are used to improve the accuracy, including the matrix square root, element-wise square root and L2 normalization.

The remainder of this paper is organized as follow: Sect. 2 reviews similar works that have been done on FER and bilinear CNN models. Section 3 gives more details about this approach. Section 4 presents our experiments, datasets and results; and Sect. 5 concludes the paper.

2 Related Work

Studies on FER using deep learning techniques used either self-built networks from scratch or fine-tuning on well-known pre-trained models. Many self-built architectures were proposed in the literature achieving various results on different datasets. For instance, multitask networks takes into consideration various factors like the head pose, illumination, facial landmarks, facial action units and subject identity. These factors are combined to conduct a simultaneous multi-task learning which may lead to model that is close to the real world conditions. Some studies like [4, 22] suggested that simultaneously conducted FER with other tasks, such as facial landmark localization and facial action units detection, can jointly improve FER performance. Other works have used network ensemble on different dataset for FER [9] achieving pretty high performance. Finally, the cascaded network, in which various modules for different tasks are combined sequentially to construct a deeper network, where the outputs of the former modules are utilized by the latter modules. In [5], Deep Belief Networks were trained to first detect faces and expression-related areas. Then, these parsed face components were classified by a stacked auto-encoder.

Self-built networks from scratch can achieve better result, but they needs to be trained on very large datasets. The dataset issue was a very limiting criteria in the beginning, because of the lack of sufficiently large datasets. But this is not the case anymore with the emergence of many large dataset containing thousands of facial expression images (e.g. FER2013 [7], ExpW [25], AffectNet [20]...etc.). An extensive survey has been proposed by Li and Deng [11] for more details.

Several methods have been proposed to improve the performance of CNNs. In [16] a bilinear pooling method for fine-grained recognition was proposed. Inspired from the second order pooling model introduced by [24], this model can capture higher interaction between image locations, which makes the model more discriminant than a simple model. This method have been used for FER by Zhou et al. [26] and noticed that they significantly outperformed their respective baselines. However, these models are high dimensional and could be impractical for a multitude of image analysis. In [6] two compact bilinear representations of these models have been proposed. They reached results as the full bilinear representation, yet with only a few thousand dimensions. This compact representations have also been used, by [21], in a multi-modal emotion recognition, combining facial expressions and voice sound. The latter was further generalized in the form of Taylor series kernel in [3]. The proposed method captures high order and non-linear feature interactions via compact explicit feature mapping. The approximated representation is fully differentiable, and the kernel composition can be learned together with a CNN in an end-to-end manner. Lin et al. have furthered their bilinear CNN model, by applying matrix normalization functions. Two matrix functions have been used, namely matrix logarithm and matrix square-root. All these methods are plugged at the end of the network, right between the convolution layers and the fully connected layers. They act as a basis expansion layers, increasing thereby the discrimination power of the fully connected layers, This discrimination power is back-propagated through the convolution layers. These methods have attracted increasing attentions, achieving better performance than classical first-order networks in a variety of tasks. Even-thought these methods increase the CNN performance, they are unable to learn by themselves and rely entirely on the CNN architecture. Furthermore, effectively introducing higher-order representation in earlier pooling layers, for improving non-linear capability of CNNs, is still an open problem.

More recently, Mahmoudi et al. [19] addressed this problem and proposed a novel pooling layer that not only reduces input information but also extracts linear and non-linear relations between features. It leverage kernel functions which allow to generalise linear pooling while capturing higher order information. Mahmoudi et al. [18] also introduced a novel FC layer based on kernel function. It applies a higher order function on its inputs instead of calculating their weighted sum. The proposed Kernelized Dense Layers (KDL) permits to improve the discrimination power of the full network and it is completely differentiable, allowing an end-to-end learning. The strength of these methods relies on the fact that they capture additional discriminant information compared to conventional pooling techniques.

To the best of our knowledge, improved bilinear CNN models have never been used for FER. We believe that these models can enhance the CNN performance also for FER, given that FER is very similar to fine grained recognition. In the following sections, we will give more details about the bilinear and the improved bilinear CNN models. We will also explore the effect of using them on FER.

3   Approach

In this section we will describe the approach we used for our FER task. This technique, called bilinear CNN model, was inspired by Lin et al. [16]. It performed very well on fine-grained visual recognition tasks, and was later improved in [15]. We will describe bellow in more details bilinear CNN models and the improved version.

3.1   Bilinear CNN Models

Bilinear pooling models were first introduced by Tenenbaum and Freeman [24]. Also called second order pooling models, they were used to separate style and content. These models have been later used for fine grained recognition and semantic segmentation using both hand-tuned and learned features.

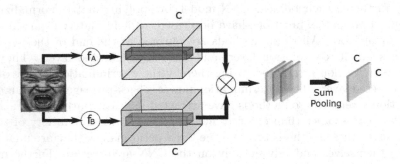

Fig. 1. A bilinear model

For image classification, we can generally formulate a bilinear model B as a quadruple $B(f_A, f_B, P, C)$ (Fig. 1). Where f_A, and f_B, are feature functions, P a pooling function and C a classification function. A feature function takes an image Img and a location $l \in Loc$ as inputs and produces a feature vectors, for each location in Loc, as follows:

$$f(l, Img) \mapsto \mathcal{R}^c \tag{1}$$

We then combine these feature functions outputs vectors using the tensor product (Eq. 2) at each location. Here, A and B are feature vectors produced by the feature functions f_A, and f_B respectively.

$$A \otimes B = \begin{bmatrix} a_1 \\ a_2 \\ . \\ . \\ . \\ a_c \end{bmatrix} \otimes \begin{bmatrix} b_1 \\ b_2 \\ . \\ . \\ . \\ y_b \end{bmatrix} = \begin{bmatrix} a_1b_1 & a_1b_2 & ... & a_1b_c \\ a_2b_1 & a_2b_2 & ... & a_2b_c \\ . & . & & . \\ . & . & & . \\ . & . & & . \\ a_nb_1 & a_nb_2 & ... & a_cb_c \end{bmatrix} \tag{2}$$

Formally, the bilinear feature combination of f_A and f_B at a location $l \in Loc$ is given by:

$$Bilinear(l, Img, f_A, f_B) = f_A(l, Img) \otimes f_B(l, Img) \tag{3}$$

The pooling function P combines the bilinear features throughout the different locations in the image (Eq. 4), which will produce a global image descriptor. One of the most used pooling functions are the sum and the max-pooling functions of all the bilinear features. Both functions ignore the location of the features and are hence orderless [16].

$$P(Loc, Img, f_A, f_B) = \sum_{l \in Loc} f_A(l, Img) \otimes f_B(l, Img) \tag{4}$$

A natural candidate for the feature function f is a CNN consisting of a succession of convolutional and pooling layers. According to [16], the use of CNNs is beneficial at many levels. It allows to use pre-trained CNNs in which we take only the convolutional layers including non-linearities as feature extractors. This can be beneficial specially when domain specific data is scarce. Another benefit of using only the convolutional layers is that the resulting CNN can process images of an arbitrary size in a single forward-propagation step. It produces outputs indexed by the location in the image and feature channel, in addition of reducing considerably the network's parameters number. Finally, the use of CNNs for a bilinear model allows this model to be trained in an end-to-end fashion. This technique has been used in a number of recognition tasks. For instance object detection, texture recognition and fine-grained classification and shown to give very good results.

Lin et al. [16] proposed bilinear CNN Models for fine-grained visual recognition (Fig. 2). The model consists of two CNNs, each trained to recognize special features. The resulting feature maps are sum-pooled to aggregate the bilinear features across the image. The resulting bilinear vector is then passed through signed square-root step, followed by L2 normalization, which improves performance in practice. Finally, the result will be fed to a classifier.

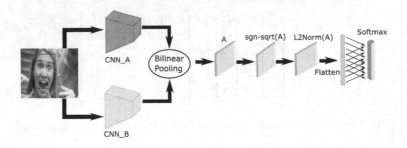

Fig. 2. Bilinear CNN architecture.

3.2 Improved Bilinear Pooling

Lin et al. [15] have also investigated various ways of normalization to improve the representation power of their bilinear model. In particular, a class of matrix functions were used to scale the spectrum (eigenvalues) of the co-variance matrix resulting of the bilinear pooling. One example of such normalization is the matrix-logarithm function defined for Symmetric Positive Definite (SPD) matrices. It maps the Riemannian manifold of SPD matrices to an Euclidean space that preserves the geodesic distance between elements in the underlying manifold (Fig. 3). An other normalization is the matrix square-root normalization which offers significant improvements and outperforms the matrix logarithm normalization when combined with element-wise square-root and L2 normalization. This improved the accuracy by 2–3% on a range of fine-grained recognition datasets leading to a new state-of-the-art.

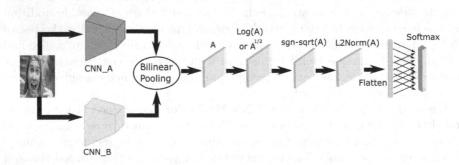

Fig. 3. Improved bilinear CNN architecture.

The strength of bilinear models relies in the fact that they capture higher interaction between image locations, which makes the model more discriminant than a simple model. This allowed them to achieve impressive results in various image recognition tasks including FER. For instance, bilinear pooling has recently been used for FER in fine-grained manner [26]. Compact bilinear pooling has also been used in a multi-modal emotion recognition combining facial expressions and voice sound [21]. But as far as we know, the improved bilinear pooling has never been used for FER. In the following section, we will explore the effect of using an improved bilinear CNN for FER. We will also implement a bilinear CNN to further appreciate the enhancement that can the improved bilinear CNN provide.

4 Experiments

In this section we will give more details about the experiments we performed in order to evaluate the approach described above. First, we give a brief description of the datasets we have used. After that, we describe architecture of the used models and training process. Finally, we discuss the obtained results.

4.1 Datasets

Our experiments have been conducted on three well-known facial expression datasets, namely the RAF-DB [13], ExpW [25] and FER2013 [7]. Facial expression datasets contain few classes that are nearly identical, which makes the recognition process more challenging.

- The RAF-DB [13] stands for the Real-world Affective Face DataBase. It is a real-world dataset that contains 29,672 highly diverse facial images downloaded from the Internet. With manually crowd-sourced annotation and reliable estimation, seven basic and eleven compound emotion labels are provided for the samples. This dataset is divided in training and validation subsets.
- The ExpW [25] stands for the EXPression in-the-Wild dataset. It contains 91,793 faces downloaded using Google image search. Each of the face images was manually annotated as one of the seven basic expression categories.
- The FER2013 database was first introduced during the ICML 2013 Challenges in Representation Learning [7]. This database contains 28709 training images, 3589 validation images and 3589 test images with seven expression labels: fear, happiness, anger, disgust, surprise, sadness and neutral.

In order to have the same dataset structure for all datasets, we divided the validation subset in RAF-DB [13] into validation and test subsets by a ratio of 0.5 each. We have also divided ExpW dataset with a ratio of 0.7 for training, 0.15 for validation and 0.15 for test.

4.2 Model Architecture and Training Process

For our experiment, we have used both a VGG-16 pre-trained on ImageNet database and a model built from scratch. For the VGG-16 we only took the convolution layers without the top fully connected ones. We added a batch normalization layer after each convolution layer (this enhances the model's accuracy by nearly 1%). We added only one fully connected layer of size 512 and a final Softmax layer of seven output classes.

On the other hand, our model architecture, as shown in Fig. 4 is quite simple and can effectively run on cost-effective GPUs. It is composed of five convolutional blocks. Each block consists of a convolution, batch normalization and rectified linear unit activation layers. The use of batch normalization [27] before the activation brings more stability to parameter initialization and achieves higher learning rate. Each of the five convolutional blocks is followed by a dropout layer. In the following we refer to this network architecture as (Model-1).

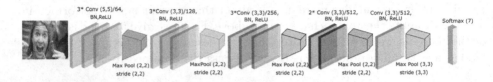

Fig. 4. Base model architecture (Model-1).

The only pre-processing which we have employed on all experiments is cropping the face region and resizing the resulting images to 100×100 pixels. We have used Adam optimiser with a learning rate varying from 0.001 to $5e-5$. This learning rate is decreased by a factor of 0.63 if the validation accuracy does not increase over ten epochs. To avoid over-fitting we have first augmented the data using a range degree for random rotations of 20, a shear intensity of 0.2, a range for random zoom of 0.2 and randomly flip inputs horizontally. We have also employed earl stopping if validation accuracy does not improve by a factor of 0.01 over 20 epochs.

4.3   Ablation Study

This section explores the impact of using bilinear pooling and improved version on the overall accuracy of the two base models (VGG-16 and Model-1). All the following experiments follow the same training process described above.

First we fine tuned the VGG-16 model on the three datasets and trained our model from scratch. Secondly, we took only the convolution part of the two trained models and add bilinear pooling (as shown in Fig. 2) with the following configurations: a) bilinear pooling on top of VGG-16, b) bilinear pooling on top of Model-1 and c) bilinear pooling on top of both VGG-16 and Model-1. We begin with fine tuning the bilinear pooling part only by freezing the underlying models. After that we train model in an end-to-end fashion. Finally, we repeated the same process of bilinear pooling with the improved version. That is to take the convolution part only of the fine-tuned VGG-16 and Model-1 and add the improved bilinear pooling (as shown in Fig. 3). We followed the same three configurations used for bilinear pooling.

Table 1 present the result of the two base models with comparison to these models with bilinear pooling and improved bilinear pooling. The VGG-16 model attains an accuracy rate of 65.23%, 67.61% and 85.23% on FER2013, ExpW and

RAF-DB respectively. Whereas Model-1 attains an accuracy of 70.13%, 75.91% and 87.05% respectvely on FER2013, ExpW and RAF-DB.

Table 1. Accuracy Rates of the proposed approach

Models	Dataset		
	FER2013	ExpW	RAF-DB
VGG-16	65.23%	67.61%	85.23%
VGG-16-BP[a]	68.15%	68.82%	85.77%
VGG-16-IBP[b]	68.71%	69.1%	86.34%
Model-1	70.13%	75.91%	87.05%
Model-1-BP[a]	71.63%	76.59%	88.48%
Model-1-IBP[b]	**72.65%**	**77.81%**	**89.02%**
(VGG-16/Model-1)-BP[a]	70.37%	73.57%	86.47%
(VGG-16/Model-1)-IBP[b]	71.22%	74.41%	87.13%

[a]BP: Bilinear Pooling.
[b]IBP: Improved Bilinear Pooling.

On the other hand one can notice that the use of bilinear pooling on top of a model increases considerably its accuracy. As reported in Table 1, the use of bilinear pooling on to of VGG-16 increases the accuracy for nearly 3% for FER2013 and more than 1% for both ExpW and RAF-DB. Similarly, the use of bilinear pooling on top of Model-1 increases the accuracy for about 1% on all datasets. However using bilinear pooling on top of both models gives an average accuracy rate between the underlying models accuracies. The resulting accuracy rates are 70.37%, 73.57% and 86.47% for FER2013, EwpW and RAF-DB respectively. This is due to the difference in accuracy between the two underlying models in the first place.

Finally, the use improved bilinear pooling increases further the accuracy rate for about 1% for all models with all datasets, compared to bilinear pooling. For instance, the accuracy rate of improved bilinear pooling on top of VGG-16 is 68.71%, 69.1% and 86.34% for FER2013, ExpW and RAF-DB respectively. Similarly, improved bilinear pooling on top of Model-1 gives 72.65%, 77.81% and 89.02% accuracy rates respectively for FER2013, ExpW and RAF-DB. The accuracy rate also increases when using improved bilinear pooling on top of both models. The later gives 71.22%, 74.41% and 87.13% on FER2013, ExpW and RAF-DB respectively.

These results demonstrate that the use of bilinear pooling and specially improved bilinear pooling, in the case of FER problem, are beneficial for the overall accuracy of the model. These techniques enhance the discriminative power of the model, compared to an ordinary fully connected layers.

4.4   Comparison with the State-of-the-Art

In this section, we compare the performance of the bilinear and improved bilinear CNN with respect to several state-of-the-art FER methods. The obtained results are reported in Table 2.

Table 2. Accuracy rate of the proposed approach and state of the art approach

Models	Dataset		
	FER2013	ExpW	RAF-DB
VGG-16-BP[a]	68.15%	68.82%	85.77%
VGG-16-IBP[b]	68.71%	69.1%	86.34%
Model-1-BP[a]	**71.63%**	**76.59%**	**88.48%**
Model-1-IBP[b]	**72.65%**	**77.81%**	**89.02%**
(VGG-16/Model-1)-BP[a]	70.37%	**73.57%**	86.47%
(VGG-16/Model-1)-IBP[b]	71.22%	**74.41%**	**87.13%**
Tang et al. [23]	71.16%	–	–
Guo et al. [8]	71.33%	–	–
Kim et al. [10]	**73.73%**	–	–
Bishay et al. [2]	–	**73.1%**	–
Lian et al. [14]	–	71.9 %	–
Acharya et al. [1]	–	–	**87%**
S Li et al. [12]	–	–	74.2%
Z. Liu et al. [17]	–	–	73.19%

[a]BP: Bilinear Pooling.
[b]IBP: Improved Bilinear Pooling.

According to Table 2, the bilinear and improved bilinear CNN outperforms the state-of-the-art methods on the ExpW dataset. The best accuracy rate is 77.81% and has been reached using the improved bilinear pooling on top of Model-1. Bilinear pooling on top of Model-1 gives, for his turn, 76.59%. Moreover bilinear and improved bilinear on top of both VGG-16 and Model-1 gives respectively 73.57% and 74.41%. Whereas bilinear pooling and the improved version on top of VGG-16 give lower rates than state-of-the-art methods [2] (**73.1%**).

On RAF-DB dataset, the accuracy of our models is also superior to state of the art methods. The best accuracy rate is 89.02% and has been reached using the improved bilinear pooling on top of Model-1. Bilinear pooling on top of Model-1 gives, for his turn, 88.48%. Moreover improved bilinear on top of both VGG-16 and Model-1 gives 87.13%. Whereas bilinear pooling and the improved version on top of VGG-16, as well as bilinear pooling on top of both VGG-16 and Model-1 give lower rates than state-of-the-art methods [1] (**87%**).

For FER2013, even thought using the bilinear and improved bilinear pooling improves considerably the models accuracy, the obtained results are still under the state of the art results. The best accuracy rate for this dataset, namely 72.65%, was reached using improved bilinear pooling on top of Model-1. Which 1% less than the state-of-the-art method [10] (**73.73%**).

5   Conclusions and Perspectives

This study proposes a FER method based on the improved bilinear CNN model. In this framework, various ways of normalization are used to improve the accuracy, including the matrix square root, element-wise square root and L2 normalization. To validate our method, we have used three large, well known, facial expression databases which are FER2013, RAF-DB and ExpW. In order to evaluate the improvement of our method, we have first implemented a CNN from scratch and fine-tuned pre-trained VGG-16 on our facial expressions datasets. After that we have implemented a bilinear model on top of the above models individually and on top of both of them. Finally, we repeated the same procedure with the improved bilinear model. The experiments show that this framework improves the overall accuracy for about 3%.

Bilinear models have been shown to achieve very good accuracy results on different visual recognition domains, like fine grained recognition, semantic segmentation and face recognition. Nevertheless, the dimensions of bilinear features are very high, usually on the order of hundreds of thousands to a few million. The reason why they are not practical for many visual recognition fields. Moreover, matrix square root function and bilinear pooling function are very memory and CPU consuming, which decrease the performance of the model. Therefore, many improvements have been applied to CNN, for instance compact bilinear pooling [6], reaching the same discriminative power as the full bilinear representation but with a representations having only a few thousand dimensions. An other improvement is the kernel pooling for CNNs [3] which is a general pooling framework that captures higher order interactions of features in the form of kernels.

Our Future work will focus on using more compact alternatives of the methods used in this work. Moreover, our perspective is to use multiple input data types (text, image and sound) in parallel, thus forming a multilinear FER model.

References

1. Acharya, D., Huang, Z., Pani Paudel, D., Van Gool, L.: Covariance pooling for facial expression recognition. In: Proceedings of the IEEE Conference on Computer Vision and Pattern Recognition Workshops, pp. 367–374 (2018)
2. Bishay, M., Palasek, P., Priebe, S., Patras, I.: SchiNet: automatic estimation of symptoms of schizophrenia from facial behaviour analysis. IEEE Trans. Affect. Comput., 1 (2019)

3. Cui, Y., Zhou, F., Wang, J., Liu, X., Lin, Y., Belongie, S.: Kernel pooling for convolutional neural networks. In: Proceedings of the IEEE Conference on Computer Vision and Pattern Recognition, pp. 2921–2930 (2017)
4. Devries, T., Biswaranjan, K., Taylor, G.W.: Multi-task learning of facial landmarks and expression. In: 2014 Canadian Conference on Computer and Robot Vision, pp. 98–103 (2014)
5. Fathallah, A., Abdi, L., Douik, A.: Facial expression recognition via deep learning. In: 2017 IEEE/ACS 14th International Conference on Computer Systems and Applications (AICCSA), pp. 745–750 (2017)
6. Gao, Y., Beijbom, O., Zhang, N., Darrell, T.: Compact bilinear pooling. In: Proceedings of the IEEE Conference on Computer Vision and Pattern Recognition, pp. 317–326 (2016)
7. Goodfellow, I.J., et al.: Challenges in representation learning: a report on three machine learning contests. In: Lee, M., Hirose, A., Hou, Z.-G., Kil, R.M. (eds.) ICONIP 2013. LNCS, vol. 8228, pp. 117–124. Springer, Heidelberg (2013). https://doi.org/10.1007/978-3-642-42051-1_16
8. Guo, Y., Tao, D., Yu, J., Xiong, H., Li, Y., Tao, D.: Deep neural networks with relativity learning for facial expression recognition. In: 2016 IEEE International Conference on Multimedia & Expo Workshops (ICMEW), pp. 1–6. IEEE (2016)
9. Hamester, D., Barros, P., Wermter, S.: Face expression recognition with a 2-channel convolutional neural network. In: 2015 International Joint Conference on Neural Networks (IJCNN), pp. 1–8 (2015)
10. Kim, B.K., Dong, S.Y., Roh, J., Kim, G., Lee, S.Y.: Fusing aligned and non-aligned face information for automatic affect recognition in the wild: a deep learning approach. In: Proceedings of the IEEE Conference on Computer Vision and Pattern Recognition Workshops, pp. 48–57 (2016)
11. Li, S., Deng, W.: Deep facial expression recognition: a survey. arXiv preprint arXiv:1804.08348 (2018)
12. Li, S., Deng, W.: Reliable crowdsourcing and deep locality-preserving learning for unconstrained facial expression recognition. IEEE Trans. Image Process. 28(1), 356–370 (2018)
13. Li, S., Deng, W., Du, J.: Reliable crowdsourcing and deep locality-preserving learning for expression recognition in the wild. In: 2017 IEEE Conference on Computer Vision and Pattern Recognition (CVPR), pp. 2584–2593. IEEE (2017)
14. Lian, Z., Li, Y., Tao, J.-H., Huang, J., Niu, M.-Y.: Expression analysis based on face regions in real-world conditions. Int. J. Autom. Comput. 17(1), 96–107 (2019). https://doi.org/10.1007/s11633-019-1176-9
15. Lin, T.Y., Maji, S.: Improved bilinear pooling with CNNs. arXiv preprint arXiv:1707.06772 (2017)
16. Lin, T.Y., RoyChowdhury, A., Maji, S.: Bilinear CNN models for fine-grained visual recognition. In: Proceedings of the IEEE International Conference on Computer Vision, pp. 1449–1457 (2015)
17. Liu, Z., Li, S., Deng, W.: Boosting-poof: boosting part based one vs one feature for facial expression recognition in the wild. In: 2017 12th IEEE International Conference on Automatic Face & Gesture Recognition (FG 2017), pp. 967–972. IEEE (2017)
18. Mahmoudi, M.A., Chetouani, A., Boufera, F., Tabia, H.: Kernelized dense layers for facial expression recognition. In: 2020 IEEE International Conference on Image Processing (ICIP), pp. 2226–2230 (2020)
19. Mahmoudi, M.A., Chetouani, A., Boufera, F., Tabia, H.: Learnable pooling weights for facial expression recognition. Pattern Recogn. Lett. 138, 644–650 (2020)

20. Mollahosseini, A., Hasani, B., Mahoor, M.H.: AffectNet: a database for facial expression, valence, and arousal computing in the wild. IEEE Trans. Affect. Comput. **10**, 18–31 (2017)
21. Nguyen, D., Nguyen, K., Sridharan, S., Dean, D., Fookes, C.: Deep spatio-temporal feature fusion with compact bilinear pooling for multimodal emotion recognition. Comput. Vis. Image Underst. **174**, 33–42 (2018)
22. Pons, G., Masip, D.: Multi-task, multi-label and multi-domain learning with residual convolutional networks for emotion recognition. arXiv preprint arXiv:1802.06664 (2018)
23. Tang, Y.: Deep learning using linear support vector machines. arXiv preprint arXiv:1306.0239 (2013)
24. Tenenbaum, J.B., Freeman, W.T.: Separating style and content with bilinear models. Neural Comput. **12**(6), 1247–1283 (2000)
25. Zhang, Z., Luo, P., Loy, C.C., Tang, X.: From facial expression recognition to interpersonal relation prediction. Int. J. Comput. Vis. **126**(5), 550–569 (2018). https://doi.org/10.1007/s11263-017-1055-1
26. Zhou, F., Kong, S., Fowlkes, C., Chen, T., Lei, B.: Fine-grained facial expression analysis using dimensional emotion model. arXiv preprint arXiv:1805.01024 (2018)
27. Zou, X., Wang, Z., Li, Q., Sheng, W.: Integration of residual network and convolutional neural network along with various activation functions and global pooling for time series classification. Neurocomputing, **367**, 39–45 (2019)

End-to-End Spectral-Temporal Fusion Using Convolutional Neural Network

Tayeb Benzenati[1,2(✉)], Abdelaziz Kallel[1,2], and Yousri Kessentini[1,3]

[1] Digital Research Center of Sfax, 3021 Sfax, Tunisia
[2] Advanced Technologies for Image and Signal Processing, University of Sfax, Sfax, Tunisia
[3] MIRACL Laboratory, University of Sfax, Sfax, Tunisia

Abstract. In the last few years, Earth Observation sensors received a large development, offering, therefore, various types of data with different temporal, spatial, spectral, and radiometric resolutions. However, due to physical and budget limitations, the acquisition of images with the best characteristics is not feasible. Image fusion becomes a valuable technique to deal with some specific applications. In particular, the vegetation area, which needs a high spectral resolution and frequent coverage. In this paper, we present a novel fusion technique based on Convolutional Neural Networks (CNN) to combine two kinds of remote sensing data with different but complement spectral and temporal characteristics, to produce one high spectral and temporal resolution product. To the best of our knowledge, this is the first attempt to deal with the spectral-temporal fusion problem. The feasibility of the proposed method is evaluated via Sentinel-2 data. The experimental results show that the proposed technique can achieve substantial gains in terms of fusion performance.

Keywords: Image fusion · Remote sensing · Convolutional neural networks · Spectral enhancement · Temporal enhancement

1 Introduction

Remote sensing (RS) generally comprises all techniques for measuring electromagnetic energy emitted from areas or objects on surface or subsurface of Earth without the need to a physical contact. In the last years, Optical Remote sensing has received a significant development thanks to the recent advancement in electronics field, allowing the acquisition of a large variety of data with a different spatial, spectral, radiometric, and temporal resolution, depending on the sensor proprieties and missions. The spatial resolution represents the size of the smallest area (pixel), the spectral resolution indicates the capability of the sensor to detect fine wavelength bands and the number of spectral channels, the temporal resolution is the period to take for revisiting the same region, and the radiometric resolution refers to the sensor's sensitivity to distinguish between smallest brightness values while capturing an image [6]. Currently, satellites offer

© Springer Nature Switzerland AG 2021
C. Djeddi et al. (Eds.): MedPRAI 2020, CCIS 1322, pp. 60–72, 2021.
https://doi.org/10.1007/978-3-030-71804-6_5

precious data about the Earth that help for detecting and monitoring in a multitude of applications. For example, vegetation monitoring [10], change detection [8], military target detection [20], and mineral exploration [21]. However, due a physical and budget limitations of satellite platforms, the acquisition of data with high characteristics for all aspects is not possible. When the technologies tackle a specific issue, researchers handle the latter with an appropriate method. Remote Sensing image fusion is a successful technique, which aims to combine one or multiple satellite images, in order to produce a fused product that includes more knowledge than each of the inputs [2]. Fusion techniques are advantageous and increase the performance in several remote sensing tasks, including object identification, segmentation, change detection, etc. The RS fusion products are in progressive increase, thanks to the growing requests from reputable companies such as Google Earth and Microsoft Visual Earth, which require very high resolution images in their commercial products, which could be done using the appropriate fusion technique.

Recently, the unavailability of products with high spatial and temporal resolution dues to the spatial-temporal limitation of optical satellites has been addressed by the reputable commercial company Planet lab [17]. Planet lab exploits more than 175 dove satellites in orbit to provide daily images from the whole Earth. Doves are nano-satellites that weight approximately 4 kg, which can acquire data at high spatial resolution of 3 m with four spectral channels (Red, Green, Blue, and near-infrared). Thanks to these satellites and its ability to offer a series of daily observation at high resolution, the need of spatio-temporal fusion has decreased. Especially, for applications that require high spatial and temporal resolutions such as the detection of rapid changes, object extraction, and object identification. Unfortunately, these satellites are characterized by a low spectral resolution as they include a limited number of bands with broad wavelengths. Besides, several agriculture applications such as monitoring vegetation seasonal dynamics, detection of leaf disease, and water consumption monitoring, need a higher number of bands with fine wavelengths, especially, in the near-infrared range. In contrast, Sentinel-2 satellite can provide a higher number of bands (13 bands), which make it the most suitable for vegetation monitoring tasks thanks to its valuable fine red-edge wavelength bands at 10 and 20 m. These bands are principally utilized to derive the vegetation indices via red-edge bands, which are significant to study the health of vegetation. However, Sentinel-2 is characterized by a low temporal resolution, as it has a long revisit circle of 5 days. Indeed, Planet and Sentinel-2 provide complementary characteristics, i.e., Planet provides a high spatial-temporal resolution but low spectral resolution, contrary to Sentinel-2, which produces images with high spectral resolution but low temporal resolution.

In this paper, we introduce a spectral-temporal fusion technique based on CNN to tackle the physical limitation of widely used satellites. To the best of our knowledge, it is the pioneering approach addressing the spectral-temporal image fusion problem. To study the feasibility of the fusion technique, only Sentinel-2 satellite is considered as a simulation tool. We assume that a low temporal resolution characterizes the fine wavelength bands at 20 m, while the broad ones at 10 m have a higher temporal resolution. The main objective of this paper is to integrate Sentinel-2 broad and fine wavelength bands on a prior date $(t-1)$, a broad wavelengths bands on prediction date (t), to produce a product at 20 m with high spectral resolution unavailable due to the technical limitation.

2   Related Works

The literature of RS fusion is rich with works proposed to address some particular image fusion problems, and the number of papers increases continuously every year. Ones of the most common RS image fusion approaches are: pansharpening [1,3] and spatio-temporal fusion [11]. Indeed, optical satellites (e.g., WorldView-3 and QuickBird) have the ability to capture two kinds of images, a low spatial Multispectral (MS) image with several fine wavelength intervals and a high spatial Panchromatic (PAN) image in one broadband (unique band). Due to a Signal-to-noise ration (SNR) constraint, the acquisition of a MS image with high spatial resolution is not realizable. This key issue has principally motivated RS researchers to develop several sophisticated pansharpening fusion techniques to deal with this system limitation. Pansharpening technique becomes a fundamental preprocessing for many RS tasks [5,12].

The majority of optical sensors that have an acceptable spatial resolution (from 5 to 60 m), like Landsat TM and Sentinel-2, offer a long revisit time (16 days for Landat and 5 days for Sentinel-2), in addition to other factors like the cloud contamination and other atmospheric conditions, which can further increase the revisit periods. Even if their fine spatial resolution is appropriate for tasks like change detection and cover mapping, the detection of rapid land cover changes at the right time becomes limited using this type of satellites. In contrast, another type of satellites, such as Sentinel-3 and MODIS, offer opposite properties. In other words, they produce images with a coarse spatial resolution, with a very short revisit time (less than 2 days). However, this coarse resolution is inappropriate for monitoring small land cover changes. As a satellite with high spatial resolution and daily observation does not exist, several works on fusion techniques have been developed, aiming to combine the two different types of satellites images, that have complementary characteristics, and fuse the latter to offer a high spatial and temporal resolution product. Therefore, the ability for monitoring and detecting land surface changes will be improved.

In the last few years, Convolutional Neural Networks (CNN) have received large attention from the computer science community in many fields, including RS image fusion [3,16], thanks to their great success in many image processing tasks, especially, super-resolution (SR) [9,13]. SR aims to reconstruct a high-resolution image from a unique low-resolution image. Recently, the authors proposed a super resolution technique based on CNN known as SRCNN [9]. SRCNN is a pioneering model that proved very competitive results compared with traditional techniques. Inspired by its great success, plenty of works adapted the latter as prepossessing in many fields that need a high spatial resolution, including pansharpening and spatial-temporal fusion techniques, as they all aim to enhance the spatial resolution of one or more low resolution images. With regard to pan-sharpening, in [16], the authors developed a SRCNN to deal with pansharpening task known as PNN. PNN aims to generate a high resolution MS image from the PAN and the MS images, that can be captured by the satellite. PNN achieved a consistent gain in performance compared with the state-of-the-art techniques. As another example, in [4], we proposed a pansharpening CNN based on Multiresolution Analysis called GIP-CNN, which aims to estimate the injection gains to control the amount of details need to be inserted into the MS image. GIP-CNN can improve the fusion quality with respect to the literature approaches, as well as the CNN-based techniques. In addition, SR success has influenced the spatial-temporal fusion. One can cite, the authors in [18] implemented an approach based on SRCNN capable to perform a complex mapping from a coarse image (captured by MODIS) to fine image (captured by Landsat) sensor, and utilize the pretrained model to predict the unavailable fine image due to the low temporal resolution of the sensor from its associated coarse image. Similarly, in [15], the authors proposed two-stream spatio-temporal fusion technique based on SRCNN. The latter focuses on learning a mapping between the corresponding fine residual image as a target and corresponding coarse images, captured in neighboring dates, ending up with two pretrained models. These models are used to produce two similar fine images; then, the outcomes are combined to generate a unique fine resolution product by applying a local weighting strategy.

3   Background

3.1   Sentinel-2 Satellite

Sentinel-2 was launched in 2015 by the European Space Association (ESA), as part of the European Copernicus program [19]. Sentinel-2 represents two identical satellites: Sentinel-2A and Sentinel-2B. They provide multispectral images with 13 bands covering the visible and near-infrared, in addition to the shortwave-infrared (SWIR) spectral region, incorporating three new spectral bands in the red-edge region (vegetation red-edge). The new bands are very useful on vegetation applications. For instance, to retrieve the canopy chlorophyll content [7]. The availability of 4 vegetation red-edge bands (B5, B6, B7, B8A) at 20 m is a unique characteristic that discriminates Sentinel-2 from other optical satellite sensors. Table 1 describes the spectral bands of Sentinel-2. In this paper, we consider the bands: B5, B6, B7, and B8a as high spectral resolution bands with low temporal resolution, and B7 and B8, as lower spectral resolution bands and higher temporal resolution.

3.2   Super-Resolution CNN

Super-Resolution is a technique to reconstruct a high-resolution (HR) images from one or more low spatial resolution (LR) images. After the considerable success of CNNs in many computer vision applications, particularly, image enhancement, such as image denoising, image inpainting, image dehazing, and super-resolution. Recently, single image super-resolution technique based on CNN

Table 1. Specifications of Sentinel-2 spectral bands

Spectral band	Central wavelength (nm)	Band width (nm)	Resolution (m)
B1	443	20	60
B2	490	65	10
B3	560	35	10
B4	665	30	10
B5	705	15	20
B6	740	15	20
B7	783	20	20
B8	842	115	10
B8a	865	20	20
B9	940	20	60
B10	1375	30	60
B11	1610	90	20
B12	2190	180	20

(SRCNN) has been proposed [9], which aims to learn a mapping from the low resolution input to the high resolution image. Even the shallowness and the simplicity of the architecture, SRCNN can achieve superior performance over the state-of-the-art techniques. SRCNN includes only three convolutional layers. As a preprocessing, the low resolution image must be interpolated to the same size of the high resolution one in order to train the network. In the next section, we propose a modified version of SRCNN adapted for the spectral-temporal fusion problem. Therefore, the inputs of the network are substituted by the concatenation of two images (multiple inputs) with different spectral and temporal characteristics instead of single input, and the output provides an improved product that combines the best features of each input (high spectral and temporal resolution).

4   The Spectral-Temporal Fusion Technique

The objective of the paper is to estimate a high spectral high temporal (HSHT) product S_{20}^t captured at date t, using the associated low spectral high temporal (LSHT) image S_{10}^t captured at the same date t, accompanied with a high spectral low temporal (HSLT) image S_{20}^{t-1} captured at a previous date $t-1$. The process results in a high spectral resolution product with higher temporal resolution (HSHT). In this work, we assume that the Sentinel bands: B5, B6, B7, and B8a constitute a HSLT image, whereas the bands: B4 and B8 are considered as LSHT resolution bands. As the considered HS and LS bands are characterized by different wavelength, the selection of LS input is based on the correlation with target HS one. For example, B4 (wavelength 650–680 nm) is used to estimate

B5 (wavelength 698–713 nm) as their spectral ranges are close to each other. Similarly, B8 (wavelength 785–900 nm) is utilized to estimate B6, B7, and B8a (wavelengths are 733–748 nm, 773–793 nm, and 855–875 nm, respectively).

The proposed technique includes a training phase and a prediction phase. Each phase is performed for each band separately respecting the same conditions.

Inspired by the great success of SRCNN in image super-resolution [9], the proposed method aims to learn an end-to-end mapping function ($F(.)$) from HSLT and LSHT images to HSHT one. As SRCNN require the same size of input and target images, the LS image (S_{10}^t) input is downsampled by a factor of 2 to the same size of HS S_{20}^t target image (Y), producing ($\hat{S}_{10}^t$); then, the latter is concatenated with the associated S_{20}^{t-1} as a single input (X). The main goal of the training phase is to optimize the following Mean Squared Error (l_2) loss function:

$$L(\theta) = \frac{1}{N} \sum_{i=1}^{N} \|F(X_i; \theta) - Y_i\|^2 \tag{1}$$

where N is the total number of the training samples, θ indicates the network weights need to be optimized, i represents the image index, and F is estimated high spectral resolution image at t. The objective function is minimized using Adam [14] with a learning initialized to 10^{-4}. To guarantee a successful training of the network, the whole image is cropped into 10000 sub-images 64 × 64 pixels, divided into training and validation parts. The former includes 80 % sub-images, and the latter comprises the rest. Figure 1 illustrates the framework of the proposed fusion technique.

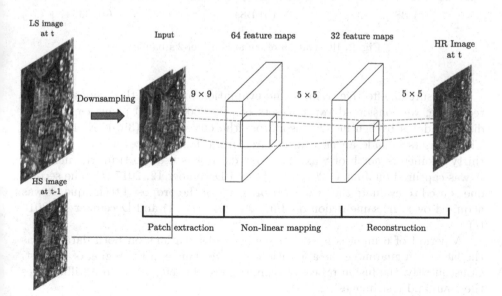

Fig. 1. The framework of the proposed fusion technique.

After the completion of the first phase, the prediction phase consists on estimating the HSHT images on another dates using the pretrained model. To this end, the training images at t and $t - 1$ by different dates $\hat{t}$ and $\hat{t} - 1$, which are previously unseen by the network, respectively, on the same region of study.

4.1 Datasets

In the experiments, we assume that the Sentinel-2 bands: B4, B8, are characterized by a low spectral resolution and high temporal resolution. In contrast, the bands: B5, B6, B7, and B8a, are considered as high spectral and low temporal resolution. Therefore, the principal objective is to estimate the high spectral bands at date t, which are assumed unavailable due to physical limitations. Figure 2 shows some considered broad and fine wavelength bands provided by Sentinel-2.

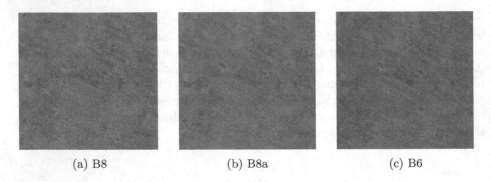

(a) B8   (b) B8a   (c) B6

Fig. 2. Illustration of some Sentinel-2's bands.

To ensure an effective training and evaluation process of the proposed fusion technique, we considered two datasets of size 2600×2600 pixels captured in different dates by Sentinel-2 sensor from the city of Sfax (35°06 N, 10°54 E). The datasets include an agriculture area from Jebiniana town, located about thirty kilometers north of Sfax. The first dataset is used to train the network. It was captured on June 6, 2017 $(t - 1)$ and December 12, 2017 (t). The second one is used to evaluate the fusion performance of the proposed technique. It was acquired over the same region on June 30, 2018 $(\hat{t} - 1)$ and December 17, 2018 $(\hat{t})$.

A period of 6 months is chosen between observations on both datasets, as the latter can guarantee the apparition of more change in the region of interest. Consequently, the fusion process becomes more challenging. Figure 3 illustrates the train and test images.

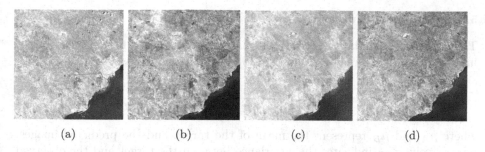

(a)   (b)   (c)   (d)

Fig. 3. Illustration of train and test datasets. (a) and (b) represent the train images on June 6, 2017 ($t-1$) and December 12, 2017, respectively. (c) and (d) are the test images on June 30, 2018 and December 17, 2018.

5   Experimental Results and Discussion

The proposed approach was compared with the state-of-the-art fusion technique: the Spatial and Temporal Adaptive Reflectance Fusion Model (STARFM) [11]. STARFM was adapted to deal with the spectral-temporal fusion problem.

In order to assess the performance of the fusion techniques, the fused images were compared with the ground-truth images at full-reference manner through the three highly used metrics: Root Mean Square Error (RMSE), Spectral Angle Mapper (SAM), and Structural Similarity (SSIM) index.

5.1   Root Mean Square Error

Root Mean Square Error (RMSE) measures the fusion distortion between the target product (A), and fused image (B). It is defined as follows:

$$RMSE(A, B) = \sqrt{E\left[(A - B)^2\right]} \tag{2}$$

where E is the expectation value. The lower RMSE, the lower distortion. Its ideal value is 0.

5.2   Spectral Angle Mapper

The Spectral Angle Mapper (SAM) [22] measures the spectral distortion between two images A and B. It is defined as follows:

$$SAM(A, B) = \arccos \frac{\langle A | B \rangle}{\|A\| \cdot \|B\|} \tag{3}$$

where $\langle . | . \rangle$ and $\|.\|$ denote the scalar product and the normalization, respectively. SAM's ideal value is 0.

5.3 Structural Similarity

The Structural Similarity (SSIM) calculates the similarity between the target image (A) and the predicted one (B) [19]. SSIM is defined as follows:

$$SSIM(A, B) = \frac{(2\mu_A\mu_B + C_1) + (2\sigma_{AB} + C_2)}{(\mu_A^2 + \mu_B^2 + C_1)(\sigma_A^2 + \sigma_B^2 + C_2)} \tag{4}$$

where μ_A and μ_B represent the mean of the target and the predicted images, respectively, σ_{AB} indicates the covariance between the target and the observed images, σ_A and σ_B are the variances of the target and the predict images, and C_1 and C_2 denote small constants utilized to avoid a null denominator when the means and variances are almost zero.

Table 2 describes the quantitative performance of the fusion products on the test dataset. Based on the results, the proposed approach overpasses the traditional technique STARFM on all bands in terms of spectral, as it obtained the best SAM value. In term of spatial fidelity, the proposed approach provides the best results on RMSE and SSIM metrics, which measures the spatial distortion. Furthermore, the proposed technique produces very competitive results in terms of RMSE with an error (less than 0.8%). Hence, this fusion result can be used for agriculture monitoring applications. The worst product in RMSE is related to the band B4, as its wavelength, compared with the other bands, is not included in the inputs low spectral resolution bands: B4 and B8. Consequently, the fusion task on this specific band is further complex for the CNN to learn.

Table 2. Quantitative performance of the fused products on test dataset.

Metric	Band	STARFM	Proposed
RMSE	B4	0.0250	**0.0072**
	B6	0.0277	**0.0069**
	B7	0.0287	**0.0057**
	B8a	0.0294	**0.0045**
SAM	B4	0.0797	**0.0242**
	B6	0.0736	**0.0179**
	B7	0.0701	**0.0137**
	B8a	0.0657	**0.0115**
SSIM	B4	0.7244	**0.9783**
	B6	0.7149	**0.9821**
	B7	0.7092	**0.9854**
	B8a	0.7045	**0.9881**

Figure 4 illustrates the fusion results and their associated ground-truth images for each band that have been described on Table 2. The ground-truth bands' images are shown in the first row, The fused images produced by STRAFM are shown in the second row, and the third row shows the fused products generated by the proposed technique. The fused images of STARFM technique provide the worst fusion performance, as the latter suffers from a blurring effect compared with the ground-truth images, and it lacks of a huge amount of spatial information. For example, the region highlighted in red suffer from blurring effect, and both details and contours are not visible. The proposed technique produces the best fusion quality as the fused results are as close as possible to the ground-truth ones, and the details and the edges are well preserved. Furthermore, it is difficult to notice any type of distortion on the fused images.

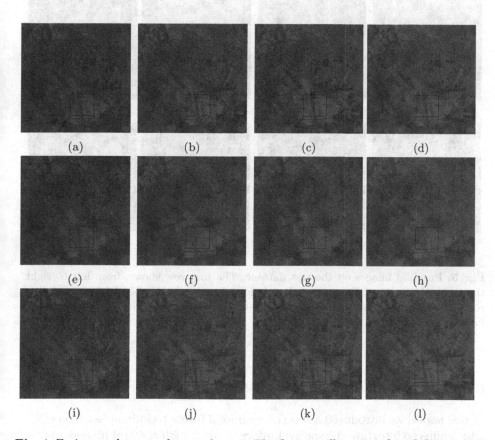

Fig. 4. Fusion products on the test dataset. The first row illustrates, from left to right, the ground-truth bands: B5, B6, B7, and B8a, respectively, the second row shows the fusion results using STARFM, and the third one shows the fusion results by the proposed technique.

Figure 5 shows the residual error images, calculated as the difference between the fused images and their associated ground-truth images for each band. The first row illustrates the residual images of the proposed technique, and the second one shows the residual images of STARFM technique. As the residual pixel values are almost zero, they were multiplied by 100 to provide more interpretability. STARFM produces the worst results, as the errors are shown on the whole residual images of each band, and it fails to reconstruct the most of spatial details of the high spectral image. The proposed approach provides better fusions results, as it successes to conserve the spatial structures of fused products. Although, the proposed technique lacks of some spatial details on heterogeneous vegetation areas that undergo small changes.

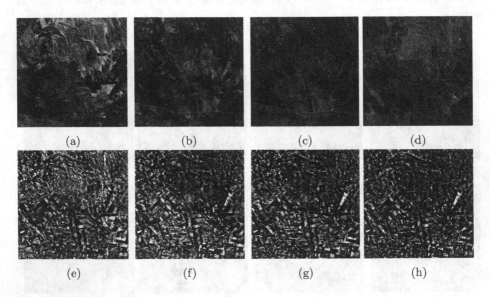

(a)　　　　　　　(b)　　　　　　　(c)　　　　　　　(d)

(e)　　　　　　　(f)　　　　　　　(g)　　　　　　　(h)

Fig. 5. Residual images on the test dataset. The first row shows, from left to right, the residual images of the proposed technique for the bands: B5, B6, B7, and B8a, respectively, the second row shows the residual images using STARFM. Brighter pixels indicate a larger error.

6　Conclusion

In this paper, we introduced a spectral-temporal fusion technique based on CNN, which aims to integrate the spectral information of high spectral images and the temporal information of high temporal resolution images. The proposed network aims to reconstruct a high spectral and temporal products from two inputs characterized by different and complementary spectral and temporal resolutions. To the best of our knowledge, it is the first work that focuses on CNN's to deal with the spectral and temporal fusion problem.

　　The qualitative and quantitative experimental results conducted on Sentinel-2 satellites using simulated images show that the proposed approach achieved comptetitive fusion quality in terms of both spectral and temporal qualities. In our future works, we intend to evaluate the proposed network to combine real data from two widely used satellites with different spectral and spatial, using deeper architecture and combining different loss functions.

Acknowledgement. We gratefully acknowledge the support of NVIDIA Corporation with the contribution of the Titan Xp GPU used for this research.

References

1. Aiazzi, B., Alparone, L., Baronti, S., Garzelli, A., Selva, M.: Twenty-five years of pansharpening: a critical review and new developments. In: Signal and Image Processing for Remote Sensing, pp. 552–599. CRC Press (2012)
2. Alparone, L., Aiazzi, B., Baronti, S., Garzelli, A.: Remote Sensing Image Fusion. CRC Press, Boca Raton (2015)
3. Benzenati, T., Kallel, A., Kessentini, Y.: Two stages pan-sharpening details injection approach based on very deep residual networks. IEEE Trans. Geosci. Remote Sens. (2020)
4. Benzenati, T., Kessentini, Y., Kallel, A., Hallabia, H.: Generalized Laplacian pyramid pan-sharpening gain injection prediction based on CNN. IEEE Geosci. Remote Sens. Lett. **17**(4), 651–655 (2019)
5. Bovolo, F., Bruzzone, L., Capobianco, L., Garzelli, A., Marchesi, S., Nencini, F.: Analysis of the effects of pansharpening in change detection on VHR images. IEEE Geosci. Remote Sens. Lett. **7**(1), 53–57 (2009)
6. Chang, N.B., Bai, K.: Multisensor Data Fusion and Machine Learning for Environmental Remote Sensing. CRC Press, Boca Raton (2018)
7. Clevers, J.G., Kooistra, L., Van den Brande, M.M.: Using Sentinel-2 data for retrieving LAI and leaf and canopy chlorophyll content of a potato crop. Remote Sens. **9**(5), 405 (2017)
8. Daudt, R.C., Le Saux, B., Boulch, A., Gousseau, Y.: Urban change detection for multispectral earth observation using convolutional neural networks. In: IGARSS 2018–2018 IEEE International Geoscience and Remote Sensing Symposium, pp. 2115–2118. IEEE (2018)
9. Dong, C., Loy, C.C., He, K., Tang, X.: Image super-resolution using deep convolutional networks. IEEE Trans. Pattern Anal. Mach. Intell. **38**(2), 295–307 (2015)
10. Frampton, W.J., Dash, J., Watmough, G., Milton, E.J.: Evaluating the capabilities of Sentinel-2 for quantitative estimation of biophysical variables in vegetation. ISPRS J. Photogramm. Remote Sens. **82**, 83–92 (2013)
11. Gao, F., Masek, J., Schwaller, M., Hall, F.: On the blending of the Landsat and MODIS surface reflectance: predicting daily Landsat surface reflectance. IEEE Trans. Geosci. Remote Sens. **44**(8), 2207–2218 (2006)
12. Gilbertson, J.K., Kemp, J., Van Niekerk, A.: Effect of pan-sharpening multi-temporal Landsat 8 imagery for crop type differentiation using different classification techniques. Comput. Electron. Agric. **134**, 151–159 (2017)
13. Kim, J., Kwon Lee, J., Mu Lee, K.: Accurate image super-resolution using very deep convolutional networks. In: Proceedings of the IEEE Conference on Computer Vision and Pattern Recognition, pp. 1646–1654 (2016)
14. Kingma, D.P., Ba, J.: Adam: a method for stochastic optimization. arXiv preprint arXiv:1412.6980 (2014)

15. Liu, X., Deng, C., Chanussot, J., Hong, D., Zhao, B.: StfNet: a two-stream convolutional neural network for spatiotemporal image fusion. IEEE Trans. Geosci. Remote Sens. **57**(9), 6552–6564 (2019)

16. Masi, G., Cozzolino, D., Verdoliva, L., Scarpa, G.: Pansharpening by convolutional neural networks. Remote Sens. **8**(7), 594 (2016)

17. Planet: Satellite Imagery and Archive. https://planet.com/products/planet-imagery/. Accessed 01 July 2020

18. Song, H., Liu, Q., Wang, G., Hang, R., Huang, B.: Spatiotemporal satellite image fusion using deep convolutional neural networks. IEEE J. Sel. Top. Appl. Earth Obs. Remote Sens. **11**(3), 821–829 (2018)

19. Wang, Z., Bovik, A.C., Sheikh, H.R., Simoncelli, E.P.: Image quality assessment: from error visibility to structural similarity. IEEE Trans. Image Process. **13**(4), 600–612 (2004)

20. Wu, H., Zhang, H., Zhang, J., Xu, F.: Typical target detection in satellite images based on convolutional neural networks. In: 2015 IEEE International Conference on Systems, Man, and Cybernetics, pp. 2956–2961. IEEE (2015)

21. Yokoya, N., Chan, J.C.W., Segl, K.: Potential of resolution-enhanced hyperspectral data for mineral mapping using simulated EnMAP and Sentinel-2 images. Remote Sens. **8**(3), 172 (2016)

22. Yuhas, R.H., Goetz, A.F., Boardman, J.W.: Discrimination among semi-arid landscape endmembers using the spectral angle mapper (SAM) algorithm (1992)

Fusing Local and Global Features for Person Re-identification Using Multi-stream Deep Neural Networks

Mahmoud Ghorbel[1,3](✉), Sourour Ammar[1,2](✉), Yousri Kessentini[1,2](✉), Mohamed Jmaiel[1,3](✉), and Ahmed Chaari[4](✉)

[1] Digital Research Center of Sfax, 3021 Sfax, Tunisia
[2] MIRACL Laboratory, Sfax University, Sfax, Tunisia
{sourour.ammar,yousri.kessentini}@crns.rnrt.tn
[3] ReDCAD Laboratory, Sfax University, Sfax, Tunisia
mohamed.jmaiel@redcad.org
[4] Anavid, Paris, France
ahmed.chaari@anavid.co

Abstract. The field of person re-identification remains a challenging topic in video surveillance and public security because it is facing many problems related to the variations of the position, background and brightness scenes. In order to minimize the impact of those variations, we introduce in this work a multi-stream re-identification system based on the fusion of local and global features. The proposed system uses first a body partition segmentation network (SEG-CNN) to segment three different body regions (the whole body part, the middle and the down body parts) that will represent local features. While the original image will be used to extract global features. Second, a multi-stream fusion framework is performed to fuse the outputs of the individual streams and generate the final predictions. We experimentally prove that the multi-stream combination method improves the recognition rates and provides better results than classic fusion methods. In the rank-1/mAP, the improvement is of $7, 24\%/9, 5$ for the Market-1501 benchmark dataset.

Keywords: Person re-identification · Semantic segmentation · Multi-steam fusion · CNN

1 Introduction

In recent years, person re-identification (re-ID) has become increasingly popular due to its important applications in many real scenarios such as video surveillance [2], robotics [23] and automated driving. Person re-ID achieves constant improvements in recent years thanks to the considerable progress of the deep learning techniques. It can be seen as an image matching problem [5]. The challenge is to match two images of the same person coming from non-overlapping camera views [7]. Despite the advances in this field, many challenges still remain

© Springer Nature Switzerland AG 2021
C. Djeddi et al. (Eds.): MedPRAI 2020, CCIS 1322, pp. 73–85, 2021.
https://doi.org/10.1007/978-3-030-71804-6_6

such as complex environment, various body poses [4], occlusion [10], background variations [6,20], illumination variations [11] and different camera views [13]. Two images of the same person can present many differences related to the variation of the background, or two different persons can be captured under the same background.

Recent re-identification approaches are generally based on deep learning techniques. They learn Convolutional Neural Networks (CNN) to extract global features from the whole image, without differentiating the different parts of the persons to be identified. Some recent works in the literature has shown that it is critically important to examine multiple highly discriminating local regions of the person's images to deal with large variances in appearance. Authors in [24] proposed a network that generate saliency maps focusing on one part and suppressing the activations on other parts of the image. In [21], the authors introduced a gating function to selectively underline such fine common local patterns by comparing the mid-level features across pairs of images. The network proposed in [3] is a multi-channel convolutional network model composed by one global convolutional layer which is divided into four equal local convolutional layers. Authors in [18] proposed a part-aware model to extract features from four body parts and generate four part vectors. [15] presented a multi-scale context-aware network to learn features from the full body and body parts in order to capture the local context knowledge. The work [12] proposed a multi-stream network that fuses feature distance extracted from the whole image, three body regions with efficient alignment and one segmented image. Besides the use of global and local features proposed by the papers cited above, we have showed in [6] that we can improve the person re-identification performance by background subtraction. Authors in [20] proposed a person-region guided pooling deep neural network based on human parsing maps in order to avoid the background bias problem. In addition to the way of extracting the characteristics from the image, some work has been devoted to the re-ranking process by considering the person re-identification as a retrieval process. The work presented in [17,27] demonstrated that re-ranking process can significantly improve the re-ID accuracy of multiple baseline methods.

In this work, we propose a multi-stream person re-ID method that combines multiple body-part streams to capture complementary information. We propose first to extract person body parts using a semantic segmentation network based on CNN. Second, we propose to fuse the predicted confidence scores of multiple body-part stream re-ID CNNs. In order to extract visual similarities from the different body parts, four streams are combined: the first one deals with the original image to extract global features while the second stream exploit a background subtracted image to avoid the background bias problem. Stream three and stream four takes as input respectively a segmented image that contains the middle and the down part of the body in order to focus on local features. To evaluate our proposed method, we conducted experiments on the large benchmark dataset Market-1501 [25].

2 Overview of the Proposed Method

In this section, we provide the details of the proposed method. Figure 1 shows
a flowchart of the whole framework. Our approach can be divided into three
separated stages. The first stage is the semantic segmentation, which consists in
extracting three images of the person body parts and an image without background from the original image. The second stage is about the feature extraction and re-ID on different streams witch takes as input four images of the same
person (original image and three segmented images) and yields as output four
similarity measures vectors. In the end, the third stage is the combination of the
four stream outputs.

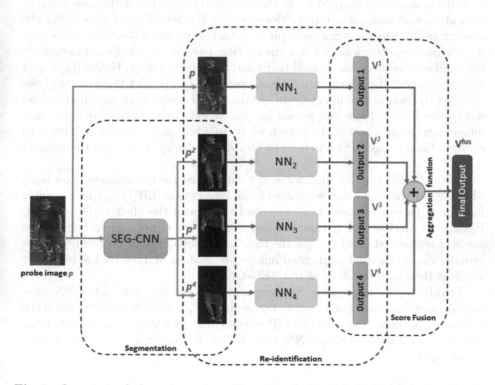

Fig. 1. Overview of the proposed multi-stream feature similarity fusion method.
(Images used are from the dataset Market-1501)

2.1 Segmentation Step

The use of the segmentation in this work has two advantages. First, it reduces the
effect of the background variation due to the person posture and the multitude
of cameras. In some cases, two images of the same person taken by two different
cameras may present some difficulties caused by the background variation. The

first image can be with a light background while the second can be with a dark background, even the texture can be different. We propose to deal with this problem by the background subtraction. Second, segmentation allows us to extract information from local parts of the image that is complementary to the global information extracted from the original image. Rather than using boxes to detect the body parts [12], we use the semantic segmentation to remove the background and to create specific body parts. The goal is to extract information only from the person body and not from the background which still present inside the box and can have an influence on the re-ID decision [20].

Our segmentation network (SEG-CNN) is inspired by the work proposed in [16]. SEG-CNN is a deep residual network based on ResNet-101 with atrous spatial pyramid pooling (ASPP) in the output layer so that it improve the segmentation and make it stronger. Moreover, in the attention of generating the context utilized in the refinement phase, two convolutions Res-5 are following. A structure-sensitive loss and a segmentation loss are also utilized to compute the similarity between the ground truth and the output image. Unlike [16] which aims to segment the person into 19 body parts and to predict the pose, we have changed the network architecture to obtain only 3 body parts: top, middle and down (See Fig. 3). From one person image, we get three different images, each image containing a part of the person body. In addition, we use those 3 parts to create a binary mask which is used to remove the background from the original image.

Since the Market-1501 dataset is not annotated for the segmentation field, SEG-CNN trained on a dataset named Look Into Person (LIP) [16] which is made for human parsing segmentation, was used to segment the Market-1501 dataset. Results on Market-1501 dataset are not satisfactory either as multiple images are over-segmented (see Fig. 2 on the right). To overcome this problem, we have visually chosen the well segmented images to create a Market-1501 sub-dataset which is then used to fine-tune our SEG-CNN.

Thanks to the fine-tuning, the segmentation results with SEG-CNN were considerably improved compared to the segmentation results obtained when the network was trained on only the LIP dataset. Figure 2 shows the improvement in the segmentation of SEG-CNN after it was fine-tuned on the Market-1501 sub-dataset.

2.2 Multi-stream Feature Extraction Method

We propose in this work to combine global and local features to enhance the re-ID performances. Our multi-stream feature extraction module is composed of four branches as shown in Fig. 1. The first branch is used to process the whole image to obtain global features (called *Full* stream). The second branch processes the background subtracted image (called *No_bk* stream) to focus only on the body part. This allows us to deal with the background variation problem. For local features, we use the last two branches that focus each on a segmented image (called *Mid* and *Dwn* streams respectively for middle and lower body parts). We empirically prove that the top body part don't contribute on the

Fig. 2. Qualitative comparison between the segmentation of SEG-CNN when it was trained on only the LIP dataset (image on the right) and SEG-CNN when it was fine-tuned on the Market-1501 sub-dataset (image on the left).

Fig. 3. Sample image of the semantic segmentation of SEG-CNN. (from the right to the left: original image, down part image, middle part image and top part image)

improvement of the final fusion score since the top part only contains the person face which is not clear because the resolution of the images is low.

Given a probe image p and a gallery set G with N images, with $G = \{g_1, g_2, ..., g_N\}$, the output of the first features extractor network is a vector $V^1 = \{S_1^1, S_2^1, ..., S_N^1\}$ of N similarity measures S_i^1 calculated between the probe image p and each image g_i of the gallery set. By the same way, the output of the three other feature extractor networks are three vectors (V^2, V^3 and V^4) that contain the similarity between the segmented probe image p^* and each segmented image g_i^* in the gallery set.

2.3   Similarity Scores Fusion

There are several score fusion strategies that have been introduced in the literature [1]. Two types of fusion can be distinguished: early fusion and late fusion. Early fusion is a fusion of feature levels in which the output of a unimodal analysis is fused before training. For the late fusion, the results of the unimodal analysis are utilized to find out distinct scores for every modality. After the fusion, a final score is computed through the combination of the outputs of every classifier. Compared with early fusion, late fusion is easier to implement and often shows effective in practice.

We propose in this work to adopt a late fusion model. It is used to aggregate the outputs of the four feature extractor networks. To compute the final similarity measure $V^{fus} = \{S_1^{fus}, S_2^{fus}, ..., S_N^{fus}\}$, the weighted sum is used in order to combine the outputs of each stream feature extractor (see Eq. 1).

$$V^{fus} = V^1 \oplus V^2 \oplus V^3 \oplus V^4 \tag{1}$$

where $S_i^{fus} = \alpha \cdot S_i^1 + \beta \cdot S_i^2 + \sigma \cdot S_i^3 + \gamma \cdot S_i^4$;
$\alpha, \beta, \sigma, \gamma \in [0, 1]$
and $\alpha + \beta + \sigma + \gamma = 1$.

In order to fix the weighted sum parameters (α, β, σ and γ), we consider a greedy search algorithm over the search space. At each iteration, we fix three weights and we vary the fourth weight according to a step, so as to always have the sum equal to 1. In this way, we went through all the possible combinations. A step of 0.05 has been chosen.

3   Experiments

We empirically evaluate the proposed method in this section. First, we introduce the used datasets, then we present the implementation details. Finally we present the experimental results of the proposed approach.

3.1   Datasets

LIP dataset [16] is a dataset focusing on semantic understanding of person. It gives a more detailed comprehension of image contents thanks to the segmentation of a human image into multiple semantics parts. It is composed by over than 50,000 annotated images with 19 semantic body parts indicating the hair, the head, the left foot, the right foot, etc. semantic part labels and 16 body joints, taken from many viewpoints, occlusions and background complexities.

Market-1501 [25] is a publicly available large-scale person re-ID dataset which is used in this work to evaluate our proposed method. The Market-1501 dataset is made up of 32,667 images of 1501 persons partitioned into 751 identities for training stage and 750 for testing stage. Images are taken by one low-resolution and five high-resolution cameras.

Three segmented databases (Images without background, images of the middle body parts and images of the down body parts) have been created from the Market-1501 database which are organized and composed exactly by the same number of images as Market-1501.

3.2   Implementation

Two neural networks architectures were used for the feature extraction and re-ID step. First, we used a ResNet-50 [8] (baseline) pre-trained on the ImageNet dataset [19] and then trained separately on different datasets (original Market-1501 dataset, Market-1501 dataset without background, middle and down part datasets). The categorical-cross-entropy was used to output a probability over all identities for each image. The stochastic Gradient descent (SGD) is utilized to minimize the loss function and then to refresh the network parameters. Moreover, we applied data augmentation to make the training dataset bigger by the use of transformations like shear-range, width-shift-range, height-shift-range and horizontal-flip. We used 90% of the images for training and the remaining 10% for validation.

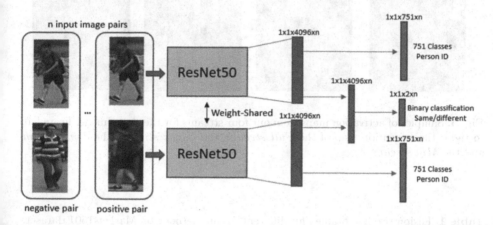

Fig. 4. In our S-CNN, two ResNet-50 are utilized to extract individually two features vectors from two images, which are utilized to predict the identity of the two input images and to predict the binary classification

The second network is a siamese network (S-CNN) [26] that combines the verification and identification losses. This network is trained to minimize three cross-entropy losses jointly, one identification loss for each siamese branch and one verification loss. We show in Fig. 4 the architecture of our siamese network. S-CNN is a two-input network formed by two parallel ResNet-50 CNNs with shared weights and bias. The final fully connected layer of the ResNet-50 network architecture is removed and three additional convolutional layers and one square layer are added [8]. Each Resnet-50 CNN is already pre-trained on different datasets. S-CNN is then trained separately on the four datasets using alternated positive and negative pairs (details of S-CNN training can be found in our previous work [6]).

To evaluate the performance of our re-identification method, we use two common evaluation metrics: the cumulative matching characteristics (CMC) at rank-1, rank-5 and rank-10 and mean average precision (mAP).

3.3 Results

We provide in this section the empirical results of the proposed method and we show the activation maps to demonstrate that using segmented images push the network to extract local features.

Extracting features from only the whole body can skip some significant information (See Fig. 5). The active region in the *No_bk stream* is larger than the active region in the *Full stream* what can cover more discriminative features. The activation map of the *dwn stream* show clearly that the use of segmented images allows us to exploit some regions of the image whose are not activated in the global stream.

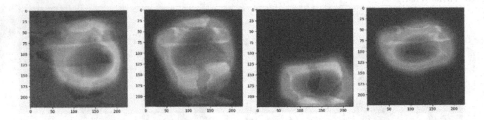

Fig. 5. Samples of activation maps from our four streams for the same image. From left to right: the activation map of the *Full stream*, the *No_bk stream*, the *dwn stream* and the *Mid stream*

Table 1. Fusion results obtained for different fusion methods on Market-1501 dataset.

Fusion method	S-CNN				ResNet50			
	Rank-1	Rank-5	Rank-10	mAP	Rank-1	Rank-5	Rank-10	mAP
Max	74.04	89.42	93.11	56.83	68.34	87.02	91.86	50.97
Sum	86.34	94.12	96.02	71.22	82.77	92.63	95.21	65.56
Accuracy weighted sum	86.54	94.23	**96.37**	71.70	82.95	92.72	95.19	65.57
Product	86.10	93.82	95.99	70.76	82.60	**92.96**	95.33	65.28
Greedy weighted sum	**87.02**	**94.26**	96.31	**71.72**	**83.87**	92.81	**95.63**	**66.15**

In the literature, there are several methods of score fusion that can be used in the context of our work [14]. In order to choose the best method, a comparative study was made. The fusion methods that have been tested are: max rule, sum rule, product rule, accuracy weighted sum and greedy weighted sum. We display in Table 1 the result of this study. Table 1 shows that the weighted sum using the greedy search technique gave the highest accuracy for both S-CNN and Resnet-50 networks. Since we have four streams with fairly different recognition rates, the weighted sum makes it possible to penalize the stream with low precision and favor the one with high precision. With greedy search technique, we can found suitable weights for our recognition model.

We show in the top of Table 2 the result of our two re-ID networks for the four streams (*Full*, *No_bk*, *Mid* and *Dwn*). We notice that S-CNN provides better results except for the stream *Mid* where S-CNN is slightly worse than the baseline. For both of S-CNN and ResNet-50, the best performance is obtained for the stream *Full* which extract information from the whole image.

Table 2. Fusion results of the multi-stream outputs on Market-1501 dataset.

Streams combination	S-CNN				ResNet50			
	Rank-1	Rank-5	Rank-10	mAP	Rank-1	Rank-5	Rank-10	mAP
Full	79.78	91.30	94.32	62.22	73.60	88.21	92.39	54.89
No_bk	73.93	88.62	92.10	58.06	67.33	84.88	90.26	50.75
Mid	47.47	68.61	75.32	29.03	47.47	68.52	75.83	28.81
Dwn	47.77	68.73	76.72	34.18	46.49	69.86	77.25	32.65
Full + No_bk + Mid + Dwn	**87.02**	**94.26**	**96.31**	**71.72**	**83.87**	**92.81**	**95.63**	**66.15**
Full + Mid + Dwn	85.71	94.00	96.22	70.70	83.16	92.78	95.21	65.16
Full + No_bk + Mid	84.88	93.40	95.51	69.01	80.10	91.83	94.56	61.66
Full + No_bk + Dwn	84.82	93.82	95.72	69.74	81.23	91.98	94.95	63.98
No_bk + Mid + Dwn	83.64	92.99	95.54	67.98	80.78	91.83	94.32	62.45
Full + Dwn	83.07	93.08	95.36	67.46	79.39	91.24	94.06	61.71
Full + Mid	83.01	92.63	94.89	66.85	77.90	90.40	93.76	58.62
Full + No_bk	82.57	92.69	95.30	67.49	77.22	90.17	93.61	59.76
No_bk + Mid	79.89	91.35	94.26	62.41	74.55	88.86	93.02	55.89
No_bk + Dwn	79.78	91.38	94.26	63.57	75.00	88.77	93.11	57.76
Mid + Dwn	78.97	90.29	93.20	60.09	76.90	89.75	92.63	56.42

In the bottom of Table 2, we present the combination results of the four stream re-ID model outputs using a weighted sum method. A greedy search method is used to get the best results on the validation dataset. The weights setting consists in choosing the best parameters: α, β, σ and γ (combination coefficients of the four streams respectively *Full*, *No_bk*, *Mid* and *Dwn*), where $\alpha + \beta + \sigma + \gamma = 1$.

Table 2 shows that the best combination is when the four streams are activated and S-CNN always provide better results than the baseline for the different combinations. With S-CNN, we get 87.02% in the rank-1 accuracy and with Resnet-50 we get 83.87%.

The obtained results show that the combination of multiple streams significantly improves the re-ID performances. Comparing to *Full* stream results, the improvement in rank-1/mAP is 7.24%/9.5% with S-CNN and 10.27%/11.26% with Resnet-50 when the four streams are combined. Less improvement values are shown when only three or two streams are combined. This improvement confirms that the features extracted from the body parts (local features) give complementary information to the whole person image features (global features).

We notice that for a re-ID model based on only three streams, the best combination is when the two streams *Mid* and *Dwn* are combined with the *Full* stream. The rank-1 accuracy respectively for S-CNN and Resnet-50 are, 85.71 and 83.16. This result confirms that local features provide additional complementary information that can enhance the re-ID decision.

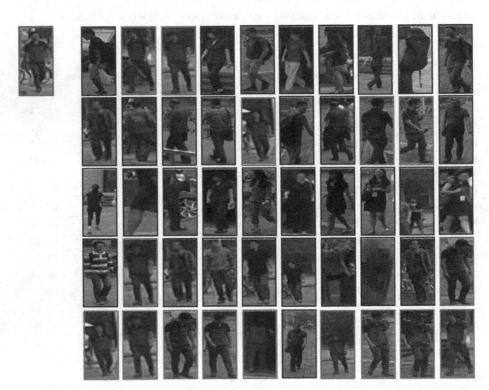

Fig. 6. Top 10 predictions for each stream and the fusion for the same query image. Person surrounded by blue box corresponds to the probe image. The first four rows correspond to the results produced by $S - CNN$ on the *Full*, *No_bk*, *Mid*, and *Dwn* streams respectively. The fifth row corresponds to the results produced by the fusion method. Person surrounded by green box denotes the same person as the probe and person surrounded by red box denotes the negative predictions. (Color figure online)

We display in Fig. 6 one qualitative result showing how the fusion of multi-stream outputs can significantly improve the prediction results. Even when all of the four streams provide a negative prediction in rank-1, the fusion method success to provide the same identity as the probe image. Some images with the same identity as the probe image can move up in the top 10 ranking list despite their absence in the top 10 of all the four streams. This result can be explained by the slight difference between the scores in some cases where the images of different people are visually difficult to distinguish. The fusion method therefore makes it possible to favor images corresponding to the probe identity at the expense of false identities.

Our method is also compared to several state-of-the-art methods for person re-ID based on multi-stream strategy. This comparative study is presented in Table 3. The obtained results highlight the performances of the proposed method and show that our method outperforms many previous works by a large margin in rank-1 accuracy and mAP. After embedding the re-ranking method [27], we obtain 89.22% in rank-1, an improvement of 2.2%.

Table 3. Comparison with the state-of-the-art approaches on Market-1501 dataset.

Method	Rank-1	mAP
Gated S-CNN [21]	65.88	39.55
PL-Net [24]	69.3	88.2
MSCAN [15]	80.31	57.53
BSTS S-CNN [6]	81.79	66.78
GPN [9]	81.94	87.07
MSCF_RK [12]	85.7	–
GLAD [22]	89.9	73.9
Ours	87.02	71.72
Ours + re-ranking	89.22	83.72

4 Conclusion

In this paper, we proposed a multi-stream method for person re-ID that aims to exploit global and local features and to avoid problems related to background variations. We propose to first perform a semantic segmentation to extract body parts, then we combine local and global feature extractor outputs to make final decision. We showed that combining multiple highly discriminative local region features of the person images leads to an accurate person re-identification system. Experiments on Market-1501 dataset clearly demonstrate that our proposed approach considerably improves the performance as compared with mono-stream methods and to the state-of-the-art approaches.

Acknowledgement. This project is carried out under the MOBIDOC scheme, funded by the EU through the EMORI program and managed by the ANPR. We thank Anavid for assistance. We gratefully acknowledge the support of NVIDIA Corporation with the donation of the Titan Xp GPU used for this research.

References

1. Atrey, P.K., Hossain, M.A., El Saddik, A., Kankanhalli, M.S.: Multimodal fusion for multimedia analysis: a survey. Multimedia Syst. **16**(6), 345–379 (2010). https://doi.org/10.1007/s00530-010-0182-0
2. Bialkowski, A., Denman, S., Sridharan, S., Fookes, C., Lucey, P.: A database for person re-identification in multi-camera surveillance networks. In: International Conference on Digital Image Computing Techniques and Applications (DICTA), pp. 1–8. IEEE (2012)
3. Cheng, D., Gong, Y., Zhou, S., Wang, J., Zheng, N.: Person re-identification by multi-channel parts-based CNN with improved triplet loss function. In: Computer Vision and Pattern Recognition (CVPR). pp. 1335–1344 (2016)
4. Cho, Y.J., Yoon, K.J.: Improving person re-identification via pose-aware multi-shot matching. In: Computer Vision and Pattern Recognition (CVPR), pp. 1354–1362 (2016)
5. Gheissari, N., Sebastian, T.B., Hartley, R.: Person reidentification using spatiotemporal appearance. In: Computer Vision and Pattern Recognition (CVPR), vol. 2, pp. 1528–1535. IEEE (2006)
6. Ghorbel, M., Ammar, S., Kessentini, Y., Jmaiel, M.: Improving person re-identification by background subtraction using two-stream convolutional networks. In: Karray, F., Campilho, A., Yu, A. (eds.) ICIAR 2019. LNCS, vol. 11662, pp. 345–356. Springer, Cham (2019). https://doi.org/10.1007/978-3-030-27202-9_31
7. Gong, S., Cristani, M., Yan, S., Loy, C.C.: Person Re-Identification, 1st edn., p. 445. springer, London (2014). https://doi.org/10.1007/978-1-4471-6296-4
8. He, K., Zhang, X., Ren, S., Sun, J.: Deep residual learning for image recognition. In: Computer Vision and Pattern Recognition (CVPR), pp. 770–778 (2016)
9. Hu, X., Jiang, Z., Guo, X., Zhou, Y.: Person re-identification by deep learning muti-part information complementary. In: IEEE International Conference on Image Processing (ICIP), pp. 848–852 (2018)
10. Huang, H., Li, D., Zhang, Z., Chen, X., Huang, K.: Adversarially occluded samples for person re-identification. In: Computer Vision and Pattern Recognition (CVPR), pp. 5098–5107 (2018)
11. Huang, Y., Zha, Z.J., Fu, X., Zhang, W.: Illumination-invariant person re-identification. In: ACM International Conference on Multimedia, pp. 365–373 (2019)
12. Huang, Z., et al.: Contribution-based multi-stream feature distance fusion method with k-distribution re-ranking for person re-identification. IEEE Access **7**, 35631–35644 (2019)
13. Karanam, S., Li, Y., Radke, R.J.: Person re-identification with discriminatively trained viewpoint invariant dictionaries. In: IEEE International Conference on Computer Vision, pp. 4516–4524 (2015)
14. Kittler, J.: Combining classifiers: a theoretical framework. Pattern Anal. Appl. **1**(1), 18–27 (1998). https://doi.org/10.1007/BF01238023
15. Li, D., Chen, X., Zhang, Z., Huang, K.: Learning deep context-aware features over body and latent parts for person re-identification. In: Computer Vision and Pattern Recognition (CVPR), pp. 384–393 (2017)
16. Liang, X., Gong, K., Shen, X., Lin, L.: Look into person: Joint body parsing & pose estimation network and a new benchmark. IEEE Trans. Pattern Anal. Mach. Intell. **41**, 871–885 (2018)

17. Mansouri, N., Ammar, S., Kessentini, Y.: Improving person re-identification by combining Siamese convolutional neural network and re-ranking process. In: IEEE International Conference on Advanced Video and Signal Based Surveillance (AVSS), pp. 1–8. IEEE (2019)

18. Quan, R., Dong, X., Wu, Y., Zhu, L., Yang, Y.: Auto-ReID: searching for a part-aware convnet for person re-identification. arXiv preprint arXiv:1903.09776 (2019)

19. Russakovsky, O., et al.: ImageNet large scale visual recognition challenge. Int. J. Comput. Vis. **115**(3), 211–252 (2015). https://doi.org/10.1007/s11263-015-0816-y

20. Tian, M., et al.: Eliminating background-bias for robust person re-identification. In: Computer Vision and Pattern Recognition (CVPR), pp. 5794–5803 (2018)

21. Varior, R.R., Haloi, M., Wang, G.: Gated Siamese convolutional neural network architecture for human re-identification. In: Leibe, B., Matas, J., Sebe, N., Welling, M. (eds.) ECCV 2016. LNCS, vol. 9912, pp. 791–808. Springer, Cham (2016). https://doi.org/10.1007/978-3-319-46484-8_48

22. Wei, L., Zhang, S., Yao, H., Gao, W., Tian, Q.: GLAD: global-local-alignment descriptor for scalable person re-identification. IEEE Trans. Multimedia **21**(4), 986–999 (2018)

23. Weinrich, C., Volkhardt, M., Gross, H.M.: Appearance-based 3D upper-body pose estimation and person re-identification on mobile robots. In: IEEE International Conference on Systems, Man, and Cybernetics, pp. 4384–4390. IEEE (2013)

24. Yao, H., Zhang, S., Hong, R., Zhang, Y., Xu, C., Tian, Q.: Deep representation learning with part loss for person re-identification. IEEE Trans. Image Process. **28**(6), 2860–2871 (2019)

25. Zheng, L., Shen, L., Tian, L., Wang, S., Wang, J., Tian, Q.: Scalable person re-identification: a benchmark. In: IEEE International Conference on Computer Vision (ICCV), pp. 1116–1124 (2015)

26. Zheng, Z., Zheng, L., Yang, Y.: A discriminatively learned CNN embedding for person reidentification. ACM Trans. Multimedia Comput. Commun. Appl. (TOMM) **14**(1), 13 (2018)

27. Zhong, Z., Zheng, L., Cao, D., Li, S.: Re-ranking person re-identification with k-reciprocal encoding. In: Computer Vision and Pattern Recognition (CVPR), pp. 1318–1327. IEEE (2017)

Analysis of Histogram of Oriented Gradients on Gait Recognition

Chirawat Wattanapanich[1], Hong Wei[1(✉)], and Wei Xu[2]

[1] University of Reading, Reading RG6 6AY, UK
wchirawat@wu.ac.th, h.wei@reading.ac.uk
[2] University of Surrey, Guildford GU2 7XH, UK
w.xu@surrey.ac.uk

Abstract. This study investigates the impact of Histogram of Oriented Gradients (HoG) on gait recognition. HoG is applied to four basic gait representations, *i.e.* Gait Energy Image (GEI), Gait Entropy Image (GEnI), Gait Gaussian Image (GGI), and newly developed Gait Gaussian Entropy Image (GGEnI). Hence their corresponding secondary gait representations, Gradient Histogram Gait Images (GHGI), are generated. Due to the nature of HoGs, the secondary gait representations contain rich information of images from different scales and orientations. The optimized HoG parameters are investigated to establish appropriate parameter settings in the HoG operations. Evaluations are conducted by using Support Vector Machines (SVM) as classifier swith CASIA dataset B. Experimental results have shown that HoG associated secondary representations are superior to the originally basic representations in gait recognition, especially in case of coping with appearance changes, such as walking with bag and walking with coat when using normal walking samples in training. GHGIs have increased the gait recognition rate approximately of 17% to GEI, 12% to GEnI, 24% to GGI and 20% to GGEnI.

Keywords: Gait representation · Histogram of oriented gradients · Model-free gait recognition

1 Introduction

Gait recognition, which is non-intrusive in identifying individuals in distance, is still challenging in biometric research. The main advantages of gait recognition are that it allows low-resolution images in recognition, can be used for long-distance detection, and has non-interference with target activities. Moreover, gait which is the personal walking characteristic is hardly hidden and spoofed.

Gait representation which presents personal gait information is one of the most important parts in gait recognition research. There are two main stages in conventional gait recognition, gait feature extraction and classification. Gait features which represent the walking characteristic can be extracted from both gait model and gait image sequence. In a model free approach, gait features are usually extracted from gait representation called compact image which is generated from a complete gait cycle. The basic compact

© Springer Nature Switzerland AG 2021
C. Djeddi et al. (Eds.): MedPRAI 2020, CCIS 1322, pp. 86–97, 2021.
https://doi.org/10.1007/978-3-030-71804-6_7

image, called Gait Energy Image (GEI) [1] or Average Silhouette [2] can be generated by an average function. GEI has been commonly used in the model free research because of its simplicity and low-cost in computation. Based on GEI, other gait compact images have been consequently established to fulfill recognition efficiency, such as Gait Entropy Image (GEnI), Gait Gaussian Image (GGI) [3], Flow Histogram Energy Image [4], Gradient Histogram Gaussian Image [5] and Gait Information Image [6]. This study has chosen GEI, GEnI, GGI and GGEnI (a Gaussian variant of GEnI) as four basic gait representations that are used to generate Gradient Histogram Gait Image (GHGI) by the Histogram of Oriented Gradients (HoG) method.

Various feature extraction methods have been used with compact images in gait recognition, such as Principal Component Analysis (PCA) [7, 8], Linear Discriminant Analysis (LDA) [9, 10] and Convolutional Neural Network (CNN) [11–14]. PCA, as a fundamental method, is chosen for dimension reduction or feature extraction in this study.

In the classification stage, various classifiers are adapted in gait recognition, such as Nearest Neighbor (NN) [3, 15, 16], Support Vector Machine (SVM) [17–19] and CNN. This study has chosen one-against-all multi-class SVM as the classifier.

GEI, GEnI, GGI and GGEnI are used as the basic gait representation image, from which Gradient Histogram Gait Images (GHGI) are generated by applying HoGs to them, followed by gait feature extraction by PCA. The classification performance is tested by multi-class SVMs on CASIA dataset B [20], that contains three types of appearance and eleven camera view angles. It aims to investigate how parameters of HoGs impact on gait recognition performance with GHGI gait representations. The rest of the paper is organized as follows. Section 2 presents the methodology for the gait recognition system. Section 3 discusses experiments and results. The conclusion is given in Sect. 4.

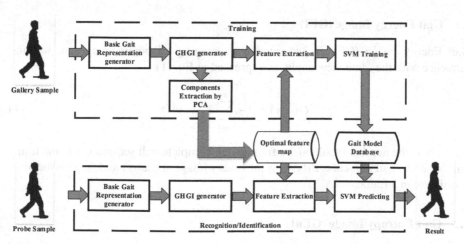

Fig. 1. General gait recognition system

2 Methodology

The gait recognition framework is shown in Fig. 1. It is a model-free gait recognition system that normally has two modes, training and testing. The training mode has four processes involved, sequence image preparation, gait representation generation, gait feature extraction, and personal model training. The testing mode comprises the similar processes as those in the training mode except that the last process is classifier's prediction. In this study, CASIA dataset B provides both training and testing images which are already processed by foreground extraction.

The study is focused on the investigation of the impact of gait representations on gait recognition performance. Four basic gait representations, GEI, GEnI, GGI and GGEnI, along with the corresponding secondary gait representations, Gradient Histogram Gait Image (GHGI) are investigated. Exemplar gait representation images are shown in Fig. 2. These gait representations are briefly described in the Sects. 2.1 to 2.5.

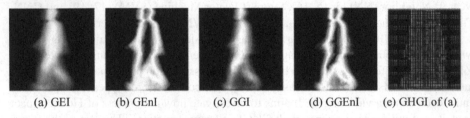

(a) GEI   (b) GEnI   (c) GGI   (d) GGEnI   (e) GHGI of (a)

Fig. 2. Examples of gait representations

2.1 Gait Energy Image (GEI)

Gait Energy Image (GEI) is generated by averaging all binary images in walking sequence with the same view angle, as expressed in Eq. (1).

$$G(x, y) = \frac{1}{N} \sum_{t=1}^{N} B_t(x, y) \tag{1}$$

where N is the number of silhouette frames in a complete gait sequence, t is the frame number in the gait sequence, $B_t(x, y)$ is the binary image at frame t and (x, y) is the pixel coordinate in a frame.

2.2 Gait Entropy Image (GEnI)

Gait Entropy Image (GEnI) [21] which aims to reduce unnecessary information with Shannon entropy theory is implemented as in Eq. (2).

$$GEnI = H(x, y) = \sum_{k=1}^{K} p_k(x, y) \log_2 p_k(x, y) \tag{2}$$

where (x, y) is a pixel coordinate and $p_k(x, y)$ is the kth probability function which has $k = 2$ because input images are a binary image. This study follows the basic concept in [21] so that $p_2(x, y) = G(x, y)$ in Eq. (1) and $p_1(x, y) = 1 - p_2(x, y)$.

2.3 Gait Gaussian Image (GGI)

GGI is similar to GEI, however, it is produced by a Gaussian function instead of the average function. This reduces the noise effect from a individual frame in the interested gait cycle. The Gaussian function is defined in Eq. (3):

$$u_i(x) = e^{-\frac{(x_i - \bar{x})^2}{2\sigma^2}} \tag{3}$$

where u_i is Gaussian membership, x_i is the respective pixel of ith frame, $\bar{x}$ is the mean of a respective pixel over all frames, and σ is the variance of the pixel vector.

Then the output pixel a_j is calculated from the average of the multiplied result between corresponding pixel and Gaussian membership, as shown in Eq. (4).

$$a_j = \frac{1}{N} \sum_{i=1}^{N} a_i u_i \tag{4}$$

where j is the pixel position, i is the frame number, a_i is the pixel value of the ith frame and N is the number of frame.

2.4 Gait Gaussian Entropy Image (GGEnI)

The aim of this newly purposed gait representation is for improving robustness against appearance changes in GGI, thus, the GEnI concept is combined with GGI in this representation. GGEnI is calculated with Eq. (2), but the probability function changes to a Gaussian membership function. GGEnI is defined as:

$$GGEnI = \sum_{k=1}^{K} p_k(x, y) log_2 p_k(x, y) \tag{5}$$

$$u_i(x, y) = e^{-\frac{\left(a_i(x,y) - \overline{a(x,y)}\right)^2}{2\sigma^2}} \tag{6}$$

$$p_2(x, y) = \frac{1}{N} \sum_{i=1}^{N} a_i(x, y) u_i(x, y) \tag{7}$$

$$p_1(x, y) = 1 - p_2(x, y) \tag{8}$$

where (x, y) is a pixel coordinate, and $p_k(x, y)$ is the kth probability, $u_i(x, y)$ is Gaussian membership of the ith frame, $a_i(x, y)$ is the pixel value of the ith frame at (x, y), $\overline{a(x, y)}$ is the mean of pixel value at (x, y) for all frames, and σ is the variance of the pixel vector.

2.5 Gradient Histogram Gait Image (GHGI)

GHEI is obtained by applying histogram of oriented gradients (HoG) to each input original image then all output frames are averaged to generate the gait representation image [22]. Differently in this study, HoG is applied to the four basic gait images to generate GHGI. GHGI is computed with the following steps.

Step 1: Compute horizontal and vertical gradients I_x and I_y.
Step 2: Compute magnitude r and orientation θ

$$r = \sqrt{I_x^2 + I_y^2} \tag{9}$$

$$\theta(x, y) = \text{atan}\left(\frac{I_x}{I_y}\right) \tag{10}$$

Step 3: Calculate cell histogram from each pixel in a cell which is a non-overlapping square region. Each cell is typically presented by 9 bin histograms.

$$\hat{\theta} = \frac{9.\theta(x, y)}{2\pi} \tag{11}$$

Cells are grouped to a block which has typically overlapped with neighbor blocks. Each block, containing 4 cells, represents a feature vector of length 36 after each cell is normalized by L1 norm.
Step 4: Combine feature vectors of all blocks which are normalized by lower-style clipped L2 norm [23].

3   Evaluation

All experiments were conducted on CASIA gait dataset B which contains videos from 124 persons. Each person had been captured in eleven view angles from 0 to 180° and three appearance variations including normal walking, walking with bag, and walking with coat. In each view angle for an individual, there are ten videos, six for normal walk, two for walking with bag, and other two for walking with coat. The datasets provide sequence images which are already processed by background subtraction, associated with the original videos. This study used only 116 persons who had complete sequence images in eleven view angles and three appearance variations.

Linear SVMs which are implemented with libSVM was chosen as classifiers for all experiments. Number of components from PCA was set as the maximum components which depend on the number of training datasets. Each personal model was trained with random error and results were averaged from five experiments.

3.1 HoG Parameters

Dalal and Triggs research [23] which suggested the optimized HoG parameters, for example number of orientation histogram bins should set to 9, is usually used as the reference for HoG parameters in Human detection research. Some research [5, 22] and some scientific program, for example MATLAB, adapt these parameters as default settings in HoGs. However, our GHGI, generated by the method described in Sect. 2.5, does not reach the maximum potential with these default settings. The initial experiments aim to find the optimized parameters for the HoG method. There are three interesting parameters, cell size, block size, and number of bins. All the experiments in this section use GEI as a basic gait representation. Personal model was trained by normal walk appearance while the recognition rate was tested by all three appearances.

The first experiment was cell size testing in which block size and number of bins were fixed as two and nine, respectively. Number of training samples or gait images per person which were used to train personal models was also considered in this experiment. Among the 6 normal walk samples of each person, we took 1, 2, 3 or 4 samples for training. Six samples per person which were two samples from each appearance were used as testing samples. The results of recognition rate are shown in Table 1.

Table 1. Cell size testing for HoG method

Cell size	Number of training samples			
	1	2	3	4
1	78.29	90.45	91.34	92.46
2	79.69	**91.31**	**91.39**	**92.46**
3	**82.52**	90.70	90.84	92.03
4	76.06	89.50	89.69	91.16
5	70.31	88.66	89.03	90.62
6	71.34	88.07	88.37	90.35
7	70.54	87.21	87.84	89.77
8	69.32	85.95	86.08	88.58

The optimized cell size for one training dataset was 3 × 3 while the rest was 2 × 2. After this optimized point, the recognition rate dropped continually. The cell size of 2 × 2 was set up as an initial parameter for the second experiment of block size testing. The number of bins was fixed as nine, the same as in the first experiment. Results are shown in Table 2.

The optimized block size was 3 × 3. When block size increases over 3 × 3, the recognition rate drops. Next, both cell size and block size were fixed to find the optimized number of bins. The testing result of number of bins against recognition rate was shown in Fig. 3. When one dataset was used in training of a personal model, it had the highest score at 87.42% with 12 bins. The rest had consequently highest scores as 92.47% (19

Table 2. Block size testing for HoG method

Block size	Number of training samples			
	1	2	3	4
1	83.14	90.97	91.42	92.58
2	84.47	91.31	91.37	92.46
3	**85.67**	**91.38**	**91.47**	**92.79**

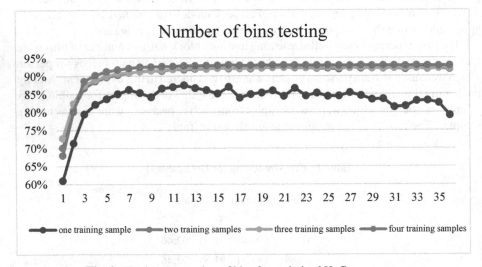

Fig. 3. Testing the number of bins for optimized HoG parameters

bins), 92.35% (25 bins) and 93.03% (16 bins) for two, three and four training samples, respectively. The optimized number of bins calculated from all testings was fifteen. As the result, the optimized parameters of the HoG method used in the experiments in this study are summarized in Table 3.

Table 3. The optimized parameter for HoG

Parameter	Number of training samples			
	1	2	3	4
Cell size	3	2	2	2
Block size	3	3	3	3
Bins	15	15	15	15

From the results demonstrated in Tables 1, 2 and 3, there is no significant difference w.r.t. recognition rate by using two or three or four training samples (only 1–2% difference). They show a similar trend whens varying the three parameters. Thus two training samples were suggested as the minimum number of training samples. In contrast, one training sample had the lowest recognition rate and it has a different pattern w.r.t. the set of best parameters, as shown in Fig. 3. It is interesting that if the parameter values were set high, the performance of GHGI was very low in terms of cell size and number of bins. The optimized parameters of HoG were applied in the other basic gait representations demonstrated in the next section.

3.2 Testing Gait Representations

Experiments involved in this section expand the HoG method to the other three basic gait representations. It shows that GHGI can improve the gait recognition rate compared to their counterparts of the basic gait representations.

Table 4. Recognition rate of the four basic gait representations and their GHGI

Represen-tations	Appeara-nces	Training samples							
		Only Basic Representation				GHGI			
		1	2	3	4	1	2	3	4
GEI	Normal	95.37	98.68	**99.21**	99.14	95.24	98.11	97.86	98.63
	Bag	60.67	68.85	69.95	71.82	83.83	90.88	91.31	**92.30**
	Coat	47.53	54.59	54.62	55.24	78.15	87.19	87.01	**88.45**
	Mixed	67.86	74.04	74.59	75.40	85.74	92.06	92.06	*93.13*
GEnI	Normal	94.99	98.74	99.02	**99.15**	94.33	97.69	98.09	98.86
	Bag	68.54	76.49	78.07	80.81	81.78	90.48	90.83	**92.15**
	Coat	51.12	57.78	57.30	60.17	76.46	86.08	86.25	**87.78**
	Mixed	71.55	77.67	78.13	80.04	84.19	91.42	91.72	**92.93**
GGI	Normal	94.93	98.13	98.78	99.09	96.27	99.28	99.63	**99.73**
	Bag	38.91	43.92	46.67	48.23	67.78	82.13	84.74	**87.39**
	Coat	20.45	26.61	28.72	29.75	41.73	58.95	61.99	**64.78**
	Mixed	51.43	56.22	58.06	59.02	68.60	80.12	82.12	**83.97**
GGEnI	Normal	94.72	98.11	98.65	98.99	95.47	99.00	99.55	**99.73**
	Bag	46.65	54.71	57.33	58.61	66.82	81.25	83.60	**85.67**
	Coat	22.76	28.96	31.51	32.40	38.97	58.60	62.00	**65.13**
	Mixed	54.71	60.59	62.50	63.33	67.09	79.62	81.72	**83.51**

Table 4 shows the recognition rate of using basic gait representations and Gradient Histogram Gait Image. Results were taken from the average of the elven view angles. GEnI was the best basic representation achieving the mixed average recognition rate of 80.04% with four normal walk training samples. All basic representations had a problem with appearance changes especially GGI and GGEnI which were generated by convolving Gaussian kernels.

From Table 4, it is clear that GHGI achieved relatively higher recognition rate over the basic representations except normal walk testing in case of GEI and GEnI. The recognition rate in cases of walking with bag and coat was significantly increased by using GHGI as gait representations. This shows that when the HoG is applied to the basic representations the new secondary representations are more robust to appearance changes. In contrast, the recognition rate in terms of normal walk was slightly decreased. GEI + HoG with four training samples had the highest averaged recognition rate of 93.13%. This confirms that GEI, which was simple and had less computation cost, was the best gait representation when combined with the HoG method.

The detailed recognition rate over 11 view angles for the secondary representations (GHGI) was shown in Fig. 4, which was resulted from four normal walk training samples. If only normal walk testing was considered, GHGI to GGI and GGEnI had the best result with the same value in every view angles. The recognition rate of 100% at 0°, 18°, 54°, 126°, 144°, 168° and 180° is shown to GGI and GGEnI, while GEI and GEnI had the best recognition rate at 99.57% (18°) and 99.89% (54°), respectively.

GHGI to both GEI and GEnI had the better recognition rate in case of walking with bag and coat. Both representations had recognition rate with bag more than 95% in 72°, 90° and 108°. And they had recognition rate with coat more than 90% in 18°, 36° and 54°. If all results from every gait presentation had been calculated together in each view angle, GHGI had the highest recognition rate at 91.23% in 72° while basic representations had the highest rate at 65.01% in 180°.

Overall, GHGI had increased the recognition rate of approximately 17% to GEI, 12% to GEnI, 24% to GGI and 20% to GGEnI. This confirms that HoG scan directly apply to the basic gait representations and increase their recognition rate especially in case of appearance changes. However, this experiment was based only on CASIA dataset B which captured each person in the similar style of coat, bag and walkway. More challenging scenarios need to be explored, such as view transformation, large population dataset, as well as in a real environment. Nevertheless, to some environments where walkway (airport gate) and cloths (hospital settings) could be controlled, the proposed gait representations should work well.

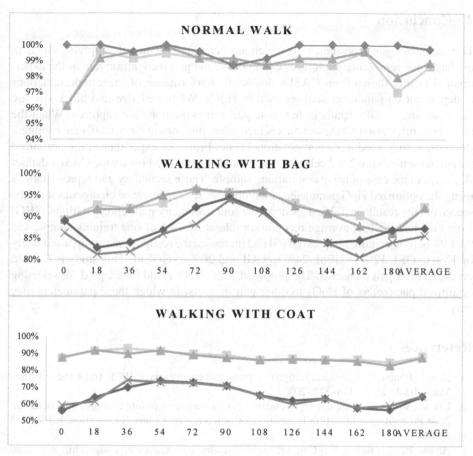

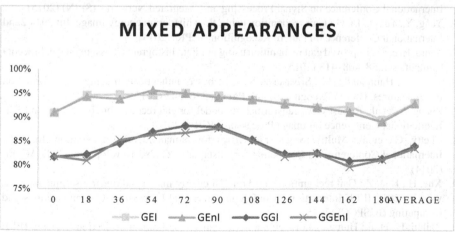

Fig. 4. Recognition rate of GHGI with different basic gait representation image

4 Conclusion

The secondary gait representations which are generated by directly applying HoGs to the basic gait representation images can improve the gait recognition rate as the experimental results shown from CASIA dataset B. Performance of these representations is dependent on parameter settings used in HoGs. When cell size and block size are decrease, small-scale details in the basic gait representations are captured. When the number of orientation histogram bins is increased, finer orientation details are captured. In contrast, they need more computational time. From our experiments, the optimized parameter settings are 2×2 cell size, 3×3 block size and 15 bins for the CASIA dataset B, except of the case of using one training sample. These secondary gait representations using the optimized HoG parameters are more robust to appearance changes as it can be seen from the results in Table 4. Among the four secondary gait representations, GHGI from GEI had the best average recognition rate at 85.74% of one training sample and 93.13% of four training samples. GHGI had increased the recognition rate approximately of 17% to GEI, 12% to GEnI, 24% to GGI and 20% to GGEnI. This study is focused on the CASIA gait dataset B. The proposed framework could be adapted for selecting optimized parameters of HoGs to other gait datasets, in which these parameters may vary.

References

1. Han, J., Bhanu, B.: Individual recognition using gait energy image. IEEE Trans. Pattern Anal. Mach. Intell. **28**(2), 316–322 (2006)
2. Liu, Z., Sarkar, S.: Simplest representation yet for gait recognition: averaged silhouette. In: 2004 Proceedings of the 17th International Conference on Pattern Recognition, ICPR 2004 (2004)
3. Arora, P., Srivastava, S.: Gait recognition using gait Gaussian image. In: 2015 2nd International Conference on Signal Processing and Integrated Networks (SPIN) (2015)
4. Yang, Y., Tu, D., Li, G.: Gait recognition using flow histogram energy image. In: 2014 22nd International Conference on Pattern Recognition (ICPR) (2014)
5. Arora, P., et al.: Improved gait recognition using gradient histogram Gaussian image. Procedia Comput. Sci. **58**, 408–413 (2015)
6. Arora, P., Hanmandlu, M., Srivastava, S.: Gait based authentication using gait information image features. Pattern Recogn. Lett. **68, Part 2**, 336–342 (2015)
7. Zheng, S., et al.: Robust view transformation model for gait recognition. In: 2011 18th IEEE International Conference on Image Processing (ICIP) (2011)
8. Chetty, G., et al.: Multiview gait biometrics for human identity recognition. In: 2014 International Conference on Computing for Sustainable Global Development (INDIACom) (2014)
9. Xue, H., Hao, Z.: Gait recognition based on gait energy image and linear discriminant analysis. In: 2015 IEEE International Conference on Signal Processing, Communications and Computing (ICSPCC) (2015)
10. Zhihui, L., et al.: Human gait recognition via sparse discriminant projection learning. IEEE Trans. Circ. Syst. Video Technol. **24**(10), 1651–1662 (2014)
11. Alotaibi, M., Mahmood, A.: Improved gait recognition based on specialized deep convolutional neural networks. In: 2015 IEEE Applied Imagery Pattern Recognition Workshop (AIPR) (2015)

12. Shiraga, K., et al.: GEINet: view-invariant gait recognition using a convolutional neural network. In: 2016 International Conference on Biometrics (ICB) (2016)
13. Wolf, T., Babaee, M., Rigoll, G.: Multi-view gait recognition using 3D convolutional neural networks. In: 2016 IEEE International Conference on Image Processing (ICIP) (2016)
14. Yan, C., Zhang, B., Coenen, F.: Multi-attributes gait identification by convolutional neural networks. In: 2015 8th International Congress on Image and Signal Processing (CISP) (2015)
15. Lan, W., et al.: Multi-view gait recognition with incomplete training data. In: 2014 IEEE International Conference on Multimedia and Expo (ICME) (2014)
16. Luo, C., Xu, W., Zhu, C.: Robust gait recognition based on partitioning and canonical correlation analysis. In: 2015 IEEE International Conference on Imaging Systems and Techniques (IST) (2015)
17. Flora, J.B., et al.: Improved gender classification using nonpathological gait kinematics in full-motion video. IEEE Trans. Hum.-Mach. Syst. 45(3), 304–314 (2015)
18. Gupta, A., et al.: Hybrid method for Gait recognition using SVM and Baysian Network. In: 2015 IEEE 8th International Workshop on Computational Intelligence and Applications (IWCIA) (2015)
19. Das, D.: Human gait classification using combined HMM & SVM hybrid classifier. In: 2015 International Conference on Electronic Design, Computer Networks & Automated Verification (EDCAV) (2015)
20. Yu, S., Tan, D., Tan, T.: A framework for evaluating the effect of view angle, clothing and carrying condition on gait recognition. In: 2006 18th International Conference on Pattern Recognition, ICPR 2006 (2006)
21. Bashir, K., Tao, X., Shaogang, G.: Gait recognition using gait entropy image. In: 3rd International Conference on Crime Detection and Prevention (ICDP 2009) (2009)
22. Hofmann, M., Rigoll, G.: Improved gait recognition using gradient histogram energy image. In: 2012 19th IEEE International Conference on Image Processing (2012)
23. Dalal, N., Triggs, B.: Histograms of oriented gradients for human detection. In: 2005 IEEE Computer Society Conference on Computer Vision and Pattern Recognition (CVPR 2005) (2005)

Possibilistic Classifier Combination
for Person Re-identification

Ilef Ben Slima[1,3]([✉]), Sourour Ammar[1,2], Mahmoud Ghorbel[1,4],
and Yousri Kessentini[1,2]

[1] Digital Research Center of Sfax, 3021 Sfax, Tunisia
[2] MIRACL Laboratory, Sfax University, Sfax, Tunisia
{sourour.ammar,yousri.kessentini}@crns.rnrt.tn
[3] LIPAH Laboratory, University of Tunis El Manar, Tunis, Tunisia
ilef.benslima@crns.rnrt.tn
[4] ReDCAD Laboratory, Sfax University, Sfax, Tunisia
mahmoud.ghorbel1991@gmail.com

Abstract. Possibility theory is particularly efficient in combining multiple information sources providing incomplete, imprecise, and conflictive knowledge. In this work, we focus on the improvement of the accuracy rate of a person re-identification system by combining multiple Deep learning classifiers based on global and local representations. In addition to the original image, we explicitly leverages background subtracted image, middle and down body parts to alleviate the pose and background variations. The proposed combination approach takes place in the framework of possibility theory, since it enables us to deal with imprecision and uncertainty factor which can be presented in the predictions of poor classifiers. This combination method can take advantage of the complementary information given by each classifier, even the weak ones. Experimental results on Market1501 publicly available dataset confirm that the proposed combination method is interesting as it can easily be generalized to different deep learning re-identification architectures and it improves the results with respect to individual classifiers.

Keywords: Deep learning · Classifier fusion · Possibility theory · CNN · Person re-identification

1 Introduction

Person re-identification (re-id) aims to identify the same person in multiple images captured from different camera views [12]. Many efforts have been dedicated to solve this problem, but person re-id still facing many challenges and can be affected by many factors such as the variation of person appearance (poses [6], illumination [16], camera views [18] and occlusion [15]) and the impact of the background scenes [10,27]. To address these challenges, many works [20,28,30] directly focus on the whole image to learn global feature description. Other works proposed to enhance the re-id accuracy of multiple baseline methods by

© Springer Nature Switzerland AG 2021
C. Djeddi et al. (Eds.): MedPRAI 2020, CCIS 1322, pp. 98–111, 2021.
https://doi.org/10.1007/978-3-030-71804-6_8

applying re-ranking process on the ranking list [21,33,37]. Using global representations generally leads to unnecessary information coming from the background while local features can be ignored. To overcome this problem, many
researches attempt to exploit local features to enhance the person re-id results
[17,19,25,29]. Some other researches try to extract local representation from
different parts of the original image. For example, [19] and [32] considered the
image as a sequence of multiple equal horizontal parts. Other works used semantic segmentation to reduce the impact of the background variations or to process
body parts separately. We cite our previous work [10] which proposed a person
re-id system based on a late fusion of a two-stream deep convolutional neural
network architecture to reduce the background bias. The first stream is the original image, and the second one is the background subtracted image belonging to
the same person. The combination method used in this work is the weighted sum
and the authors demonstrated that combining the output of these two streams
can enhance the person re-id performances.

In this paper, we extend our previous work by combining different body
part streams with the original and background subtracted images in order to
integrate local representations and alleviate the pose and background variations.
Traditional combination methods are not generally efficient when combining
multiple information sources providing incomplete, imprecise, and conflictive
knowledge. To overcome this limitation, we propose in this paper a possibilistic
combination method to aggregate the output of multiple person re-identification
classifiers.

The possibility theory, introduced by Zadeh [34], is an uncertainty representation framework which deals with uncertainty by means of fuzzy sets [7].
It naturally complements fuzzy set theory for handling uncertainty induced by
fuzzy knowledge [4]. Possibility theory has been used in many works in order to
improve the performance of classifiers in the context of uncertain and poor data.
For example, the authors in [5] developed possibilistic Bayesian classifiers which
showed a good performance in the case of poor data. The aggregation between
two possibilistic classifiers has been also proposed in this work in order to take
advantages of different classifiers and further improve their accuracy. Besides,
the authors in [3] used a probability-to-possibility transform-based possibilistic
approach in order to deal with decision-making under uncertainty.

Recently, an aggregation approach was proposed in [1], named SPOCC
method, which combines different learner predictions in the possibility theory
framework and may be applied on any type of classifier. It assumes that the
possibility distributions framework reflects how likely the classifier prediction is
correct and considers the uncertainty factor of the classifier and the imprecision
of the used data.

Inspired by the work of [1], we propose in this paper a combination method
based on possibility theory to deal with the imprecision of our different classifiers
and to aggregate their predictions in the context of person re-identification. Thus,
the main contributions of this paper are as follows:

- At first, we propose to consider different body part streams as input of our Convolutional Neural Network (CNN) classifier. Thus, different classifiers are applied and different predictions could be obtained for a query image.
- Secondly, we propose a combination method that is based on possibility theory and is composed of two main phases; the construction and the aggregation of possibility distributions for each classifier.
- Finally, we evaluate this combination method on the Market-1501 benchmark dataset using two different deep CNN architectures and we prove that our method is especially interesting in the case of using poor classifiers.

This paper is organized as follows. We present in Sect. 2 an overview of our proposed method and we provide the implementation details. Then, we present the experimental results in Sect. 3. Finally, we conclude in Sect. 4.

2   Overview of the Proposed Method

We depict in this section the details of the proposed method. We recall that our work takes place in the context of person re-identification which aims to identify the same person in multiple images captured from different camera views. Given a probe person image p and a gallery set G with N images belonging to l different identities (class labels), with $G = \{g_i \mid i = 1 \dots N\}$ and $\Omega = \{m_j \mid j = 1 \dots l\}$, the aim of person re-id method is to compare p with all the gallery images g_i in G in order to determine the identity m_j in Ω of p.

We propose in this work to extend our work [10] by considering four different variations of the input image: the original and background subtracted images and the middle and down body parts images.

We show in Fig. 1 a flowchart describing the three processing steps. The proposed framework takes as input the original image p. In the first step, we use the semantic segmentation model (SEG-CNN) proposed in our previous work [10] to generate three segmented images: background subtracted image, middle and down body parts. Four images are then given as input to the second step (re-identification step), where we apply a deep learning classifier on each input image and generate the corresponding output m^p_{k-pred}, where $k - pred$ is the predicted identity by the kth classifier. The third step, called *possibilistic fusion*, consists on aggregating these outputs ($\{m^p_{k-pred}\}_{k=1\dots4}$) to provide the final result using the possibilistic distribution of each classifier. In this paper, we focus on the third step, namely the possibilistic fusion. The aim of this method is to combine multiple classifier outputs in order to provide robust person re-identification results.

Our possibilistic fusion method consists on two main phases as shown in Fig. 3: 1) the construction of possibility distributions and 2) the aggregation of these distributions to make a final decision.

For the first phase, we apply each classifier on the validation set and we create the corresponding confusion matrix (see Fig. 2). The four confusion matrices $M^{(k)}; k = 1 \dots 4$ are used as input of our combination method, precisely for the

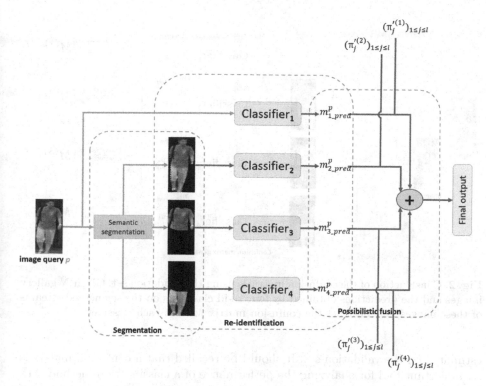

Fig. 1. Overview of the proposed framework with 3 main steps: the first step is the segmentation of the query image in order to obtain local representations of the body parts. The second one considers each segmented image (and the original image) as input of a re-id classifier and gives four different predictions. And the final step consists in the aggregation of these four predictions using the possibility distribution of each classifier.

construction of the possibility distributions (see Sect. 2.1). Because of in re-id process, learning and testing datasets contain always different identities, we use in this step the gallery images G as validation data to generate the confusion matrix for each classifier. Then, in the second phase, the above generated possibility distributions of the four classifiers are aggregated to make the final decision (see Sect. 2.2). We provide in next sections the details of these steps.

2.1 Construction of Possibility Distributions

The first phase of the proposed combination method is to construct the possibility distributions of each classifier. This method is inspired from the work of [1] where the possibility distributions are obtained from the confusion matrices of the corresponding classifiers. These confusion matrices are obtained by applying a re-id classifier on the validation set (see Fig. 2) which reflects how likely each classifier prediction is correct regarding the frequentist probabilities

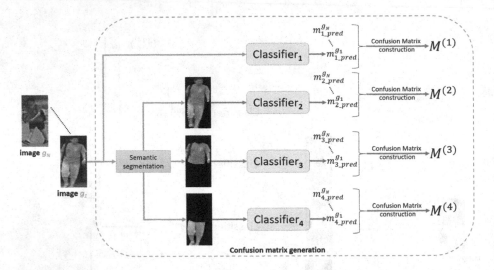

Fig. 2. Construction of the confusion matrices using the validation set. Given N gallery images and the predictions obtained by four re-id classifiers on the segmented streams of these images, we construct the confusion matrix $M^{(k)}$ of each classifier k.

estimated on the validation set. It should be recalled that a confusion matrix is an important tool for analyzing the performance of a classification method [11]. It is a two-dimensional matrix which contains information about the actual and the predicted classes and which summarizes the number of correct and incorrect predictions [24].

Using the obtained confusion matrices $M^{(k)}$, we construct the possibility distributions of each classifier using three different steps (as presented in the first part of Fig. 3).

Normalization of the Confusion Matrices: It should be noted that a considerable disparity between the distribution of images in each class can exist in many datasets. In this case, the possibility distributions generated from the confusion matrices can be biased due to this disparity. For that reason, we propose to normalize the values of each cell $M_{ij}^{(k)}$ in each confusion matrix $M^{(k)}$ according to the number of instances in each class, so that the new values of the matrix will be in the same order of magnitude. This normalization step is given by the following formula:

$$M_{ij}'^{(k)} = \frac{M_{ij}^{(k)}}{M_{\cdot j}^{(k)}}; \quad \forall i, j \tag{1}$$

where $M_{\cdot j}^{(k)} = \sum_{h=1}^{l} M_{hj}^{(k)}$

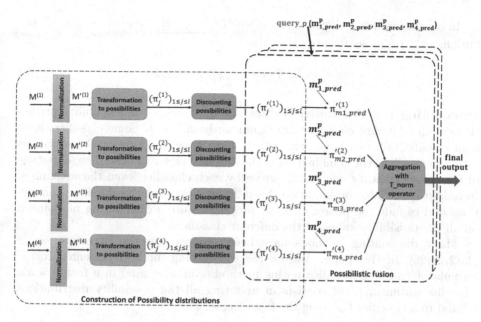

Fig. 3. Overview of the proposed possibilistic combination method. This method contains two main phases: The first phase is the construction of possibility distributions from the confusion matrices $M^{(k)}$ (of each classifier C_k; $k = 1..4$) which leads to possibility distributions $(\pi_j^{'(k)})_{1 \le j \le l}$. The second phase is the fusion of possibility distributions $\pi_{m_{k-pred}}^{'(k)}$ which corresponds to the predicted class m_{k-pred}^p of the classifier C_k for a query image p.

Construction of Possibility Distributions: In order to construct possibility distributions, we propose to transform the confusion matrix of each classifier into possibility distributions. To do so, the first step is to normalize the jth column of the confusion matrix to obtain an estimation of the probability distribution $p(Y = i/m_k = j)$ where Y is the actual class and m_k is the class predicted by the classifier C_k. This probability distribution of the column j is denoted by $p_{Y/m_k=j}$. Then, we use the Dubois and Prade Transformation method (DPT) [8] to transform the probability distributions into possibility distributions. So, for each classifier C_k and for each column j, the possibility distributions $\pi_j^{(k)}$ are obtained from the probability distributions $p_{Y/m_k=j}$ after ordering them in descending order. The DPT transforming method is given by this formula:

$$
\pi_i = \begin{cases} 1 & \text{if } i = 1 \\ \pi_{i-1} & \text{if } i > 1 \text{ and } p_i = p_{i-1} \\ \sum\limits_{q=i}^{\ell} p_q & \text{otherwise} \end{cases}
\tag{2}
$$

where the p_i are ordered in the descending order ($p_1 \ge p_2 \ge ... \ge p_l$).

In conclusion, for each classifier C_k, we obtain the different possibility distributions $(\pi_j^{(k)})_{1 \leq j \leq l}$ as follows:

$$\pi_j^{(k)} = DPT\{p_{Y/m_k=j}\}; \forall j = 1..l \tag{3}$$

Discounting the Possibility Values: In most cases, the capability predictions of the different classifiers are significantly different. Some classifiers have high classification rates and some others have a weak accuracy. Otherwise, as mentioned earlier, the combination of the different classifiers can take advantage of the complementary information given by each classifier, even the weak ones. In order to take into consideration this difference between the classifiers' predictions and to fade the poorer ones, we propose to use a discounting mechanism on all the possibility values of the different classifiers.

Many discounting methods have been proposed in the literature, as in [2,22,23,26]. In this paper, we use the discounting method presented in the formulas 4 and 5. Other discounting methods could be used in a future work. The discounting method consists in updating all the possibility distributions related to a classifier C_k using the following formula:

$$\pi_j'^{(k)} = (1 - \alpha_k) \times \pi_j^{(k)} + \alpha_k \tag{4}$$

The variable α_k is a coefficient relative to the classifier C_k which is given as follows:

$$\alpha_k = 1 - \left(\frac{1 - r\,[C_k]}{1 - \min_{k'} r\,[C_{k'}]} \right)^\rho \tag{5}$$

where $r\,[C_k]$ is the estimated error rate of the classifier C_k on the validation set and ρ is a hyper-parameter to tune by grid search.

Using the above equation, it should be noted that the best base classifier is not discounted since the value of its α_k is equal to 0.

2.2 Aggregation of Possibility Distributions

After constructing all the possibility distributions of the different classifiers, the next phase is to combine these possibility distributions in order to classify a new query image.

As presented in Fig. 3, for each query p, we consider the class (m_{k-pred}^p) predicted by each classifier C_k. This prediction corresponds to the Top 1 identity predicted by the classifier. Then, for each classifier, and given its own prediction, we consider the possibility distribution which corresponds to the predicted class m_{k-pred}^p among all the possibility distributions constructed in the above phase. Thus, only the four possibility distributions $\pi_{m_{k-pred}}'^{(k)}$ are considered and will be aggregated in order to make the final prediction.

As other measures in the fuzzy set theory, the possibility distributions can be aggregated using a T-norm operator. T-norms are examples of aggregation functions; they are widely used in knowledge uncertainty treatment [31]. Among different T-norm operators proposed in the literature [9], we propose to use the elementwise Product T-norm ($T_\times$) in this work.

Therefore, if $\pi_{k_1 k_2}$ is the aggregated possibility distribution obtained by applying a T-norm to the distributions π_{k_1} and π_{k_2}, then, $\pi_{k_1 k_2}$ is obtained as follows:

$$\pi_{k_1 k_2}(y) = T_\times(\pi_{k_1}(y), \pi_{k_2}(y)) = \pi_{k_1}(y) \times \pi_{k_1}(y); \forall y \tag{6}$$

Since the T-norm Product operator is a commutative and associative operator, it is obviously applied in the case of more than two factors. Consequently, the possibility distribution of the ensemble of aggregated classifiers is obtained as follows:

$$\pi_{ens} = T_\times(\pi_{m_1-pred}^{'(1)}, \pi_{m_2-pred}^{'(2)}, \pi_{m_3-pred}^{'(3)}, \pi_{m_4-pred}^{'(4)}) \tag{7}$$

Finally, the final prediction of a query p by the ensemble of classifiers is the class c_{ens} given by:

$$c_{ens}(p) = \arg\max_{y \in \Omega} \pi_{ens}(y) \tag{8}$$

3 Experiments

In this section, we empirically evaluate the proposed method and we show how possibilistic combination can enhance person re-id results. Experiments are carried out on a publicly available large-scale person re-identification dataset Market1501 [35]. This dataset is composed of 32,667 images divided into 19,372 gallery images, 3,368 query images and 12,396 training images related to 1501 person identities distributed in 751 identities for training phase and 750 for testing phase. Images are captured by one low-resolution and five high-resolution cameras.

We implemented the different steps of the proposed combination method and we applied them on the classification results obtained by two different deep convolutional neural network architectures: the Siamese CNN architecture (S-CNN) [36] and the ResNet50 architecture [13]. First, the confusion matrices are obtained by applying the two classifiers on the gallery set (the 19,372 gallery images), as presented in Fig. 2. Then, these two classifiers and the combination method are applied on the test set according to the person re-identification protocol (query set containing 3368 images and gallery set containing 19,372 images) (see Fig. 1). As mentioned in Sect. 2.1, we used a grid search method to find the best value of the ρ parameter used in the formula 5.

To evaluate the performance of our combination method, we use the accuracy metric which reflects the number of correct classifications among all the classified query images. In this paper, we only focus on the Top 1 predicted class.

The results obtained by applying the two different CNN classifiers (S-CNN and ResNet50) are shown respectively in Figs. 4 and 5. We remind that we propose to use four different re-id streams for each CNN classifier:

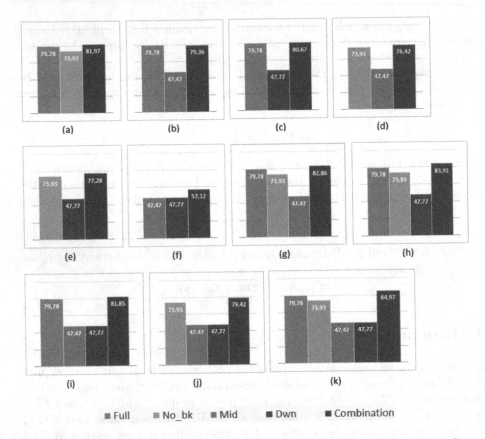

Fig. 4. Possibilistic Fusion results using S-CNN classifier on Market-1501 dataset. Since we have four stream classifiers, we provide in this figure the fusion result of different possible combination of 2–4 streams. Red bar indicates the fusion result of corresponding streams. (Color figure online)

- the original image (denoted by *Full*)
- the image with no background (*No_bk*)
- the middle body part (*Mid*)
- the down body part (*Dwn*)

In each graphic of Fig. 4 and Fig. 5, the reported *Combination* refers to the accuracy obtained by fusing the output of the corresponding stream classifiers. For example, in the first graphic (a) of Fig. 4, we present the results of the classifier using the *Full* stream (the light blue bar), the result of the classifier using the *No_bk* stream (the grey bar) and finally the result of our fusion method using these two streams *Full+No_bk* (the red bar). In the same way, we present in the last graphic (k) of Fig. 4 the results of the classifiers using the four streams individually (*Full* in light blue, *No_bk* in grey, *Mid* in orange and *Dwn* in blue) followed by the result of our fusion method using these four streams (in red bar).

It should be noted that, among the four individually streams, the *Full* stream (which extract information from the whole image) gives the best classification rates when using both classifiers (For example, in the case of S-CNN classifier, we obtain 79.78% with the *Full* stream against 73.93% with *No_bk* stream, 47.47% with the *Mid* stream and 47.77% with the *Dwn* stream). We should also note that the results of individual streams are better when we use the S-CNN classifier (the *Full* stream gives 79.78% when we use S-CNN and 73.60% when we use ResNet50).

Based on the results showed in Fig. 4 and 5, we notice that our fusion method outperforms the individually-stream classifiers in almost all the cases (except one single case in the diagram (b) of Fig. 4).

We also mention that the best accuracy rate is obtained when we combine the four streams (84.97% is obtained when we use the four streams and the S-CNN classifier (diagram (k) in Fig. 4) and 84.08% with the ResNet50 classifier (diagram (k) in Fig. 5)). When compared with the *Full* stream (which gives the best results among the four streams), our possibilistic combination method makes an improvement of 6.5% when using the S-CNN classifier and of 14.23% when using the ResNet50 classifier.

From the results showed in Fig. 4 and 5, we also remark that our proposed possibilistic combination method is more efficient when using poor classifiers. We remind that the Resnet50 classifier gives less accurate results than the S-CNN classifier. However, our combination method makes a better improvement when using the Resnet50 classifier (an improvement of 14.23% compared to the *Full* stream (see diagram (k) in Fig. 5)) than that obtained when using the S-CNN classifier (an improvement of 6.5% compared to the *Full* stream (see diagram (k) in Fig. 4)). On the other hand, we remark that when we combine the two poorer classifiers, *Mid* + *Dwn*, we obtain a highest improvement of 19.57% when using S-CNN classifier compared to the *Dwn* stream which gives a performance of 47.77% (see diagram (f) in Fig. 4) and of 21.46% when using ResNet50 classifier compared to the *Mid* stream which gives a performance of 47.47% (see diagram (f) in Fig. 5). In contrast, the combination of the two better streams, *Full* + *No_bk* (see diagrams (a) in Fig. 4 and 5), does not make a great improvement especially in the case of S-CNN classifier (2.47% compared to the *Full* classifier).

To summarize, the proposed combination method based on the possibilistic framework is able to improve the performance obtained by each classifier separately. It is able to take advantages of the opinions of even the poorer classifiers in order to make a better decision. In addition, the experimental results elaborated on the Market-1501 dataset with two different classification methods confirm that the possibilistic based combination method is especially interesting in the case of poor classifiers.

We also compared our method with other state-of-the-art methods of person re-id applied on the Market-1501 dataset. We especially focus on methods based on multi-stream approaches. Table 1 presents a comparative study of these methods. As we focus in our approach on the Rank-1 predicted identity, we consider in this comparison only the Rank-1 result predicted by each method. The

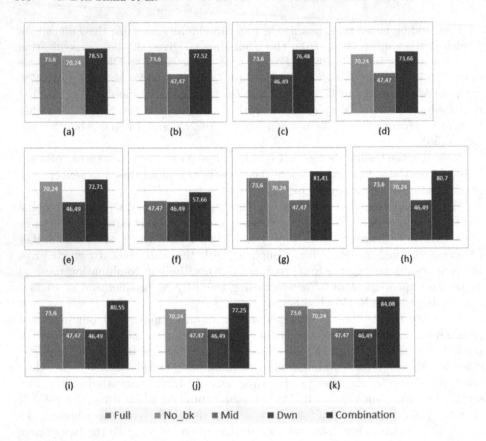

Fig. 5. Possibilistic Fusion results using ResNet50 classifier on Market-1501 dataset. Since we have four stream classifiers, we provide in this figure the fusion result of different possible combination of 2–4 streams. Red bar indicates the fusion result of corresponding streams. (Color figure online)

results in Table 1 show that our method outperforms most of other methods by a large margin. For example, it makes an improvement of 3.8% compared to the BSTS S-CNN method and of 22.6% compared to PL-Net method. This confirms that the usage of multiple classifiers on different streams can improve the classification rates; and that our possibilistic combination method is able to take advantage of the decision of the different classifiers, even the poorer ones (the middle and down).

Table 1. Comparison with the state-of-the-art approaches on Market-1501 dataset.

Method	Rank-1
Gated S-CNN [28]	65.88
PL-Net [32]	69.3
MSCAN [19]	80.31
BSTS S-CNN [10]	81.79
GPN [14]	81.94
Ours	**84.97**

4   Conclusion

In this paper, we proposed a possibilistic combination method which aims to merge the outputs of multiple Deep learning classifiers based on global and local representations in order to enhance the performance of a person re-identification system. The proposed combination method takes place in the framework of possibility theory, since it enables us to deal with imprecision and uncertainty. Experimental tests were performed on the Market-1501 dataset and have led to very satisfactory results compared to the results obtained by each classifier separately, especially in the case of using poor classifiers. It should be noted that we considered in this paper the Top 1 identity predicted by each classifier. It would be then interesting to extend this work to take into account the Top 5 or Top 10 predicted identities in a future work. In addition, we used in this paper the product T-norm when fusing the possibility distributions of the different classifiers. As a perspective, we envisage to test other T-norms as the Lukasiewicz or the Drastique T-norms [9]. Finally, another interesting perspective is to propose other discounting methods to take into account the differences between the classifiers and to fade the poorer ones [2,22,23].

Acknowledgement. We gratefully acknowledge the support of NVIDIA Corporation with the donation of the Titan Xp GPU used for this research.

References

1. Albardan, M., Klein, J., Colot, O.: SPOCC: scalable possibilistic classifier combination-toward robust aggregation of classifiers. Expert Syst. Appl. **150**, 113332 (2020)
2. Anderson, R., Koh, Y.S., Dobbie, G.: CPF: concept profiling framework for recurring drifts in data streams. In: Kang, B.H., Bai, Q. (eds.) AI 2016. LNCS (LNAI), vol. 9992, pp. 203–214. Springer, Cham (2016). https://doi.org/10.1007/978-3-319-50127-7_17
3. Baati, K., Hamdani, T.M., Alimi, A.M., Abraham, A.: A new possibilistic classifier for mixed categorical and numerical data based on a bi-module possibilistic estimation and the generalized minimum-based algorithm. Intell. Fuzzy Syst. **36**(4), 3513–3523 (2019)

4. Bouchon-Meunier, B., Dubois, D., Godo, L., Prade, H.: Fuzzy sets and possibility theory in approximate and plausible reasoning. In: Bezdek, J.C., Dubois, D., Prade, H. (eds.) Fuzzy Sets in Approximate Reasoning and Information Systems, pp. 15–190. Springer, Boston (1999). https://doi.org/10.1007/978-1-4615-5243-7_2

5. Bounhas, M., Mellouli, K., Prade, H., Serrurier, M.: Possibilistic classifiers for numerical data. Soft Comput. **17**(5), 733–751 (2013)

6. Cho, Y.J., Yoon, K.J.: Improving person re-identification via pose-aware multi-shot matching. In: IEEE Conference on Computer Vision and Pattern Recognition (CVPR), pp. 1354–1362 (2016)

7. Dubois, D., Foulloy, L., Mauris, G., Prade, H.: Probability-possibility transformations, triangular fuzzy sets, and probabilistic inequalities. Reliable Comput. **10**(4), 273–297 (2004)

8. Dubois, D., Prade, H.: On several representations of an uncertain body of evidence. In: Fuzzy Information and Decision Processes, pp. 167–181 (1982)

9. Farahbod, F., Eftekhari, M.: Comparison of different t-norm operators in classification problems. Fuzzy Logic Syst. **2**(3) (2012)

10. Ghorbel, M., Ammar, S., Kessentini, Y., Jmaiel, M.: Improving person re-identification by background subtraction using two-stream convolutional networks. In: Karray, F., Campilho, A., Yu, A. (eds.) ICIAR 2019. LNCS, vol. 11662, pp. 345–356. Springer, Cham (2019). https://doi.org/10.1007/978-3-030-27202-9_31

11. Giannakopoulos, T., Pikrakis, A.: Audio classification. In: Introduction to Audio Analysis, Chapter 5, pp. 107–151. Academic Press (2014)

12. Gong, S., Cristani, M., Yan, S., Loy, C.C. (eds.): Person Re-Identification. ACVPR. Springer, London (2014). https://doi.org/10.1007/978-1-4471-6296-4

13. He, K., Zhang, X., Ren, S., Sun, J.: Deep residual learning for image recognition. In: IEEE Conference on Computer Vision and Pattern Recognition (CVPR), pp. 770–778 (2016)

14. Hu, X., Jiang, Z., Guo, X., Zhou, Y.: Person re-identification by deep learning muti-part information complementary. In: IEEE International Conference on Image Processing (ICIP), pp. 848–852. IEEE (2018)

15. Huang, H., Li, D., Zhang, Z., Chen, X., Huang, K.: Adversarially occluded samples for person re-identification. In: IEEE Conference on Computer Vision and Pattern Recognition (CVPR), pp. 5098–5107 (2018)

16. Huang, Y., Zha, Z.J., Fu, X., Zhang, W.: Illumination-invariant person re-identification. In: ACM International Conference on Multimedia, pp. 365–373 (2019)

17. Huang, Z., et al.: Contribution-based multi-stream feature distance fusion method with k-distribution re-ranking for person re-identification. IEEE Access **7**, 35631–35644 (2019)

18. Karanam, S., Li, Y., Radke, R.J.: Person re-identification with discriminatively trained viewpoint invariant dictionaries. In: IEEE International Conference on Computer Vision, pp. 4516–4524 (2015)

19. Li, D., Chen, X., Zhang, Z., Huang, K.: Learning deep context-aware features over body and latent parts for person re-identification. In: IEEE Conference on Computer Vision and Pattern Recognition (CVPR), pp. 384–393 (2017)

20. Li, W., Zhao, R., Xiao, T., Wang, X.: DeepReID: deep filter pairing neural network for person re-identification. In: IEEE Conference on Computer Vision and Pattern Recognition (CVPR), pp. 152–159 (2014)

21. Mansouri, N., Ammar, S., Kessentini, Y.: Improving person re-identification by combining Siamese convolutional neural network and re-ranking process. In: IEEE International Conference on Advanced Video and Signal Based Surveillance (AVSS), pp. 1–8. IEEE (2019)
22. Mercier, D., Elouedi, Z., Lefevre, E.: Sur l'affaiblissement d'une fonction de croyance par une matrice de confusion. Rencontres Francophones sur la Logique Floue et Ses Applications, pp. 277–283 (2010)
23. Mercier, D., Quost, B., Denœux, T.: Refined modeling of sensor reliability in the belief function framework using contextual discounting. Inf. Fusion 9(2), 246–258 (2008)
24. Meyer-Baese, A., Schmid, V.: Foundations of neural networks. In: Pattern Recognition and Signal Analysis in Medical Imaging, 2nd edn., pp. 197–243. Academic Press (2014)
25. Quan, R., Dong, X., Wu, Y., Zhu, L., Yang, Y.: Auto-ReID: searching for a part-aware convnet for person re-identification. In: IEEE International Conference on Computer Vision, pp. 3749–3758 (2019)
26. Shafer, G.: A Mathematical Theory of Evidence, vol. 42. Princeton University Press, Princeton (1976)
27. Tian, M., et al.: Eliminating background-bias for robust person re-identification. In: IEEE Conference on Computer Vision and Pattern Recognition (CVPR), pp. 5794–5803 (2018)
28. Varior, R.R., Haloi, M., Wang, G.: Gated Siamese convolutional neural network architecture for human re-identification. In: Leibe, B., Matas, J., Sebe, N., Welling, M. (eds.) ECCV 2016. LNCS, vol. 9912, pp. 791–808. Springer, Cham (2016). https://doi.org/10.1007/978-3-319-46484-8_48
29. Wang, P., Qing, C., Xu, X., Cai, B., Jin, J., Ren, J.: Local-global extraction unit for person re-identification. In: International Conference on Brain Inspired Cognitive Systems, pp. 402–411 (2018)
30. Xiao, T., Li, H., Ouyang, W., Wang, X.: Learning deep feature representations with domain guided dropout for person re-identification. In: IEEE Conference on Computer Vision and Pattern Recognition (CVPR), pp. 1249–1258 (2016)
31. Yager, R., Gupta, M., Kandel, A., Bandler, W., Kiszka, J.: Forms of multi-criteria decision functions and preference information types. In: Approximate Reasoning in Expert Systems, pp. 167–177 (1985)
32. Yao, H., Zhang, S., Hong, R., Zhang, Y., Xu, C., Tian, Q.: Deep representation learning with part loss for person re-identification. IEEE Trans. Image Process. 28(6), 2860–2871 (2019)
33. Yu, R., Zhou, Z., Bai, S., Bai, X.: Divide and fuse: a re-ranking approach for person re-identification. In: The British Machine Vision Conference (BMVC), pp. 135.1–135.13. BMVA Press (2017)
34. Zadeh, L.A.: Fuzzy sets as a basis for a theory of possibility. Fuzzy Sets Syst. 1(1), 3–28 (1978)
35. Zheng, L., Shen, L., Tian, L., Wang, S., Wang, J., Tian, Q.: Scalable person re-identification: a benchmark. In: IEEE International Conference on Computer Vision, pp. 1116–1124 (2015)
36. Zheng, Z., Zheng, L., Yang, Y.: A discriminatively learned CNN embedding for person reidentification. ACM Trans. Multimed. Comput. Commun. Appl. (TOMM) 14(1), 1–20 (2017)
37. Zhong, Z., Zheng, L., Cao, D., Li, S.: Re-ranking person re-identification with k-reciprocal encoding. In: IEEE International Conference on Computer Vision and Pattern Recognition (CVPR), pp. 1318–1327. IEEE (2017)

Implementation of Open-Source Image Analysis Techniques in Commercial Quality Control Systems

Ross Ockmore[1,2], Wei Xu[1,2](✉), and Hong Wei[1,2]

[1] University of Surrey, Guildford GU2 7XH, UK
{w.xu,h.wei}@surrey.ac.uk
[2] University of Reading, Reading Berkshire RG6 6AH, UK

Abstract. Using image pattern matching techniques, this paper presents the development of an open-source based quality control program that can distinguish between sample pages in a book printing/production environment, intended to enable automatic rejection of incorrect pages from the binding process. Novel adaptations are made to an ORB (**O**riented FAST and **R**otated **B**rief) based image matching system that deals with quantifying the confidence of a match to ensure that even identical pages in the incorrect orientation are rejected during book binding operations. The program is subjected to a variety of quantitative tests to evaluate its performance and from these tests the effects of various parameters used in the program are discovered, allowing tuning to be performed. Potential paths for development of the analysis program are discussed, with the implementation of machine learning, highlighted as a possibility, to provide automated parameter tuning, and suggestions for further optimisation of the software are made, with a view to creating an even more bespoke version that retains performance whilst cutting computational overhead to a minimum.

1 Introduction

Quality control and assurance are an essential part of any manufacturing operation. Preventing the release of defective goods for public consumption is imperative for retention of both company reputation and a healthy customer base. When dealing with end-consumers, a lack of quality assurance leads to dissatisfaction, often resulting in decreased return custom; a publisher receiving a large number of complaints from readers may decide to terminate a contract with a manufacturer/supplier and may pursue reimbursement for lost profits. Losing clients is a major blow to many manufacturers, and it can trigger reviews by remaining clients to ensure that problems with quality are not a companywide issue. To inspire confidence with clients, and to win new business, companies typically aim to achieve ISO 9000 accreditations, which require the implementation of procedures and documentation to carefully control the consistency of output (UKEssays 2018). In the modern era, production techniques have become highly automated in nature, as output speeds and volumes increase to meet demand in the global market. It only makes sense therefore, that the quality assurance process is

C. Djeddi et al. (Eds.): MedPRAI 2020, CCIS 1322, pp. 112–124, 2021.
https://doi.org/10.1007/978-3-030-71804-6_9

also automated to a similar or the same degree, allowing for tight controls and more accurate checking of goods.

Book binding is a process by which leaves of paper are joined together to form a cohesive codex. Dating back thousands of years, this process is still utilised across the world – despite the rise of digital media, traditional paper-based novels and textbooks still account for a large proportion of total book sales (Parker 2018). There is a preference for the physical form and tactile nature of paper-based books in society, and as such it can be assumed that production is likely to continue for many years. Due to this continued demand, it is sensible to develop control measures for book production lines, to bring the industry in line with the latest technological developments, increasing efficiency.

Any device that is intended to be utilised in a production setting for page sorting must be capable of monitoring the orientation and 'correctness', making evaluations and determining whether a sheet is suitable for advancement to the stacking/sheaf stage of production. Evaluation of advancement criteria should mimic the human visual inspection process of goods and decision-making abilities, and therefore relies on the capture and processing of images. The prevalence of image processing has risen rapidly in recent years with the advancement of smartphone technology. As digital control of production lines is pervasive within the industry it is reasonable to expect that algorithms/software that can, in combination with a camera sensor, rapidly analyse sample photos of pages and determine whether they should be rejected or accepted are already used by companies. However, it is also likely that companies are paying licensing fees for these capabilities and as such are losing out on potential profit. The creation of a program with similar capabilities was explored, which is instead based upon open-source development, thus removing license fees for the industry.

2 Methodology

Image feature matching is a well-developed field with open-source libraries. Algorithms such as ORB (Oriented FAST and Rotated BRIEF), which was specifically created to offer similar functionality to replace the widely used SIFT algorithm without licensing issues for the end-user (Rublee et al. 2011) are integrated into the library to be used as tools when solving image matching problems.

These tools are designed to extract features that can be used in a matching process from images, firstly by identifying 'keypoints' within the image data, and then by producing an image descriptor for the area around the keypoint (Mordvintsev and Abid 2013). This method is analogous to the human process of studying an image, in which different aspects of the image will draw the eye – a building in a natural landscape will likely have a notable difference in composition to its surroundings, with sharp, defined edges and corners.

These tools do require augmentation with further techniques depending on the application and using the Python platform, several additional processing steps were implemented to achieve a good level of functionality for this particular quality control task, as can be seen in the flowchart above in Fig. 1. Firstly, Lowe's ratio test is applied to reduce the number of false/poor matches passed to the latter stages. As explained in Lowe's paper, this is implemented by matching each query image feature to its two

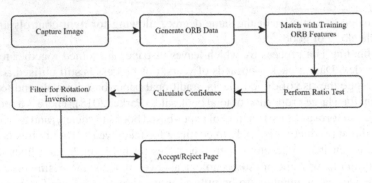

Fig. 1. Image analysis procedure

closest counterparts from the training dataset and then comparing the likeness of each to determine if a good match has been made (Lowe 2004). Once these matches have been determined, if a sufficient number of matches have been identified the next step of the process is to calculate a confidence score – whilst the ratio test filters matches, it provides no metric of how alike two pages are, and could produce matches between identical letters/words at different locations on a page. 'Homography' is the term used to describe the relationship between a deformed image and its master, such that any pixel in the master image transformed according to the homographic relationship will be located in the correct position in the deformed image space (CorrMap 2013). This information is typically employed in photographic manipulation when 'stitching' separate images of the same scene, taken from different perspectives, or when attempting to identify an object that is viewed at a different angle from the sample image that produced training features for that object. In the context of this project, homography offers a method by which to create a confidence score for the likeness of two processed pages, which can be used to reject a page from the production line.

The principle behind the calculation of a confidence score stems from the assumption that in a good match scenario both the train and query subjects are identical. As such, it is expected that after a ratio test has filtered subpar pairings, all points remaining should share a common translational and rotational homography between the two images. This is unlikely to be the case as the majority should fit the common homography if the match truly is correct. As such, the proportion of matches that are inliers can be considered against the total number of matches submitted to the algorithm that calculates homography, and this gives a confidence metric. Similarly, to how the ratio can be set for Lowe's test, this metric has a threshold that is set by the end-user, and so some degree of fine-tuning can be performed depending on testing in different production environments.

Homography can be found using a statistical technique known as Random Sample Consensus (RANSAC), which sorts through data sets generating estimates of fitting parameters from small samples and then testing the application of the fitting parameters to the dataset (Fischler and Bolles 1981). In this case, RANSAC examines pairings and attempts to find the most applicable homography for the majority of pairs. RANSAC is robust against the effects of strong outliers, that is to say, outliers that are very far from the expected result and are prone to skew averaging/norming methods.

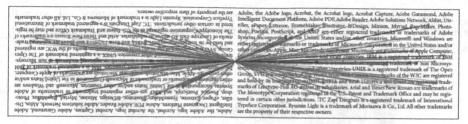

Fig. 2. High confidence match with upside-down query (False positive)

As ORB is designed to be accepting of rotational variation, it is ultimately lacking the ability to reject a page in an incorrect orientation for the binding process. This issue is demonstrated above in Fig. 2 where an inverted query subject has been compared to the train image, producing a large number of matches and a high confidence score. As it is can be assumed that both train and query images shall be captured in-plane in the quality control process, then a purely in-plane rotation value can be used to remove false positives from the matching algorithm, and thus reject pages off of the production line. Whilst the homography found previously contains all of the transformation data linking the two images, it can be difficult to extract a purely in-plane rotational value.

Fortunately, the oriented FAST keypoint data used by ORB is retained throughout the calculations made in the analysis process, and within this data, the keypoint orientation is stored. As long as the page can only translate and rotate on one plane, and the assumption can be made that after the ratio and homography filtration that each keypoint pair is correct, this orientation data can be directly compared within pairs and a rotational value computed. An average rotation value can thus be calculated from the set of correctly matched pairs, and whilst this has an amount of variation, it is a reliable indicator for a large rotation. The threshold for rotation can be set at a high value such as 90° so that only an inverted page is rejected.

3 Evaluation

3.1 Testing Setup and Aims

For all testing, a laptop was used with an i5-1035G1 Intel processor clocked at 1.19 GHz, with the ability to boost to 3.6 GHz under load. It is unlikely that the analysis program will use more than one core and so should yield good results in terms of allocating processing power to the program. For image capture during testing, a Microsoft LifeCam HD-3000 USB camera was used. The laptop was using a 64-Bit Windows 10 operating system in all experiments. Python 3.7.4 was used to run the analysis program, and version 4.1.2.30 of OpenCV was used, in conjunction with NumPy version 1.18.1. The latest available driver was installed for the USB camera used and all images captured from the USB camera were 640 × 480 pixels in resolution.

As shown in Fig. 3 the test samples consisted of two with text-heavy and two with a mixture of text and images, henceforth be referred to as Sample 1 (top left in figure), Sample 2 (top right), Sample 3 (bottom left), and Sample 4 (bottom right).

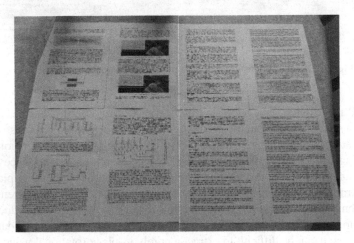

Fig. 3. Sample test media

Testing was primarily based around the user tuneable parameters involved in the analysis process and external factors affecting the program. This information could then be used to calibrate the program, allowing its performance to be assessed in a quality control capacity. Measurements were taken at least five times for each trial, and averages were established to help control random error. More detailed descriptions of testing procedures are listed in the following sections, with results.

3.2   Influence of Magnitude of ORB Feature Generation

As ORB features are the data that is used in comparisons of images, it is reasonable to expect that a change in the number of features generated may have an effect on the number of matches and thus the quality of a comparison. Conversely, generating more features could have an impact on processing, and as such, it is likely that an optimal compromise exists. To test this, the ratio test value was set and held at a nominal value of 0.7, selected arbitrarily from the near optimal region, found in Lowe's paper.

A comparison was performed by capturing train and query images of Sample 1. The confidence threshold was removed, and the program was set to report the confidence of a true image match, as well as the time taken to complete the analysis, and the number of keypoint matches generated. This data was then recorded.

Figure 4 Below demonstrates the change in both yield and processing time as the number of ORB features generated changes. Yield, in this case, refers to the number of matches accepted as good as compared to the number of features generated. Initially, the yield tends to remain constant as the number of features produced increases, but after a certain point decreases drastically. The yield value would be expected to remain reasonably constant, as the comparison images are identical, however, the decline behaviour may be explained by considering the nature of a feature.

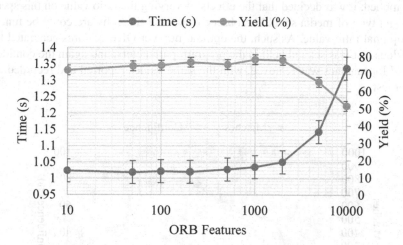

Fig. 4. Variation of match yield and processing time due to ORB feature count change

Features are described around key points of interest, and in any image there are only a finite amount of points that a human would consider distinctive. Once all of these points have been found and described, extraneous keypoints will be based on decreasingly distinct features, until minor variations in the mathematical calculations performed by the computer on identical images can result in different key points being identified and described. As such, these extraneous features are unlikely to have matching correspondent points in the opposite dataset, so cannot be matched. Therefore, the number of significantly distinct points (and matches) remains the same, as the number of features increases, thus reducing yield.

The execution time increase exhibited by the program as the number of features increases is logical; the generation of each feature requires computation, as does each match. Therefore, the production of more features will increase the amount of operations the laptop has to execute before the dataset is complete and will increase the amount of points to be compared during matching. The time to compute does, however, remain fairly consistent, with only small increases up to 1000 features.

As a compromise, it is sensible to move forward using 1000 features despite the small increase in delay, as the generation of more features within the train target zone should allow for more tolerance to offset/movement of the query image out of the same relative frame, as there are more points to match in the first place. Using more than 1000 features causes large relative increases in delay and using too few features may affect comparison abilities for offset, identical samples.

3.3 Influence of Ratio Test Value

The ratio test can be either overly discriminate or accepting of keypoint matches depending on the value chosen. Whilst Lowe's work identified a general range of values that can be applied, it was decided that the effects of varying the ratio value on this specific system and type of media should be observed, so that the software could be tuned to a near optimal ratio value. As such, the optimal number ORB features generated from the previous test was set and held in the program parameters, and again the confidence threshold for matches was removed, with the same values reported and recorded as in the prior test.

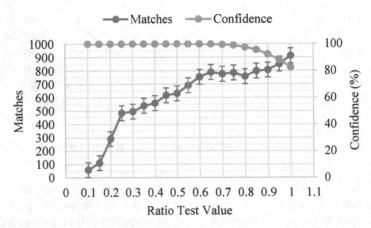

Fig. 5. Variation of returned matches and comparison confidence metric due to change in ratio test value

Figure 5 above demonstrates the changes in returned matches and the confidence value achieved in comparison, as ratio test value varies. An increase in returned matches as the ratio test criteria is loosened to be expected, as it is intended to be a filter for bad matches. If the definition of what is a 'bad match' is altered to include more matches, then more matches will be classified as 'good'. In the case of the analysis program, the confidence metric, based on how many matches agree with the homography generated from the datasets, can be viewed as a confirmation of whether a match is 'good' or not.

When identical images are compared, if the match passes the ratio test but does not fit the general transform that relates the other matches for the train/query feature set then it is clearly erroneous; the images are directly related by a transform and all key points should have a partner with the same description and transformed key point location. The opposite situation can occur when the ratio test is tightened, as it could wrongly exclude a match that would have otherwise fit the homography perfectly and is therefore wasting a potential 'good' match.

Similarly to the ORB feature generation increase, which increases the number of features that can be used to make a positive identification between an offset image and a train from an identical sample, increasing the number of matches allowed through the ratio test should aid in providing a definitive acceptance. Every good match excluded is one less match from which to generate homography, and if the total number of matches is reduced significantly due to large offset then this one match may have a significant effect on the result of the confidence assessment.

As before it is best to make a compromise between decreasing the confidence by letting bad matches through and restricting the number of good matches passed on by the ratio test. Too many bad matches in the dataset could skew the results of the RANSAC procedure despite its tolerance for outliers, and as stated above, too few good matches leave RANSAC with no data to work from.

It can clearly be seen from the graph that confidence does not notably decrease until the ratio test value reaches 0.7, and all values lower than this result in a reduction of matches with no gain of confidence. After 0.7, increased values return reduced confidence, therefore the matches gained are bad, and offer no positive benefit to the program. Therefore, it is logical to continue using 0.7 for this parameter, as used in previous tests, since a large proportion of matches are already gained by this point compared to the lowest ratio test values.

3.4 Influence of Offset

Only a small area of approximately 220 mm × 160 mm on the test media is captured by the overhead camera. The key points are generated and described in this area. When the paper moves through the production line, it is conceivable that the query image could change enough to produce a false positive when compared to the train sample area, and as such could cause a page to be mistakenly rejected.

To quantify the degree to which the analysis program is affected by offset when processing the media it is expected to be used upon, two tests were carried out using Sample 1 and Sample 2 to represent a mixture of page content. As before, each test was carried out comparing train and query image captures from the same page, whilst the ratio value and ORB feature count were held constant at the optimal values found in the previous two tests. Similarly, the confidence threshold was removed, and the same values of confidence and matched pairs were reported as in previous tests as the position of the samples was adjusted to introduce x-axis offset, as well as processing time. Once complete, a confidence threshold can be chosen from a desired offset tolerance (Fig. 6).

Figure 7 shows that offsetting the samples for comparison in the x-axis has a major effect on analysis results. Testing did not consider y-axis variation as it is assumed to be controlled by a production system that feeds paper in a linear fashion.

Both confidence and number of matches returned appear to fall off in a reasonably predictable manner as an offset is increased, although the data is more sparse than desirable for the calculation of an approximate function to describe the behaviour for either attribute. Despite the large reduction in both values, the result from such a test would appear to be fairly reliable, with a fair number of matches generating a reasonable confidence score. It is unlikely in this scenario that an incorrect page would be falsely recognised as acceptable.

This combined score is an attempt to generalise the behaviour of the program, although with a small sample size it is not a particularly robust model. The text-heavy Sample 2 suffers a much more drastic reduction in performance, as shown in Fig. 8.

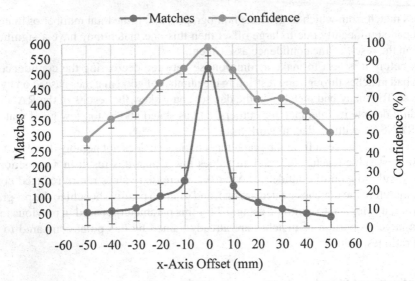

Fig. 6. Variation of returned matches and comparison confidence metric due to offset (Sample 1&2 Combined)

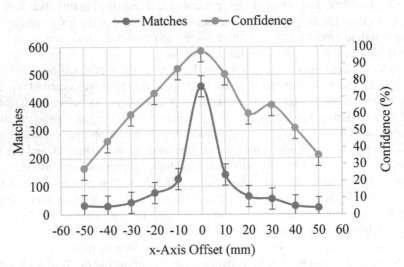

Fig. 7. Variation of returned matches and comparison confidence metric due to offset (Sample 2, Text Heavy)

Figure 7 also demonstrates some minor inconsistency in results that arose during testing. The differing of confidence measurements from the general trend at 20 mm offset has a large influence on the combined result graph. This difference could be attributed to a subtle change in lighting that may not have been noticeable to the naked eye but was significant enough to influence matching performance.

Bearing the results of this test in mind, it is sensible to account for a specific tolerance of offset by design; 5% x-axis offset tolerance on an A3 page allows for around 20 mm of movement, which is 10% of the image capture area width, whilst maintaining 60% confidence. It can be seen in Fig. 8 that this remains true for text-heavy samples, and so one solution to this issue is to design the processing machinery to place a page within this tolerance, or to simply move the camera's position so that the proportion of the page that is captured is increased. Thus, the 10% tolerance on image capture area offset allows a larger tolerance on overall page position.

3.5 Influence of Illumination

For the testing described above, all work was carried out in consistent lighting condition, however, the changeable conditions could affect the ability of the program to differentiate between samples. As such, a test was devised using a diffused artificial light source, the intensity of which could be varied. An LDR/potential divider sensor circuit was used to measure a relative value of light intensity in the target area. Starting at the brightest value, which was approximately equivalent to good ambient daylight, the light was stepped down between trials, with ORB features and ratio test value held constant as before. Again, measures of confidence, matched pairs and processing time were observed.

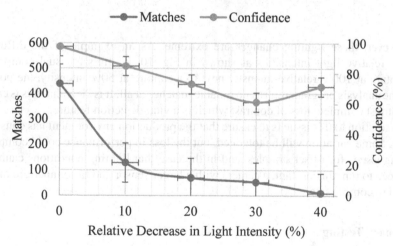

Fig. 8. Variation of returned matches and comparison confidence metric due to change in light intensity

Light intensity was shown to have a large effect on both the confidence metric and on the number of returned matches, as shown in Fig. 9. In spite of this large change, confidence does remain sufficiently high for a positive identification to be made, but this may have been because of the lack of movement of the identical test sample. Whilst the number of matches remains high enough to be considered a good sample size for RANSAC to work upon and produce homography from, by the time a 40% decrease in relative light intensity is reached, the number of samples has dropped significantly.

The drop is such that it is debatable, despite high confidence values, whether it can be concluded that the result of a positive match is statistically sound. It is important to note that if no minimum threshold is set for returned matches, it should theoretically be possible to generate a homography from only two matches, and this is problematic as any two matches can be related by a transform with 100% confidence attached to it. Adding a third match that doesn't fit the transform in this scenario would only decrease the confidence by 33%.

Fig. 9. Daylight equivalent, reference (Left) compared to 50% relative reduction in light intensity (Right)

However, these lighting changes are extreme. As an example of the difference between relative light intensities as shown in Fig. 10, it offers a visual comparison of a capture at 100% relative intensity next to a capture at 50% intensity, the point at which the analysis program returns no reliable matches at all. It is clear that this is caused by an almost complete loss of contrast which is a vital detection feature.

The solution to this issue is to ensure that the production environment has consistent lighting. Some variation will be tolerated, but the loss in performance could compound matching issues for offset samples, and in the case that lighting conditions cannot be guaranteed to remain constant, a camera with a larger sensor and faster aperture may be required to compensate.

3.6 Binary Testing

To determine the performance of the system, binary tests were performed, comparing samples pages to one another. In 160 tests, only one incorrect matching judgement was made. A larger sample would be needed to confirm, though this initial testing indicates a basic degree of accuracy and repeatability has been achieved.

3.7 Processing Speed

During testing of the analysis program, from all available test data recorded where timing data was noted, an average processing time of just over one second per image comparison task was calculated. This is abnormally high for a system using ORB, as research suggested that it was an algorithm capable of real time analysis of video feeds. During scripting of the analysis program, testing was carried out and processing times were considerably lower than one second. It was initially believed that the added complexity of homography and inversion checks was responsible for the slow down.

However, upon further investigation of this issue, it appears that the camera capture is responsible for added processing time. It transpires when the camera captures an image, it needs to be initialised each time before a photo is taken.

It is confirmed by tests using a short Python script, the initiation process adds the time as shown in Table 1. The average time to grab a frame from the camera is around one millisecond, as opposed to over one second for the full initialisation and shutdown process.

Table 1. The average time to grab a frame from the camera

Operation	Test					
	1	2	3	4	5	Avg.
Frame Grab (s)	0.0010	0.0009	0.0010	0.0033	0.0009	0.0014
Start, Grab, Release (s)	1.2990	1.2080	1.2010	1.1476	1.2650	1.2241

4 Conclusion

The primary task of the work presented in this paper was to develop open-source based software for replacement of visual inspection in a book production quality control system. It can be concluded from the testing performed that the analysis program is effective, with a low binary test failure rate. Whilst the program is currently slower than the desired speed for real-time on-line inspection, the cause of this issue has been identified as a hardware interaction issue and can be rectified to bring processing time down, facilitating multiple image comparisons per second.

Optimisation of the program can be performed. Employing ORB as it currently does, the program removes the intolerance of angular variation of BRIEF, and then a filter must be applied later on to stop inverted image acceptance. Both of these steps add a small amount of computational time, but the suitability of ORB to this scenario has been proven. The study shows that only the most relevant parts of the algorithm are used in a new process bespoke to the quality control task. It may prove fruitful to move the program to a new programming language that is non-interpreted. This should, again, help to improve processing speed, but may also open up the possibility of combining both the low-level controller and the analysis program on a microprocessor-based system. Furthermore, the tuning performed in this work could be adapted into an automated process, adopting a rudimentary form of machine learning where the end-user trains the program on a large dataset of media similar to that which is intended to be analysed. This may yield more refined tuning parameters than a human input to the system does, and as these parameters have demonstrated to have such a large effect on system performance, a set of better tuned parameters could offer further enhancement to the system.

References

CorrMapp: The Homography transformation, March 2013.https://www.corrmap.com/features/homography_transformation.php. Accessed 14 May 2020

Fischler, M., Bolles, R.: Random sample consensus: a paradigm for model fitting with applications to image analysis and automated cartography. Commun. ACM **24**(6), 381–395 (1981)

Lowe, D.: Distinctive image features from scale-invariant keypoints (2004). https://www.cs.ubc.ca/~lowe/papers/ijcv04.pdf. Accessed 11 May 2020

Mordvintsev, A., Abid, K.: Understanding Features, August 2013. https://opencv-python-tutroals.readthedocs.io/en/latest/py_tutorials/py_feature2d/py_features_meaning/py_features_meaning.html. Accessed 10 May 2020

Parker, O.: Print books vs. e-books – an update, March 2018. https://graphicartsmag.com/articles/2018/03/print-books-vs-e-books-update/. Accessed 13 Nov 2019

Rublee, E., Rabaud, V., Konolige, K., Bradski, G.: ORB: an efficient alternative to SIFT or SURF. In: Proceedings of the IEEE International Conference on Computer Vision, pp. 2564–2571, November 2011. https://doi.org/10.1109/ICCV.2011.6126544

UKEssays: Importance of ISO 9000, November 2018. https://www.ukessays.com/essays/engineering/importance-of-iso.php?vref=1. Accessed 13 Nov 2019

Ensemble Classification Using Entropy-Based Features for MRI Tissue Segmentation

Nadjet Bouchaour[(✉)] and Smaine Mazouzi

LICUS Lab, University 20 Aout 1955, BP 26 Route el Hadaik, 21000 Skikda, Algeria
n.bouchaour@univ-skikda.dz

Abstract. It is still hard to deal with artifacts in magnetic resonance images (MRIs), particularly when the latter are to be segmented. This paper introduces a novel feature, namely the spatial entropy of intensity that allows a pattern-based representation which enhances the MRI segmentation despite presence of high levels of noise and intensity non uniformity (INU) within MRI data. Moreover, we bring out that ensembles of classifiers used with the proposed feature have significantly enhanced structured MRI segmentation. Thus, to conduct experiments, MRIs with different artifact levels were extracted and exploited from the Brain Web MRI database. The obtained results reveal that the proposed feature, especially when used with ensembles of classifiers has significantly enhanced the overall MRI segmentation.

Keywords: MRI tissue segmentation · Spatial entropy · Classifier boosting · Ada-Boost

1 Introduction

Pattern-based classification has wined more interest in the last decade. According to such approach, not only data are used to infer features, but also patterns that exist within data. These patterns are also used for classification and feature definition. It has been stated in several works [5] that pattern mining can help to enhance data classification, mainly with structured domains, such as object recognition and image analysis. Consequently, for several applications in the aforementioned fields, patterns can be defined as sequences of graphs in the raw data [18,26]. So defining pattern-based classification models undoubtedly allows to enhance classification, rather than using models, based solely on raw data.

Furthermore, combining classifiers and training them together with good partition of the training data, has allowed to enhance the overall classification results. Also, all the works having used the ensemble classifiers have yielded better results than those using single classifiers, regardless the weak elementary classifier that was used as constructing element of the ensemble. It has been stated in several works in the literature that combining classifiers according to

© Springer Nature Switzerland AG 2021
C. Djeddi et al. (Eds.): MedPRAI 2020, CCIS 1322, pp. 125–139, 2021.
https://doi.org/10.1007/978-3-030-71804-6_10

various ensemble methods allows to avoid several classical flaws in data classification. The most known flaw is the over-training problem, mainly when the volume of training data is too large. Furthermore, classifier combining allows to deals with the problem of the early convergence of the algorithm when the classification is optimization-based such as in the neural based methods [9,14].

In this work, we are interested in the classification of the MRI data using an ensemble of classifiers, namely the boosting algorithm [8]. In contrast to most of the published works, and instead of using the raw image data, taken individually at the different voxels, we consider a pattern-based representation where the neighboring voxels are aggregated to form patterns, and then use these latter as features for classification. To construct the pattern which will be used as the classification feature, we use an energy based coding, assuming that the energy defined within the neighborhood of a voxel represents well the voxel separation. Therefore, the model is based on defining within a neighborhood of a voxel an energy function represented as a spatial entropy of voxels' intensities. Such an energy function allows to consider, in addition to the image intensity, the local geometrical spatial relations that exist in the MRI data. We show that the aggregation of data according to the considered pattern, especially with energy coding, as well as the classification of these patterns with the most used ensemble of classifiers: the Adaboost, allows to significantly improve the results of classification of MRI data.

The next parts of the paper are structured as follows: firstly, in Sect. 2 we present a review of segmentation methods in medical imaging, including those based on machine learning, in addition to the main works in the literature that are close to the ours. Secondly, in Sect. 3 we provide details of our approach by presenting both the used pattern through energy coding, and the use of the Adaboost algorithm for MRI segmentation. Then, Sect. 4 is dedicated to the experimentation of our method, where we present both the used dataset and the obtained results, as well as a comparison with some methods of the literature. Finally, a concise conclusion to summarize our contribution and highlights some potential perspectives.

2   Related Work

Image segmentation is one of the most important tasks in the process of pattern recognition using visual data. It consists of subdividing the pixels/voxels of an image into distinct and homogeneous regions. There are dozens of different methods of segmentation. However, all these methods can be classified according to three main families:

1. Contour-based methods: the common principle of these methods is to detect discontinuities in visual data. These discontinuities represent the edges in the image. The detected edges are generally disjoint and open, and therefore they must be joined and closed for proper use in the subsequent recognition process.

2. Region-based methods: their principle consists in grouping the pixels/voxels of the image having the same features, in disjoint but homogeneous subsets according to a certain homogeneity criterion. These homogeneous subsets are called regions.

3. Methods by classification: their major asset is that they allow the learning from the labeled data, forming the ground truth. Segmentation by classification consists of assigning a label to any pixel/voxel of the image using a classifier (single or ensemble). Given that we are interested in this last family in this work, we devote the remainder of this section to introduce some methods of MRI segmentation by data classification methods.

First, classification-based segmentation methods can be further subdivided into two sub-categories:

1. Heuristic-based methods: where one or more heuristics are considered to define a pixel/voxel labeling criterion. The heuristics consider a given prior, relative to the image, to the noise, or to the distortions that the image could undergo during its acquisition. For instance, we can cite the Fuzzy C-Mean [3] algorithm, where the classification prior consists in considering for the pixels/voxels at the borders of the regions and elsewhere that there exists a mixture of information, each one relating to one of the data classes. Markovian methods [12] consider the prior of *smoothness*, where the data are considered homogeneous by parts, and any part corresponds to a homogeneous region of the image. Also, Markovian representations can express some spatial constraints that the data must respect.

2. Methods by learning: where machine learning techniques are used. The principle is to proceed by learning classifiers using labeled data, so-called training set, then use the trained classifiers to classify the data, in this case called test set. According to the latter approach, several new methods based on the combination of classifiers have emerged. The ensemble of classifiers is one of these methods, and it is based on the aggregation of a set of classifiers, called weak classifiers, trained separately according to some particular sampling, allowing on the one hand the improvement of the performance of the classification and on the other hand, dealing with some problems inherent to machine learning, where the most known is the over-training problem.

Magnetic resonance imaging (MRI) is of great importance for the establishment of correct diagnoses and thus the prescription of appropriate treatments. MRI segmentation in order to extract tissues and establish diagnostic remains an active research field [23]. The segmentation of an MRI consists in extracting the main tissues for which physicians and radiologists are mainly interested. These tissues are respectively CSF (Cerebrospinal Fluid), GM (Gray Matter) and WM (White Matter), for structural MRI, and also LM (Lesional Matter) for pathological MRI. Several methods for MRI segmentation have been published, starting with contour detectors, passing through region extractors, and ending with machine-learning based methods. Richard et al. [17] used a distributed approach with Markovian and Bayesian categorization of MRI tissues.

The principle of their method is to segment the volume into sub volumes and then make autonomous agents cooperate to produce an overall image segmentation. The method suffer from several problems including the ad-hoc subdivision of volumes. Also, the Markovian methods are known by their minimization iterative methods that are very time consuming. By adopting the same paradigm, Scherrer et al. [20] proposed a distributed Markov model for the classification of MRI data. In their work, the authors were able to formalize the classification by using both a multi-agent system for data distribution and processing, and a Markovian representation of MRI data, allowing classification using Markovian classifiers and dealing with spatial constraints at the same time.

Several works have proposed machine-learning methods for MRI segmentation. However, few of them have used ensemble of classifiers, where mainly the unique used feature was the voxel intensity. Some authors have proceeded to feature extraction then using the obtained features with ensemble classifiers to process MRI data. Rajasree et al. have considered a fractal representation of MRI data, by using the Brownian move technique [16]. The adopted features are then used with the Adaboost algorithm to detect tumors in MRI data. Gustavo et al. have combined Genetic Algorithms (GA) and Adaboost clustering to detect the tumor area in the MRIs [13]. After a data thresholding using the GA algorithm in order to delimit the tumor area, Adaboost is trained using the obtained classification by the GA algorithm, then used to finally detect the tumor as the largest connected component in the whole image.

Recently, deep learning techniques, mainly convolutional neural networks (CNN) were widely proposed for MRI data processing. Their strong advantage is that they do not need for feature representation and extraction. In such techniques MRI data in the input are convolved to kernels in the middle layers, so features are automatically produced. Output layers classify voxels according the produced features [4, 24].

As far as we know, entropy-based features for MRI processing are rare in the literature. Sarita et al. have combined probabilistic neural network and wavelet entropy for feature extraction to classify MRI data [19]. Entropy-based features were also used with optimization-based clustering, such as in the work introduced by Pham et al. [15], where authors combined fuzzy entropy clustering and multi-objective particle swarm optimization. In order to extend data representation, some authors such as Bahadure et al. [2] have transformed data from spatial domain to frequency domain, then proceed by the SVM classifier to segment such represented MRI data.

In our work, a novel representation by the spatial entropy of the voxel intensities is introduced. Contrary to the previous cited works, the proposed entropy thanks to its spatial expression, takes into account both spatial and radiometric interactions of data within the MRIs.

3   Pattern-Based Features for MRI Data Classification

In this section, we define a pattern-based feature that will be tested for brain tissue classification in MRIs. A set of weak classifiers (Support Vector Machine

(SVM) or Naïve Byes) are combined according the boosting algorithm to be trained and to be used to label the voxels of the MRI volume. Boosting is beneficial for MRI data segmentation because it allows to avoid the over-training problem by distributing the training data over several weak classifiers. Furthermore, Adaboost algorithm allows an adaptive distribution of data which is well appropriate for MRI data, given that MRI data distribution model is not beforehand known. At first, the MR image is pre-processed using a skull-strip algorithm, namely FSL Brain Extraction Tool (BET) [10,22], to remove the non brain tissues. In our case we have preferred to avoid the noise filtering, given that, firstly, the MRI data are usually altered on the boundaries between the different tissues by the partial volume effect, where an averaging of the intensities at these voxels aggravate such effect. Secondly, because the proposed pattern allows the noise reduction on voxel classification even without MRI data smoothing. Such characteristic of the proposed method is explained by the fact that the used entropy-based pattern around a given voxel is a combination of the whole voxels belonging to the voxel neighborhood. Before introducing details how our method proceeds to label voxels, firstly, we present in the following section the Adaboost algorithm for two-classes classifiers, and then we pursue with how such an algorithm can be generalized for problems with more than two classes.

3.1   AdaBoost for MRI Data Classification

AdaBoost is a meta algorithm for data classification. It consists of an ensemble of classifiers, called weak in this case, that adaptively boost the performance of the ensemble classifier [8]. The outputs of the latter are combined according to a set of weights obtained according to the training data, providing the final AdaBoost classifier. Adaptation in such meta algorithm refers to that fact that the weak classifiers are adjusted by the subsets of the training data that were wrongly classified at the previous iterations. The algorithm bellow is an Adaboost implementation with a binary weak classifier h. After the learning of the ensemble classifier using the training set $(x_1, y_1), ...(x_m, y_m)$ the whole hypothesis of the ensemble classifier is expressed by the function $H(x)$, where x is an instance from the test set to be labeled $y \in \{-1, +1\}$.

To deal with problems with more than two classes, lets M classes, $M - 1$ binary weak classifiers are used to substitute one weak M-classes' classifier. There are two well known methods that allow combining binary classifiers to build a multi-class classifier. The first method proceeds according to the principle *winner takes all* [21], where the kth classifier allows to distinguish the class k from all the other classes. For the second method, a classifier is dedicated to each couple of classes [11], where its role is to distinguish the two classes for which it is dedicated. We note that the two methods are implemented in the most of the machine-learning platforms.

Algorithm 1: Adaboost

Result: H(x)

Given:$(x_1, y_1), ..., (x_m, y_m)$ where $x_i \in X, y_i \in \{-1, +1\}$;

Initialisation:$D_1(i) = \frac{1}{m}$ for $i = 1, ..., m$;

for *t=1,..., T* **do**

Train weak learner using distribution D_t;

Get weak hypothesis $h_t : X \rightarrow \{-1, +1\}$;

Aim : select h_t with low weighted error:

$$\varepsilon = \text{Pr}_{i \sim D_t}[h_t(x_i) \neq y_i];$$

Choose $\alpha = \frac{1}{2} \ln\left(\frac{\varepsilon}{1-\varepsilon}\right)$;

Update, for $i = 1, ..., m$:

$$D_{t+1}(i) = \frac{D_t(i) \exp(-\alpha_t y_i h_t(x_i))}{Z_t};$$

where Z_t is a normalization factor (chosen so that D_{t+1} will be a distribution).

end

Output the final hypothesis:

$$H(x) = \text{sign}\left(\sum_{t=1}^{T} \alpha_t h_t(x)\right)$$

3.2 MRI Data

The MRI volume obtained after skull-striping is a set of voxels that each one can belong to one of the three remaining tissues, namely, the Cerebrospinal Fluid (CSF), the Gray Matter (GM), and the White Matter (WM). Each of them is characterized by its mean intensity and the corresponding standard-deviation (μ_c, σ_c) , $c \in \{CSF, GM, WM\}$. We also assume that the intensity distribution in each tissue is Gaussian (see Formula 1).

$$f_c(x_i, \mu_c, \sigma_c) = \frac{1}{\sigma_c \sqrt{2\pi}} e^{\frac{1}{2}(x_i - \mu_c)^2 / 2\sigma_c^2} \tag{1}$$

where x_i is the intensity of the voxel at the location i.

3.3 Energy Coding-Based Classification

Our proposed entropy-based pattern aims to capture interactions between the voxels belonging to a local neighborhood. Such interactions can be represented according to an energy function. So, the proposed pattern for a given voxel i in the MRI volume is a vector of three components, where each component represents the spatial entropy of the intensities of the similar voxels in the neighborhood. Such subsets of similar voxels are obtained by the k-means algorithm, applied on the voxel's neighborhood with three classes (CSF, GW, WM) (see Eq. 2).

$$E_c = -\sum_{D_c} P_i \times log_2 P_i \tag{2}$$

where D_c denotes the set of the voxels belonging to the class c, and P_i is the probability that the voxel belongs to the class c:

$$P_i = \frac{\frac{1}{\sigma_c \sqrt{2\pi}} e^{\frac{1}{2}(x_i - \mu_c)^2 / 2\sigma_c^2}}{\sum_c \frac{1}{\sigma_c \sqrt{2\pi}} e^{\frac{1}{2}(x_i - \mu_c)^2 / 2\sigma_c^2}} \tag{3}$$

μ_c, σ_c are respectively the mean and the standard-deviation of the intensities of the voxels belonging to the class c and situated in the neighborhood of the voxel in question (i). So, a clustering by the k-means algorithm is performed at the voxel neighborhood, so the three subsets of voxels and their respective couples of (μ_c, σ_c), $c \in \{CSF, GM, WM\}$ are obtained. We notice that for the training MRIs we do not need for clustering in voxel neighborhood because we have the ground truth that allows to know the voxels of each cluster what allows to calculate the three spacial entropies.

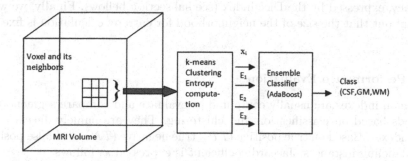

Fig. 1. Principle of the proposed energy-coding-based classification.

As it can be noticed on Fig. 1, the vector of features that will be used for classification by the SVM or the Naïve Byes is composed, in addition to the voxel's intensity x_i, of the three spatial entropies E_1, E_2 and E_3, obtained according to the clustering of the set of the voxels forming the local neighborhood. Such a pattern captures well the interactions of the voxels, and expresses well the spatial constraints that exist within the MRI data. The entropies E_1, E_2, and E_3 allow to distinguish the cases where the voxel is in the neighborhood of a tissue border or not. Also, they allow distinguishing if a voxel is affected by a high deviation due to noise. Obviously, the intensity of the voxel in question is considered for classification, so the resulting class is likely that of the tissue with the mean intensity is the closest, but adjusted if needed by the interaction with voxels in the neighborhood, expressed by the introduced spatial entropies.

4   Experimentation and Evaluation

The experimentation of the proposed pattern has been done using MRI volumes from the well known database brain web [7]. This database provide a large set of MRI volumes with their ground truth labeling, enabling authors to use machine-learning based methods, and quantitatively evaluate the proposed methods. Furthermore MRIs can be obtained according to various levels of artifacts, namely noise, and INU. All MRIs are $181 \times 217 \times 181$ voxels of size. In this work, they are considered only MRIs with T1 modality. As in most of works in the literature of the field, we have used 70% of data for training and 30% for testing.

4.1   Parameter Selection

Only one parameter is to be set in the proposed method. It consists of the number of iterations of the Adaboost algorithm, which corresponds also to the number of weak classifiers that will be combined to classify the MRI voxels. This parameter is quantitatively adjusted by testing a set of values and then we choose that from which there is no more significant enhancement of classification accuracy, expressed by the Dice index (see subsection bellow). Finally, we want to point out that the size of the neighborhood for entropy calculation is fixed at 3×3.

4.2   Performance Evaluation

Two main indexes are usually computed to evaluate and compare segmentation methods based on classification and clustering. They are namely Jaccard and Dice indexes. Based on true positive (TP), true negative (TN), and false positive (FP) labeling instances, Jaccard coefficient is expressed as follows:

$$Jaccard = \frac{TP}{TP + TN + FP} \tag{4}$$

Dice coefficient can be expressed as:

$$Dice = \frac{2TP}{2TP + TN + FP} \tag{5}$$

We opted for Dice index for two main reasons: the first one is that it is the most cited in the literature and the second one is that it has been considered by works with which we compare ours.

4.3   Experimental Results

As it has been cited above, we have experimented the proposed features by using two different weak classifiers, namely the SVM classifier and Naïve Bayes classifier. Indeed, we have started our experimentation by testing several classifier models and we have noticed that the retained classifiers yielded score better. So, the introduced results corresponds to the use of two sets of weak classifiers, combined each one according the AdaBoost algorithm. We have considered two different classifiers, and we have compared our results to those of previous works,

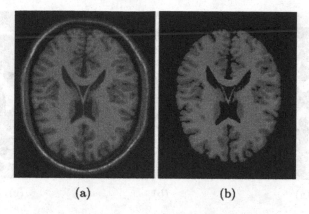

Fig. 2. A MRI sample form brain web database. (a) Raw MRI with 3% noise level and 20% INU level, (b) Extracted brain by Brain Extractor from FSL.

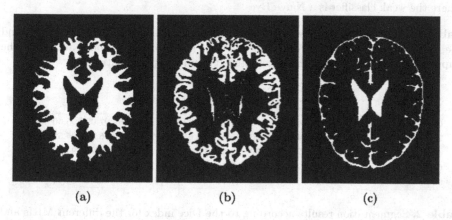

Fig. 3. MRI segmentation results with noise level set to 1% and INU set to 0%. (a), (b), (c) are respectively the White matter, the Gray matter and the CSF for the case where the weak classifier is a SVM.

in order to show that the improvement of the results is not due to the classifier itself, but to the proposed features, namely the spatial entropy.

First, we introduce in Figs. 2, 3, and 4 respectively the MRI obtained with 1% noise level and 0% INU level, the three brain tissues using SVM as weak classifier, and the three brain tissues using Naïve Bayes as weak classifier. We can visually notice, by comparing with the MRI image, that the obtained tissues are well delimited.

Table 1 shows the segmentation results according to the Dice index using a the SVM classifier as a weak classifier with the voxel intensity and its spatial entropies as the classification features.

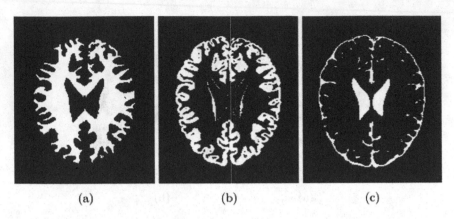

(a)   (b)   (c)

Fig. 4. MRI segmentation results with noise level set to 1% and INU set to 0%. (a), (b), (c) are respectively the White matter, the Gray matter and the CSF for the case where the weak classifier is a Naïve Byes.

Table 1. Segmentation results according to the Dice index for the different MRIs and the different brain matters (WM, GM and CSF). The classification features by the Support Vector Machine are the voxel intensity and its spatial entropies.

N INU	WM				GM				CSF			
	1	3	5	7	1	3	5	7	1	3	5	7
0%	99.17	98.10	96.60	94.08	98.23	96.21	93.53	89.25	98.46	97.09	95.60	93.63
20%	98.40	97.70	96.26	94.30	96.86	95.51	93.05	89.47	97.78	96.85	95.59	93.73
40%	97.02	96.55	94.95	92.75	94.59	93.67	90.80	87.02	96.92	96.29	94.69	92.99
60%	93.58	91.79	89.48	87.3	86.37	83.78	79.41	73.97	87.94	87.07	85.32	81.04
90%	90.40	89.08	87.42	85.78	83.05	80.17	76.66	71.44	87.89	86.32	84.04	80.38

Table 2. Segmentation results according to the Dice index for the different MRIs and the different brain matters (WM, GM and CSF). The Adaboost of the Naïve Bayes classifier with the spatial entropies of the voxel and its intensity as the classification features.

N INU	WM				GM				CSF			
	1	3	5	7	1	3	5	7	1	3	5	7
0%	98.90	97.53	95.17	91.48	97.41	94.88	90.30	82.45	97.36	96.05	94.18	91.96
20%	98.08	97.14	94.32	91.55	95.94	94.15	88.98	82.57	96.72	95.73	94.45	92.15
40%	96.19	94.52	92.30	89.67	92.56	89.54	84.63	78.68	95.39	94.78	92.95	91.72
60%	90.09	88.58	87.08	86.24	77.73	73.94	69.88	68.08	86.29	85.47	83.97	80.68
90%	86.18	85.70	85.24	84.89	67.67	66.91	65.69	65.31	83.97	84.05	82.16	79.96

Table 2 shows the segmentation results according to the Dice index using a Naïve Bayes as a weak classifier with the voxel intensity and its spatial entropies as the classification features.

According the results introduced in Table 1 and Table 2, we notice the high scores of segmentation when the spatial entropy is used as a classification feature.

This improvement can be explained by the capture of the interactions between neighboring voxels. These interactions are expressed thanks to an energy, formulated as a spatial entropy. A voxel is not classified solely according to its value (gray level) but according to the strength of its interactions with its neighboring voxels.

According the introduced results, we can notice that the method has well scored, and it presents a strong robustness against noise and INU, where Dice index was not drastically fall with high levels of these two artifacts. For instance, for white matter, the variation of the Dice index is from 98.40 to 96.26 with the SVM classifier for a variation in noise from 1% to 5%, with INU fixed to 20%. We can notice the same robustness against the INU. The variation is from 99.17 to 93.58 for the INU varying from 0% to 60% with a noise level set at 1%. With the Naïve Byes classifier, the method scores also well, and presents also good robustness against noise and INU. For CSF, the variation of the Dice index is from 97.78 to 95.59 with the SVM classifier for a variation in noise from 1% to 5%, with INU fixed to 20%. Also, the same robustness is noticed against the INU. The variation is from 98.46 to 96.92 for the INU varying from 0% to 40% with a noise level set at 1%.

Figures 5 and 6 introduce the variations of the Dice index according the number of iterations of AdaBoost algorithm, respectively in the two cases: using the SVM, or using the Naïve Bayes as weak classifier. We can notice that Dice index uniformly grows with the SVM classifier for the three tissues, and becomes stable from the 9th iteration. It is the same case for the Naïve Bayes classifier, however the latter become stable little early that the SVM one, namely from the 8th iteration. According to the two cases, we ca, conclude that the Adaboost algorithm does not require many iterations (less than 10 iterations) to be trained. Such a low number of iterations allows us to conclude that the classification of voxels according the proposed methods is too fast and can be envisaged for realtime applications.

In order to show the effectiveness of the proposed features, we introduce in Table 3 a comparison between the obtained MRI data classification results with SVM as weak classifier and those of some well cited works from the literature. We have considered MRI with 20% INU and different noise levels, and we compared results for WM and GM tissues.

Table 3. Comparison results according Dice index with some work from the literature.

	WM				GM			
Noise method	1	3	5	7	1	3	5	7
Fast%	97	95	94	92	96	94	91	91
SMP5%	94	94	90	86	93	92	90	87
NL-FCM%	94	91	90	83	94	93	90	87
Boosted spatial entropy (with SVM)%	98	98	96	94	97	96	93	89

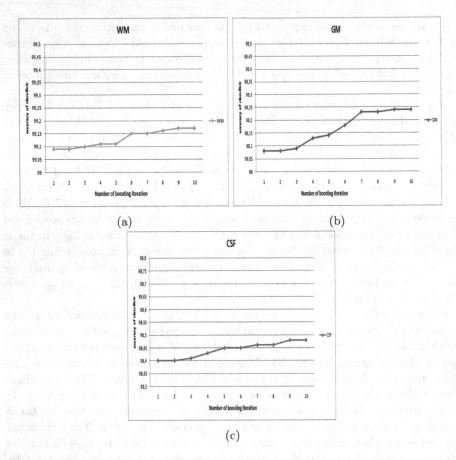

Fig. 5. Variation of the accuracy of classification based on the SVM weak classifier according to the number iterations of Adaboost. (a): WM, (b): GM, (c): CSF.

We can notice from the previous table that our method scores nearly better than all the cited methods. They are more close to Fast [25], considered the best, compared to the others [1,6]. Such results confirm that the proposed features when they are used with an ensemble classifier, such as Adaboost, are well appropriate to represent local patterns in MRIs data, especially when the latter are to be segmented.

4.4 Results Analysis and Discussion

According to the different results introduced below, we notice the strong improvement in segmentation results when spatial entropy is used as classification features, in addition to intensities of voxels. The use of the spatial entropy of the voxel with its intensity has allowed a large increase in the values of the Dice index, even with high levels of noise and INU. This can be explained by

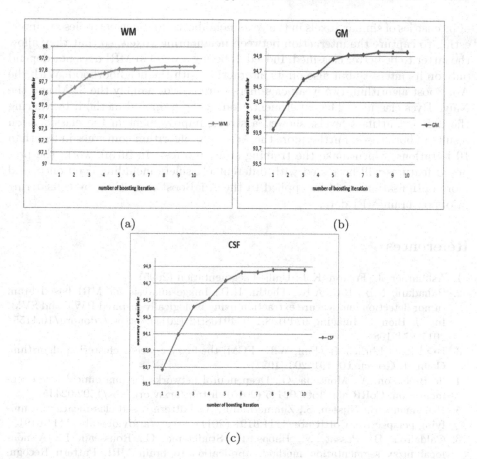

Fig. 6. Variation of the accuracy of classification based on the Naïve Bayes weak classifier according to the number iterations of Adaboost. (a): WM, (b): GM, (c): CSF.

the fact that the proposed spatial entropy, in addition to its ability to consider the voxel and its neighborhood, and as it has an energy nature, it expresses the interaction force between the voxels in the MRIs. Thus, a voxel is not classified solely according to its value, but also according to the force of interaction of the voxel with its neighborhood. Taking into account the spatial entropy has shown better robustness against noise and INU, especially when the levels of these artifacts are high. Such a result can be explained by the widening of the voxel's field of interaction beyond its local neighborhood.

5   Conclusion

In this paper, we have introduced a new pattern-based set of features of MRI data and how it was used with an ensemble classifier for voxel classification. The introduced features consist, in addition to the voxel's intensity, of the spatial entropies of intensities of similar voxels in the voxel neighborhood. Such entropies are interesting to capture the interaction between neighboring voxels, so that they allow the latter to be better classified. Indeed, labeling a voxel in MRI does not depend only on its intensity but also on its interaction with the neighborhood. With the AdaBoost algorithm, two weak classifiers were tested, namely the SVM and the Naïve Byes classifier. The experimentation of the proposed method, by varying the different artifact levels, showed a strong improvement in the classification results in both cases. Furthermore the Adaboost algorithm converges in less than 10 iterations, which make the training stage too fast. In future work, the proposed features will be tested with different classifiers including deep ones, and more optimisation could be applied to the AdaBoost algorithm, by considering priors on brain MRI data.

References

1. Ashburner, J., Friston, K.J.: Unified segmentation (2005)
2. Bahadure, N.B., Ray, A.K., Thethi, H.P.: Image analysis for MRI based brain tumor detection and feature extraction using biologically inspired BWT and SVM. Int. J. Biomed. Imaging 9749108:1–9749108:12 (2017). https://doi.org/10.1155/2017/9749108
3. Bezdek, J., Ehrlich, R., Full, W.E.: FCM: the fuzzy c-means clustering algorithm. Comput. Geosci. **10**, 191–203 (1984)
4. de Brébisson, A., Montana, G.: Deep neural networks for anatomical brain segmentation. CoRR abs/1502.02445 (2015). http://arxiv.org/abs/1502.02445
5. Bringmann, B., Nijssen, S., Zimmermann, A.: Pattern-based classification: a unifying perspective. CoRR abs/1111.6191 (2011). http://arxiv.org/abs/1111.6191
6. Caldairou, B., Passat, N., Habas, P., Studholme, C., Rousseau, F.: A nonlocal fuzzy segmentation method: application to brain MRI. Pattern Recogn. **44**(9), 1916–1927 (2011). https://doi.org/10.1016/j.patcog.2010.06.006, https://hal.archives-ouvertes.fr/hal-00476587
7. Cocosco, C., Kollokian, V., Kwan, R.S., Evans, A.: Simulated brain database homepage. https://brainweb.bic.mni.mcgill.ca/brainweb. Accessed 03 June 2020
8. Freund, Y., Schapire, R.: A short introduction to boosting (1999)
9. Hornik, K.: Approximation capabilities of multilayer feedforward networks. Neural Networks **4**(2), 251–257 (1991). https://doi.org/10.1016/0893-6080(91)90009-T
10. Jenkinson, M.: Bet2 : MR-based estimation of brain, skull and scalp surfaces. In: Eleventh Annual Meeting of the Organization for Human Brain Mapping (2005). https://ci.nii.ac.jp/naid/10030066593/en/
11. Knerr, S., Personnaz, L., Dreyfus, G.: Single-layer learning revisited: a stepwise procedure for building and training a neural network. In: Fogelman Soulié, F., Hérault, J. (eds.) Neurocomputing: Algorithms, Architectures and Applications. NATO ASI Series, vol. F68, pp. 41–50. Springer-Verlag, Heidelberg (1990). https://doi.org/10.1007/978-3-642-76153-9_5
12. Li, S.: Markov random field modeling in image analysis. In: Advances in Pattern Recognition (2009)

13. Oliveira., G.C., Varoto., R., Jr., A.C.: Brain tumor segmentation in magnetic resonance images using genetic algorithm clustering and adaboost classifier. In: Proceedings of the 11th International Joint Conference on Biomedical Engineering Systems and Technologies. BIOIMAGING: BIOIMAGING, vol. 2, pp. 77–82. INSTICC, SciTePress (2018). https://doi.org/10.5220/0006534900770082

14. Park, J., Sandberg, I.W.: Approximation and radial-basis-function networks. Neural Comput. **5**(2), 305–316 (1993). https://doi.org/10.1162/neco.1993.5.2.305

15. Pham, T.X., Siarry, P., Oulhadj, H.: A multi-objective optimization approach for brain MRI segmentation using fuzzy entropy clustering and region-based active contour methods. Magn. Resonance Imaging **61**, 41–65 (2019)

16. Rajasree, R., Columbus, C.C.: Brain tumour image segmentation and classification system based on the modified adaboost classifier. Int. J. Appl. Eng. Res. **10**(14) (2015)

17. Richard, N., Dojat, M., Garbay, C.: Distributed markovian segmentation: application to MR brain scans. Pattern Recogn. **40**(12), 3467–3480 (2007). https://doi.org/10.1016/j.patcog.2007.03.019

18. Roma, A.A., et al.: Invasive endocervical adenocarcinoma: a new pattern-based classification system with important clinical significance. Am. J. Surg. Pathol. **39**(5), 667–672 (2015). https://doi.org/10.1097/pas.0000000000000402

19. Saritha, M., Paul Joseph, K., Mathew, A.T.: Classification of mri brain images using combined wavelet entropy based spider web plots and probabilistic neural network. Pattern Recogn. Lett. **34**(16), 2151–2156 (2013). https://doi.org/10.1016/j.patrec.2013.08.017

20. Scherrer, B., Forbes, F., Garbay, C., Dojat, M.: Distributed local MRF models for tissue and structure brain segmentation. IEEE Trans. Med. Imaging **28**(8), 1278–1295 (2009)

21. Schölkopf, B., Burges, C., Vapnik, V.: Extracting support data for a given task. In: KDD (1995)

22. Smith, S.: Fast robust automated brain extraction. Human Brain Mapp. **17** (2002)

23. Yamanakkanavar, N., Choi, J.Y., Lee, B.: MRI segmentation and classification of human brain using deep learning for diagnosis of Alzheimer's disease: a survey. Sensors **20**(11), 3243 (2020). https://doi.org/10.3390/s20113243

24. Zhang, W., et al.: Deep convolutional neural networks for multi-modality isointense infant brain image segmentation. NeuroImage **108**, 214–224 (2015)

25. Zhang, Y., Brady, M., Smith, S.: Segmentation of brain MR images through a hidden markov random field model and the expectation-maximization algorithm. IEEE Trans. Med. Imaging **20**, 45–57 (2001)

26. Zhou, C., Cule, B., Goethals, B.: Pattern based sequence classification. IEEE Trans. Knowl. Data Eng. **28**, 1285–1298 (2016)

From a Textual Narrative to a Visual Story

Imran Shafiq Ahmad[✉][iD], Havish Kadiyala[✉][iD],
and Boubakeur Boufama[✉][iD]

School of Computer Science, University of Windsor, Windsor, ON N9B 3P4, Canada
{imran,kadiyalh,boufama}@uwindsor.ca

Abstract. Much of our daily learning is done through visual information. Visual information is an indispensable part of our life and tends to convey a lot more details than either speech or text. A visual portrayal of a story is generally more appealing and convincing. It is also useful in a variety of applications, such as an accident/crime scene analysis, education and treatment of various psychological or mental disorders like Post-Traumatic Stress Disorder (PTSD). Some individuals develop PTSD due to their exposure to some dangerous or shocking life experience, such as military conflict, physical or sexual assault, traffic or fire accident, natural disasters, etc. People suffering from PTSD can be treated using Virtual Reality Exposure Therapy (VRET), where they are immersed in a virtual environment to face feared situations that may not be safe to encounter in real life. In addition, generated 3D scenes can also be used as a visual aid for teaching children. Since crating 3D context and scenarios for such situations is tedious, time-consuming and requires special expertise in 3D application development environments and software, there is a need for automatic 3D scene generation systems from simple text descriptions. In this paper, we present a new framework for creating 3D scenes from a user-provided simple text. This proposed framework allows us to incorporate motion as well as special effects into the created scenes. In particular, the framework extracts the objects and entities that are present in a given textual narrative as well as spatial relationships. Depending on the description, it then creates either a 3D scene or a 3D scene with corresponding animation. This framework allows creation of a visualization using a set of pre-existing objects using $AutodeskMaya^{®}$ as an implementation environment.

Keywords: 3D scene generation from text · Spatial relations · Text to scene creation · Multimedia · Computer graphics · Animation

1 Introduction

A connected series of events, either real or fictional, is generally presented as a story using textual description either in written or oral form. Visual story telling, on the other hand, is a presentation of the same information using simple visual

© Springer Nature Switzerland AG 2021
C. Djeddi et al. (Eds.): MedPRAI 2020, CCIS 1322, pp. 140–151, 2021.
https://doi.org/10.1007/978-3-030-71804-6_11

aids and has been around for years. The old English proverb says "A picture is worth a thousand words" because a picture can concisely describe a concept, a situation, or an abstract idea which may need many words to get the point across. Many different application areas benefit from visual representation of a situation that is generally described in words. Examples of such areas include, but are not limited to, creation of an accident/crime scene for detailed analysis and investigation, education, training, proof-of-concept marketing or advertising campaigns, and treatment of many complex psychological or mental disorders, such as Post Traumatic Stress Disorder (PTSD).

Post-traumatic stress disorder (PTSD) is a serious mental disorder. In many cases, it is a result of either experiencing or witnessing some terrifying event. Symptoms may include a constant feeling of fear, flashbacks, nightmares and severe anxiety, as well as uncontrollable thoughts about the event [1,14]. Virtual Reality Exposure Therapy (VRET) is a possible therapeutic treatment for patients suffering from PTSD [1] and is said to help the emotional plight of patients during exposures. Since it is neither possible to recreate life-threatening incidents nor to know what exactly a person with PTSD may have felt during the incident, patients suffering from PTSD can be immersed in a virtual environment and the health practitioners can observe their emotional and mental state during any such incident. VRET has been used in treating some war veterans experiencing PTSD [13]. Creating a virtual environment requires a lot of time because scenarios faced by individuals often vary significantly. For this reason, it necessary to automatically create 3D scenes from simple text descriptions. Similarly, many crime scene and accident investigations require 3D creation of an actual scene as narrated by witnesses for detailed analysis and for helping understand complex situations during legal proceedings. 3D scenes or 3D animations of such instances may not only provide a very clear picture, but can also be used to help them understand how the incident may have unfolded.

To describe a situation or to narrate a story, the medium of communication is generally some natural language. The individual(s) reading or listening to this story generally create(s) a visual image of the objects, the environment, the scene and the story in their mind in order to understand and extrapolate the contents. However, in many other situations, a 3D scene can enable them to understand the situation or concept and make them familiar with the necessary information. As an example, a 3D scene can allow children to become more interested in the topics they are exposed to. Creating such a 3D scene that represents a story is a time-consuming and challenging process. It involves the creation of objects, their careful placement in the scene to mimic the actual scene and the application of the appropriate material for each object. Moreover, in many situations, as the story evolves, its proper representation requires 3D animation to make it even more complicated. Therefore, there is a need to develop methods to automatically create 3D scenes and 3D animations from a given text.

In this paper, we propose a system to generate 3D scenes from simple text input. We use Natural Language Tool Kit (NLTK) to extract names of objects from the provided text and to identify objects. We also identify the spatial relations associated with these objects to determine their physical location in the scene. This paper also provides an object positioning framework to place objects in a scene by calculating their bounding box values of the objects and considering the spatial relationships between them, as well as adding motion and special effects in the established static scene to create animations.

The rest of the paper is organized as follows. Section 2 provides information about some of the related work. In Sect. 3, we propose and discuss our framework. Section 4 provides a brief overview of the text processing component of the framework for analyzing the input text for identification and retrieval of key objects and their spatial relationships. Section 5 provides our object placement and scene generation approach. Section 6 provides some experimental results while Sect. 7 provides a few concluding remarks and possible future work.

2   Related Work

To generate a visual representation from provided text, many of the earlier proposed techniques require either the use of annotated objects or pre-formatted input, like XML. In some cases, such systems may also require the user to "learn complex manipulation interfaces through which objects are constructed and precisely positioned within scenes" [3]. The 3D models representing real-world items may also need to be annotated different set of characteristics to describe their spatial relationships with other objects. Spatial relations not only play a crucial role in the placement of objects in a scene but also in describing their association with other objects. Prior research assumes that somehow this knowledge has been provided during the manual annotation process and is accessible.

WordsEye [5] is a system to generate 3D scenes from textual descriptions. It primarily provides a user a blank slate to represent a picture using words such that the representation contains both the actions performed by the objects in the scene as well as their spatial relations. With the help of tagging and parsing, it essentially converts the provided text into semantic representation, which can be portrayed by choosing and arranging models from a model database to form a 3D scene. WordsEye's authors have continued to improve the system, with subsequent documents to give more information about how the system operates. WordsEye consists of a library of approximately 3,000 3D objects and roughly 10,000 2D images, which are tied to a lexicon of about 15,000 nouns [15]. WordEye is publicly accessible through the URL: http://www.wordseye.com.

Put [4] is generally considered as one of the first proposed text-to-scene system. It is a language-based interactive system that changes the location of the objects in a scene by taking input in the form of an expression. Therefore, every statement needs to be in the form Put(X P Y), where X and Y are the objects and P is a spatial relationship between them. As an example, one might issue a command "Put the chair in room at location (x, z)" or "Put the ball in front of the square table" [4].

In [8], Li et al. also presented a system to generate 3D scenes from text. The proposed system is based on $AutodeskMaya^{®}$ such that the input text is in the form of XML. This system consists of three main components: language engine, object database and graphics engine. In the language engine, the user generates an XML file from the provided input text using different tags to describe object names and spatial relationships among them. The system then places the objects in the scene based on their spatial relationships with other objects. The object database contains 3D objects. Based on the requirements of the user input, these objects can be imported into the scene. The graphics engine is responsible of importing and repositioning objects in the scene. To reduce collisions among objects and to prevent overlapping, Lu et al. [10] used the concept of bounding box which itself is an extension to the approach suggested by Li [8]. Chang et al. [3] used natural language descriptions for each 3D scene in their indoor scenes dataset. The system learns from this dataset and recommends a set of suitable 3D scenes according to the spatial constraints and objects provided in the given input text. Depending on the probability of words that are matched between the input text and the description of the scene, the system provides the layouts of a 3D scene in descending order of the probability. An extension of his work is proposed by the same authors as SCEENSEER [2], where the user can iteratively change the location of an object in the selected scene through the input text.

Unlike text to 3D scene generation systems, the text to animation is even more complex. In addition to the challenges that the static scene generation systems face, the text to animation systems also need to recognize the set of actions associated with the objects in the text. Such systems should also be able to assign movement to the object while making sure that the objects neither collide with nor overlap other objects in the scene. The system proposed by Ruqian Lu et al. [11] takes a very limited subset of Chinese natural language as an input which is then transformed into a frame-based semantic description language. The system then constructs a qualitative script consisting of a sequence of scenes with camera movements and lighting for each scene. This qualitative script is then converted into a quantitative script which specifies a series of static image frames to be generated. Finally, the quantitative script is converted to an animation script to get the final animation. CarSim [6] is another system that involves animation. It takes accident reports, written in French, as its input and generates a 3D animation. The system performs linguistic analysis on the text and categorizes the objects into motionless objects, moving objects and collisions. Based on the input text, the system creates animations for accident scenes. Glass et al. [7] system takes annotated fictional text as its input. Constraints like layout, appearance and motion associated with the objects are present in the annotated text. These constraints are converted into mathematical constraints to generate 3D animation. Oshita et al. [12] developed a system that maintains a database of motion clips. For each motion in the input text, one query frame is generated which searches the database for its respective motion clip. Time duration for all of these motion clips are stored in a motion time-table and is used to create the final animation.

3   Framework

To create a visual story from textual narratives, our proposed framework consists of two stages: (i) text processing, and (ii) object positioning as shown on Fig. 1. In the text processing stage, the input, which generally involves a description of a scene or a story, is processed to identify and extract names of object and their spatial relationships. In the second stage, the system retrieves previously identified objects from the system library of 3D objects and imports them into the scene. After importing these objects, the system tries to establish the dimensions of each object (height, width and length) through its bounding box information. In conjunction with the extracted spatial relationships, these dimensions are used to properly place objects in the scene. After placing objects, any motion associated with them is added to the scene by specifying keyframes with respect to time. Unlike previously proposed models, in our framework we specify individual motion functions to add keyframes to each of the object, according to the type of movement indicated in the input text.

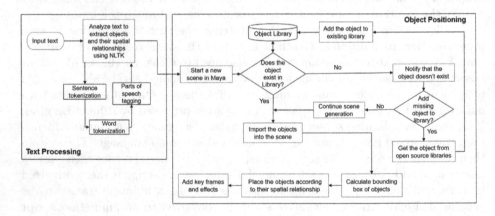

Fig. 1. Proposed framework

4   Text Processing

In principle, the user-provided input text in this framework is a description of a scene that contains objects and their spatial relationships. In order to process text input, we use Natural Language Tool Kit (NLTK) in Python (available from https://www.nltk.org/). NLTK is an open-source library that is written in Python and runs on all operating systems (Windows, MAC OS and Linux) and is supported by Python. It includes both symbolic and statistical natural language. It also provides easy-to-use interfaces to over 50 annotated corpora and lexical resources along with a suite of text processing libraries for classification, tokenization, parsing, and semantic reasoning [9]. Furthermore, it contains implementations of many different algorithms to provide various different functionalities and are used in many research implementations and projects.

These algorithms are trained on a structured set of texts. Using NLTK, every word in the text is tagged such that the input text is first split into sentences and then to individual words. The process of classifying words into their parts of speech and labeling them accordingly is known as part-of-speech (POS) tagging. With the help of these tags, nouns and positions, i.e., the object names and the inter-object spatial relationships are extracted. A simple example of text processing for basic 3D objects is shown on Fig. 2. The final outcome of text processing is a list containing the names of objects that are present in the scene to be created, as well as their spatial relationships.

text= "Sphere on cube and cone on sphere"

sentence_tokenized = nltk.sentence_tokenize (text)   *//splitting the input text into sentences*

⇨ ['Sphere on cube","cone on sphere']

word_tokenized=nltk.word_tokenize(sentence_tokenized)   *//splitting each sentence into words*

⇨ [['Sphere', 'on', 'cube'], ['cone', 'on', 'sphere']]

parts_of_speech_tagging=nltk.pos_tag(word_tokenized)   *//tagging parts of speech to every word*

⇨ [('sphere', 'NN'), ('on', 'IN'), ('cube', 'NN')]
⇨ [('cone', 'NN'), ('on', 'IN'), ('sphere', 'NN')]

//where NN stands for noun and IN stands for preposition

Fig. 2. Example of text processing

5   Object Positioning

In this section, we discuss the suggested approach to use output from the text processing stage to generate a 3D scene.

5.1   Bounding Box

In a 3D animation software, a bounding box stores the values of X_{min}, Y_{min}, Z_{min}, X_{max}, Y_{max} and Z_{max} of a 3D object, with respect to the X, Y and $Z - axis$. These values provide us not only the physical dimensions of a 3D object but allows us to prevent overlapping of objects during their placement in the scene. For example, the dimensions (length, height and width) of a table object in 3D space can be found by simply using $X_{max} - X_{min}$, $Y_{max} - Y_{min}$ and $Z_{max} - Z_{min}$, respectively (Fig. 3).

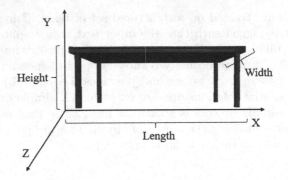

Fig. 3. Calculating the dimensions of a 3D object - a table

5.2   Spatial Relationships

Spatial relationships provide information about the position of two or more objects in space, relative to oneself and to each other. Spatial relationships provide the ability to understand locations and directions through specific words. In text-to-scene generation systems, these words are vital to specify both the position of an object and its relationships to other objects in the scene. Table 1 shows a few of the different spatial relationships that are supported by our system. We have classified spatial relationships in two categories: location and direction. This classification is based on the distance at which an object is placed relative to the position of another object in the scene. For the location spatial relationships, one face of the object is in contact with another object's face and the location spatial relationships are on, under, in front of, left, right, inside, behind, above and below. For directional spatial relationships, an object is placed at a certain distance from another one and the direction spatial relationships are east, west, north, south, southeast, southwest, northeast and northwest.

Table 1. Spatial relations

Location-based spatial relationship	Direction-based spatial relationship
on, under, in front of, left, right, behind,	east, west, north, south,
inside, above, below, next	southeast, southwest, northeast, northwest

6   Scene Generation

AutodeskMaya® is a very popular and a leading 3D computer graphics application software that is capable of handling complete animation production pipeline and runs on all three major platforms, i.e., Microsoft Windows, MacOS and Linux. It is a 3D modeling and animation software and has very strong capability to generate realistic special effects and high quality rendering through a set of menus. It provides C++ Application Programmers Interface (API) and also allows to extend the functionality by providing access to Maya Embedded Language (MEL), as well as Python. With the help of MEL or Python, users are able to write a script or develop a plugin to accommodate repetitive tasks by running them within Maya. We have used Maya to generate 3D scenes. With the output from text processing stage containing names of objects and their spatial relationships, the system imports these objects from its own object library. These objects can be resized and their visual characteristics such as colours or texture can be changed to reflect the resemblance with that of the objects in the textual story, either before or after generation of the final scene. New objects can be added to the library as well as existing objects can be replaced with the new ones. During the process of scene generation, if the object is not present in the library, the user gets a choice to either add a new object to the library or continue the scene generation without that object. The objects are initially imported into the scene and placed at the origin, i.e., position (0, 0, 0) in the 3D space. Thereafter, by using the bounding box, the system extracts the dimension (X_{min}, Y_{min}, Z_{min}, X_{max}, Y_{max} and Z_{max}). Depending on the spatial relationships between the objects, the system calculates either 1D or 2D relationship among length, height and width, since every spatial relationship may not require all the three dimensions. For example, the location spatial relationship 'on' involves the height of the object, while the direction spatial relationship 'northeast' involves both length and depth of the objects to place them in the scene. Figure 4 shows different object locations with respect to different spatial relationships.

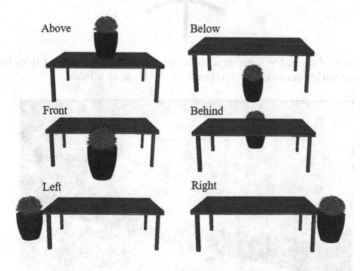

Fig. 4. Spatial relations with respect to table

The next step after object positioning is to add animation and any special effects to the objects. Autodesk Maya allows different animation techniques to add motion to an object. The most common among them is the keyframe animation, in which the object's spatial location as well as key attributes are saved with respect to the time. We have movements with different characteristics that can be assigned to any of the objects in the scene. However, it is important to note that not all objects will have exact or similar movements. As an example, consider a scene a walking person and a moving car. In a realistic scenario, the walk will be much slower than the speed of movement of the car. Consequently, the distance traveled by both for the same period of time will be different and as such should be indicated in the animation. Finally, the system adds any special

Fig. 5. In front of the table there is a chair. There is a book on the table. Left of the book is a vase with flowers in it. Northeast of the book is a lamp.

Fig. 6. There is a car on road and car is moving. There is a walkway on the left of the road. There is a building to the left of the footpath. The building is facing towards footpath. The building is on fire.

effects that are associated with the objects or the scene. Figure 5 is an example of a 3D scene generated using our framework for the input text as shown in the figure (Figs. 6, 7, 8 and 9).

Fig. 7. During sunrise, the sky is full of clouds and birds are flying above the mountains.

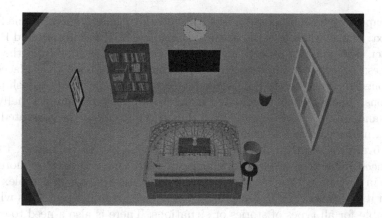

Fig. 8. There is a table inside a room and a couch in front of the table with a Stool right to the couch. There is a lamp on the stool and a vase on the table and flowers in the vase. Northeast of the table there is a plant. Northwest of table there is a bookcase. A carpet is on the floor. A clock is on the front wall and a TV below the clock. A photo frame is on the left wall.

Fig. 9. Odette building is on the right of the Sunset Avenue and the Erie hall is on the left of the Sunset Avenue. Next to the Erie Hall, there is Lambton Tower and Chrysler Hall is north of the Lambton Tower. North of the Odette Building is Toldo Building. Students are walking on the Sunset avenue.

7   Conclusion and Future Work

In this paper, we have proposed a new framework to generate a 3D scene from a given text. Our method uses the Natural Language Tool Kit library and Python to extract the names of objects and their spatial relationships from the input text. These objects are imported from our database and are then placed and repositioned in the generated 3D scene based on their spatial relationships and dimensions. The latter are calculated using bounding box values. Finally, animations and special effects are added to the objects to make the generated scene dynamic, more realistic and complete.

The overall system can be improved in many ways. In particular, there is a clear need for better handling of the input text. One can develop more NLP libraries in Python within Maya to perform semantic analysis of complex input texts. In its current form, it is capable of processing smaller sentences which is not suitable for all types of stories or situations. There is also a need to extract information from relatively larger passages to build a scene.

References

1. Anagnostopoulos, C.N., Anagnostopoulos, I., Loumos, V., Kayafas, E.: The primary care PTSD screen (PC-PTSD): development and operating characteristics. Primary Care Psychiatry **9**(1), 9–14 (2003)
2. Chang, A.X., Eric, M., Savva, M., Manning, C.D.: SceneSeer: 3D scene design with natural language. ArXiv abs/1703.00050 (2017)
3. Chang, A.X., Savva, M., Manning, C.D.: Interactive learning of spatial knowledge for text to 3D scene generation. In: Proceedings of the Workshop on Interactive Language Learning, Visualization, and Interfaces, pp. 14–21 (2014)

4. Clay, S.R., Wilhelms, J.P.: Put: language-based interactive manipulation of objects. IEEE Comput. Graph. Appl. **16**(2), 31–39 (1996)
5. Coyne, B., Sproat, R.: WordsEye: an automatic text-to-scene conversion system. In: Proceedings of the 28th Annual Conference on Computer Graphics and Interactive Techniques, pp. 487–496 (2001)
6. Dupuy, S., Egges, A., Legendre, V., Nugues, P.: Generating a 3D simulation of a car accident from a written description in natural language: the CarSim system. In: Proceedings of the Workshop on Temporal and Spatial Information Processing, vol. 13, pp. 1–8 (2001)
7. Glass, K.R., Bangay, S.: Automating the creation of 3D animation from annotated fiction text. In: Proceedings of the IADIS International Conference on Computer Graphics and Visualization, pp. 3–10 (2008)
8. Li, C., Yin, C., Lu, J., Ma, L.: Automatic 3D scene generation based on Maya. In: Proceedings of 2009 IEEE 10th International Conference on Computer-Aided Industrial Design Conceptual Design, pp. 981–985 (2009)
9. Loper, E., Bird, S.: NLTK: the natural language toolkit. ArXiv arXiv preprint cs/0205028 (2002)
10. Lu, J., Li, C., Yin, C., Ma, L.: A new framework for automatic 3D scene construction from text description. In: Proceedings of the 2010 IEEE International Conference on Progress in Informatics and Computing, vol. 2, pp. 964–968 (2010)
11. Lu, R., Zhang, S.: Automatic generation of computer animation: using AI for movie animation (2002)
12. Oshita, M.: Generating animation from natural language texts and semantic analysis for motion search and scheduling. Vis. Comput. **26**(5), 339–352 (2010)
13. Rizzo, A., et al.: A virtual reality exposure therapy application for Iraq war military personnel with post traumatic stress disorder: from training to toy to treatment. In: NATO Advanced Research Workshop on Novel Approaches to the Diagnosis and Treatment of Posttraumatic Stress Disorder (2006)
14. Roy, M.J., Rizzo, A., Difede, J., Rothbaum, B.O.: Virtual reality exposure therapy for PTSD (2016)
15. Ulinski, M., Coyne, B., Hirschberg, J.: Evaluating the WordsEye text-to-scene system: imaginative and realistic sentences. In: Proceedings of the 11th International Conference on Language Resources and Evaluation (LREC 2018), Miyazaki, Japan, May 2018

Document and Media Analysis

Personality Traits Identification Through Handwriting Analysis

Tahar Mekhaznia[1]([⊠]) [iD], Chawki Djeddi[1], and Sobhan Sarkar[2]

[1] University of Tebessa, Tebessa, Algeria
tahar.mekhaznia@univ-tebessa.dz
[2] University of Edinburgh, Edinburgh, UK

Abstract. Personality traits are of paramount importance in identifying the human's behavior. They represent a useful information source for forensic control, recruitment profiling, medical symptoms, and other applications. Personality traits are identified through various physical aspects, including sense, honesty, and other emotions. These aspects can be revealed through handwritten features. Since handwriting is unique for everyone, its identification process is not as straight forward as it appears; rather it involves efficient tools for extraction and classification of features. The process has been the subject of various research works. However, results reported remain unsatisfactory due to mainly dissimilarities in handwriting. In this paper, we present an approach of recognition of personality traits based on textural features extracted from handwritten samples. Experiments are carried out using artificial neural networks and the TxPI-u database. Results deliver a significant recognition rate which endorses its effectiveness against similar works.

Keywords: Handwriting analysis · Personality identification · Neural networks · Feature classification

1 Introduction

Handwriting is viewed as a combined psycho-mechanic process achieved by the writer's hand according to his brain commands. It is, to some extent, his/her private seal and trademark, which cannot be reproduced by others. Such effect is endorsed by two natural factors that contribute to the script individuality; first, the genetic factor, which is responsible for the hand bio-mechanical structure, muscular strength and brain system proprieties, while the second, a mimetic factor, relative to the training concept acquired through the basic education and cultural environment influence. By another way, individual writing is subject to several improvements during the lifetime; it starts with a basic behavior in classroom copybook style, progressively affected by new attributes depending on personal life events, skills, etc. Finally, it becomes, specific to its owner.

By another way, personal handwriting is a part of the global human aspects as walking behavior and voice speech. They allowed in some way, disclosing

C. Djeddi et al. (Eds.): MedPRAI 2020, CCIS 1322, pp. 155–169, 2021.
https://doi.org/10.1007/978-3-030-71804-6_12

the psychological state of their owner. They accordingly represent a useful data source for forensic control, recruitment profiling, medical diagnostic symptoms and wide other applications. Related research area adopted the *Graphology* as a science of recognition of human traits and emotional outlay [1]. It allows revealing enough about the writer psychology and assessment based on handwriting features and in this way, the *handwriting recognition* emerged.

Handwriting recognition, known also as *character recognition* is a study, consists of the process of conversion of manual texts to codes of symbols usable within a computer. The process is achieved by appropriate applications, including machine learning and OCR engines; it involves the script extraction, segmentation and classification of features. The useful information is stored on referential databases, known as classifiers, used afterward as an identification tool of the writer manuscript samples.

The writer identification, called also the *personality traits identification* refers to the scientific methodology that understanding and evaluating personality emotion. It operates via the structure and patterns of handwriting and intends to build the writer personality through a piece of his handwriting. The identification process is unstable anywhere. It obeys to the concept that no two people write exactly similar and no one reproduces the same writing twice and depends essentially on the analyst's experience and his/her skills; however, the related results are quite often costly and prone to errors. Consequently, experts turn to the automated handwriting analysis which seems to be effective for trait personality prediction. It performs a one-to-many search with samples of authorship in a given classifier and gives back the most similar results which, may be processed manually afterward.

To solve the handwriting recognition problem, we propose an approach of evaluation of personality traits through various handwriting characteristics. Its principle consists of the extraction of handwriting sample features and their classification using artificial neural network (ANN) algorithm. The results allow leading to recognize various personality traits in regard of the *Five-Factor Model* (FFM). The handwriting features proposed are based on *edge directional, run length and ink distribution*. The experimental process is accomplished using a new resource database called TxPI-u with 534 samples, performed by several writers; represent a common set of personality traits. A part on the database contents is used in the training process. It is noteworthy to mention that the full identification of personality traits is never reached. This may be due to the diversity of writer's manuscripts, the scan-quality of documents and foreground/background separation problems. In addition, the character recognition rate within a given document cannot be viewed as a valid result due to the lack of a standard evaluation context.

The rest of the paper is organized into five sections: After an introduction and a literature review in Sects. 1 and 2, the proposed approach is described in Sect. 3. Section 4 illustrates some preliminary experiments and statistical analysis of results. Finally, the paper is concluded in Sect. 5; it summarizes the paper contents and provides valuable ideas about avenues for further investigation of the problem.

2   Literature Review

Personality traits identification based handwriting remains a thriving research field. Its prominence emerges in pattern recognition, classification and in general, in the artificial intelligence (AI) field. Accordingly, researchers adopted diverse strategies for features extraction of symbols, conducting the retention of just effective information and then, decreasing the dimension of classifiers [2]. Before that, the *staff lines* problem must be fixed; it refers to the writing guidelines, encountered especially in old documents and often overlaps symbols parts. Staff lines removal must be processed before or after the segmentation stage with the risk of losing parts of useful data. It involves specific transformations and symbols reconstruction which conducts to useless results in various cases.

Literature in this context are abundant; the earliest works date backs to 90s where Sheikholeslami et al. [3] proposed a computer-aided graphology system for extraction and analysis of handwriting with reduced data and limited results. In the 2000s, various similar works have emerged. They performed their experiments upon data-sets of numerous writers' samples [4]. Researchers and for their experiments, extract a variety of features: characters dimensions, slants and loops frequency [5]; document and paragraph layout, pixels density [6]; document layout, pen pressure, words spacing [7]; baseline behavior and t-bar, y-loop characteristics [8]; "*f*" and "*i*" letters characteristics [9]; baseline layout, slants, margins [10]; isolated characters behavior [11]. About the classification, researchers adopted various alternatives: neural network [9,12]; grey-level co-occurrence matrix, Gabor filters [13], crisp and fuzzy approach [14]; fuzzy inference [15]; other specific tools [16]; machine learning tool with KNN [17]; combination of CNN and SVM classifiers [18].

In term of effectiveness, if a part of the cited approaches has yielded promising results, various other attempts remain unfruitful [19]. Their steering toward just the Latin-derived alphabets is undoubtedly the main cause, coupled with their ineptitude to deal with actual databases. Besides that, we noticed the significant amount of training data required by certain approaches which constitute a drawback of their efficiency. Overall, and in lack of a standard for predicting behavior based on handwriting, the most obtained results still dependent to their experimental environment.

3   Proposed Methodology

3.1   The Approach Overview

The proposed approach is based on three layers of Artificial neural network (ANN) architecture; it uses the contents of a handwriting database for evaluating the personality traits of the writer according to the FFM model. It focuses on analyzing off lines samples, a suitable alternative that replaces the questionnaire and psychological interview, used in classical processes.

The handwriting samples are produced in a consistent format, recognized easily by the computer with a high degree of accuracy. Writing features are then considered and classified according to a predefined model. First, a part of the features is used as training mode that enhances the recognition accuracy. Figure 1 depicts the main approach steps for recognition.

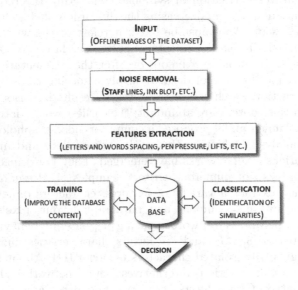

Fig. 1. Main steps of recognition process

3.2   Dataset

The dataset used for the evaluation of the present work consists of a new standardized multimodal corpus, baptised Text for *Personality Identification of Undergraduates*, baptised *TxPI-u* [20], dedicated to experience the personality traits problem. Its contents consist of samples of manuscripts from a group of 418 of undergraduate Mexican students. It presented as a set of images samples of various academic programs (management, humanity, social studies, communication, etc.). An associated class 1 or 0 is affected to each sample; it corresponds to a present level of a specific personality trait (extroversion, agreeableness, conscientiousness, emotional stability and openness) according to the FFM. An image sample is illustrated in Fig. 2.

3.3   Noise Removal

Staff lines (called also ruled paper) consist of a series of horizontal continuous lines used as a guide, helping readers and especially writers to maintain their writing on a straight line and their drawing on a paging order (Figs. 2 and 3). The ruling layout is determined according to the style defined by the manuscript's author or the entity for which it is intended. Staff lines are intended to maintain

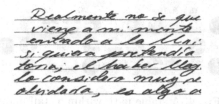

Fig. 2. An extract of TxPI-u image sample

notes pitch for school notebooks and musical supports. Nowadays, they have gradually disappeared from documents due the use of mechanical writing, but still present within archives, and old manuscripts.

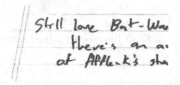

Fig. 3. A manuscript pattern with staff lines

Noise removal consists of removing staff lines and other unwanted data as extra symbols, ink blots that do not offer any useful information. It allows instant character recognition and in consequence, improves the quality of the image. In general, staff lines are performed with the same color of writing pen and sometimes, overlapped parts of writing symbols. Therefore, their automatic removal is susceptible to alter relevant data. Moreover, the issue is compounded by the support texture quality and the writer handwriting which partly modify the standard behavior of characters. In literature, staff lines identification and removal have envisaged under various aspects: thickness, distance between lines, straight behavior and exploration of the contrast between fonts and paper [21–24]. We adopted in this paper the idea illustrated by Dos Cardoso et al. [25]; it forward the notion of a stable path, defined as the shortest horizontal line that relays two pixels u and v enclosed in two distinct sub-graphs Ω_1 and Ω_2 situated respectively on both margins of the music score (Fig. 4). A staff line is then viewed as an extensive object of black pixels with a homogenous width supported by a given shortest path. Staff lines thickness is modeled as an average of contiguous stable paths (Fig. 5). Several runs are needed on the same series of pixels to fix the staff space height.

Finally, the removal of staff lines consists just on swapping their pixels with white color and keeping intact other objects exceeding the considered width.

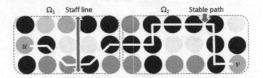

Fig. 4. A stable path within a staff line

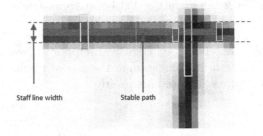

Fig. 5. Staff line width adjustment

3.4 Feature Extraction

The feature extraction is a very important step in pattern recognition systems; it partially emulates human thinking about the direction in handwritten traces. Handwriting features are various: line regularity, letters and words spacing, pen pressure, lifts, etc. They appear as dominant factors in visual appearance of handwritten shapes and are independent of the amount of the written material and the variations of the writer's life behavior. In the context of the present work, we retain for experiments the slants, writing direction, and the ink trace features as illustrated below.

Edge-Hinge Distribution (f1). The Edge-hinge distribution, *EHD* in short, is a statistical feature that illustrates the direction orientation of a handwriting pattern. It reproduces the behavior of a pair of neighborhood edge fragments starting from a central pixel and evolving in two distinct directions, oriented respectively at angles φ_1 and φ_2 with the horizontal line as showed in Fig. 6. The probability distribution $p(\varphi_1, \varphi_2)$ is extracted over a wide sample of pixels pairs that appear in the opposite corners of a square window moving over an edge-detected handwriting piece; it solely concerns just one scale direction instead of multiple ones.

The EDD is the main feature of writing stroke that materializing more accurate about writer identification features as illustrated below.

Run-Length Distributions (f2/f5). The run-length distribution, *RLD* in short, involves the behavior of the text direction, loop size and curvature [27]. The method principle consists on scanning pixel's columns on various directions

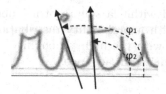

Fig. 6. The orientation of segments emerged from a central point

within a binary image and computes the number of dark pixels (which correspond to ink width) at any direction after removing salt and pepper noise. The best values are used to construct a template distribution. Once dark pixels are processed, the histogram of run lengths is normalized and interpreted as a probability distribution. In experiments, we consider the RLD for both black pixels (f2) and white pixels (f5) which seem informative about symbols and words spacing.

Auto-regressive Model (f3). The auto-regressive model, AR in short, is a statistical tool for depicting the dynamic characteristics of discrete data within textures and images. AR describes the intensity of a given pixel depending on the intensity of its neighbors of a certain distance in all directions. It is then used to achieve the contents of a missing area within an image shape. The pixel intensity is represented as a linear combination of neighborhood pixels' intensities according to Eq. 1.

$$\dot{I} = \sum_{x,y_{min}}^{x,y_{max}} a_{ij} I_{i-p,j-p} + n_{xy} \tag{1}$$

with $\dot{I}_{xy}$, the complete sample at the location (x, y), the (i, j) denotes the known neighborhood values. The $[x_{min}, y_{min}, x_{max}, y_{max}]$ refer to the model order, generally represented by a square window Ω, a corresponds to the prediction coefficient and n, represents the white noise process. AR model has been successfully applied for modeling texture synthesis, segmentation and image classifications [28,29].

The Edge-Direction Distribution (f4). The edge-direction distribution, EDD in short, is a texture descriptor which consists of an edge convolution with two orthogonal differential kernels followed by thresholding [26]. Such feature has been long used as the main component of handwriting trace [30,31]. It is extracted by considering the line that relays two adjacent edge points k and $k + 1$ with (x_k, y_k) and (x_{k+1}, y_{k+1}) as their respective coordinates in a binary image in which only the edge pixels are visible. The considered line forms with the horizontal straight line an angle φ [32], computed as Eq. 2.

$$\varphi = \arctan(\frac{y_{k+1} - y_k}{x_{k+1} - x_k}) \tag{2}$$

The EDD is considered within a square of neighborhood pixels in various directions (Fig. 7), each with a probability distribution $p(\varphi)$. In experiments, we consider just the EDD with the high probability since the direction of the writer's pen cannot be predicted in advance.

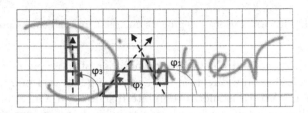

Fig. 7. Edge-direction distribution from 4 pixels-long edge fragments

3.5   Classification

In the classification stage, the considered features are arranged into sets according to the personality traits. Various classifiers are available for this purpose They are devoted, each for a dedicated task-dependent of its specificities: fast recognition [33], parameter setting rules [34], automatic retrieval feature [18], etc. Their performance depends on the ability of input processing [35], training background [36], and the way of the user adjusts and manages the considered database [24]. Most classifiers are built upon an architecture of neural networks [37]; They have found application in a wide variety of problems, including pattern recognition.

We have adopted the ANN due to its flexible architecture, connection weights evaluation, and activation functions. It also seems well adapted at handwritten styles recognition [38]. It consists of three main types of layers arranged in a feed-forward structure and fully interconnected. The base layer acquires the handwriting sample features as data vectors. The intermediary hidden layers build a map of neurons connection based on handwriting learning features where the last layer generates distinct feature spaces according to the Big Five personality traits. We have five outputs that correspond to the FFM model, whereas, the input dimension is variable and depends on the feature vectors size as shown in Table 1.

The considered classifier achieves both training and test stages. In the training process, the it earmarked a part of the extract features to enrich a comprehensive database. In the test process, each feature vector is compared with the classifier patterns to locate closest similar features. The retained data may, in principle, match closely to the corresponding writer personality aspects.

4   Experimental Evaluation

Evaluation is conducted on the database presented in Sect. 3 where its contents are split into three disjoint sets, assigned separately for training, validation, and test processes.

4.1   Methodology Principle

The main experimental process consists of three phases, namely the noise removal, the construction of feature vectors, and the features classification.

In the first phase, the idea presented in Sect. 3.3 is performed on each image of the database. As it showed in Fig. 8a, staff lines within the used database' images are relatively clear, concise and exhibit a regular vertical spacing. So it is not hard to locate the sub-graphs Ω_1 and Ω_2 related to each staff line. Also, they are straight and with equal length; it then easily leads to the construction of stable paths. Nevertheless, lines width is defined as an average of contiguous stable paths, so, it does not reflect the real thickness of each line. Hence, their removal may alter, in some cases parts of the overlapped data, especially for lines with inhomogeneous thickness. Despite that, the lost data concern just letters extended to lower zone as g, j, p, etc. which constitutes no more than 5% of the written contents; such fact cannot alter the whole image features. A staff removed lines model is observed in Fig. 8.

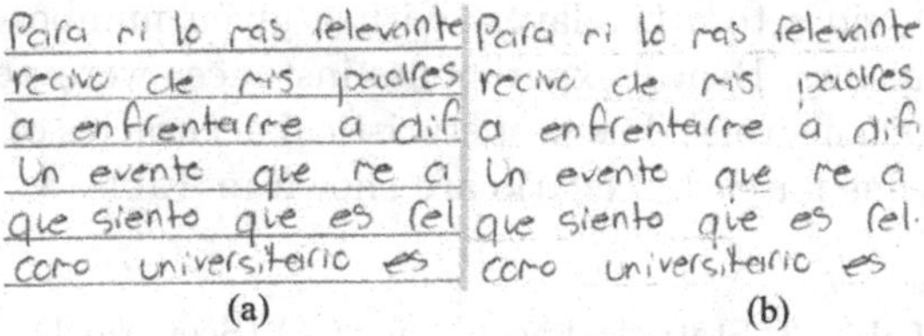

Fig. 8. Fragment of an image of the database. (a) with staff lines. (b) Staff lines removed

The second phase is dedicated to the features extraction. As described in Sect. 3.4, five feature methods have been explored in this study (f1 to f5). Each method builds its feature vector based on the characteristics extracts from characters of the database. The goal of the operation is to identify each character with a minimum of characteristics. Given the variable nature of the handwriting characters, feature vectors have distinct sizes which correspond to the number of characteristics of characters according to each feature. Table 1 summarizes the sizes of vectors (as presented in Sect. 3.4). We propose four experimental scenarios with various amounts of data for each process as shown in Table 2.

Table 1. Vectors dimension of the extracted features

Feature	Description	Size
f1	Edge hinge Dist./ chip of 7 pixels	3136
f2	Run Length Dist. for black segments	400
f3	Auto Reg. Model for black pixels	24
f4	Edge Direction Dist.	40
f5	Run Length Dist. for white segments	400

Table 2. Experimental scenarios

Scenario n°	% of dataset amount		
	Training	Validation	Test
1	50	25	25
2	60	20	20
3	70	15	15
4	80	10	10

The proposed classifier involves three layers with feed-forward architecture. The input layer is a set of five neurons; it accepts data of the five feature vectors f1 to f5. The output layer is doted also with five neurons; it delivers a result that corresponds to the five personality traits. We consider a hidden layer, fully connected on both sides to other layers with a given number of neurons that leads to the best results. Hence, experiments instances were performed using a range of 1000 to 5000 neurons. The best statistical accuracies of trait personality averaged over 10 runs for each scenario are shown in Tables 3, 4, 5 and 6.

Table 3. Statistical accuracies (%) (Scenario 1)

Feature set	Number of neurons in the hidden layer				
	1200	2500	2600	2700	2800
f1	62,98	61,03	64,13	59,67	59,74
f2	57,35	53,81	53,74	50,13	57,20
f3	58,38	52,27	60,48	49,58	57,94
f4	57,16	57,53	59,85	60,04	51,93
f5	60,41	52,85	**67,99**	57,72	60,63

The overall results vary from 50% to 60%. The best accuracies (more than 65%) were noted for features f1 and f5. They were observed when the hidden layer size varies from 2500 to 3500 neurons. Furthermore, most experiments provide roughly alike results for all presented scenarios as shown in Fig. 9.

Table 4. Statistical accuracies (%) (Scenario 2)

Feature set	Number of neurons in the hidden layer				
	3300	3400	3500	3600	3700
f1	61,20	57,60	67,80	**71,00**	54,70
f2	53,90	51,70	54,00	56,40	59,40
f3	54,70	59,00	54,60	60,20	58,20
f4	57,00	53,40	56,40	55,00	56,50
f5	**71,90**	59,70	59,80	48,60	59,20

Table 5. Statistical accuracies (%) (Scenario 3)

Feature set	Number of neurons in the hidden layer				
	3200	3300	3400	3500	3600
f1	57,68	54,33	51,60	57,64	59,23
f2	50,42	62,80	54,73	48,77	52,12
f3	50,68	48,69	53,37	56,83	54,62
f4	54,62	53,63	46,63	53,15	56,83
f5	**67,22**	53,63	51,12	51,09	66,89

Table 6. Statistical accuracies (%) (Scenario 4)

Method	Number of neurons in the hidden layer				
	3500	3600	3700	3800	3900
f1	50,61	65,12	58,12	59,67	56,69
f2	57,27	53,26	52,85	49,72	52,78
f3	57,64	55,76	56,94	49,06	49,69
f4	56,02	53,70	50,13	56,28	54,55
f5	50,61	**65,12**	58,12	59,67	56,69

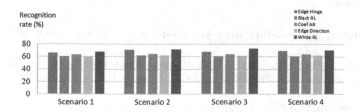

Fig. 9. Statistical accuracies for each scenario

4.2   Analysis and Evaluation

The experiments showed that the run-length of white segments (f5) exhibits a better performance than other features. It provides more informative results against the black segments feature (f2). By another way, the overall best results are obtained with a hidden layer of 3200 to 3600 neurons. Furthermore, a significant variation of outcome has been observed with distinct parts of data within the database, for different features or when varying the proportions of training and test sets.

In regard to recent literature, similar works provide divergent results due to their specific test environments: 47 to 75% [39], 48% [40], 62 to 85% [41], 60 to 90% [42–45], 76% [46,47] and more 90% [48–50]. Consequently, a comparative study with these works seems without interest.

5   Conclusion

The personality trait identification is a methodology of evaluating human emotions based on a piece of his/her handwriting. It allows in some aspect, disclosing the insight psychological state of the writer. Such fact offers a useful data source for forensic control, recruitment profiling, medical diagnostic symptoms and wide other applications.

The personality trait identification consists of handwriting pattern analysis, characters feature extraction and classification. The ideas actually, is an active research subject but results still far from satisfaction. This is due to the writing patterns complexity and the variation of writers styles.

In this paper, a personality trait identification approach has been proposed where a set of writing level features have been evaluated. Experiments have been carried out on a database of 543 handwritten samples. The result showed a prediction accuracy of more than 70% for both edge-hinge distribution and run-length distribution and more than 55% for other features, which seems to be effective regarding similar literature works.

By another way, we think the approach performs well if the experimental space will be expanded to include more features and classifiers. It hence opens avenues for further studies that improve handwriting recognition accuracy.

References

1. Desbarrolles, A., Jean-Hippolyte: Les mystères de l'ecriture, 2eme edition. Paris (1872)
2. Lauer, F., Suen, C.Y., Bloch, G.: A trainable feature extractor for handwritten digit recognition. Pattern Recogn. (2007). https://doi.org/10.1016/j.patcog.2006.10.011
3. Sheikholeslami, G.S.N.V.: Computer aided graphology (1997)
4. LeCun, Y., Cortes, C., Burges, C.: The MNIST database of handwritten digits. Courant Institute of Mathematical Sciences (1998)

5. Zois, E.N., Anastassopoulos, V.: Morphological waveform coding for writer identifi-cation. Pattern Recogn. (2000). https://doi.org/10.1016/S0031-3203(99)00063-1
6. Cha, S.-H., Srihari, S.N.: Writer identification: statistical analysis and dichotomizer. In: Ferri, F.J., Iñesta, J.M., Amin, A., Pudil, P. (eds.) SSPR /SPR 2000. LNCS, vol. 1876, pp. 123–132. Springer, Heidelberg (2000). https://doi.org/10.1007/3-540-44522-6_13
7. Kamath, V., Ramaswamy, N., Navin Karanth, P., Desai, V., Kulkarni, S.M.: Devel-opment of an automated handwriting analysis system. J. Eng. Appl. Sci. 6 (2011)
8. Champa, H.N., AnandaKumar, K.R.: Automated human behavior prediction through handwriting analysis. In: Proceedings - 1st International Conference on Integrated Intelligent Computing, ICIIC 2010 (2010). https://doi.org/10.1109/ICIIC.2010.29
9. Grewal, P.K., Prashar, D.: Behavior prediction through handwriting analysis. In: IJCST (2012)
10. Mukherjee, S., De, I.: Feature extraction from handwritten documents for person-ality analysis. In: 2016 International Conference on Computer, Electrical and Com-munication Engineering, ICCECE 2016 (2017). https://doi.org/10.1109/ICCECE.2016.8009580
11. Zafar, M.F., Mohamad, D., Anwar, M.M.: Recognition of online isolated hand-written characters by backpropagation neural nets using sub-character primitive features. In: 10th IEEE International Multitopic Conference, INMIC 2006 (2006). https://doi.org/10.1109/INMIC.2006.358154
12. Cha, S.H., Tappert, C.C.: Automatic detection of handwriting forgery. In: Proceed-ings - International Workshop on Frontiers in Handwriting Recognition, IWFHR (2002). https://doi.org/10.1109/IWFHR.2002.1030920
13. Said, H.E.S., Baker, K.D., Tan, T.N.: Personal identification based on handwriting (2002). https://doi.org/10.1109/icpr.1998.712068
14. Mogharreban, N., Rahimi, S., Sabharwal, M.: A combined crisp and fuzzy approach for handwriting analysis. In: Annual Conference of the North American Fuzzy Information Processing Society - NAFIPS (2004). https://doi.org/10.1109/nafips.2004.1336307
15. Mutalib, S., Ramli, R., Rahman, S.A., Yusoff, M., Mohamed, A.: Towards emo-tional control recognition through handwriting using fuzzy inference. In: Proceed-ings - International Symposium on Information Technology, ITSim (2008). https://doi.org/10.1109/ITSIM.2008.4631735
16. Abdul Rahiman, M., Varghese, D., Kumar, M.: HABIT: handwritten analysis based individualistic traits prediction (2013)
17. Joshi, P., Agarwal, A., Dhavale, A., Suryavanshi, R., Kodolikar, S.: Handwriting analysis for detection of personality traits using machine learning approach. Int. J. Comput. Appl. (2015). https://doi.org/10.5120/ijca2015907189
18. Niu, X.X., Suen, C.Y.: A novel hybrid CNN-SVM classifier for recognizing hand-written digits. Pattern Recogn. (2012). https://doi.org/10.1016/j.patcog.2011.09.021
19. Chaudhari, K., Thakkar, A.: Survey on handwriting-based personality trait iden-tification. Expert Syst. Appl. (2019). https://doi.org/10.1016/j.eswa.2019.01.028
20. Ramírez-De-La-Rosa, G., Villatoro-Tello, E., Jiménez-Salazar, H.: TxPI-u: a resource for Personality Identification of undergraduates. J. Intell. Fuzzy Syst. (2018). https://doi.org/10.3233/JIFS-169484
21. Blostein, D., Baird, H.S.: A critical survey of music image analysis. In: Structured Document Image Analysis (2011)

22. Dutta, A., Pal, U., Fornés, A., Lladós, J.: An efficient staff removal approach from printed musical documents. In: Proceedings - International Conference on Pattern Recognition (2010). https://doi.org/10.1109/ICPR.2010.484
23. Pinto, T., Rebelo, A., Giraldi, G., Cardoso, J.S.: Music score binarization based on domain knowledge. In: Vitrià, J., Sanches, J.M., Hernández, M. (eds.) IbPRIA 2011. LNCS, vol. 6669, pp. 700–708. Springer, Heidelberg (2011). https://doi.org/10.1007/978-3-642-21257-4_87
24. Phangtriastu, M.R., Harefa, J., Tanoto, D.F.: Comparison between neural network and support vector machine in optical character recognition. In: Procedia Computer Science (2017). https://doi.org/10.1016/j.procs.2017.10.061
25. dos Santos Cardoso, J., Capela, A., Rebelo, A., Guedes, C., Pinto da Costa, J.: Staff detection with stable paths. IEEE Trans. Pattern Anal. Mach. Intell. (2009). https://doi.org/10.1109/TPAMI.2009.34
26. Bulacu, M., Schomaker, L., Vuurpijl, L.: Writer identification using edge-based directional features. In: Proceedings of the International Conference on Document Analysis and Recognition, ICDAR (2003). https://doi.org/10.1109/ICDAR.2003.1227797
27. Arazi, B.: Handwriting identification by means of run-length measurements. IEEE Trans. Syst. Man Cybern. (1977). https://doi.org/10.1109/TSMC.1977.4309648
28. Köppel, M., Doshkov, D., Racape, F., Ndjiki-Nya, P., Wiegand, T.: On the usage of the 2D-AR-model in texture completion scenarios with causal boundary conditions: a tutorial. Signal Process Image Commun. (2015). https://doi.org/10.1016/j.image.2015.01.010
29. de Souza, P.: Texture recognition via auto regression. Pattern Recogn. (1982). https://doi.org/10.1016/0031-3203(82)90025-5
30. Bulacu, M., Schomaker, L.: Writer style from oriented edge fragments. In: Petkov, N., Westenberg, M.A. (eds.) CAIP 2003. LNCS, vol. 2756, pp. 460–469. Springer, Heidelberg (2003). https://doi.org/10.1007/978-3-540-45179-2_57
31. Crettea, J.P.: A set of handwriting families: style recognition. In: Proceedings of the International Conference on Document Analysis and Recognition, ICDAR (1995). https://doi.org/10.1109/ICDAR.1995.599041
32. Li, H., Toh, K.A., Li, L.: Advanced Topics in Biometrics. World Scientific, Singapore (2011)
33. Sarkhel, R., Das, N., Das, A., Kundu, M., Nasipuri, M.: A multi-scale deep quad tree based feature extraction method for the recognition of isolated handwritten characters of popular Indic scripts. Pattern Recogn. (2017) https://doi.org/10.1016/j.patcog.2017.05.022
34. Breiman, L.: Random forests. Mach. Learn. (2001). https://doi.org/10.1023/A:1010933404324
35. Pramanik, R., Raj, V., Bag, S.: Finding the optimum classifier: classification of segmentable components in offline handwritten Devanagari words. In: Proceedings of the 4th IEEE International Conference on Recent Advances in Information Technology, RAIT 2018 (2018). https://doi.org/10.1109/RAIT.2018.8389032
36. Elleuch, M., Zouari, R., Kherallah, M.: Feature extractor based deep method to enhance online Arabic handwritten recognition system. In: Villa, A.E.P., Masulli, P., Pons Rivero, A.J. (eds.) ICANN 2016. LNCS, vol. 9887, pp. 136–144. Springer, Cham (2016). https://doi.org/10.1007/978-3-319-44781-0_17
37. David, G.S., Duda, R.O., Hart, P.E.: Pattern classification, 2nd edn. Wiley, Hoboken (2012)
38. Duval, F.: Artificial Neural Networks: Concepts, Tools and Techniques Explained for Absolute Beginners. 2018

39. Al Maadeed, S., Hassaine, A.: Automatic prediction of age, gender, and nationality in offline handwriting. EURASIP J. Image Video Process. **2014**(1), 1–10 (2014). https://doi.org/10.1186/1687-5281-2014-10
40. Majumdar, A., Krishnan, P., Jawahar, C.V.: Visual aesthetic analysis for handwritten document images. In: Proceedings of International Conference on Frontiers in Handwriting Recognition, ICFHR (2016). https://doi.org/10.1109/ICFHR.2016.0085
41. Chen, Z., Lin, T.: Automatic personality identification using writing behaviours: an exploratory study. Behav. Inf. Technol. (2017). https://doi.org/10.1080/0144929X.2017.1304994
42. Mutalib, S., Rahman, S.A., Yusoff, M., Mohamed, A.: Personality analysis based on letter 't ' using back propagation neural network. In: Proceedings of the International Conference on Electrical Engineering and Informatics Institut Teknologi Bandung (2007)
43. Gavrilescu, M.: Study on determining the Myers-Briggs personality type based on individual's handwriting. In: 2015 E-Health and Bioengineering Conference, EHB 2015 (2016). https://doi.org/10.1109/EHB.2015.7391603
44. Asra, S., Shubhangi, D.C.: Human behavior recognition based on hand written cursives by SVM classifier. In: International Conference on Electrical, Electronics, Communication Computer Technologies and Optimization Techniques, ICEEC-COT 2017 (2018). https://doi.org/10.1109/ICEECCOT.2017.8284679
45. Wijaya, W., Tolle, H., Utaminingrum, F.: Personality analysis through handwriting detection using android based mobile device. J. Inf. Technol. Comput. Sci. (2018) https://doi.org/10.25126/jitecs.20172237
46. Arica, N., Yarman-Vural, F.T.: An overview of character recognition focused on off-line handwriting. IEEE Trans. Syst. Man Cybern. Part C Appl. Rev. (2001). https://doi.org/10.1109/5326.941845
47. Fallah, B., Khotanlou, H.: Detecting features of human personality based on handwriting using learning algorithms Adv. Comput. Sci. Int. J. **4**, 31–37 (2015)
48. Sen, A., Shah, H.: Automated handwriting analysis system using principles of graphology and image processing. In: Proceedings of 2017 International Conference on Innovations in Information, Embedded and Communication Systems, ICIIECS 2017 (2018). https://doi.org/10.1109/ICIIECS.2017.8276061
49. Bal, A., Saha, R.: An improved method for handwritten document analysis using segmentation, baseline recognition and writing pressure detection. Procedia Comput. Sci. (2016). https://doi.org/10.1016/j.procs.2016.07.227
50. Prasad, S., Singh, V.K., Sapre, A.: Handwriting analysis based on segmentation method for prediction of human personality using support vector machine. Int. J. Comput. Appl. (2010). https://doi.org/10.5120/1256-1758

Efficient Service Selection in Multimedia Documents Adaptation Processes

Zakaria Laboudi[1]([✉]), Abdelkader Moudjari[2], Asma Saighi[1],
and Hamana Nazim Hamri[1]

[1] RELA(CS)2 Laboratory, University of Oum El-Bouaghi, Route de Constantine BP
321, 04000 Oum El-Bouaghi, DZ, Algeria
laboudi.zakaria@univ-oeb.dz
[2] MISC Laboratory, University of Constantine, 2, Nouvelle ville Ali Mendjeli BP
67A, 25100 Constantine, DZ, Algeria

Abstract. Pervasive systems help access to multimedia documents at
any time, from anywhere and through several devices (smart TV, laptop, tablet, etc.). Nevertheless, due to changes in users' contexts (e.g.
noisy environment, preferred language, public place, etc.), restrictions
on correct access to these documents may be imposed. One possible
solution is to adapt their contents using adaptation services so that they
comply, as far as possible, with the current constraints. In this respect,
several adaptation approaches have been proposed. However, when it
comes to selecting the required adaptation services, they often carry out
this task according to predefined configurations or deterministic algorithms. Actually, the efficient selection of adaptation services is one of
the key-elements involved in improving the quality of service in adaptation processes. To deal with this issue (i.e. the efficient selection of
adaptation services), we first provide an enriched problem formulation
as well as methods that we use in problem-solving. Then, we involve
standard and compact evolutionary algorithms to find efficient adaptation plans. The standard version is usually adopted in systems that are
not subject to specific constraints. The compact one is used in systems
for which constraints on computational resources and execution time are
considered. The proposal is validated through simulation, experiments
and comparisons according to performance, execution time and energy
consumption. The obtained results are satisfactory and encouraging.

Keywords: Context-aware pervasive systems · Multimedia documents
adaptation · QoS-aware adaptation service selection · Evolutionary
algorithms

1 Introduction

Pervasive computing is one of the latest emerging trends of technology. It aims at
creating an environment endowed with communication and computation capabilities. In contrast to desktop computing paradigm, pervasive systems can be

C. Djeddi et al. (Eds.): MedPRAI 2020, CCIS 1322, pp. 170–187, 2021.
https://doi.org/10.1007/978-3-030-71804-6_13

implemented in any device, in any place and at any time. This helps mobile systems to sense their environment and thus to adapt their behavior accordingly. Indeed, the technological progress is contributing in making smart devices as a way to understand the context of collected data and concern activity due to their ability to send, collect, store, process and communicate data [23]. In such cases, the context is associated with three important aspects [30]: *where you are; who you are with and what resources are nearby (smart objects, networks, etc.).*

This study focuses on efficient access to multimedia documents in context-aware pervasive systems. These documents include media objects of different natures: texts, images, audios, videos, etc. In practice, they are used in many fields such as e-learning, healthcare, news and tourism. In fact, pervasive computing can improve their presentation since it helps ensure multi/cross-device compatibility (e.g. smart TV, laptops, smartphones). In spite of this, as users' contexts are subject to changes over time, some restrictions may be imposed on proper access to these documents. One possible solution is to adapt their contents so that they conform as much as possible to the current context; below a scenario for illustration.

Sarah is a University student. In the morning, she has to go to the University and wants to consult courses through her smartphone in the bus. These documents contain a mixture of texts and illustrative videos, audios and images. Thus, she may use the cellular network, which is a paid service. The system identifies that: 1) the screen size of the smartphone is not suitable for playing the current content, 2) auditory contents should be avoided in the bus since it is a public place and 3) Sarah should avoid playing large data contents (e.g. videos) to save access to the data through Internet. Immediately, a notification is shown on Sarah's smartphone suggesting to adapt the document by enlarging and rearranging media objects, converting auditory contents into texts and using low quality media objects.

The above scenario depicts the importance of understanding the context to infer the current users' contextual constraints and thus to perform useful actions. In the literature, there exist several approaches for multimedia documents adaptation (MDA) in pervasive environments [6, 8–12, 14, 15, 17, 27–29]. In general, the adaptation processes within these approaches begin with sensing users' context information. Then, they analyze these information to identify the constraints that make the context non-compliant with the original documents' features. Finally, they infer the adaptation actions and perform them using adaptation services to provide adapted documents.

Even so, most of the existing works in the field do not address the efficient selection of services among a large set of candidates, especially when quality parameters must be taken into account (e.g. price, reliability, etc.) [6]. As discussed in [7], this aspect is a key-element for improving the quality of service (QoS) in adaptation processes. Practically speaking, when it comes to selecting a subset of required services, most of adaptation approaches, whatever their nature, often carry out this task through a pre-established selection or deterministic algorithms. Currently, the number of adaptation services has become important so that they are delivered under various forms and models. In particular, for the same functionality, there may exist many instances that differ in the technical details and non-functional features. This makes their selection difficult.

To deal with this issue, we first provide an enriched formulation to model the considered problem. This is a combinatory problem that depends on the numbers of services and providers, hence the optimization of a function over a set of values. Therefore, we involve *quantum-inspired evolutionary algorithms* since they allow both local and global search. Also, *conventional* and *compact* versions of *genetic algorithms* are used. The compact versions are adopted in systems where constraints on resources and execution time are considered. The proposal is validated through simulation, experiments and comparisons according to performance, execution time and energy consumption. Overall, the obtained results are promising and encouraging. In fact, although there are several proposals to deal with services selection in other fields (e.g. web/cloud service selection), this work is different since: 1) it uses an enriched problem formulation compared to the ones used in the literature, 2) the solving method involves compact metaheuristics. To the best of our knowledge, this is the first initiative of its kind to deal with this issue.

The remainder of this paper is organized as follows. Section 2 reviews the state-of-the-art about MDA in context-aware pervasive systems as well as the issues related to the selection of adaptation services. Section 3 provides the problem formulation of the efficient selection of adaptation services. It also gives details about the methods and algorithms proposed for problem solving. Section 4 discusses the experiments and the obtained results. Finally, Sect. 5 gives some concluding remarks and ongoing works.

2   Multimedia Documents Adaptation: State-of-the-Art

2.1   Multimedia Documents Adaptation in Pervasive Systems

MDA in context-aware pervasive systems has been the subject of much research that selects and executes adaptation services to provide adapted documents [6,8–12,14,15,17,27–29]. As reported in [23], context-aware pervasive systems include three basic elements: *sensing, thinking* and *acting*. Next, we detail these elements in the field of MDA. It should be noted that, though there exist several adaptation approaches, they differ only in the way they implement these elements and in the documents' models they deal with.

- **Sensing**: it is defined as the acquisition of data about the physical world used by the pervasive systems through sources of information like sensors and sensing devices. The context includes several sensed information that can be organized into categories [23]: **physical context** (e.g. noise level), **user context** (e.g. location), **computational context** (e.g. battery level) and **temporal context** (e.g. agenda). These information are arranged according to a context model. For more details about context modeling, the reader should refer to [33].

- **Thinking**: the information gathered from the sensors is unprocessed; it should then be analyzed further to take desired actions. The values of the context elements contribute in identifying the constraints impeding the proper execution of documents (see Table 1). The aim is to infer the conflicts for which users' contexts do not comply with documents' features, often through *"if...else"* rules; the semantic web rule language is an example [14,29]

Table 1. Typical context elements, constraints and conflicts

Context element	Value	Constraints	Conflicts
Location	Lab	Constrained place	Auditory content should be avoided
Preferred language	English	Unsuitable language	The user cannot understand the content
Current activity	Driving	Visual deficiency	Hands and eyes cannot be used properly

- **Acting**: the last step is to infer and execute adaptation actions as per the current conflicts, to provide adapted documents (see Table 2). Each action is carried out through a set of abstract tasks applied to media objects. Then, *adaptation plans* (*paths*) are built by binding each abstract task to one service from a repository of adaptation services. These latter are described by specific properties such as service id, *input/output parameters*, *action type* (e.g. transmoding, transcoding, transformation, etc.) and *quality parameters* (e.g. price, reliability, etc.), and implemented using several services' types (e.g. web and cloud services) [12].

Table 2. Description of typical adaption actions

Adaption actions	Description
Exclude audio	Converting audio objects into texts and, muting and subtitling videos
Language translation	Translating the original document from one language to another preferred by the user or to sign language for dumb persons
Voice-commands	Set of vocal commands used when users' hands cannot be used

2.2 Classification of Multimedia Adaptation Approaches

Depending on where the decision-making and adaptation actions take place, multimedia adaptation approaches are divided into four categories as well as their hybridization [6]. The choice regarding which category to use depends on many factors such as devices' computing power, the available resources, etc.

- **Server-side adaptation**: the devices playing the documents represent the client-side that sends adaptation requests to a server. This latter takes charge of the whole operation of documents adaptation (e.g. [29]).
- **Client-side adaptation**: the devices playing the documents are supposed to be able to perform the adaptation process by themselves (e.g. [8]).
- **Proxy-based adaptation**: the adaptation process involves a proxy between the client and the server which acts as a mediator (e.g. [11]).
- **Peer-to-peer adaptation**: the devices playing the multimedia documents may communicate with each other but also with several platforms, to execute adaptation services (e.g. [12]).

2.3   Adaptation Services Selection Issues

As reported in [7], the QoS in any given adaptation process is defined through an evaluation of the adaptation services according to two kinds of quality parameters: the *cost* and *benefit*. The cost depends on services' features such as pricing, response time, etc. The benefit depends on media objects' features such as image resolution, video speed, etc. Globally, the QoS relies on user's preferences and its context usage while the quality of outputs is related to the nature of objects.

By reviewing several MDA approaches, we could note that most of their QoS methods focus mainly on the benefit aspect. In other words, they do not care about the efficient selection of adaptation services according to their costs (i.e. adaptation service QoS parameters). Hence, they adopt either a pre-established selection or deterministic algorithms (e.g. [14,15,29]). Actually, a good adaptation system should not aim only at dealing with users' contexts and preferences, but also optimizing adaptation service QoS values.

Currently, multimedia services are available in different types and in large numbers, covering a wide range of features. We cite as examples Aylien APIs for media intelligence [1], MeaningCloud APIs for text processing [2], Google Cloud for media and entertainment [3] and media services on Amazon Web Services [4]. Such providers offer their services to consumers according to different models such as on-fly, on-demand, real-time, scheduled, etc. The aim is to converge towards everything as a service. This wealth has led to a significant diversity so that for the same functionality, there may exist several candidate services that differ in details and characteristics. It follows that the adaptation process should select adaptation services from a multitude of instances, those that best meet both functional and non-functional features of adaptation plans.

Much research has been done on QoS-aware service composition, in particular for web and cloud services [31,38]. It is defined as an NP-hard problem, usually modeled as a multi-choice and multi-dimension 0–1 knapsack problem. The composition process is carried out following a workflow model that involves abstract descriptions of services. The main forms of workflow structures are sequence, choice, parallel split and loop. For each abstract task, it is asked to select one concrete service among a set of candidates. Several methods are proposed to deal with this issue; we distinguish *static* and *adaptive* approaches [32].

- **Static approaches**: they perform the service composition according to a prior knowledge about QoS values without considering dynamic changes in QoS (e.g. [20,21,25,26,35,37]). They belong to three subcategories:
  - **Exact methods**: they seek optimal solutions using deterministic methods such as constraint programming and linear integer programming; however, the computational complexity does not always allow finding them.
  - **Approximate approaches**: they allow finding approximate solutions using heuristics and meta-heuristics; the particle swarm optimization and genetic algorithms are good examples.
  - **Pareto-optimization approaches**: they involve the Pareto optimality which introduces a set of potential solutions that are optimal with respect to one or more objective functions, but not all.
- **Adaptive approaches**: these approaches have extended the service composition problem to finding optimal solutions in cases where QoS values are not known prior (e.g. [22,24,34,36]). They can adapt to changes in QoS values of the service environment. These approaches belong to two subcategories:
  - **Internal composition approaches**: they react to environmental changes by rebuilding a service composition either from ground up or from the point of fault within the composite service. They use several techniques such as artificial intelligence planning techniques and reinforced learning.
  - **External composition approaches**: they use adjustable adapters that bridge the gap between the service workflow and the dynamically changing service environment. They use several techniques such as social network analysis and protocol-based approaches.

3   Contributions

This section introduces our contributions for the efficient selection of adaptation services.

3.1   Context and Motivations

This work deals with the efficient selection of adaptation services so as to improve the QoS in MDA processes. It particularly focuses on the cost aspect by considering the *price*, *response time* and *reliability*. The price depends on the budget allocated for invoking paid services. The response time is linked to the performance of services. Finally, the reliability refers to the degree of maintaining the quality regarding the network and the queries processed by services.

In fact, many researchers have embarked on a frantic race to apply optimization methods to services' selection paradigm. Certainly, this is a key-element but it should not be an end in itself; because, what is more important is to put such algorithms in contexts. In this line of thinking, our work aims at integrating the optimization of service selection within an adaptation system. As part of ongoing works, we are working on designing a generic architecture that can be adapted to a wide range of the approaches discussed above. To do so, we involve Multi-Agents Systems (MAS) to model the three basic elements of context-aware pervasive systems. Indeed, MAS are a very good tool for the effective management of environmental changes, in particular *sensing, perception, adaptability, communication, autonomy, cooperation, negotiation, intentionality* and *distribution*. These features are advantageous for context-aware pervasive systems that involve properties such as *proactiveness, context understanding (surrounding), smartness, mobility, cross-platform, self-tuning, adaptation, etc..* The idea consists in placing the agents depending on the approach's category adopted while keeping the same communication protocols between them. The service selection methods will then be used once the negotiation process between the providers and consumers agents is finished.

The main contributions of this paper are summarized as follows:

1. *An enriched problem formulation* in the light of the objectives sought as well as solving methods that meet the problem definition. Starting from the fact that existing formulations of the services selection paradigm deal with QoS parameters through benchmarks or probability distributions (simulation) (e.g. [20,25,34,36]), our formulation reinforces the problem definition by modeling the offers provided by services' providers. This is an influential aspect since it reflects many real-world situations in practice. It is noteworthy that, as the present work does not depend on any specific approach, only sequential composition workflows are considered. The other models can be transformed into the sequential model using transformation techniques [18].

2. *Synthetic methods* for generating adaptation service QoS values according to scenarios based on the degree of competition amongst adaptation services providers. This makes the problem modeling closer to real-world situations; especially that it still lacks benchmarks for making tests and comparisons. Indeed, there are currently few tools dedicated to the description of adaptation services [7]. In fact, most of existing works that deal with the services selection paradigm generate datasets (QoS values) through probability distributions or benchmarks without considering the correlation between these values (e.g. [20,25,34,36]). We argue then that the proposed synthetic methods allow dealing with large, dynamic and various datasets leading to more reliable and deeper analysis and comparisons between solving-methods. On another side, although benchmarks enable making comparisons between solving-methods performances, they allow, however, dealing only with a set of predefined values for QoS parameters. Thus, synthetic methods may be more suitable for solving-methods analysis comparing to benchmarks.

3. *Optimization methods* for providing a composition of services that converges towards the optimal adaptation paths. Depending on the adaptation approach category, the adaptation services' selection may be performed either by the devices playing the documents or by remote machines. Unlike most of existing services selection methods that focus mainly on optimizing the cost function, in the context of adaptation services selection, further vital concerns

should be taken into account such as the available computational resources and execution time constraints. For instance, although Pareto optimization approaches are expected to achieve better results, they are however unsuitable for devices endowed with limited computational resources since they are generally CPU-time and memory consuming operations. This leads us to care about three aspects: performance, execution time and energy consumption. Accordingly, approximate approaches are more suitable since they vary from local to global search methods using one or multiple solutions, unlike Pareto optimization that considers only the global search. Thus, it is useful to compare between several approximate approaches according to the number of solutions they deal with. In such a context, evolutionary algorithms may excel since they are one of the most adopted approaches for web and cloud service selection [31, 38], in particular that they include both standard and compact versions. The former deal with many solutions; thus, they run generally on systems that are not subject to specific constraints. The latter deal with very few number of solutions; thus they can run on systems for which constraints on resources (CPU, memory, battery, etc.) and execution time are considered. They also show a simplicity of implementation and ease in setting parameters [19]. In fact, the current number of optimization methods is very large. It would then be possible for us to consider other approaches expect that the time constraints did not allow us to test them all. We keep this point for future works.

3.2 Problem Statement and Modeling

Now, we formulate the problem of efficient selection of adaptation services. For this purpose, we adopt some of the basic concepts and notations used in [18].

1. *Service class*: we denote by $S = \{S_1, S_2, \ldots, S_k\}$ the set of k abstract tasks composing the *abstract composite service* (ACS) inferred by the adaptation process, where $S_{i=\{1..k\}} \in S$ refers to a single task;
2. *Concrete service*: each abstract task $S_i \in S$ represents a functionality that can be implemented by one concrete service among a subset of candidates, denoted by $I_i = cs_{ij}$, from the repository of all available adaptation services. The concrete composite service (CCS) (adaptation path) is an instance of the ACS that binds each abstract task $S_i \in S$ to a concrete service $cs_{ij} \in I_i$.
3. *Service provider*: Each concrete service $cs_{ij} \in I_{i=1..k}$ comes from one and only one provider. The set of all providers is denoted by $P = \{P_1, P_2, \ldots, P_m\}$, where m is the number of providers. For each provider $P_{u=1..m}$, the adaptation services offered are grouped into a set denoted by $SP_u = \{csp_{uv}\}$.
4. *QoS criteria*: three non-functional criteria are considered: the price, response time and reliability. For any given concrete service $cs_{ij} \in I_{i=1..k,}$, these criteria are defined as a vector $Q(cs_{ij}) = [q_p(cs_{ij}), q_t(cs_{ij}), q_r(cs_{ij})]$, which represents the price, response time and reliability, respectively. The QoS criteria of the CCS are defined as a vector $Q(CCS) = [q_p(CCS), q_t(CCS), q_r(CCS)]$ representing the price, response time and reliability, respectively.

5. *Fitness functions*: it aims at finding the optimal CCS by selecting services that minimize functions $f_{p,t}$ and maximize f_r, as given in equations (1,2,3):

$$f_{p,t}(x) = \sum_{i=i}^{K} \sum_{cs_{ij} \in I_i} x_{ij} \times q_{p,t}(x_{ij}) - g_{p,t}(x) \tag{1}$$

with $g_{p,t}(x) = \sum_{u=1}^{m} g_u(x)$

$$f_r(x) = \prod_{i=1}^{k} \sum_{cs_{ij} \in I_i} x_{ij} \times q_r(cs_{ij}) \tag{2}$$

Subject to:

$$f_{p,t}(x) \leq C_{max}, \ f_r(x) \geq R_{min} \ and \ \sum_{cs_{ij} \in I_i} x_{ij} \leq 1 \tag{3}$$

where $x = ((x_{11}, x_{12}, \ldots, x_{1|I_i|}), (x_{21}, x_{22}, \ldots, x_{2|I_i|}), \ldots, (x_{1k}, x_{2k}, \ldots, x_{k|I_k|}))$, $x_{ij} \in \{0, 1\}$ indicates the absence / presence of concrete services $c_{ij} \in I_{i=1..k}$ in the CCS. $C_{max} \in \{P_{max}, T_{max}\}$ is a maximum cost for the price and response time not to be exceeded while R_{min} is a minimum lower bound for the reliability. In addition, to each provider $P_{u=1..m}$ is assigned an extra profit, denoted by $g_{u=1..m}$. It is earned in accordance with the price and response time of services $csp_{uv} \in SP_{u=1..m}$; details are given on Sect. 3.3. For example, if the consumer invokes multiple services coming from provider P_u, this latter may make reduction on the total price or offer more resources and privileges to improve the response time. This increases the degree of competition amongst the providers. To evaluate the quality of the CCS, the *Simple Additive Weighting (SAW)* technique is used [18]. It converts vector $Q(CCS)$ into a single normalized real value as follows:

$$w_1 \frac{Q_{max\_p}(ACS) - f_p(x)}{Q_{max\_p}(ACS)} + w_2 \frac{Q_{max\_t}(ACS) - f_t(x)}{Q_{max\_t}(ACS)} + w_3 \frac{f_r(x) - Q_{min\_r}(ACS)}{1 - Q_{min\_r}(ACS)} \tag{4}$$

Where $w_1 + w_2 + w_3 = 1$.

Q_{max} and Q_{min} represent the minimum and maximum values of QoS criteria in all possible instances of the ACS, calculated as shown in equations (5,6).

$$Q_{min\_r} = \prod_{i=1}^{k} min_{cs_{ij} \in I_{i=1..k}} q_p \times (CS_{ij}) \tag{5}$$

$$Q_{max\_p,t} = \sum_{i=1}^{k} max_{cs_{ij} \in I_{i=1..k}} q_{p,t} \times (CS_{ij}) \tag{6}$$

3.3   Solving Methods

For large problem's instances, approximate and Pareto optimization approaches
are more suitable. In this case, for each candidate solution x, functions $f_{p,t,r}$
are calculated according to a vector x' obtained through a repair function. This
latter withdraws some concrete services from vector x until the constraints on
price, response time and reliability become satisfied (P_{max}, T_{max} and R_{min}).
Two repair methods are proposed: *random repair* and *greedy repair*.

– **Random repair (*Rep1*):** the repair function withdraws randomly concrete
  services from vector x as much as necessary until there is no cost overrun.
– **Greedy repair (*Rep2*):** the repair function withdraws concrete service cs_{ij}
  which maximizes $|Q(x) - Q(x')|$. The process is repeated as much as necessary
  until there is no cost overrun. In this way, we keep a maximum number of
  services hoping that we provide good quality adapted documents.

All that remains is to define the gain function g. Three methods are proposed:
No gain, the gain based on exemption and *the gain based on cost reduction.*

– **No gain:** Providers do not offer any benefit based on the services requested.
– **The gain based on exemption (buy n, get one free):** each provider
  $P_u \in P$ may make exemptions by offering the lower-cost service for free if the
  customer requests more than n services from set SP_u.
– **The gain based on cost reduction (buy n, benefit from cost reduction):** each provider $P_u \in P$ may offer a discount (cost reductions) for the
  customer according to a rate $DR \in [0, 1]$ if more than n services are requested
  from set SP_u.

3.4   Synthetic Methods to Simulate Adaptation Service QoS Values

To simulate adaptation service QoS values, we need methods to generate them.
To this end, we inspire from the methods used in studying the knapsack problem
[16]. The difficulty of problem-solving depends on the number of abstract tasks
and the available concrete services. It also depends on the degree of correlation
between QoS values; the more they are correlated (i.e. close each other's), the
more the problem-solving is expected to be difficult. In addition, if each provider
offers multiple concrete services to consumers, then the selection will be even
more difficult since it leads competitive offers between providers.

Three types of correlations between adaptation service QoS values are proposed: *uncorrelated costs, weakly correlated costs* and *strongly correlated costs*,
as given on Table 3. Let r and v be two positive parameters chosen empirically.
Also, let $q_{p_i=1..k}$, $q_{t_i=1..k}$ and $q_{r_i=1..k}$ be random values generated following a
uniform distribution over the interval $[1, v]$ (denoted by uniform $(1, v)$).

Higher correlation leads to smaller value for the difference: $(max_{i=1..k}$
$\{q_{p,t,r}(cs_{ij})\}$ - $min_{i=1..k}\{q_{p,t,r}(cs_{ij})\})$, and thus for the standard deviation. Note
that in the case of *weak correlation 1*, the price, response time and reliability
of concrete services $cs_{ij} \in I_{i=1..k}$ related to each abstract task $S_{i=1..k} \in S$ are

Table 3. Synthetic methods for generating adaptation service QoS values

Correlation types	Price $q_p(cs_{ij})$	Response time $q_t(cs_{ij})$	Reliability $q_r(cs_{ij})$
Uncorrelated	uniform $(1, v)$	uniform $(1, v)$	uniform $(1, v)/v$
Weak correlation 1	q_{p_i} $+ uniform(-r, r)$	$q_{t\_i} +$ $uniform(-r, r)$	$q_{r\_i} +$ uniform $(-r, r)/(v + r)$
Weak correlation 2	–	$q_p(cs_{ij}) +$ $uniform(-r, r)$	$q_p(cs_{ij}) +$ $uniform(-r, r)/(q_p(cs_{ij}) + r)$
Strong correlation	–	$q_p(cs_{ij}) + r$	$q_p(cs_{ij}) +$ $r/(q_p(cs_{ij}) +$ $r + uniform(0, r))$
Constraints types	$Pmax$	$Tmax$	$Rmin$
Unbounded cost (C_{max1})	$+\infty$	$+\infty$	0
Average cost (C_{max2})	$\frac{1}{2}Q_{max\_p}(CCS)$	$\frac{1}{2}Q_{max\_t}(CCS)$	$\sqrt{Q_{min\_r}(CCS)}$

weakly correlated. In the case of *weak correlation 2* and *strong correlation*, the response time and reliability of any given concrete service cs_{ij} are correlated with its price.

On another side, by using the *unbounded cost* option, the solution will include all concrete services requested (there will be no constraints on costs). Otherwise, it will include about half of the services selected, which influences negatively on the adapted content with respect to the current context.

3.5   Finding Approximate Solutions Using Evolutionary Algorithms

Evolutionary algorithms (*EA*) are a class of meta-heuristics that have proven to be effective for finding approximate solutions to several optimization problems. They deal with populations of candidate solutions (individuals) encoded in accordance with the current problem. The evolution process follows an iterative procedure where at each iteration, the individuals are evaluated according to a fitness function, selected and recombined in order to generate new population. The subclasses of EA differ in the way they encode the individuals as well as in the way they implement the selection and recombination operators.

In the present work, three EAs are used: *quantum-inspired evolutionary algorithms (QIEA)* [16], *genetic algorithms (GA)* [16] and *compact genetic algorithms (CGA)* [19]. QEIAs combine principles inspired from EA and quantum computing. They encode the solutions as quantum registers composed of qubits (superposition of states), which is, in fact, a probabilistic model. The recombination of individuals is performed through quantum operators such as the measure and the interference. QIEAs allow both local and global search over solutions' spaces (they can work on populations of size ranging from one to many solutions). GAs are based on principles inspired from natural selection and modern genetics theories. They encode the individuals as chromosomes that are recombined through crossover and mutation operators. Unlike standard GAs, a CGA uses estimated probability density functions to manipulate a virtual population encoded as a probability vector, which represents in fact a compacted population of size N_p. At each iteration, two chromosomes are randomly generated using the probability vector and evaluated. The pair of individuals *[winner, loser]* is then used to update the probability vector. To further improve the performances, we propose to apply the crossover and mutation operators to the pair *[winner, loser]*. Details about these EAs are omitted for space reasons (further details can be found in [16,19]).

Each candidate solution $x = ((x_{11},..,x_{1|I_i|}),(x_{21},..,x_{2|I_i|}),..,(x_{1k},..,x_{k|I_k|}))$, $x_{ij} \in \{0,1\}$ is encoded as a binary chromosome composed of k genes; k is the number of abstract tasks in the inferred ACS [21]. Each gene $g_{i=1..k}$ corresponds to service class S_i. The length of gene g_i depends on the number of services in set I_i. Each chromosome is evaluated according to the formulas and methods presented above. The structure of chromosomes allows building quantum registers and probability vectors that keep the same form by substituting only every bit by a qubit and a probability value, as shown in Fig. 1.

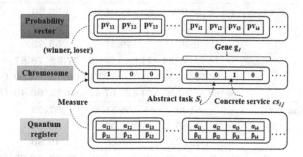

Fig. 1. Individuals encoding for GA, CGA and QIEA.

4   Experiments, Numerical Results and Discussion

Our proposal is validated by making experiments, gathering the results and analyzing them. For this purpose, four instances of EA - denoted by $\#GA$, $\#CGA$, $\#QIEA_1$ and $\#QIEA_2$ - are executed for a sufficient number of runs (over 50 runs) by covering all possible cases. Each of them is iterated for a maximum number of 100 iterations. We mention that by performing more than 50 runs, this made no difference. The hardware and software configurations are as follows: laptop endowed with *i7 3537U CPU (2.5 GHz)* and *8 Gb* of memory, the Java language and the Eclipse IDE. The parameters settings are given below.

- **Optimization problem parameters**: number of abstract tasks $k = 8$; number of concrete services $nb = 70$; number of providers $m = 15$; $v = 10$; $r = 5$; $w_{i=1..3} = 0.5$, 0.4 and 0.1, respectively; the gain is based on cost reduction with discount rates $DR_{p,t}$ generated as uniform $(0.1, 0.2)$; threshold for discounting $n = 3$.
- $\#QIEA_{1,2}$ **parameters**: the population size N_p is equal to 5 for $\#QIEA_1$ and to 1 for $\#QIEA_2$. The initial amplitudes of qubits (α_i, β_i) are set to $\sqrt{1/2}$. The interference operator is the same as in [13].

– #CGA and #GA **parameters**: both virtual and real populations are of size $N_p = 52$. In addition, instances #CGA and #GA use elitist selection, one cut-point crossover, swap mutation with rate of 2% and total replacement.

The parameters settings were configured experimentally. In fact, by executing several instances that differed in parameters' values and scenarios regarding providers' gain policies, the results did not show us any improvements. Tables 4 and 5 show the fitness and execution times for each EA instance; b, m and w refer to *best*, *mean* and *worst* results recorded over the 50 runs, respectively.

Table 4. Performances of GA, CGA and QIEA (%).

Correlation	Cost type		#GA		#CGA		#$QIEA_1$		#$QIEA_2$	
			Rep1	Rep2	Rep1	Rep2	Rep1	Rep2	Rep1	Rep2
No correlation	C_{max1}	b	58.03		58.04		**59.83**		57.77	
		m	51.09		53.40		**56.97**		53.81	
		w	46.37		49.84		**53.22**		49.62	
	C_{max2}	b	74.71	76.83	74.06	77.68	**77.68**	**78.87**	74.54	77.68
		m	64.59	65.80	68.79	72.93	**69.72**	**73.80**	65.81	69.14
		w	60.46	61.97	64.12	67.47	**64.72**	**66.40**	60.58	61.59
Weak-correlation 1	C_{max1}	b	53.32		56.31		**57.26**		55.56	
		m	46.86		50.36		**53.27**		50.39	
		w	42.82		46.58		**49.80**		46.63	
	C_{max2}	b	76.19	78.58	76.59	78.58	**77.90**	**78.92**	76.84	**78.92**
		m	66.93	69.38	71.07	73.40	**72.13**	**76.85**	68.68	73.15
		w	61.38	64.35	66.58	69.23	**67.24**	**72.39**	63.48	67.00
Weak-correlation 2	C_{max1}	b	58.67		59.84		**62.18**		60.96	
		m	52.84		56.03		**58.98**		55.96	
		w	48.25		53.32		**56.65**		52.31	
	C_{max2}	b	79.83	83.87	82.74	**84.09**	83.87	**84.09**	**84.09**	**84.09**
		m	69.17	77.71	75.74	81.45	**77.34**	**82.92**	70.84	80.94
		w	59.71	71.71	69.30	77.96	**70.32**	**80.22**	64.69	77.08
Strong correlation	C_{max1}	b	54.66		57.45		**61.63**		59.63	
		m	45.29		50.50		**56.41**		51.66	
		w	39.75		44.90		**51.22**		40.37	
	C_{max2}	b	81.58	**85.49**	81.63	84.87	**83.98**	**85.49**	83.01	**85.49**
		m	68.79	79.02	75.44	82.73	**77.52**	**84.46**	70.89	82.21
		w	62.49	71.05	**69.59**	79.25	69.47	**82.38**	64.03	75.45

Table 5. Execution time for GA, CGA and QIEA (recorded in seconds)

Correlation	Cost type		#GA		#CGA		#QIEA$_1$		#QIEA$_2$	
			Rep1	Rep2	Rep1	Rep2	Rep1	Rep2	Rep1	Rep2
No correlation	C_{max1}	b	0.1880		0.0280		0.0340		0.0060	
		m	0.1948		0.0300		0.0359		0.0070	
		w	0.2250		0.0490		0.0410		0.0080	
	C_{max2}	b	0.2530	1.8630	0.0360	0.3200	0.0440	0.3900	0.0090	0.0770
		m	0.2618	2.0552	0.0382	0.3335	0.0466	0.4203	0.0093	0.0863
		w	0.2920	2.5520	0.0430	0.3500	0.0520	0.4590	0.0110	0.0960

Discussion and Analysis

Table 4 shows that CGA and $QIEA$ perform better than GA, with a preference to #$QIEA_1$. By analyzing the behavior of these algorithms, it was found that the probabilistic models of CGA and $QIEA$ are more suitable for the exploration and exploitation of the search space. Table 4 draws also our attention to the effect of the repair mechanisms on the evolutionary process within all EAs. Indeed, one can compare the results obtained when considering C_{max1} (repair methods are not used since the costs are unbounded) and C_{max2} (repair methods are involved since the costs are restricted) in all correlation methods. In particular, the greedy repair shows more efficiency than random repair since the services are selectively withdrawn. We point out that, in the case of C_{max1}, the fitness is negatively influenced by the reliability value that decreases when the number of selected services grows.

Overall, the execution time for GA is greater than for CGA and $QIEA$. This is expected since the number of individuals evaluated at each iteration is about of $N_p/2$ while #CGA and #$QIEA_1$ deal only with 4 and 5 individuals, respectively; especially that the largest portion of the execution time has elapsed in the evaluation phase. Another observation is that the execution time in greedy repair method is greater than in random repair. This is because the greedy repair makes many tests before withdrawing services, which increases the computational complexity.

Regarding the energy consumption (E), Abdelhafez et al. showed in a recent work [5] that for sequential GAs, it is directly proportional to time (T) and power (P): $E \approx P \times T$. According to Table 5, one observes that: $T_{GA} \approx a \times TC_{GA} \approx b \times T_{QIEA_1} \approx c \times T_{QIEA_2}$; a, b and c are constants greater than 1. As a result, the energy consumption can be rewritten as follows: $E_{GA} \approx a \times E_{CGA} \approx b \times E_{QIEA_1} \approx c \times T_{QIEA_2}$. Undoubtedly, CGA and $QIEA$ may really consume less energy compared to GA.

In view of the foregoing, #CGA and #$QIEA$ are more efficient than #GA while consuming less energy and computational resources. This makes them suitable to the adaptation approaches categories discussed above, in particular when these algorithms are performed by mobile and battery-based devices. Actually, we could not do more in-depth analysis due to space reasons.

Finally, we assess our proposal against other research-works. Unfortunately, the performances of our algorithms could not be compared with other approaches due to the lack of benchmarks. In addition, the adopted problem formulation is different. The main advantages are summarized as follows:

- Most of existing approaches dedicated to services selection paradigm target mainly the optimization of QoS parameters and the improvement of execution time (see for instance [20,25,26,34–36]). This is necessary but not sufficient on its own. For instance, the authors in [26] have made a comparative study of many-objective evolutionary algorithms for efficient composition of QoS-aware web services. Even though these approaches could achieve better results, the excessive computational cost could still limit the general adoption of such algorithms, in particular for devices endowed with limited computational resources. Thus, our proposal considers further aspects such as the available computational resources and time constraints which are essential in the context of MDA.
- Although there are several works applying metaheuristics for problems dealing with energy minimization in a target scenario such as energy consumption of web and cloud services (e.g. [35]), very few works focus on analyzing energy consumption of metaheuristics themselves [5]. This is relevant for green computing since the adaptation services' selection may be frequently performed by MDA processes, especially when the number of users grows.
- The proposal can be viewed as a complementary element to existing MDA approaches since most of them do not take into account the cost aspect.
- The proposal shows adaptability insofar as it treats the service selection problem at a high level of abstraction, regardless of any specific approach.
- The proposal is flexible since it allows several options for selecting adaptation services in accordance with the available computational resources.
  Our proposal shows also some limitations which are recapped as follows:
- The proposed methods belong to static service selection approaches and thus they do not show adaptation to changes in QoS values over time.
- The collection of services involves the creation of a repository that must be maintained continuously. This may require service discovery mechanisms.

Nevertheless, as this study has not yet reached its end, we plan to overcome these limitations using MAS, which is actually a work that we have already started.

5   Conclusion

The aim of this paper was to propose new mechanisms for the efficient selection of adaptation services used by MDA processes. For this purpose, the problem was first modeled as an optimization problem following an enriched formulation. Then, synthetic methods are proposed to generate QoS values due to the lack of benchmarks. Finally, standard and compact versions of evolutionary algorithms are used in order to efficiently select adaptation paths according to price, response time and reliability of services. The proposal was validated through simulations and experiments. The numerical results showed us that CGA and QIEA are more efficient than GA in terms of performance and execution time while consuming less energy and computational resources.

Currently, we are working on design a generic MAS-based architecture that can be configured to several adaptation approaches. The agent paradigm is involved to model the elements of context-aware pervasive systems namely *sensing, thinking* and *acting* as well as the efficient management of adaptation services. We will also perform more experiments by implementing, analyzing and comparing several services selection approaches ranging from Pareto-based to exact methods, with a special focus on those involving MAS to deal with changes in services' environments (e.g. [25,37]).

Acknowledgments. We would like to thank the Direction Generale de la Recherche Scientifique et du Developpement Technologique (DGRSDT) in Algeria, for supporting this research work. Also, the authors would like to thank Dr. Amer Draa from MISC Laboratory - University of Constantine 2, Algeria, for the feedback and discussions on optimization concerns and issues.

References

1. https://aylien.com/media-monitoring-api/
2. https://www.meaningcloud.com/
3. https://cloud.google.com/solutions/media-entertainment
4. https://aws.amazon.com/fr/media-services/
5. Abdelhafez, A., Alba, E., Luque, G.: A component-based study of energy consumption for sequential and parallel genetic algorithms. J. Supercomput. **75**(10), 6194–6219 (2019). https://doi.org/10.1007/s11227-019-02843-4
6. Adel, A., Philippe, R., Sébastien, L.: Multimedia documents adaptation based on semantic multi-partite social context-aware networks. Int. J. Virtual Commun. Soc. Netw. (IJVCSN) **9**(3), 44–59 (2017)
7. Adel, A., Sébastien, L., Philippe, R.: Enrich the expressiveness of multimedia document adaptation processes. In: Semantic Multimedia Analysis and Processing, pp. 185–218. CRC Press (2017)
8. Belhadad, Y., Refoufi, A., Roose, P.: Spatial reasoning about multimedia document for a profile based adaptation. Multimedia Tools Appl. **77**(23), 30437–30474 (2018). https://doi.org/10.1007/s11042-018-6080-8
9. Bettou, F., Boufaida, M.: An adaptation architecture dedicated to personalized management of multimedia documents. Int. J. Multimedia Data Eng. Manage. (IJMDEM) **8**(1), 21–41 (2017)
10. Derdour, M., Roose, P., Dalmau, M., Ghoualmi-Zine, N.: An adaptation platform for multimedia applications CSC (component, service, connector). J. Syst. Inf. Technol. **14**(1), 4–22 (2012)
11. Dromzée, C., Laborie, S., Roose, P.: A semantic generic profile for multimedia document adaptation. In: Intelligent Multimedia Technologies for Networking Applications: Techniques and Tools: Techniques and Tools, pp. 225–246 (2013)
12. Hai, Q.P., Laborie, S., Roose, P.: On-the-fly multimedia document adaptation architecture. Procedia Comput. Sci. **10**, 1188–1193 (2012)

13. Han, K.H., Kim, J.H.: Quantum-inspired evolutionary algorithm for a class of combinatorial optimization. IEEE Trans. Evol. Comput. **6**(6), 580–593 (2002)
14. Jannach, D., Leopold, K.: Knowledge-based multimedia adaptation for ubiquitous multimedia consumption. J. Netw. Comput. Appl. **30**(3), 958–982 (2007)
15. Khallouki, H., Bahaj, M.: Multimedia documents adaptive platform using multi-agent system and mobile ubiquitous environment. In: 2017 Intelligent Systems and Computer Vision (ISCV), pp. 1–5. IEEE (2017)
16. Laboudi, Z., Chikhi, S.: Comparison of genetic algorithm and quantum genetic algorithm. Int. Arab J. Inf. Technol. **9**(3), 243–249 (2012)
17. Lakehal, A., Alti, A., Laborie, S., Philippe, R.: Ontology-based context-aware recommendation approach for dynamic situations enrichment. In: 2018 13th International Workshop on Semantic and Social Media Adaptation and Personalization (SMAP), pp. 81–86. IEEE (2018)
18. Le, D.-N., Nguyen, G.N.: A new ant-based approach for optimal service selection with E2E QoS constraints. In: Intan, R., Chi, C.-H., Palit, H.N., Santoso, L.W. (eds.) ICSIIT 2015. CCIS, vol. 516, pp. 98–109. Springer, Heidelberg (2015). https://doi.org/10.1007/978-3-662-46742-8_9
19. Lee, J.Y., Kim, M.S., Lee, J.J.: Compact genetic algorithms using belief vectors. Appl. Soft Comput. **11**(4), 3385–3401 (2011)
20. Li, C., Li, J., Chen, H.: A meta-heuristic-based approach for QoS-aware service composition. IEEE Access **8**, 69579–69592 (2020)
21. Li, Y., Yao, X., Liu, M.: Cloud manufacturing service composition optimization with improved genetic algorithm. Math. Probl. Eng. NA **2019**, 1–19 (2019)
22. Liu, J.W., Hu, L.Q., Cai, Z.Q., Xing, L.N., Tan, X.: Large-scale and adaptive service composition based on deep reinforcement learning. J. Vis. Commun. Image Represent. **65**, 102687 (2019)
23. Mahalle, P.N., Dhotre, P.S.: Context-aware pervasive systems. Context-Aware Pervasive Systems and Applications. ISRL, vol. 169, pp. 49–66. Springer, Singapore (2020). https://doi.org/10.1007/978-981-32-9952-8_3
24. Medeiros Campos, G.M., Souto Rosa, N., Ferreira Pires, L.: Adaptive service composition based on runtime verification of formal properties. In: Proceedings of the 50th Hawaii International Conference on System Sciences (2017)
25. Naseri, A., Navimipour, N.J.: A new agent-based method for QoS-aware cloud service composition using particle swarm optimization algorithm. J. Ambient Intell. Hum. Comput. **10**(5), 1851–1864 (2019). https://doi.org/10.1007/s12652-018-0773-8
26. Ramírez, A., Parejo, J.A., Romero, J.R., Segura, S., Ruiz-Cortés, A.: Evolutionary composition of QoS-aware web services: a many-objective perspective. Expert Syst. Appl. **72**, 357–370 (2017)
27. Saighi, A., Laboudi, Z.: A novel self-organizing multi agent-based approach for multimedia documents adaptation. In: 2020 International Conference on Electrical, Communication, and Computer Engineering (ICECCE), pp. 1–6. IEEE (2020)
28. Saighi, A., Laboudi, Z., Roose, P., Laborie, S., Ghoualmi-Zine, N.: On using multiple disabilities profiles to adapt multimedia documents: a novel graph-based method. Int. J. Inf. Technol. Web Eng. (IJITWE) **15**(3), 34–60 (2020)
29. Saighi, A., Philippe, R., Ghoualmi, N., Laborie, S., Laboudi, Z.: HaMA: a handicap-based architecture for multimedia document adaptation. Int. J. Multimedia Data Eng. Manage.(IJMDEM) **8**(3), 55–96 (2017)
30. Schilit, B., Adams, N., Want, R.: Context-aware computing applications. In: 1994 First Workshop on Mobile Computing Systems and Applications, pp. 85–90. IEEE (1994)

31. She, Q., Wei, X., Nie, G., Chen, D.: QoS-aware cloud service composition: a systematic mapping study from the perspective of computational intelligence. Expert Syst. Appl. **138**, 112804 (2019)
32. Shehu, U.G., Epiphaniou, G., Safdar, G.A.: A survey of QoS-aware web service composition techniques. Int. J. Comput. Appl. **89**, 10–17 (2014)
33. Strang, T., Linnhoff-Popien, C.: A context modeling survey. In: Workshop on Advanced Context Modelling Reasoning and Management (2004)
34. Thangaraj, P., Balasubramanie, P.: Meta heuristic QoS based service composition for service computing. J. Ambient Intell. Hum. Comput., 1–7 (2020). https://doi.org/10.1007/s12652-020-02083-y
35. Wang, S., Zhou, A., Bao, R., Chou, W., Yau, S.S.: Towards green service composition approach in the cloud. IEEE Trans. Serv. Comput. **99**, 1–14 (2018)
36. Yuan, Y., Zhang, W., Zhang, X., Zhai, H.: Dynamic service selection based on adaptive global QoS constraints decomposition. Symmetry **11**(3), 403 (2019)
37. Zertal, S., Batouche, M., Laboudi, Z.: A novel hybrid optimization-based approach for efficient development of business-applications in cloud. Int. J. Inf. Syst. Serv. Sect. (IJISSS) **12**(4), 14–35 (2020)
38. Zhao, X., Li, R., Zuo, X.: Advances on QoS-aware web service selection and composition with nature-inspired computing. CAAI Trans. Intell. Technol. **4**(3), 159–174 (2019)

Offline Writer Identification Based on CLBP and VLBP

Faycel Abbas[1,2(✉)], Abdeljalil Gattal[1], Chawki Djeddi[1], Ameur Bensefia[3], Akhtar Jamil[4], and Kamel Saoudi[5]

[1] Department of Mathematics and Computer Science, Larbi Tebessi University, Tebessa, Algeria
{faycel.abbas,abdeljalil.gattal,c.djeddi}@univ-tebessa.dz
[2] LIMPAF Laboratory, Computer Sciences Department, Faculty of Sciences and Applied Sciences, Mohand Akli University, Bouira, Algeria
[3] Higher Colleges of Technology, CIS Division, Abu Dhabi, UAE
abensefia@hct.ac.ae
[4] Department of Computer Engineering, Istanbul Sabahattin Zaim University, Istanbul, Turkey
akhtar.jamil@izu.edu.tr
[5] Department of Electrical Engineering, Mohand Akli University, Bouira, Algeria
k.saoudi@univ-bouira.dz

Abstract. Writer identification from handwriting is still considered to be challenging task due to homogeneous vision comparing writer of handwritten documents. This paper presents a new method based on two LBPs kinds: Complete Local Binary Patterns (CLBP) and Local Binary Pattern Variance (LBPV) for extracting the features from handwriting documents. The feature vector is then normalized using Probability Density Function (PDF). Classifications are based on the minimization of a similarity criteria based on a distance between two features vectors. A series of evaluations using different combinations of distances metrics are realized high identification rates which are compared with the methods that are participated in the ICDAR 2013 competition.

Keywords: Writer identification · CLBP · LBPV · PDF · Distances metrics

1 Introduction

Document analysis and classification has been an interesting research area for many decades and has attracted a large number of applications including writer identification, writer retrieval, gender classification and many more. Writer identification has been an active field of research and a number of systems realizing promising results have been reported in the literature. Consequently, a number of studies have investigated the correlation between handwriting of writer. Among these, writer identification and verification from handwriting has been most widely studied and also makes the subject of our presented research.

© Springer Nature Switzerland AG 2021
C. Djeddi et al. (Eds.): MedPRAI 2020, CCIS 1322, pp. 188–199, 2021.
https://doi.org/10.1007/978-3-030-71804-6_14

In this paper, we will mainly focus on writer identification which is finding the writer of a query document comparing it with a set of writers known by the system.

Furthermore, in writer identification, there may exist large differences in the handwriting according the writing style such as the existence of noise, variability and variation in handwriting and the limited amount of handwriting images.

In the past few years, various researchers have been proposed a wide variety of features to identify the writer of a questioned document. Usually, we can categorize the writer identification approaches based on different features such as LBP, LTP [1], LPQ [2], curvature features [3], RootSIFT descriptors [4] into two main categories: The text-independent methods identify the writer of a document independent of its semantic content. On the other hand, the text samples to be compared are required to be containing the same fixed content in text-dependent methods. The text-dependent researches on writer recognition are principally motivated by forensic applications; one of the most comprehensive studies in this area has been presented in [5, 10].

Numerous competitions with the objective to identify the handwriting were organized at well-known conferences such as the International Conference on Document Analysis and Recognition (ICDAR) and the International Conference on Frontiers in Handwriting Recognition (ICFHR). However, the competition on Writer Identification using the English and Greek handwriting samples have been held in conjunction with ICDAR 2013 [11]. This paper analyses how current state-of-the-art methods in Writer Identification perform on handwritten document dataset of ICDAR 2013 competition [11]. The best method in this competition named "CS-UMD-a" is used the gradients taken from the contour of the segments of words spliced by sewing cuts to form a feature vector. In the next step, features are grouped together to find a representative character set. The similarity is determined by the use of feature vectors sets taken from the cluster centers from two images.

The proposed system ranked first used different configurations of Complete Local Binary Patterns (CLBP) and Local Binary Pattern Variance (LBPV), and various combinations of distances metrics to identify writer from handwriting document. Hence, the features vectors normalized using Probability Density Function (PDF). The proposed system uses a leave-one-out strategy for ranking according to the similarity between two handwritings. An overview of the proposed method is illustrated in (Fig. 1). A detailed comparison and analysis of results of these competitions and those realized by the proposed technique is presented in Sect. 3.

The rest of the paper is organized as follows. We first present some of the most relevant works in the writer identification approaches. Second, we discuss the feature employed in our study, followed by the handwritten document matching mechanism. Section 5 details the experiment conducted along with a comparative analysis and discussion on the realized results. Finally, we conclude the paper with a discussion on future perspectives on the subject.

2   Related Work

Different literature reviews have been conducted in the field of writer identification [12], where the handwriting variability and its impact on both the writer recognition task and text recognition task have been discussed [13]. Under the umbrella of the writer recognition, two main approaches exist: Identification task and the verification (authentication) task. In the identification task, the system takes as input a handwriting sample and must associate it to an identity from those registered in the system; at the opposite in the verification task, the system takes two handwriting samples and must decide if they have been written by the same hand or not. In this section we will discuss some works conducted in the writer identification task.

All the writer identification approaches reported in the literature converge in the same structure, articulated around a feature's extraction module and a decision module. The role of the pre-processing module, when it is present, is limited to image binarization and connected component extraction.

The central module, where divergences can be observed between the different writer identification approaches is the features' extraction module, where the features used can be classified into local features(structural) and global(textural) features.

Textural features have been considered in [2] where the authors have extracted, from handwriting blocks, features based on Local Binary Patterns (LBP) and Local Phase Quantization (LPQ). The approach was evaluated on the IAM dataset and the Brazilian Forensic Letter (BFL) dataset with an SVM classifier, where 99% of good identification rate is announced by the authors. Another approach based on textural features was proposed by [1], where the handwriting images are divided into fragments, considered as a texture, and from which LBP features were extracted in addition to Local Ternary Patterns features(LTP); a variant of LBP less sensitive to noise and distortion, and Local Phase Quantization features (LPQ); which relies on the local phase information extracted from the short-term Fourier transform. The approach has also been evaluated with two different datasets, IAM and IFN/ENIT datasets, with performances rates of 89.5% and 94.9%, respectively.

As stated previously, other writer identification approaches were based on locale features, such as the graphemes, resulting from handwriting words segmentation process [14], and the codebook [15]. The codebook has been widely considered in the literature. Indeed, in [16] the authors used it to characterize the handwriting's junctions; the approach was evaluated on two different datasets: IAM and Fire maker, where 94% of good identification rate was obtained. The authors in [17] have also used the codebook with their fragmented connected-component contours (FCO3), extracted from character fragments. The approach was evaluated with the Fire maker dataset, with a rate of 97% of good identification.

It has to be noted that most of the analysis of the writer identification reported in the literature are built on textural features extraction, due to their ability to describe the main characteristics of writers based on handwriting blocks. In this study, we investigate the relevance of using a couple of features: the CLBP and the VLBP, presented in the following section.

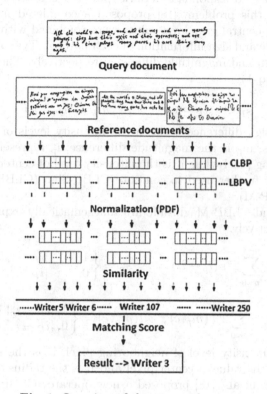

Fig. 1. Overview of the proposed system.

3   Feature Extraction

In our study on handwritten document writer classification, we have selected to use both features: CLBP feature and LBPV feature. These features allow capturing the curvature information and textural information in handwritten document for a discriminatory representation. These descriptors have been successfully applied to various problems related to document analysis. These features are discussed in the following sub-sections

3.1   Complete Local Binary Patterns (CLBP)

Local Binary Patterns consider the local structure of the image only discarding the difference of magnitude between the central pixel and its neighboring pixels. In [18] authors argued that since LBP considers only the difference between two gray values, it often tends to generate inconsistent codes. The binary code generated by the LBP operator for a central pixel with intensity value. The generated LPB code corresponds to a dark spot that is not true in this case.

To cope with this problem, [18] proposed a completed modeling of LBP called CLBP. The central gray level values were combined with the local differences of magnitude and sign information of each pattern. Two bits are employed to capture the sign and magnitude difference respectively. The computation is summarized in (Eq. 1).

$$s_P = s(i_P - i_c) \qquad m_P = |i_P - i_c| \qquad (1)$$

Where s_p is the sign difference between the intensity levels of the central and neighboring pixels, m_p is the magnitude difference; i_p represents the intensity level of neighboring pixel while i_c is the intensity level of center pixel.

s_p and m_p are further used to compute CLBP-Sign (CLBP-S) and CLBP-Magnitude (CLBP-M).

CLBP Sign and CLBP Magnitude are mathematically expressed in (Eq. 2) and (Eq. 3) respectively.

$$CLBP\,S_{(P,R)} = \sum_{p=0}^{p-1} 2^p s\,(i_p - i_c)\,, \qquad s_p = \begin{cases} 1, & |i_P - i_c| \ge c \\ 0, & |i_P - i_c| < c \end{cases} \qquad (2)$$

$$CLBP\,M_{(P,R)} = \sum_{p=0}^{p-1} 2^p t\,(m_p, c)\,, \qquad t(m_p, c) = \begin{cases} 1, |i_P - i_c| \ge c \\ 0, |i_P - i_c| < c \end{cases} \qquad (3)$$

Where i_p is the intensity level of neighboring pixel, i_c is the intensity level of center pixel, P is the value of center pixel and R is the radius of neighborhood.

Moreover, Guo et al. [18] proposed a new operator CLBP Center CLBPC by using gray level of each pattern (Eq. 4).

$$CLBPC_{(P,R)} = t(i_c, c_i) \qquad (4)$$

Where i_c is the gray level value of central pixel and c_i is the average gray level of whole image.

The final CLPB descriptor is formed by concatenating the three descriptors and outperformed the classical LBP for texture classification problems [18].

3.2   Local Binary Pattern Variance (LBPV)

Local Binary Pattern Variance (LBPV) is proposed to exploits the complementary information of local contrast into the one dimensional LBP histogram [19]. A rotation invariant measure of the local variance (VAR) is quantized using the threshold values from the test images, these threshold values are computed the total distribution by calculating feature distributions from all training images. It can be defined as:

$$VAR_{(P,R)} = \frac{1}{p}\sum_{p=0}^{p-1} (i_p - u)^2 \qquad Where \quad u = \frac{1}{p}\sum_{p=0}^{p-1} i_p \qquad (5)$$

Some threshold values are computed to partition the total distribution into N bins with an equal number of entries.

The LBPV is a simplified but efficient joint LBP and contrast distribution method. Therefore, the variance VAR can be used as an adaptive weight to adjust the contribution of the LBP code in histogram calculation. Furthermore, LBPV does not need any quantization and it is totally training-free. The LBPV histogram is computed as:

$$LBPV_{(P,R)}(K) = \sum_{I=1}^{N} \sum_{j=0}^{M} W\left(LBP_{(P,R)}(i,j),k\right), k \in [0,k] \tag{6}$$

Where:

$$W(LBP_{P,R}(i,j),k) = \begin{cases} VAR_{P,R}(i,j) , & LBP_{P,R}(i,j) = k \\ 0 & , & otherwise \end{cases} \tag{7}$$

In addition, these feature vectors are normalized using Probability Density Function (PDF) of an exponential distribution for providing a significant improvement for writer classification.

Probability Density Function of an exponential distribution is used frequently in queuing theory to model the random time lapses between events. If the times between events follow an exponential distribution, then the number of events in a specific interval of time follows a so-called Poisson distribution.

The exponential distribution has mean parameter μ which must be greater than zero and evaluated at the values x in the vector X.

The exponential PDF is :

$$f_x(x|\mu) = \begin{cases} \frac{1}{\mu} \exp^{-\frac{1}{\mu}x} & for & x > 0 \\ 0 & for & x \leq 0 \end{cases} \quad where \ \mu > 0 \tag{8}$$

4 Decision Strategy

In an attempt to enhance the reliability of the accuracy rates of the proposed system, a decision module is designed to produce the final decision according to the results from a classification step based on distances metrics such as the Euclidean distance, city block distance, correlation distance, cosine distance and Spearman distance.

During the matching step, features extracted from the query handwritten document are compared to the feature vector of reference documents, which the final result of matching score reports the minimum distance is chosen that are closest matches to a query handwritten document.

For combination distance metrics, the standard statistical reasoning measures based on the minimum product distance from the best distance metrics is used to arrive at final decision by taking into account the decision of many distance metrics. In our study, we took for the purpose of increase classification rate.

In the next section, we present the experimental settings and the corresponding results.

5   Experimental Results

We carried out a series of experiments to evaluate the effectiveness of the proposed system for writer identification on off-line handwritten documents using the ICDAR 2013competition dataset [11].

In the first experiment, the proposed method was tested using the entire benchmarking dataset containing 1000 document images (04 documents per writer) [11].

The performance measurement used is the precision Top1 which is a standard evaluation metric for information retrieval.

The experiments aim to study the effect of the mean parameter μ of exponential distribution in normalizing the Complete Local Binary Patterns (CLBP) and Local Binary Pattern Variance (LBPV) features from the binarized image. In addition, the Euclidean distance measure is used for classifying each document. The realized Top1 is illustrated in Fig. 2 and Fig. 3.

It can be seen that the CLBP16,4, CLBP 16,8 and LBPV 16,8 features while $\mu = 78$ outperform the others features configuration. Therefore, these features are extracted from the complete handwriting image.

In addition to Euclidean distance, we also evaluated the optimal features using different distance metrics such as the correlation distance, cosine distance, Spearman distance and city block distance, to improve the classification rates.

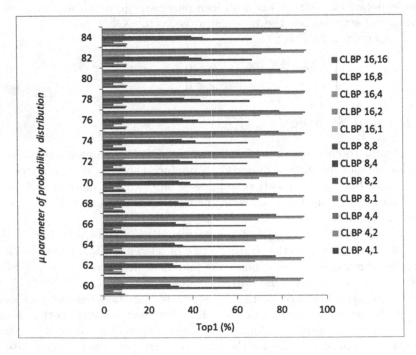

Fig. 2. Top1 rates on ICDAR 2013 competition using CLBP.

Table 1. Writer identification rates with different features using the different distance metrics.

	Feature histogram description		
	CLBP 16,4	CLBP 16,8	LBPV 16,8
DIM	486	486	243
EUCL	87.70	88.90	82.10
CORR	**90.40**	**91.30**	**90.30**
COSINE	90.00	90.90	85.10
SPEARMAN	89.50	93.70	90.60
CITYBLOCK	87.20	88.50	84.00

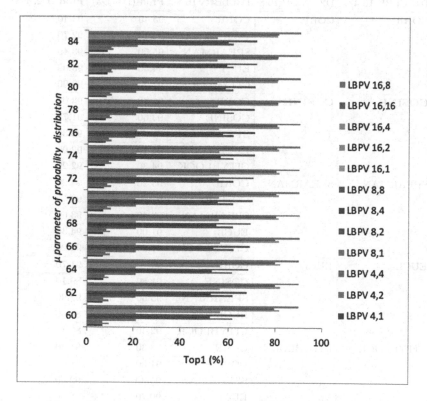

Fig. 3. Top1 rates on ICDAR 2013 competition using LBPV.

Tables 1 summarize the performance of these features using the different distance metrics. A highest precision Top1 of 90.40%, 91.30% and 90.30 % from CLBP(16, 4), CLBP(16, 8) and CLBP(16, 8), respectively, provided using correlation distance.

We also computed the precision Top1 for various combinations of best distance metrics to improve the classification rate. The performance of the proposed method was studies using the minimum of the product (Prod) of the different distance metrics with corresponding features.

Table 2 summarizes the results obtained using these combination schemes. In general, the classification rates of combination scheme based on the minimum of product of the cosine distance of CLBP 16,4 and Spearman distance of LBPV 16,8 are relatively high as compared to other combinations distance metrics as well achieving the precision Top1 of 95.70%.

Table 2. Writer identification rates for various combination schemes.

Combination schemes			Top 1 (%)	
D1: CLBP 16,4	D2: CLBP 16,8	D3: LBPV16,8	Prod (D1, D3)	Prod (D2, D3)
CORR	CORR	CORR	95.40	93.40
		COSINE	94.10	92.70
		SPEARMAN	95.50	93.40
		EUCL	94.50	93.00
		CITYBLOCK	94.40	93.00
COSINE	**COSINE**	CORR	95.30	93.00
		COSINE	93.60	91.70
		SPEARMAN	**95.70**	93.30
		EUCL	94.10	92.00
		CITYBLOCK	94.30	92.20
SPEARMAN	SPEARMAN	CORR	93.20	94.20
		COSINE	91.80	93.50
		SPEARMAN	92.40	93.60
		EUCL	91.00	94.30
		CITYBLOCK	91.60	94.20
EUCL	EUCL	CORR	94.40	91.70
		COSINE	91.80	89.10
		SPEARMAN	95.50	92.90
		EUCL	92.40	89.00
		CITYBLOCK	92.40	89.10
CITYBLOCK	CITYBLOCK	CORR	93.30	91.40
		COSINE	91.00	88.80
		SPEARMAN	95.30	92.50
		EUCL	90.70	88.50
		CITYBLOCK	91.50	88.90

According the previous results, we are evaluated the proposed method using the optimal decision strategy compared with the four (4) best systems submitted to ICDAR 2013 competition on Writer Identification. Table 3 reports the comparison of the proposed method with the same as that of the ICDAR 2013 competition (1000 document images (Greek and English)).

Table 3. Comparison of proposed method with ICDAR 2013 methods.

Rank	Method	Top1
1	**Proposed method**	**95.70**
2	CS-UMD-a	95.10
3	CS-UMD-b	95.00
4	HIT-ICG	94.80
5	TEBESSA-c	93.40

It can be seen from Table 3 that the proposed method outperforms other methods. These results validate the effectiveness of the texture features with optimal combination schemes for Writer Identification.

The second experiment was conducted using only the Greek part of the benchmarking dataset (500 images) and only the English part of the benchmarking dataset (500 images). The evaluation results of proposed system with optimal combination shames for each language independently described in the Table 4.

Table 4. Writer identification rates using only the Greek part and the English part of the benchmarking dataset.

Rank	Method	Script	Top1	Average
1	**Proposed method**	Greek	**97.20**	**95.20**
		English	93.20	
2	CS-UMD-a	Greek	95.60	95.10
		English	**94.60**	
3	CS-UMD-b	Greek	95.20	94.80
		English	94.40	
4	HIT-ICG	Greek	93.80	93.00
		English	92.20	
5	TEBESSA-c	Greek	92.60	91.20
		English	91.20	

It can be seen from Table 4 that the proposed method outperforms other methods using for each language independently (script-dependent) Greek and English. It should however be noted that the proposed system does not require any preprocessing and the features are directly extracted from document images.

6   Conclusions and Future Works

An effective technique for characterizing writer from handwriting is presented that exploits CLBP and LBPV histograms as features. Different configurations of both features are investigated with combination distance metrics. The system evaluated using the same experimental protocol as that of the ICDAR 2013 outperformed the submitted methods reported in the competition.

In our further study on this problem, we intend to investigate other textural measures to characterize writer from handwriting and exploration of feature selection techniques to identify the most appropriate textural descriptors for this problem is also planned. Moreover, the classification step of the present study is very much traditional. We plan to enhance the classification module based on classical distance metrics by using new distance metric.

References

1. Hannad, Y., Siddiqi, I., El Kettani, M.: Writer identification using texture descriptors of handwritten fragments. Expert Syst. Appl. **47**, 14–22 (2016)
2. Bertolini, D., Oliveira, L., Justino, E., Sabourin, R.: Texture-based descriptors for writer identification and verification. Expert Syst. Appl. **40**, 2069–2080 (2013)
3. Siddiqi, I., Vincent, N.: Text independent writer recognition using redundant writing patterns with contour-based orientation and curvature features. Pattern Recogn. **43**, 3853–3865 (2010)
4. Christlein, V., Bernecker, D., Hönig, F., Maier, A., Angelopoulou, E.: Writer identification using GMM supervectors and exemplar-SVMs. Pattern Recogn. **63**, 258–267 (2017)
5. Djeddi, C., Al-Maadeed, S., Gattal, A., Siddiqi, I., Souici-Meslati, L., El Abed, H.: ICDAR2015 competition on multi-script writer identification and gender classification using 'QUWI' database. 13th International Conference on Document Analysis and Recognition (ICDAR), Tunis, pp. 1191–1195. IEEE (2015)
6. Djeddi, C., Al-Maadeed, S., Gattal, A., Siddiqi, I., Ennaji, A., El Abed, H.: ICFHR2016 Competition on multi-script writer demographics classification using "QUWI" database. In: 15th International Conference on Frontiers in Handwriting Recognition (ICFHR), China, pp. 602–606. IEEE (2016)
7. He, S., Schomaker, L.: Writer identification using curvature-free features. Pattern Recogn. **63**, 451–464 (2017)
8. He, S., Schomaker, L.: Delta-n Hinge: rotation-invariant features for writer identification. In: 22nd International Conference on Pattern Recognition, Stockholm, Sweden, 24–28 August 2014, pp. 2023–2028. ICPR (2014)
9. Bulacu, M., Schomaker, L.: Text-independent writer identification and verification using textural and allographic features. IEEE Trans. Pattern Anal. Mach. Intell. **29**, 701–717 (2007)
10. Brink, A., Smit, J., Bulacu, M., Schomaker, L.: Writer identification using directional ink-trace width measurements. Pattern Recogn. **45**, 162–171 (2012)
11. Louloudis, G., Gatos, B., Stamatopoulos, N., Papandreou, A. : ICDAR 2013 competition on writer identification. In: 12th International Conference on Document Analysis and Recognition (ICDAR), Washington DC, pp. 1397–1401. IEEE (2013)
12. Tan, G., Sulong, G., Rahim, M.: Writer identification: a comparative study across three world major languages. Forensic Sci. Int. **279**, 41–52 (2017)
13. Srihari, S., Cha, S., Arora, H., Lee, S.: Individuality of handwriting. J. Forensic Sci. **47**, 15447J (2002)

14. Bensefia, A., Paquet, T., Heutte, L.: Grapheme based writer verification. In: 11th Conference of the International Graphonomics Society (IGS2003), pp. 274–277 (2003)
15. Brink, A., Niels, R., van Batenburg, R., van den Heuvel, C., Schomaker, L.: Towards robust writer verification by correcting unnatural slant. Pattern Recogn. Lett. **32**, 449–457 (2011)
16. He, S., Wiering, M., Schomaker, L.: Junction detection in handwritten documents and its application to writer identification. Pattern Recogn. **48**, 4036–4048 (2015)
17. Schomaker, L., Franke, K., Bulacu, M.: Using codebooks of fragmented connected-component contours in forensic and historic writer identification. Pattern Recogn. Lett. **28**, 719–727 (2007)
18. Guo, Z., Zhang, L., Zhang, D.: A completed modeling of local binary pattern operator for texture classification. IEEE Trans. Image Process. **19**, 1657–1663 (2010)
19. Guo, Z., Zhang, L., Zhang, D.: Rotation invariant texture classification using LBP variance (LBPV) with global matching. Pattern Recogn. **43**, 706–719 (2010)

Deep Learning Architecture for Off-Line Recognition of Handwritten Math Symbols

Kawther Khazri Ayeb, Yosra Meguebli, and Afef Kacem Echi[✉]

ENSIT-LaTICE, University of Tunis, Tunis, Tunisia
afef.kacem@ensit.rnu.tn
http://www.latice.rnu.tn/francais/presentation.htm

Abstract. Real scientific challenge, handwritten math formula recognition is an attractive field of pattern recognition leading to practical applications. Hundreds of alphanumeric and math symbols need to be recognized, many are so similar in appearance that some use of context is necessary for disambiguation. Analysis of the spatial relationships between symbols is challenging. In this work, we focus on handwritten math symbols and propose to recognize them by a deep learning approach. The symbol images, used for train, validation, and test are generated from Competition on Recognition of Online Handwritten Mathematical Expressions dataset (CROHME) 2019's online patterns of mathematical symbols. As the large dataset is crucial for the performance of the deep learning model and it is labor-intensive to obtain a large amount of labeled data in real applications, we first augmented the database. Standing on the transfer learning technique, we then tested and compared several pre-trained Convolutional Neural networks (CNNs) like VGGNet, SqueezeNet, DenseNet, and Xception network and we tuned them to better fit our data. An accurate classification of 91.88% (train), 88.82% (validation), and 83.68% (test) for 101 classes is achieved, using only off-line features of the symbols.

Keywords: Handwriting math symbol recognition · Data augmentation · Transfer learning · Deep learning · CNN · Xception · VGGNet · SqueezeNet · DenseNet

1 Introduction

Handwritten math formula recognition is attracting interest due to its practical applications for consumers and academics in many areas such as education, office automation, etc. It offers an easy and direct way to input math formulas into computers, and therefore improves productivity for scientific writers. However, it is a challenging field due to the variety of writing styles and math formulas structures. Hundreds of alphanumeric and math symbols need to be recognized,

© Springer Nature Switzerland AG 2021
C. Djeddi et al. (Eds.): MedPRAI 2020, CCIS 1322, pp. 200–214, 2021.
https://doi.org/10.1007/978-3-030-71804-6_15

and also the two-dimensional structures, specifically the relationships between a pair of symbols, for example, superscript and subscript, both of them increase the difficulty of this recognition problem.

Many on-line techniques have been studied for handwritten math formula recognition. But when the recognition is carried out from a document image, therefore off-line techniques must be considered. In the last decade, most of the research has focused on typeset formulas but little research is published. The main difference between on-line and off-line recognition of math formulas is the temporal information that conveys the former problem that is lost in the latter problem. Math formula recognition can be divided into main steps: symbol recognition and structure analysis. Note that an accurate math formula recognition system greatly depends on an efficient symbol recognizer. Recently, deep learning marks the state of the art for math symbol classification problems, especially those including multiple layers of nonlinear information processing that automatically solve problems without using any prior knowledge. The results of recent researchers studies, summarized in Table 1 prove that Deep neural networks enhance mathematical recognition symbols [5] comparing to previous methods like Modified Quadratic Discriminant Functions (MQDFs) [4] with Bidirectional Long Short-term Memory (BLSTM) and Hidden Markov Models (HMM) [9].

The focus in this work is on handwritten math symbol recognition. It is one of the application in pattern classification: the task of labeling the symbol candidates to assign each of them a symbol class. It is as well a difficult task because the number of classes are quite important, more than one hundred different symbols including digits, alphabet, operators, Greek letters and some special math symbols (see Fig. 1).

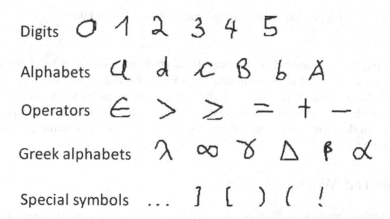

Fig. 1. Samples of math symbols.

It exists an overlapping between some symbol classes (inter-class variability): for instance, some symbols belonging to different classes might look about the same when considering different handwritten samples. There is also a high intra-class variability because each writer has his writing style (see Fig. 2). Besides, the challenges coming with the off-line. Many results showed that on-line recognition reached higher accuracy than off-line recognition [9], because of the absence of tracking coordinate of the symbol from start to stop, used to recognize it properly. So, it is important to design robust and efficient classifiers and to use a representative training data set. Nowadays, most of the proposed solutions use machine learning algorithms such as artificial neural networks or support vector machines.

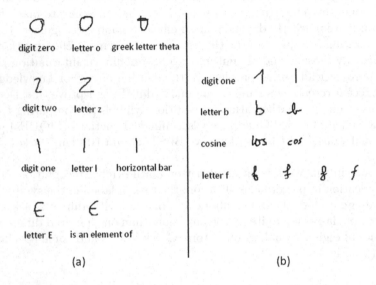

Fig. 2. Inter-class (a) and intra-class (b) variability.

This paper is organized as follows. In Sect. 2, we present a brief review in the field of math symbol recognition. In Sect. 3, we detail architectures of the proposed deep learning models and the used data augmentation and learning transfer mechanisms. In Sect. 4, we discuss the obtained results and compare the proposed models and some related works. In Sect. 5, we give some conclusions and prospects.

2   Related Works

In this section, we briefly discuss all advances in the area of math symbol recognition, as summarized in Table 1. The focus is on deep learning-based models.

In [1], authors define their proper CNN with a simple architecture composed of two convolutional layers, two pooling layers, a fully connected and a softmax layer to classify off-line handwritten math symbols. To improve their results, they tuned the performance of CNN by changing the number of feature maps

Table 1. Comparison between some related works.

Ref.	System	Model	Classes	Database	Accuracy (%)
[1]	Off-line Handwritten Math Symbols Classification	proper CNN	102	CROHME 2014 - train: 85781 - test: 10061	- 93.27 - 87.72
[2]	Off-line Handwritten Math Symbols Classification	HMS-VGGNet	- 101: CROHME - 369: HASYv2	- train: 403729 CROHME 2016 + HASYv2 (part) - val: 6081 CROHME 2013 test - test: 10061 CROHME 2014 test - test: 10019 CROHME 2016 test - train: 366566 ± 1356 HASYv2 train - test: 16827 ± 166 HASYv2 test	 - 88.46 - 91.82 - 92.42 - 85.05
[3]	Off-line Handwritten Math Symbols Classification	- modified LeNet - pretrained SqueezeNet	- 87 - 101	- MNIST: 6000 - Set of Handwritten Digit Images: 2000	- 90 (modified LeNet) - 90 (SqueezeNet)
[4]	Online handwritten Math Expression Recognition	Online: Markov Random Field(MRF) Off-line: modified quadratic discriminant function (MQDF)	101	- Hands-Math dataset - Crohme 2016 [6]	- 88.24 - 86.05
[5]	Online Handwritten Math Symbols Detection	Inception v2, Resnet 50, Resnet 101, Inception Resnet v2	- 7 - 101	- flowchart dataset [7] - Crohme 2016	Inception Resnet v2: - 99 (val) 97 (test) - 89.7 (val) 86.8 (test)
[9]	Online Handwritten Math Expression Recognition	- structure recognition: 2D stochastic context-free grammars - symbol recognition: HMM (online and offline features)	- 100 - 37 - 57	- MathBrush [8] - CROHME 2011 Part1 - CROHME 2011 Part2	- 86.49 (W. dep.) 84.11 (W. Ind.) - 88.07 - 87.82

in convolutional layers, the number of nodes in a fully-connected layer, and the size of the input image. The authors used CROHME 2014 for training and evaluation. Authors declare obtaining 93.27% as train accuracy and 87.72% as a test, but they didn't show any accuracy or loss curve, which is necessary to add more credibility to their work. In [2], authors proposed a CNN, called HMS-VGGNet, for off-line recognition of handwritten math symbols. It is inspired by VGGNet, with smaller image sizes and additional batch normalization layers. The authors also used global average pooling layers to replace the fully connected layers. To prevent the lack of off-line data, the authors used elastic distortion to enrich the training set. Their proposed CNN uses only off-line features of the symbols and achieved an accuracy of 92.42% using CROHME 2016 test set. In [3], authors described an approach for off-line recognition of handwritten math symbols. They used Simple Linear Iterative Clustering for symbol segmentation and different methods: k-Nearest Neighbors (k-NN), LeNet, and SqueezeNet for symbol classification. The best-obtained accuracy using k-NN is 84% with 66 classes of symbols. Using modified LeNet, they achieved an accuracy of 90% with 87 classes. Finally, they reached 90% with a pre-trained SqueezeNet for 101 classes. The authors mentioned that they used the 6000 MNIST images from the CROHME dataset and 2000 images from the set of Handwritten Digit Images published by Computer Vision Group of the University of Sao Paulo, but they did not give details about the number of used instances for train, validation, and test and the cited accuracies. Recently, researchers used the off-line features extracted from the symbol images in combination with the online features to recognize the online math symbols and got great achievements. MyScript [6], the winner of CROHME 2016 extracted both online and off-line features and processed with a combination of Deep Multilayer Perceptron and Recurrent Neural Networks. MyScript achieved 92.81% in CROHME 2016 test set.

From our study of the state-of-the-art, we noted that the combination of online and off-line features betters the symbol recognition task performance and that the off-line recognition of math symbol should be more considered if we aim to reach the best performance. We also noted that many classification techniques are previously used, but there are very few works that compare different classification techniques on the same database and with the same experimental conditions.

3   Proposed System

We explored different architectures of CNNs, trained, and tested them using CROHME 2019 dataset. The objective is to find out the appropriate model for the off-line math symbol recognition. For that, we followed some steps, as described below.

3.1   Data Generation and Tuning

In CROHME 2019, there are 101 different classes of math symbols. The online data is given in Ink Markup Language (InkML) where each symbol is presented by an InkML file. This latter contains the set of symbol traces, knowing that a trace consists of a set of timing sampling points, and each point records its position. When generating symbol images from online data, we connected the points of the same trace with a single line. The generation of symbol images from InkML files is performed by a tool provided with the CROHME 2019 dataset. We then made some changes to ensure the automatic distribution of images on folders named with the class names. To train the proposed CNN models, we generated 30993 symbol images of size 38×38. To built the train and validation dataset, we automatically split the images dataset to have 24758 images for the train and 6235 for the validation. For the test, we generated and created ground truth of 15483 images from the 15483 CROHME test dataset. As it is known, improving the performance of a deep learning model depends either on tuning the applied model or tuning the used data. Since training deep learning models need several hours, we thought about normalizing the generated symbol dataset by binarizing and inverting them.

3.2   Model Tuning

To classify math symbols using a deep learning model, we have to choose one of these three alternatives: 1) to define a new model and train it on our data. 2) to use a predefined model, tune and train it on our data, or 3) to reuse a pre-trained model on other data and train it on our data. Based on the first tests and limited by the available data and computational resources, we have chosen the third alternative. One of the most common problems that we encountered while training these deep networks is overfitting. Recall that overfitting happens when a model learns the detail and noise in the training data to the extent that it negatively impacts the performance of the model on new data. To prevent such a problem, mainly due to overly complex models with too many parameters, we added a global average pooling layer where all the parameters in one feature map are averaged as a result. As deep networks need to be trained on large scale datasets and it is labor-intensive to obtain a large amount of labeled data in real applications, we first augmented the database. Standing on the transfer learning technique, we then tested and compared several pre-trained CNNs. This is will be dealt with in more detail in the next subsections.

Data Augmentation. Having a large dataset is crucial for the performance of the deep learning model. However, we can improve the performance of the model by augmenting the data we already have. Deep learning frameworks usually have built-in data augmentation utilities. Accordingly, to perform augmentation on a dataset of handwritten math symbols, it must be considered that it does not change the symbol meaning, for example, <when is vertically flipped, it is converted to>. Therefore, some augmentation techniques cannot be run on all symbols. In this work, we applied rotation with a random angle in the range of $[-15, 15]$ and horizontal and vertical shift augmentation techniques which are almost safe for handwritten math symbol recognition. Figure 3 shows several symbol image samples generated by the used augmentation techniques.

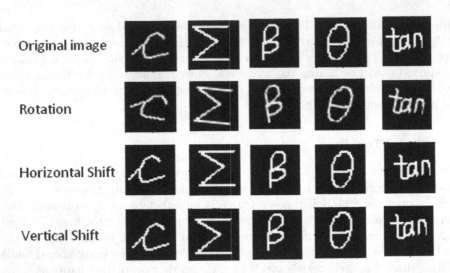

Fig. 3. Samples of symbol images result of data augmentation.

Used Models. Deep learning models need high computational resources with a huge dataset to obtain good results. One of the solutions to use deep learning-based models for symbol classification is to reuse pre-trained models and to test them with different parameters to improve accuracy. In our work, we have tried four pre-trained CNN models: VGGNet, SqueezeNet, Xception Network, and DenseNet. To these deep networks, we added two layers: 1) an average pooling layer to overcome the problem of over-fitting by averaging the parameters, and 2) a dense layer with regularization for math symbol class prediction. We started our tests from the smallest to the deeper network:

- Squeezenet: is a CNN with 18 layers deep, it is characterized by its compressed architecture design based on fire modules. A fire module is a combination of squeeze layers (1×1 convolution filters) and expand layers (a mix of 1×1 and 3×3 convolution filters)
- VGGNet19 [10]: is a CNN with 19 layers deep, it is composed of 16 convolutional layers and 3 fully connected layers
- Xception [11]: is a CNN with 71 layers deep it is based entirely on depthwise separable convolution layers.
- Densenet121 [12]: is a CNN with 121 layers deep. Recent work has shown that CNN can be deeper, more accurate, and efficient to train if they contain shorter connections between layers and this is what characterises in fact the Densenet. Each layer in Densenet is connected to every other layer in a feed-forward fashion. Whereas traditional CNN with L layers have L connections, one between each layer and its subsequent layer, Densenet has $L(L + 1)/2$ direct connections. DenseNets have several advantages: they strengthen feature propagation, encourage feature reuse, and reduce the number of

parameters. The efficiency of this model is proven by the tests that we did for the recognition of math symbols.

Table 2 and Fig. 4 show the architectures of the different models.

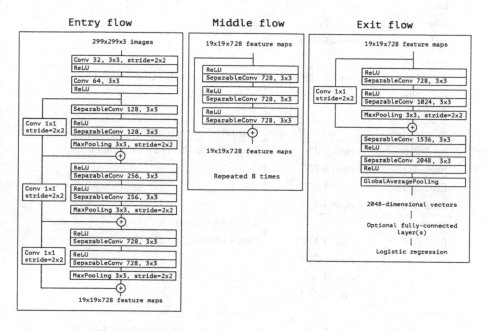

Fig. 4. Architecture of the Xception network.

Transfer Learning. In computer vision, transfer learning is expressed through the use of pre-trained models. A pre-trained model is a model that was trained on a large dataset to solve a problem similar to the one that we want to solve. It allows us to build accurate models in a timesaving way [13]. To well apply transfer learning and reuse some pre-trained model, we first have to correctly classify the treated problem, considering the size of the dataset and its similarity to the used dataset to train the pre-trained model. Figure 5 shows the size-similarity matrix that controls the choice of the model and guides us to fine-tune it to get successful results.

Table 2. Architecture of SqueezeNet, VGGNet and DenseNet

SqueezeNet	VGGNet19	DenseNet121
18 weight layers	19 weight layers	121 weight layers
Input		
conv1-64 Relu	conv3-64 conv3-64	con1-3
maxpool		
fire2-128 fire3-128 fire4-256	conv3-128 conv3-128	DenseBlock-64 (6×ConvBlock)
maxpool		TransitionLayer (conv1+Average pool)
fire5-256 fire6-384 fire7-384 fire8-512	conv3-256 conv3-256 conv3-256 conv3-256	DenseBlock-128 (12×Convblock)
maxpool		TransitionLayer
fire9-512	conv3-512 conv3-512 conv3-512 conv3-512	DenseBlock-256 (24×ConvBlock)
maxpool		TransitionLayer
con1-1000	conv3-512 conv3-512 conv3-512 conv3-512	DenseBlock-512 (16×ConvBlock)
average pool	maxpool	average pool
	FC-4096	
	FC-4096	
	FC-1000	
Softmax		

Fine-Tuning. Having situated our problem according to the size-similarity matrix, we can choose the adequate fine-tuning alternatives. Figure 6 represents a CNN model as a succession of two blocks: a convolutional base for feature extraction in the top and a classifier in the bottom. Following the size-similarity matrix, four fine-tuning decisions can be taken.

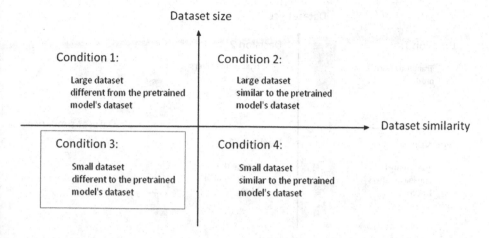

Fig. 5. Size similarity matrix.

4 Experimental Results

4.1 CROHME Dataset

Since the datasets of off-line handwritten mathematical symbols are rare, we used the online data of CROHME 2019 to generate symbol images for off-line symbol recognition. The number of symbol classes in the CROHME dataset is 102, including a junk class for erroneous symbols. To evaluate the proposed CNN models, we generated 30993 symbol images. To built the train and validation datasets, we automatically split the images dataset to have 24758 images for the train and 6235 for the validation. For the tests, we generated and created ground truth of 6820 images from CROHME 2019 test dataset.

4.2 Experimental Setup

Our experiments were performed on an Intel(R)Core (TM) with a CPU of 2.5 GHz and a memory of 8 GB. We trained our system using pre-trained deep learning models from the Tensorflow library, trained over the ImageNet dataset. Although our generated images are different from the natural images of the ImageNet dataset, we found that training using the pre-trained models allows for much faster convergence than training from scratch, especially with the presence of a small dataset. Regarding the size-similarity matrix presented in Fig. 5, we found that our classification problem satisfied the third condition (small dataset and different from the pre-trained model's dataset, that is why we fine-tuned

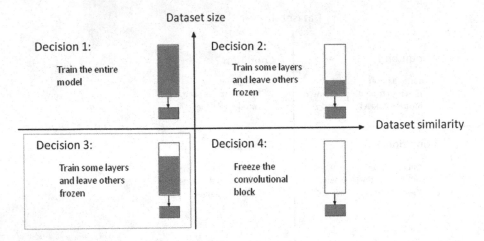

Fig. 6. Decision map for fine-tuning pre-trained models.

our model by freezing the ten first layers of the convolutional block responsible of the extraction of generic features and train the rest on our data. The initial learning rate was 0.001, the Batch Size was set to 32. We initialized the number of the epoch at 200 and we implemented early stopping callbacks.

4.3   Results and Discussion

We trained different CNN models with various parameters on our dataset. Figure 7 shows the accuracy and loss curves of the different CNN models. Our best obtained experimental results are shown in Table 3.

We can see that DenseNet121 achieves the state-of-the-art and outperforms the other models. This can be explained as follows: 1) This network is remarkably deeper than the others (121 layers), and 2) Adding more instances to the dataset enhances the capabilities of the model (using a dataset of 24758 train images and 6235 validation images improves the accuracy from 91.73% to 91.88% for the training and from 84.07% to 88.82% for the validation). Evaluating our model on the test dataset, we obtained an accuracy of 83.68%. Table 4 shows the performance measures: Precision, Recall and F1-score of the different classes and the overall system.

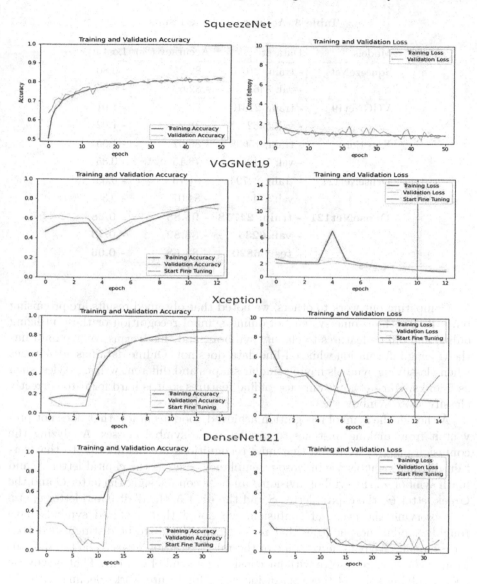

Fig. 7. Accuracy and loss curves.

Table 3. Accuracy and loss results.

Models	Dataset	Accuracy (%)	Loss
SqueezeNet	- train: 21610	- 82.25	- 0.80
	- val: 5462	- 82.6	- 0.35
VGGNet19	- train: 21610	- 72	- 1.01
	- val: 5462	- 78	- 1.02
Xception	- train: 15698	- 86.02	- 1.55
	- val: 7012	- 78.15	- 0.85
DenseNet121	- train: 22794	- 91.73	- 0.33
	- val: 5745	- 84.07	- 0.36
DenseNet121	**- train: 24758**	**- 91.88**	**- 0.28**
	- val: 6235	**- 88.82**	**- 0.20**
	- test: 6820	**- 83.68**	**- 0.06**

Comparing our work to others, we noted that obtained results are promising but still less than some systems of online symbol recognition or those utilizing online and offline features to classify symbols, and this because online data has the tracing information while off-line data does not. Online data has advantages when classifying symbols having similar shapes and different writing styles, such as 5 and s. Our networks only use offline features so it is hard for it to correctly classify those symbols.

Although the symbol recognition achieved good accuracy, that does not prevent it from making mistakes to predict some symbol classes. Analyzing the confusion matrix, we found that miss recognitions are mainly due to that certain distinct symbols are in close resemblance, such as the capital letter X and math symbol $\times$, the symbol division / and the comma sign, the letter O and the Greek letter Θ, the capital letter S and the digit 5, the digit 9 and letter g, etc.

Observing the event of confusion, we noted that confused symbols have roughly similar morphologies that make them difficult to be distinguished even for a human. We considered some of the misrecognition cases to be too difficult for any classifier to resolve without considering symbol context. That is why we keep resolving some of these confusion cases for future works dealing with the entire math formula recognition.

Table 4. Model performance evaluation.

Class	Prec.	Recall	F1-score	Nb.	Class	Prec.	Recall	F1-score	Nb.
!	0.67	1.00	0.80	2	forall	1.00	1.00	1.00	1
(	0.95	0.88	0.92	190	g	0.22	1.00	0.36	6
)	0.96	0.83	0.89	236	gamma	0.86	0.50	0.63	12
+	0.98	0.95	0.97	601	geq	0.88	1.00	0.93	7
−	1.00	0.92	0.96	723	gt	1.00	1.00	11.00	5
0	0.97	0.96	0.96	118	h	0.60	0.60	0.60	5
1	0.53	0.96	0.68	215	i	0.72	0.96	0.82	24
2	0.81	0.98	0.89	326	in	0.75	1.00	0.86	3
3	0.94	0.99	0.96	137	infty	0.92	0.92	0.92	12
4	0.90	0.86	0.88	81	int	0.89	0.64	0.74	25
5	0.92	0.80	0.85	95	j	0.84	0.67	0.74	24
6	0.94	0.83	0.88	41	junk	0.86	0.90	0.88	1350
7	0.90	0.90	0.90	31	k	0.79	0.96	0.87	24
8	0.90	0.90	0.90	31	l	0.33	0.17	0.22	6
9	0.79	0.39	0.53	79	lambda	0.50	1.00	0.67	1
=	0.98	0.95	0.96	273	ldots	0.77	1.00	0.87	10
A	1.00	0.75	0.86	16	leq	1.00	1.00	1.00	16
B	1.00	1.00	1.00	9	lim	0.41	0.88	0.56	8
comma	0.28	0.38	0.32	53	log	0.67	0.92	0.77	13
C	1.00	0.60	0.75	62	lt	0.67	1.00	0.80	2
Delta	1.00	1.00	1.00	1	m	0.77	0.71	0.74	28
E	1.00	1.00	1.00	11	mu	0.00	0.00	0.00	4
F	0.71	0.83	0.77	6	n	0.79	0.94	0.86	81
G	0.00	0.00	0.00	2	neq	0.67	0.33	0.44	6
H	0.57	1.00	0.73	4	o	0.00	0.00	0.00	8
I	1.00	1.00	1.00	2	p	0.11	0.33	0.17	3
L	1.00	0.60	0.75	20	phi	0.00	0.00	0.00	1
M	0.75	0.75	0.75	4	pi	0.79	0.96	0.86	23
N	0.43	0.50	0.46	6	pm	0.00	0.00	0.00	4
P	0.78	0.52	0.62	27	point	0.87	1.00	0.93	13
R	1.00	1.00	1.00	15	prime	0.00	0.00	0.00	4
S	0.53	0.82	0.65	28	q	0.20	0.29	0.24	17
T	0.67	1.00	0.80	4	r	0.30	0.58	0.40	12
V	1.00	0.70	0.82	10	rightarrow	0.55	0.86	0.67	7
X	0.06	0.30	0.10	27	s	1.00	1.00	1.00	1
Y	0.62	0.93	0.74	14	sigma	0.12	1.00	0.22	1
[	0.92	0.82	0.87	28	sin	0.86	0.86	0.86	22
]	0.94	0.60	0.73	25	sqrt	0.95	0.78	0.86	96
a	0.87	0.97	0.92	100	sum	1.00	0.88	0.94	25
alpha	0.91	0.86	0.89	36	t	0.80	0.77	0.79	31
b	0.89	1.00	0.94	59	tan	0.88	0.54	0.67	13
bar	0.00	0.00	0.00	131	theta	0.62	0.91	0.74	11
beta	1.00	0.93	0.97	15	times	1.00	0.08	0.15	173
c	0.05	1.00	0.10	1	u	0.48	1.00	0.65	12
cos	0.92	0.83	0.87	29	v	1.00	1.00	1.00	3
d	0.96	0.96	0.96	94	w	0.83	1.00	0.91	5
div	0.89	0.89	0.89	9	x	0.83	0.98	0.90	339
division	0.15	0.06	0.09	31	y	0.81	0.92	0.86	62
e	0.96	1.00	0.98	25	z	0.96	0.56	0.70	144
exists	1.00	1.00	1.00	1	{	1.00	0.50	0.67	4
f	0.91	0.40	0.56	25	}	1.00	1.00	1.00	4

5 Conclusion and Future Work

In this paper, we addressed the problem of offline recognition of handwritten mathematical symbols. We used a deep learning recognition method based on the Densenet model to which we did some modification. Our symbol recognition system has shown its efficiency on a reasonable number of handwritten symbols from Crohme 2019 dataset with an accuracy rate of 83.71%. In further works, we plan to improve the performance of the model by augmenting the data we already have. We will also work out on treating the case of junk symbol by making the focus on finding why they are considered junk, and how to treat them based on cause analysis.

References

1. Ramadhan, I., Purnama, B., Al Faraby, S.: Convolutional neural networks applied to handwritten mathematical symbols classification. In: Fourth International Conference on Information and Communication Technologies (ICoICT) (2016)
2. Dong, L., Liu, H.: Recognition of offline handwritten mathematical symbols using convolutional neural networks. In: Zhao, Y., Kong, X., Taubman, D. (eds.) ICIG 2017. LNCS, vol. 10666, pp. 149–161. Springer, Cham (2017). https://doi.org/10.1007/978-3-319-71607-7_14
3. Nazemi, A., Tavakolian, N., Fitzpatrick, D., Fernando, C., Suen, C.Y.: Offline handwritten mathematical symbol recognition utilising deep learning, cs.CV (2019)
4. Phan, K.M., Le, A.D., Indurkhya, B., Nakagawa, M.: Augmented incremental recognition of online handwritten mathematical expressions. Int. J. Doc. Anal. Recogn. (IJDAR) **21**(4), 253–268 (2018). https://doi.org/10.1007/s10032-018-0306-1
5. Julca-Aguilar, F.D., Hirata, N.S.T.: Symbol detection in online handwritten graphics using Faster R-CNN. In: International Workshop on Document Analysis Systems (DAS) (2018)
6. Mouchere, H., Viard-Gaudin, C., Zanibbi, R., Garain, U.: ICFHR2016 CROHME: competition on recognition of online handwritten mathematical expressions (2016)
7. Awal, A.M., Feng, G., Mouchere, H., Viard-Gaudin, C.: First experiments on a new online handwritten flowchart database. In: Document Recognition and Retrieval XVIII (2011)
8. MacLean, S., Labahn, G., Lank, E., Marzouk, M., Tausky, D.: Grammar-based techniques for creating ground-truthed sketch corpora. Int. J. Doc. Anal. Recogn. **14**, 65–74 (2011). https://doi.org/10.1007/s10032-010-0118-4
9. Alvaro, F., Sanchez, J.A., Benedi, J.M.: Recognition of on-line handwritten mathematical expressions using 2D stochastic context-free grammars and hidden Markov models. Pattern Recogn. Lett. **35**, 58–67 (2014)
10. Simonyan, K., Zisserman, A.: Very deep convolutional neural networks for large-scale image recognition. In: ICLR (2015)
11. Chollet, F.: Xception: deep learning with depthwise separable convolutions, cs.CV (2017)
12. Huang, G., Liu, Z., Maaten, L., Weinberger, K.: Densely connected convolutional networks, cs.CV (2018)
13. Rawat, W., Wang, Z.: Deep convolutional neural networks for image classification: a comprehensive review. Neural Comput. **29**(9), 2352–2449 (2017)

A Conditional GAN Based Approach for Distorted Camera Captured Documents Recovery

Mohamed Ali Souibgui[1(✉)], Yousri Kessentini[2], and Alicia Fornés[1]

[1] Computer Vision Center Computer Science Department,
Universitat Autònoma de Barcelona, Bellaterra, Spain
{msouibgui,afornes}@cvc.uab.es

[2] Digital Research Center of Sfax, 3021 MIRACL Laboratory,
Sfax University, Sfax, Tunisia
yousri.kessentini@crns.rnrt.tn

Abstract. Many of the existing documents are digitized using smart phone's cameras. These are highly vulnerable to capturing distortions (perspective angle, shadow, blur, warping, etc.), making them hard to be read by a human or by an OCR engine. In this paper, we tackle this problem by proposing a conditional generative adversarial network that maps the distorted images from its domain into a readable domain. Our model integrates a recognizer in the discriminator part for better distinguishing the generated images. Our proposed approach demonstrates to be able to enhance highly degraded images from its condition into a cleaner and more readable form.

Keywords: Mobile phone captured images · Document enhancement · Generative adversarial networks

1 Introduction

With the increasing daily use of smartphones and the advancement of its applications, they start replacing other tools and machines in many different tasks, such as scanning. Nowadays, smartphones could be used to digitize a document paper by simply taking a photo from its camera. Indeed, smartphones allow to scan anywhere compared to a classic scanning machine that is not mobile due to its size and weight. However, despite the mobility advantage, problems are occurring in most of the camera based scans: bad perspective angles, shadows, blur, light unbalance, warping, etc. [17]. Consequently, the extracted text from these document images by directly using a standard Optical Character Recognition (OCR) system becomes unreliable. Lately, thanks to the success of deep and machine learning models, some recent works show a higher robustness when reading distorted documents (at line level). Anyway, some of these methods apply a preprocessing step to segment the scanned text images into separated

© Springer Nature Switzerland AG 2021
C. Djeddi et al. (Eds.): MedPRAI 2020, CCIS 1322, pp. 215–228, 2021.
https://doi.org/10.1007/978-3-030-71804-6_16

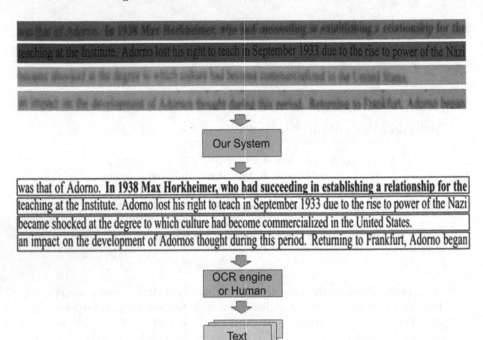

Fig. 1. The proposed reading process: the role of our system is to preprocess the images to be read by an OCR system or by a human.

lines. For example, [2] applied the Long Short-Term Memory (LSTM) networks directly on the gray-scale text line images (without removing the distortions), to avoid error-prone binarization of blurred documents, as the authors claimed. Similarly, [3] used Convolutional Neural Networks (CNN) to extract the features from the lines and pass it thought a LSTM to read the text. All these approaches lead indeed to a better performance comparing to using a standard OCR engine in this specific domain (i.e. distorted line image). Those neural networks could be seen as direct mapping functions from the distorted lines to the text. This means that they are not providing a clean version of the image lines to be read by a human, or by the widely used OCR systems that are much powerful when dealing with clean images because they are trained on a huge amount of data from different domains and languages. For this reason, we believe that restoring the lines images, i.e. mapping it from the distorted domain to a readable domain (by an OCR system or by a human) is a better solution. Figure 1 illustrates our approach: a preprocessing module to improve the posterior reading step (either manual or automatic).

Knowing that the OCR accuracy has largely depended on the preprocessing step since it was generally the first step in any pattern recognition problem, a lot of research has addressed the preprocessing stage (i.e. document binarization and enhancement) during the last decades. The goal of this step is to transform the document image into a better or cleaner version. In our case, this means to remove (or minimize) the distortions is these lines (e.g. shadows, blur and warping). The most common step to clean a text image is binarization, which is usually done by finding either locally or globally thresholds to separate the text pixels from the distorted ones (including background noise) using the classic Image Processing (IP) techniques [18,19,21]. These approaches could be used to remove the shadows and fix the light distortion, but, they usually fail to restore the blurred images or to fix the baselines. Thus, machine learning techniques for image domain translation have been recently used for the this purpose. These methods mainly consist of CNN auto-encoders [4,14,16] and Generative Adversarial Networks (GANs) [7,11,22,23]. The latter is leading to a better performance comparing to the classic IP techniques because they can handle more complex distortion scenarios like: dense watermarked [22], shadowed [8,13], highly blurred [10,22] and warped [15] document images.

But, despite the success of the mentioned machine learning approaches for images domain translation, they are still addressing those distortion scenarios separately. Contrary, in this paper we are providing a single model to solve different types of degradation in camera captured documents [6,17]. Moreover, in those image domain translation approaches, the goal is mapping an image to a desired domain depending only on the visual pixels information loss. In our case, when translating the text images, they should not only look clean, but also, legible. It must be noted that, sometimes, the model could consider the resultant images as text, but in fact they are just random pixels that emulate the visual shape characteristics of text, or random text characters that are constructing a wrong and random script. For this reason, current machine learning text generation models are using a recognition loss in addition to the visual loss to validate the readability of a generated text image [1,12]. Similarly, we add a recognizer in our proposed conditional GAN model to guide the generator in producing readable images (by the human or the OCR) when translating them from the distortion domain to the clean domain. This simple idea shall lead to a better recovery of our distorted lines.

The rest of the paper is organized as follows. Our proposed model is described in the next Section. Afterwards, we evaluate it comparing with related approaches in Sect. 3. Finally, a brief conclusion is added in Sect. 4.

2   Proposed Method

The proposed architecture is illustrated in Fig. 2. It is mainly composed of three components: A regular generator G, a discriminator D (with the assigned trainable parameters θ_G and θ_D, respectively) and an OCR system R, which will not be trainable since it will only be used to validate the generations. It must be noted that we used the same generator and discriminator architectures as [22], because of the superiority that they showed in document enhancement tasks.

During training, the generator is taking as an input the distorted image, noted by I_d and outputting a generated image I_g, hence: $I_g = G_{\theta_G}(I_d)$. Then,

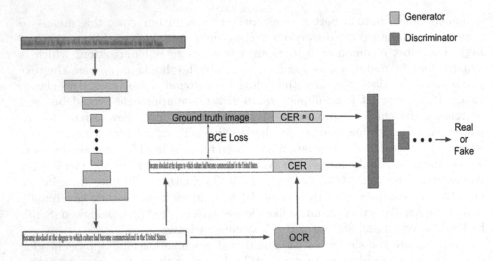

Fig. 2. The proposed architecture.

the generated image is passed through the recognizer (OCR system) to get the recognition accuracy measured by the Character Error Rate (CER) $CER_g = R(I_g)$. After that, a matrix having the same shape of I_g is created and filled with the resultant CER_g. The matrix is concatenated with I_g over the depth and passed to the discriminator with the label Fake to train it. The discriminator is looking, of course, to the Ground Truth (GT) images I_{gt} which are concatenated with a CER that is close to zero and labeled as real.

Clearly, concatenating a matrix with the same number of pixels as the generated image could be replaced by attaching a simple loss directly to the CER and force it to be reduced. However, the choice of a CER matrix was done to let the method be extendable on measuring the error rate from each word (even character or pixel) separately. Thus, we can provide a better feedback to the model, so that it can focus on enhancing the parts with high CER in the image (which could be known from the matrix), while keeping the parts of the image line that were correctly recovered (with low CER in the matrix).

The discriminator is then used to predict the degree of 'reality' (i.e. how realistic) of the generated image, where $P(Real) = D_{\theta_D}(I_g, CER_g)$. We noted that it is better to assign a high CER for the GT images at the beginning of the training stage and then starting to decrease it after some epochs. Thus, we start with a weak discriminator that we progressively enhance it in parallel with the generator to get a better adversarial training. The whole adversarial training could be formalized, hence, with the following loss:

$$L_{GAN}(\theta_G, \theta_D) = \mathbb{E}_{I_d, I_{gt}} \log[D_{\theta_D}(I_d, I_{gt}, CER$$
$$\approx 0)] + \mathbb{E}_{I_d} \log[1 - D_{\theta_D}(I_d, G_{\theta_G}(I_d), CER_g)] \tag{1}$$

To speed up the convergence of the generator parameters θ_G, we use an additional loss which is the usual Binary Cross Entropy (BCE) between the generated images and the ground truth images. The whole Loss becomes:

$$L(\theta_G, \theta_D) = min_{\theta_G} max_{\theta_D} L_{GAN}(\theta_G, \theta_D) + BCE(\theta_G) \tag{2}$$

For a better understanding, we describe in what follows each architecture of the used components.

2.1 Generator

Similar to [22], the used generator is following the U-net encoder-decoder architecture detailed in [20]. It consists of 17 fully convolutional layers with the encoder-decoder fashion, 8 layers for the encoder (down-sampling with max-pooling every two layers) until getting to the 9th layer, followed by a 10th for the decoder (up-sampling every two layers), with an employed skip connections (a concatenation between the layers). Table 1 presents the architecture. As it can be seen, the output is an image with 1 channel since we are providing a grey scale image.

Table 1. Generator architecture: the channels and skip connections are presented. In the U-net model all the convolutions have the kernel size 3×3.

Layer	1	2	3	4	5	6	7	8	9	10	11	12	13	14	15	16	17	18	19
Channels	64	64	128	128	256	256	512	512	512	512	512	256	256	128	128	64	64	2	1
Skip-con	–	16	–	14	–	12	–	10	–	8	–	6	–	4	–	2	–	–	–

2.2 Recognizer

We used Tesseract 4.0 as a recognizer. This OCR engine version is based on deep learning techniques (LSTM), which show a good recognition performance. The recognizer takes an image as input and outputs its predicted text. Anyway, it must be noted that any other OCR system could be used for this purpose.

2.3 Discriminator

The defined discriminator is composed of 6 convolutional layers described in Table 2, which outputs a 2D matrix containing probabilities of the generated image denoting its realistic degree. The discriminator receives three inputs: the degraded image, its cleaned version (ground truth or cleaned by the generator) and the obtained CER. Those inputs are concatenated together in a $H \times W \times 3$ shape. Then, the obtained volume is propagated in the model to end up in a $\frac{H}{16} \times \frac{W}{16} \times 1$ matrix in the last layer. This matrix contains probabilities that should be, to the discriminator, 1 if the clean image represents the ground truth and 0 if it is coming from the generator. Therefore, the last layer takes a sigmoid as an activation function. Once the training is finished, this discriminator is no longer used. Given a distorted image, we only use the generative network to recover it. However, the discriminator shall force the generator during training to produce a realistic result, in addition to the BCE loss with the GT images.

Table 2. Discriminator architecture. All the convolutions are with kernel size 4×4. A max-pooling is performed after each layer, except the last one.

Layer	1	2	3	4	5	6
Channels	64	128	256	256	256	1

3   Experiments and Results

As mentioned above, the goal of this study is to provide a mapping from the distorted document into a clean and readable version. For evaluation, we compare our proposed approach with the relevant methods that can handle the same task in this Section.

3.1   Dataset and Training Details

For a fair comparison, all the methods will be tested on the same dataset containing the distorted lines images and its clean version. This data was taken from SmartDoc-QA [17], which is constituted from smartphone's camera captured document images, under varying capture conditions (light, shadow, different types of blur and perspective angles). SmartDoc-QA is categorized in three subsets of documents: contemporary documents, old administrative documents and shop's receipts. For computational reasons, we use only the contemporary documents category in our experiments. An example of those documents is presented in Fig. 3.

A preprocessing step was done to segment those documents at line level and construct our desired dataset. First, we extract the document paper from the background by applying a Canny edge detector [5] and finding the four corners of the document. Then, a geometric transformation is done for dewarping. Finally, the horizontal projection was applied to detect the lines. This results in 17000 lines images pairs (distorted and clean); from them, 10200 pairs were taken for training the different approaches and 6800 pairs for testing.

The training was done for 80 epochs with a batch size of 32, and the Adam optimization algorithm was used with a learning rate of 1e−4.

3.2   Evaluated Approaches and Metrics

We study the performance of our developed method by comparing it with the following existing approaches, which were widely used for similar tasks:

- DE-GAN [22]: This method uses our same architecture, but without a recognizer (only a generator and a discriminator). In this way, we can evaluate if adding the recognizer helps to provide cleaner documents.

Fig. 3. Examples of two documents from QmartDoc-QA dataset

- Pix2Pix-HD [23]: This method extends [11] to provide a higher resolution and more realistic images. Anyway, both methods falls in the set of the widely used approaches to translate images between different domains.
- CNN [10]: In this approach, a CNN is used to clean the image. Concretely, it was proposed for the goal of text images deblurring.

The comparison is performed using two types of metrics: The first type is for measuring the visual similarity between the predicted images and the GT images. For this purpose, we use the Peak signal-to-noise ratio (PSNR) and Structural Similarity Index Measure (SSIM) [9]. The second metric type is for measuring the readability of the provided image. For this purpose, we simply use the CER metric after passing the cleaned images through Tesseract 4.0. The CER metric is defined as $CER = \frac{S+D+I}{N}$, where S is the number of substitutions, D of deletions, I of insertions and N the ground-truth's length. So, the lower the CER value, the better.

3.3   Results

Table 3. Comparative results between the different approaches.

Approach	SSIM	PSNR	CER
Distorted lines	0.33	9.08	0.25
CNN [10]	**0.54**	**13.54**	0.29
DE-GAN [22]	0.51	12.03	0.26
Pix2pix-HD [23]	0.45	11.45	0.66
Our approach	0.52	12.26	**0.18**

The obtained results are presented in Table 3. As it can be seen, cleaning the distorted images using the different approaches leads to a higher SSIM and PSNR compared to the degraded lines (without any cleaning). This means that we are able to recover a visually enhanced version of the lines images using any of these approaches, with a slightly better performance using the CNN [10] approach. But, this does not means that all these approaches are leading to better versions of the line images. Because, the text is also an important factor to evaluate the cleaning.

Anyway, the CER of the distorted images is much better than the cleaned ones when using the CNN, pix2pix-HD and DE-GAN approaches. As stated before, the reason is that the text in those methods is degrading during the mapping to the clean space. Since the model is only enhancing the visual form of the distorted line images. Contrary, when using our proposed approach, we observe that the CER is also boosted with 7% compared to the distorted images. This demonstrates the utility of using the recognition rate input in our proposed model, which cleans the image while taking the text preservation into account. Thus, from the found results, we can conclude that our model is the best way to perform the distorted to clean text image mapping among the different compared approaches.

Moreover, To illustratively compare the performance of the different methods, we show in what follows some qualitative results. In Fig. 4, we present the recovering of a slightly distorted line. This means that it could be correctly read by the OCR even without any preprocessing, since the distortion is only consists in the baseline due to the warped document and in the background color. It could be observed from the figure that applying the CNN, pix2pix-HD and DE-GAN methods is fixing the baseline and cleaning the background, but deteriorating the text quality and leads to some character errors when reading by the OCR. Contrary, our proposed approach is the one that mostly preserves the text readability while visually enhancing the text line. Another example of a slightly blurred and warped line is also presented in Fig. 5. Despite the fact that the OCR result on the distorted image is still similar to applying it on our generated line (with a clear superiority compared to the CNN and pix2pix-HD methods), it is

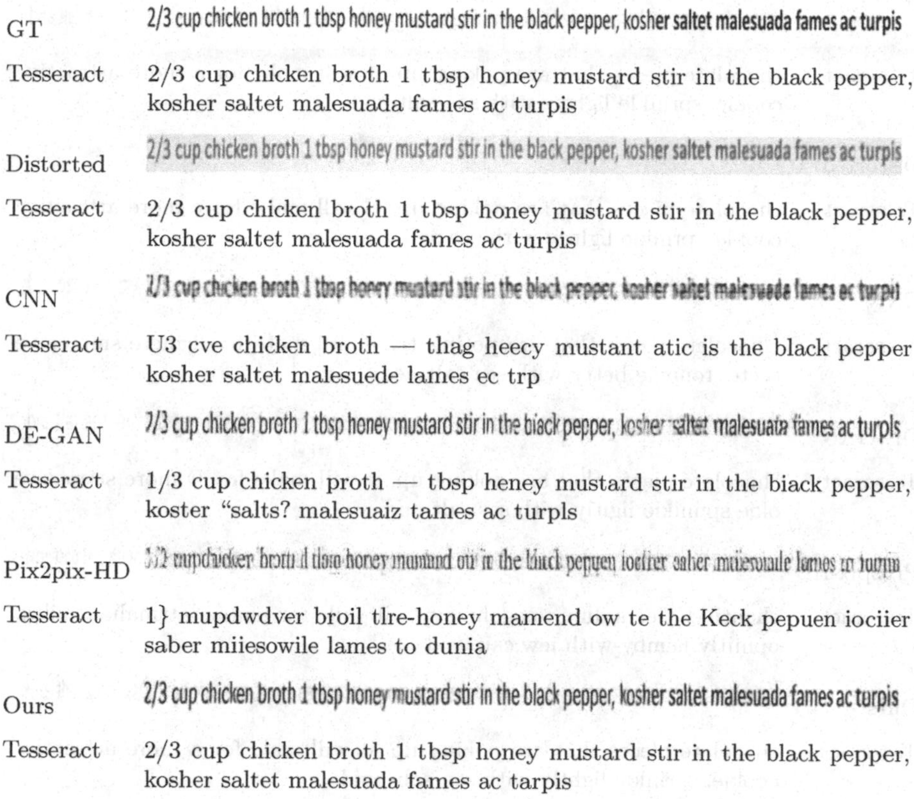

GT   2/3 cup chicken broth 1 tbsp honey mustard stir in the black pepper, kosher saltet malesuada fames ac turpis

Tesseract   2/3 cup chicken broth 1 tbsp honey mustard stir in the black pepper, kosher saltet malesuada fames ac turpis

Distorted   2/3 cup chicken broth 1 tbsp honey mustard stir in the black pepper, kosher saltet malesuada fames ac turpis

Tesseract   2/3 cup chicken broth 1 tbsp honey mustard stir in the black pepper, kosher saltet malesuada fames ac turpis

CNN   2/3 cup chicken broth 1 tbsp honey mustard stir in the black pepper, kosher saltet malesuada fames ec turpis

Tesseract   U3 cve chicken broth — thag heecy mustant atic is the black pepper kosher saltet malesuede lames ec trp

DE-GAN   7/3 cup chicken broth 1 tbsp honey mustard stir in the black pepper, kosher saltet malesuata fames ac turpls

Tesseract   1/3 cup chicken proth — tbsp heney mustard stir in the black pepper, koster "salts? malesuaiz tames ac turpls

Pix2pix-HD   5/3 mupdwdver broti il tisro honey mumind otir ir the biuck pepuen ioeiier saber miiesowile lames to turpin

Tesseract   1} mupdwdver broil tlre-honey mamend ow te the Keck pepuen iociier saber miiesowile lames to dunia

Ours   2/3 cup chicken broth 1 tbsp honey mustard stir in the black pepper, kosher saltet malesuada fames ac turpis

Tesseract   2/3 cup chicken broth 1 tbsp honey mustard stir in the black pepper, kosher saltet malesuada fames ac tarpis

Fig. 4. Results of the different approaches for fixing a warped line image. Errors made by the Tesseract reading engine are shown at character level using the red color. (Color figure online)

clear that our model is producing a much easier image to read by a human, since it is successfully deblurring and unwarping it. We also note in this example that the use of the regular DE-GAN (our same architecture except the recognizer) is resulting in a weak discriminator, which could be fooled by a wrong generation. This can be observed from comparing the visual similarity between our approach and DE-GAN. But, when reading the text, more DE-GAN's character errors are made compared to our generated text.

Next, we show the recovery of some highly distorted lines in Fig. 6. In this case, we tried to recover two distorted lines containing high blur, shadows and warping. Obviously, reading those lines directly with Tesseract is the worst option since it is clearly leading to a bad result by missing a lot of words which results in a high CER. However, by applying the different cleaning approaches, we are able to remove the distortion and produce a better text. Same as previous experiments, it can be seen that our proposed model is achieving the highest results by giving the best line image recovery. Our produced image is visually

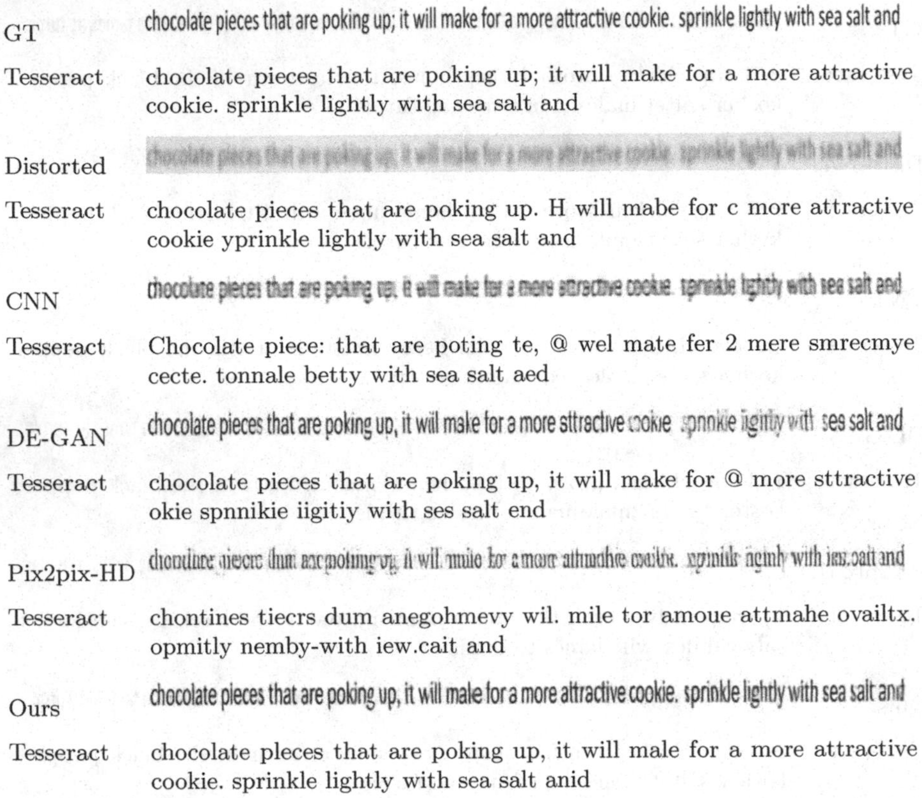

GT	chocolate pieces that are poking up; it will make for a more attractive cookie. sprinkle lightly with sea salt and
Tesseract	chocolate pieces that are poking up; it will make for a more attractive cookie. sprinkle lightly with sea salt and
Distorted	chocolate pieces that are poking up; it will make for a more attractive cookie. sprinkle lightly with sea salt and
Tesseract	chocolate pieces that are poking up. H will mabe for c more attractive cookie yprinkle lightly with sea salt and
CNN	chocolate pieces that are poking up, it will make for a more attractive cookie. sprinkle lightly with sea salt and
Tesseract	Chocolate piece: that are poting te, @ wel mate fer 2 mere smrecmye cecte. tonnale betty with sea salt aed
DE-GAN	chocolate pieces that are poking up, it will make for a more sttractive cookie sprnkle iigitiy with ses salt and
Tesseract	chocolate pieces that are poking up, it will make for @ more sttractive okie spnnikie iigitiy with ses salt end
Pix2pix-HD	chontines tiecrs dum ancpoting up, it wil. mile tor a moue attmahe ovailtx. spmitly nemby with iew.oait and
Tesseract	chontines tiecrs dum anegohmevy wil. mile tor amoue attmahe ovailtx. opmitly nemby-with iew.cait and
Ours	chocolate pieces that are poking up, it will male for a more attractive cookie. sprinkle lightly with sea salt and
Tesseract	chocolate pleces that are poking up, it will male for a more attractive cookie. sprinkle lightly with sea salt anid

Fig. 5. Results of the different approaches for fixing a blurred and warped line image, errors made by Tesseract reading engine are shown in character level with the red color. (Color figure online)

closed to the GT image, with a preserved text, that can be seen from the low CER compared to different methods.

Finally, it is worth to mention that our proposed model was sometimes failing to produce readable lines. This was happening when dealing with the extremely distorted lines. Some examples of this particular case are presented in Fig. 7. As can be seen, despite the fact that some words have been correctly enhanced and recognized by the OCR after applying our method, the line images are still visually degraded and unsatisfactory. Of course, this is happening due to the extreme complexity of fixing such lines, which are hard to be read even by the human naked eye.

GT	audiences personal needs to use media and responds to the media, which determined by
Distorted	audiences personal needs to use media and responds to the media, which determined by
Tesseract	WS 0 WBE Ia and responds (6 the media. which determined by
CNN	audiences personal needs to use media and responds to the media. which determined by
Tesseract	guciences setsona needs io use media and responcs io the media. wich determned ie
DE-GAN	audiences personal needs io use media and responds to the media, which detennined by
Tesseract	audiences personal needs io woe mecie and responds to the medi, wri detennined ny
Pix2pix-HD	audiences personal reads to use ments and rsaponde io the medls, which datermined Up
Tesseract	1} audiences perional reads fo use ments and rszeonde io the medis, witich determined tia
Ours	audiences personal reads to use ments and rsaponds to the medls, which determined Up
Tesseract	auclences persond! needs fo use medie and responds to the media, which deterttiined yr

GT	mounds of dough (the size of generous golf balls) onto baking sheet, making sure to turn horizontally any
Distorted	mounds of dough (the size of generous golf balls) onto baking sheet, making sure to turn horizontally any
Tesseract	wen horizontally any
CNN	mounds of dough (the size of generous golf balls) onto baking sheet, making sure to turn horizontally any
Tesseract	moune: of Gowgh fihe mae of pemereet get balai eees bate thet mating rere te ture hormontaily any
DE-GAN	mounds of dough (the sise of generous golf salls) sem baking sheet, msking sure te turn homentally ary
Tesseract	mounds of dough {the sie et cenereat gol! ssl sem bakig sheet, mskinz sure te tum homentaly ary
Pix2pix-HD	mounds of bough the due of generios grrl! hald tom lating cheer, mnding aure to hum horizontal\y ani
Tesseract	predt a? bout. .tbe due of geewerios gut! neckd wir tating cheer, muting aare te lum keotteerath, an
Ours	mounds of dough (the sise of generous golf balls) este baking sheet, making sure to tum horizontally any
Tesseract	mounds of dough ithe sire ef generaus goll bald este bakiog sheet, making sure te tum horivontally any

Fig. 6. Results of the different approaches for fixing two distorted line images. Errors made by the Tesseract reading engine are shown at character level in red color. (Color figure online)

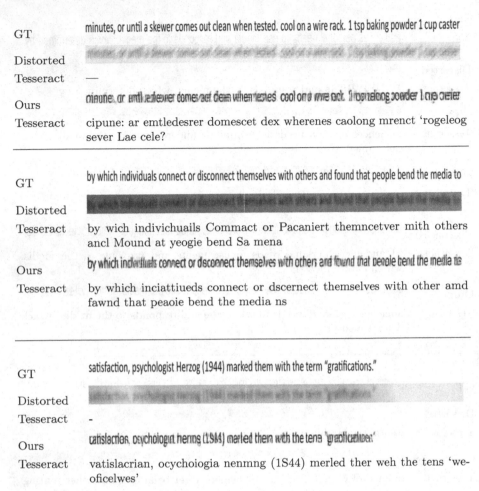

Fig. 7. Results of our approach for cleaning the extremely distorted line images. Errors made by the Tesseract reading engine are shown at word level in red color. (Color figure online)

4   Conclusion

In this paper we have proposed an approach for recovering distorted camera captured documents. The goal is to provide a clean and readable version of the document images. Our method integrates an OCR to cGAN model to preserve the readability while translating the document domain. As a result, our method leads to a better CER compared to the widely used methods for this task.

As future work, our proposed model could be extended to handle full pages instead of lines. Furthermore, the CER matrix provided for the discriminator could include the error rates at local level instead of passing the CER of the whole text line. This could help the discriminator to provide a better feedback to the generative model, and thus, improve the overall model performance. Finally, it will be interesting to test the model on historically handwritten degraded documents, using of course, a Handwritten Text Recognition system instead of the OCR system.

Acknowledgment. This work has been partially supported by the Swedish Research Council (grant 2018-06074, DECRYPT), the Spanish project RTI2018-095645-B-C21, the Ramon y Cajal Fellowship RYC-2014-16831 and the CERCA Program/Generalitat de Catalunya.

References

1. Alonso, E., Moysset, B., Messina, R.: Adversarial generation of handwritten text images conditioned on sequences. In: 15th International Conference on Document Analysis and Recognition (ICDAR) (2019). https://doi.org/10.1109/ICDAR.2019.00083
2. Asad, F., Ul-Hasan, A., Shafait, F., Dengel, A.: High performance OCR for camera-captured blurred documents with LSTM networks. In: 12th IAPR Workshop on Document Analysis Systems (DAS) (2016). https://doi.org/10.1109/DAS.2016.69
3. El Bahi, H., Zatni, A.: Text recognition in document images obtained by a smartphone based on deep convolutional and recurrent neural network. Multimed. Tools Appl. **78**(18), 26453–26481 (2019). https://doi.org/10.1007/s11042-019-07855-z
4. Calvo-Zaragoza, J., Gallego, A.J.: A selectional auto-encoder approach for document image binarization. Pattern Recogn. **86**, 37–47 (2019)
5. Canny, J.: A computational approach to edge detection. IEEE Trans. Pattern Anal. Mach. Intell. 679–698 (1986). https://doi.org/10.1109/TPAMI.1986.4767851
6. Chabchoub, F., Kessentini, Y., Kanoun, S., Eglin, V., Lebourgeois, F.: SmartATID: a mobile captured Arabic text images dataset for multi-purpose recognition tasks. In: 2016 15th International Conference on Frontiers in Handwriting Recognition (ICFHR), pp. 120–125 (2016)
7. Choi, Y., Choi, M., Kim, M., Ha, J.W., Kim, S., Choo, J.: StarGAN: unified generative adversarial networks for multi-domain image-to-image translation. In: The IEEE Conference on Computer Vision and Pattern Recognition (CVPR) (2018)
8. Fan, H., Han, M., Li, J.: Image shadow removal using end-to-end deep convolutional neural networks. Appl. Sci. **9**, 1–17 (2019). https://doi.org/10.3390/app9051009
9. Horé, A., Ziou, D.: Image quality metrics: PSNR vs. SSIM. In: 20th International Conference on Pattern Recognition (ICPR) (2010). https://doi.org/10.1109/ICPR.2010.579
10. Hradiš, M., Kotera, J., Zemčík, P., Šroubek, F.: Convolutional neural networks for direct text deblurring. In: British Machine Vision Conference (BMVC), pp. 6.1–6.13, September 2015. https://doi.org/10.5244/C.29.6
11. Isola, P., Zhu, J.Y., Zhou, T., Efros, A.A.: Image-to-image translation with conditional adversarial networks. In: The IEEE Conference on Computer Vision and Pattern Recognition (CVPR) (2017)
12. Kang, L., Riba, P., Wang, Y., Rusiñol, M., Fornés, A., Villegas, M.: GANwriting: content-conditioned generation of styled handwritten word images. Arxiv preprint (2020)
13. Le, H., Samaras, D.: Shadow removal via shadow image decomposition. In: The IEEE International Conference on Computer Vision (ICCV), October 2019

14. Lore, K.G., Akintayo, A., Sarkar, S.: LLNet: a deep autoencoder approach to natural low-light image enhancement. Pattern Recogn. **61**, 650–662 (2017)
15. Ma, K., Shu, Z., Bai, X., Wang, J., Samaras, D.: DocUNet: document image unwarping via a stacked U-Net. In: The IEEE Conference on Computer Vision and Pattern Recognition (CVPR), June 2018
16. Meng, G., Yuan, K., Wu, Y., Xiang, S., Pan, C.: Deep networks for degraded document image binarization through pyramid reconstruction. In: 14th IAPR International Conference on Document Analysis and Recognition (ICDAR), pp. 2379–2140 (2017). https://doi.org/10.1109/ICDAR.2017.124
17. Nayef, N., Luqman, M.M., Prum, S., Eskenazi, S., Chazalon, J., Ogier, J.M.: SmartDoc-QA: a dataset for quality assessment of smartphone captured document images - single and multiple distortions. In: 13th International Conference on Document Analysis and Recognition (ICDAR) (2015). https://doi.org/10.1109/ICDAR.2015.7333960
18. Niblack, W.: An Introduction to Digital Image Processing. Strandberg Publishing Company, Birkeroed (1985)
19. Otsu, N.: A threshold selection method from gray-level histograms. IEEE Trans. Syst. Man Cybern. **9**, 62–66 (1979). https://doi.org/10.1109/TSMC.1979.4310076
20. Ronneberger, O., Fischer, P., Brox, T.: U-Net: convolutional networks for biomedical image segmentation. Arxiv preprint (2015)
21. Sauvola, J., Pietik, M.: Adaptive document image binarization. Pattern Recogn. **33**, 225–236 (2000)
22. Souibgui, M.A., Kessentini, Y.: DE-GAN: a conditional generative adversarial network for document enhancement. IEEE Trans. Pattern Anal. Mach. Intell. (2020). https://doi.org/10.1109/TPAMI.2020.3022406
23. Wang, T.C., Liu, M.Y., Zhu, J.Y., Tao, A., Kautz, J., Catanzaro, B.: High-resolution image synthesis and semantic manipulation with conditional GANs. In: The IEEE Conference on Computer Vision and Pattern Recognition (CVPR) (2018)

Learning Features for Writer Identification from Handwriting on Papyri

Sidra Nasir[✉] and Imran Siddiqi[✉]

Vision and Learning Lab, Bahria University, Islamabad, Pakistan
rnsidra7@gmail.com, imran.siddiqi@bahria.edu.pk

Abstract. Computerized analysis of historical documents has remained an interesting research area for the pattern classification community for many decades. From the perspective of computerized analysis, key challenges in the historical manuscripts include automatic transcription, dating, retrieval, classification of writing styles and identification of scribes etc. Among these, the focus of our current study lies on identification of writers from the digitized manuscripts. We exploit convolutional neural networks for extraction of features and characterization of writer. The ConvNets are first trained on contemporary handwriting samples and then fine-tuned to the limited set of historical manuscripts considered in our study. Dense sampling is carried out over a given manuscript producing a set of small writing patches for each document. Decisions on patches are combined using a majority vote to conclude the authorship of a query document. Preliminary experiments on a set of challenging and degraded manuscripts report promising performance.

Keywords: Writer identification · ConvNets · IAM dataset · Papyrus

1 Introduction

Historical documents contain rich information and provide useful insight into the past. Drawings, embellishments, shapes, letters and signatures not only provide explicit details on the content but, diverse cultural and social attributes are also manifested in the style of writing and its evolution. Paleographers are particularly interested in tasks like identifying the scribe, determining the date and place of origin of a manuscript and so on. Such problems, naturally, require significant experience and domain knowledge.

Over the last few decades, there has been a significant increase in the trend to digitize ancient documents [1,2]. The digitization not only aims at preserving the cultural heritage and to make it publicly accessible but also allows research on these rich collections without the need to physically access them. This, in turn, has exposed the pattern classification researchers in general and the document and handwriting recognition community in particular to a whole new set of

© Springer Nature Switzerland AG 2021
C. Djeddi et al. (Eds.): MedPRAI 2020, CCIS 1322, pp. 229–241, 2021.
https://doi.org/10.1007/978-3-030-71804-6_17

challenging problems [3]. Few of the prominent digitization projects include the International Dunhuang Project (IDP) [4], The Monk system [5], Madonne [3] and NAVIDOMASS (NAVIgation in Document MASSes). Besides digitization, these projects are also supported by development of automated tools to assist the paleographers in tasks like spotting keywords in manuscripts or retrieving documents with a particular writing style or a dropcap etc. The SPI (System for Paleographic Inspection) [6] Software, for instance, has been employed by experts to compare and analyze paleographic content morphologically. Such systems help paleographers in inferring the origin of a manuscript as morphologically similar strokes are likely to originate from similar temporal and cultural environments. The notion of similarity can also be exploited to identify the scribe of a given manuscript.

In the past, paleographers and historians have been hesitant in accepting computerized solutions. The key contributing factor to this resistance has been the lack of 'trust' in machine based solutions. In the recent years, however, thanks to the advancements in different areas of image analysis and machine learning as well as the success of joint ventures between paleographers and computer scientists, the experts are more open to accepting automated solutions in their practices [7]. The main motivation of such solutions is to assist and not replace the human experts. These tools can be exploited to narrow down the search space so that the experts can focus on limited set of samples for detailed and in-depth analysis [8].

Among various challenges in computerized analysis of historical manuscript, identification of scribes carries significant importance. Identifying the writer can also be exploited to estimate the date and region in which the manuscript was produced by correlating with the 'active' period of the scribe [9]. Writer of a document can be categorized by capturing the writing style which is known to be specific for each individual [10]. Writing style is typically exploited through a global (page or paragraph) scale of observation. Textural features, for example, have been extensively employed to capture the writing style [11–13]. Another series of methods employs low level statistical measures computed from relatively closer scale of observation (characters or graphemes for example) [10]. Studying the frequency of certain writing patterns in a given handwriting has also been exploited to characterize writers under the category of codebook based writer identification [14, 15]. In the recent years, feature learning using deep convolutional neural networks (CNNs) has also been investigated to characterize the writer [16]. A major proportion of work on writer identification targets contemporary documents which do not offer the challenges encountered when dealing with ancient manuscripts. Noise removal, segmentation of text from background, segmentation of handwriting into smaller units for feature extraction etc. are few of the challenges that hinder the direct application of many established writer identification methods to historical manuscripts. Another important factor is the medium on which writing is produced that has evolved over time (stone, clay, papyrus, parchment, paper etc.). Each medium has its own unique challenges that must be addressed to effectively identify the scribe.

This paper addresses the problem of writer identification from handwriting on papyrus. The digitized images of handwriting are pre-processed and divided into patches using a dense sampling. Machine learned features are extracted from each patch using a number of pre-trained ConvNets. Since handwriting images are very different from the images on which most of the publicly available CNNs are trained, the networks are first fine tuned using a large dataset of contemporary writings. These networks are further tuned on the papyrus images to identify the scribe. Experimental study is carried out on the GRK-Papyri [17] dataset and results are reported at patch as well as document level (by applying a majority vote on patch level decisions).

We first present an overview of recent studies on similar problems in Sect. 2. Section 3 introduces the dataset and presents the details of the proposed technique. Details of experiments along with a discussion on the reported results are presented in Sect. 4. At the end, we summarize our findings in Sect. 5.

2   Related Work

In the recent years, computerized analysis of ancient handwriting has gained significant attention from the document recognition community [18–21]. The key challenge in the automatic writer identification (AWI) is the selection of distinguishable features which effectively extract the writing style of the scribe from the handwriting images. The scale of observation at which features are computed is also critical as features can be extracted from complete pages, small patches of handwriting, text lines, words, characters or even graphemes. These units represent different scale of observations at which the handwriting is analyzed.

As discussed in the introductory discussion, a recent trend in writer identification from contemporary documents is to learn features from data, typically using ConvNets. In our discussion, we will be focusing more on machine learning based methods for writer identification. Readers interested in comprehensive reviews on this problem can find details in the relevant survey papers [22,23].

From the perspective of feature learning, ConvNets are either trained from scratch or pre-trained models are adapted to writer identification problem using transfer learning. Rehman et al. [18], for instance, employed the well-known AlexNet [24] architecture pre-trained on ImageNet [25] dataset as feature extractor. Handwriting images are fed to the trained model and extracted features are fed to an SVM for classification. In another deep learning based solution, Xing and Qiao [19] introduced a deep multi-stream CNN termed as DeepWriter. Small patches of handwriting are fed as input to the network that is trained with softmax classification. Experiments on English and Chinese writing samples report high identification rates. Authors also demonstrate that joint training on both scripts leads to better performances.

Among other significant contributions, Tang and Wu [26] employ a CNN for feature extraction and the joint Bayesian technique for identification. To enhance the size of training data, writing samples are split into words and their random combinations are used to produce text lines. The technique is evaluated through experimental study on the ICDAR2013 and the CVL dataset and Top-1 identification rates of more than 99% are reported in different experiments. In another similar work, writer identification is carried out from Japanese hand-written characters using a AlexNet as the pre-trained model [27]. Fiel et al. [28] mapped handwriting images to feature vectors using a CNN and carried out identification using a nearest neighbor classifier. Christlein et al. [20] investigate unsupervised feature learning using SIFT descriptors and a residual network. Likewise, authors in [29] employ a semi-supervised learning approach with ResNet. Weighted Label Smoothing Regularization (WLSR) was introduced to regulate the unlabeled data. Words in the CVL dataset were used as the original data while IAM words as the unlabeled set of data in the experimental study.

While CNNs are mostly employed in the classification framework for writer identification, Keglevic et al. [21] propose to learn similarity between handwriting patches using a triplet network. The network is trained by minimizing the intra class and maximizing the inter class distances and the writing patches are represented by the learned features. A relatively recent trend is to exploit hyperspectral imaging to capture handwriting images, mainly for forensic applications. Authors in [30] demonstrate the effectiveness of employing multiple spectral responses of a single pixel to characterize the writer. These responses are fed to a CNN to identify the writer. Experiments on the UWA Writing Inks Hyperspectral Images (WIHSI) dataset reveal the potential of this interesting area for forensic and retrieval applications.

From the perspective of writer identification in historical manuscripts, the literature is relatively limited as opposed to contemporary documents [31,32]. In some cases, standard writer identification techniques have also been adapted for historical manuscripts [33]. A recent work is reported in [34] that targets writer identification in medieval manuscripts (Avila Bible). Transfer learning is employed to detect text lines (rows) from images and the writer against each line is identified. Majority voting is subsequently applied on the row-wise decisions to assign a writer to the corresponding page and, page-level accuracy of more than 96% is reported. Sutder et al. [35] present a comprehensive empirical study to investigate the performance of multiple pre-trained CNNs on analysis of historical manuscripts. The networks were investigated for problems like character recognition, dating and handwriting style classification.

In another similar work, Cilia et al. [36] propose a two-step transfer learning based system to identify writers from historical manuscripts. The text rows in images are first extracted using an object detection system based on MobileNet. The CNN pre-trained on ImageNet is subsequently employed for writer identification on digitized images from a Bible of the XII century. Mohammed et al. [37] adapt a known writer identification method (Local Naïve Bayes Nearest-Neighbour classifier [38]) for degraded documents and demonstrate high identification rates on 100 pages from the Stiftsbibliothek library of St. Gall collection [39]. The same technique was applied to the GRK-Papyri dataset [17] with FAST keypoints and reported a low identification rate of 30% (using a leave-one-out evaluation protocol).

After having discussed the recent contributions to writer identification in general and historical documents in particular, we now present the proposed methods in the next section.

3   Materials and Methods

We now present the details of the proposed method for characterization of writers from the challenging papyrus handwriting. We first introduce the dataset employed in our study followed by the details of pre-processing, sampling and writer identification through ConvNets. The approach primarily relies on characterizing small patches of handwriting using machine-learned features in a two-step fine tuning process. An overview of the key steps is presented in Fig. 1 while each of these steps is discussed in detail in the subsequent sections.

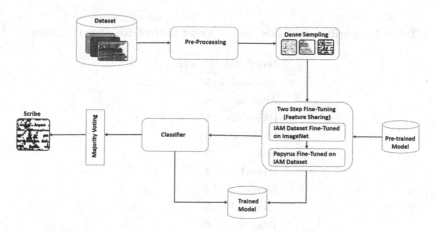

Fig. 1. An overview of key processing steps in the system

3.1   Dataset

The experimental study of the system is carried out on the GRK-Papyri dataset presented in [17]. The dataset consists of 50 handwriting samples of 10 different scribes on papyri. All writings are in Greek and come from the 6th century A.D. The dataset has been made available for research along with the ground truth information of writers. Sample images from the dataset are shown in Fig. 2.

All images are digitized as JPEGs and height of images varies from 796 to 6818 pixels while the width values are in the range 177 to 7938 pixels. The DPI also varies from a minimum of 96 to a maximum of 2000. Few of the images are digitized as gray scale with others are three channel RGB images. The samples suffer from sever degradation including low contrast, holes and glass reflection etc. (Fig. 2). The background contains papyrus fibers with varying sizes and

Fig. 2. Sample images of GRK-Papyri dataset [17]

frequencies adding further complexity from the perspective of automated processing. The samples are not uniformly distributed across the 10 scribes and the number varies from 4 to 7 samples per writer as presented in Table 1.

Table 1. Distribution of samples per writer in the GRK-Papyri dataset

Writer ID	Samples
Abraamios	5
Andreas	4
Dioscorus	5
Hermauos	5
Isak	5
Kyros1	4
Kyros3	4
Menas	5
Pilatos	6
Victor	7

3.2 Pre-processing

Prior to feeding the images to ConvNets for feature extraction, we need to process the images. Since the dataset comprises both colored and gray scale images with diverse backgrounds of papyrus fiber, directly feeding raw images may lead to learning features that could be linked with the background information rather than handwriting. We therefore first convert all images to gray scale and preprocess them in different ways to investigate which of the representations could yield better performance. These include:

- Binarization using adaptive (Sauvoloa [40]) thresholding.
- Application of Canny edge detector to preserve edges of writing strokes only.

- Edge detection on adaptively binarized images.
- Binarization of images using a recent deep learning based technique – DeepOtsu [41].

The output images resulting from these different types of processing are illustrated in Figure 3.

Adaptive Binarization	Edge Detection	Edge Detection on Binarized images	Deep Otsu

Fig. 3. Output images resulting from different types of pre-processing

3.3 Data Preparation Using Dense Sampling

When employing pre-trained ConvNets in a transfer learning framework (fine tuning them on the target dataset), the resolution of images must match the input expected at the network. Naturally, resizing the complete page to a small square and feeding it to a network is not very meaningful as not only all writer-specific information is likely to be lost but the aspect ratio is also highly disturbed. We, therefore, carry out a dense sampling of the complete image using overlapping squared windows. The size of window determines the scale of observation and extracting square windows ensures that the aspect ratio is not disturbed once the extracted patches are resized to match the input layer of pre-trained CNN. Figure 4 illustrates few patches of size 512×512 extracted from one of the images in the dataset.

Full Image   Patches 512 x 512

Fig. 4. Patches extracted from a binarized image in the dataset

3.4   Two-Step Fine Tuning of ConvNets

As discussed in the earlier sections, deep ConvNets have become the gold standard for feature extraction as well as classification. Designing a new architecture and training CNNs from scratch for every problem, however, is neither required not feasible. In most cases, architectures and weights of ConvNets can be borrowed from those trained on millions of images and made publicly available by the research community. This concept is commonly termed as transfer learning and has been successfully applied to a number of recognition tasks.

Pre-trained ConvNets can be employed only as feature extractors in conjunction with another classifier (SVM for example) or, they can be fine-tuned to the target dataset by changing the softmax layer (to match classes under study) and continuing back propagation. Fine-tuning can be employed to update weights of all or a subset of layers by freezing few of the initial layers. Most of the pre-trained networks publicly available are trained on the ImageNet [25] dataset and have been fine-tuned to solve many other problems.

In our study, we employ the pre-trained ConvNets by fine-tuning them to our problem. More specifically, we employ three standard architectures namely VGG16 [42], Inceptionv3 [43] and ResNet50 [44] trained on the ImageNet dataset. Since we deal with handwriting images which are different from the images in the ImageNet dataset, we employ a two-step fine-tuning. First we fine-tune the networks using IAM handwriting dataset [45] which contains writing samples of more than 650 writers. Although these are contemporary samples and do not offer the same challenges as those encountered in historical documents, nevertheless, since these images contain handwriting, we expect an enhanced feature learning. Once the networks are fine-tuned on IAM handwriting samples, we further tune them on the writing patches in our papyri dataset. The softmax layer of the final network is changed to match 10 scribes in our problem.

4   Experiments and Results

We now present the experimental protocol, the details of experiments and the reported results. The GRK-Papyri dataset is provided to carry out writer identification task in two experimental settings.

– Leave-one-out Approach
– A training set of 20 and a test set of 30 images

Since we employ a machine learning based technique, experiments under a leave-one-out approach would mean training the system 50 times for each evaluation. We, therefore, chose to employ the training and test set distribution provided in the database i.e. 20 images in the train and 30 in the test set.

We first present the identification rates as a function of different preprocessing techniques. These classification rates are computed by fine-tuning Inceptionv3 first on IAM dataset and subsequently on the training images in the GRK-Papyri dataset. Results are reported at patch level as well as document level by applying a majority vote on the patch level decisions. It can be seen from Table 2 that among the different pre-processing techniques investigated, DeepOtsu reports the highest identification rates of 27% at patch level and 48% at document level. The subsequent experiments are therefore carried out using DeepOtsu as the pre-processing technique.

Table 2. Writer identification rates for different pre-processing techniques (two-step fine-tuning of Inceptionv3)

	Patch level	Document level
Adaptive Binarization [40]	0.11	0.32
Canny Edge Detection [46]	0.10	0.27
Edge Detection+Binarization	0.38	0.16
Deep Otsu [41]	**0.27**	**0.48**

Table 3 presents a comparison of the three pre-trained models VGG16, Inceptionv3 and ResNet50 employed in our study.

Table 3. Performance of single and two step fine tuning on different pre-trained ConvNets

	Fine-tuning scheme	Patch level	Document level
VGG16 [42]	ImageNet→Papyri	0.14	0.36
	ImageNet→IAM→Papyri	0.16	0.38
Inceptionv3 [43]	ImageNet→Papyri	0.24	0.42
	ImageNet→IAM→Papyri	0.27	0.48
ResNet50 [44]	ImageNet→Papyri	0.30	0.51
	ImageNet→IAM→Papyri	**0.33**	**0.54**

We present the identification rates by directly fine-tuning the models from ImageNet to our dataset (single step tuning) as well as by first tuning them on the IAM dataset and subsequently on the paypri dataset (two step tuning). It can be seen that in all cases two-step fine tuning serves to enhance the identification rates by 2 to 6%. The highest document level identification rate is reported by fine tuning ResNet50 and reads 54%. Considering the complexity of the problem and the small set of training samples, the reported identification rate is indeed very promising.

We also study the impact of patch size (scale of observation) on the identification rates. Document level identification rates with two step fine-tuning of Inceptionv3 and ResNet50 as a function of patch size are summarized in Fig. 5. It is interesting to observe that both the models exhibit more or less similar trend and the highest identification rates are reported at a patch size of 512×512, i.e. 48% and 54% for Inception and ResNet respectively. Too small or too large patches naturally report relatively lower identification rates indicating that scale of observation is a critical parameter that must be carefully chosen.

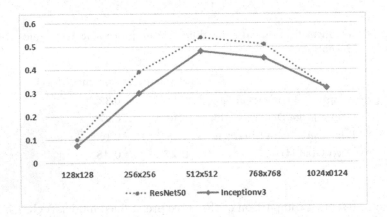

Fig. 5. Writer identification rates as a function of patch size

From the view point of comparison, writer identification rates are reported on this dataset using Normalized Local Naïve Bayes Nearest-Neighbor with FAST key points in [17]. Authors report an identification rate of 30.0% with leave-one-out protocol and, 26.6% identification rate with distribution of data into training and test set. Using the same distribution of 20 images in the training and 30 in the test set, we report an identification rate of 54% which seems to be quite encouraging.

5   Conclusion

This study aimed at identification of scribes from historical manuscripts. More specifically, we investigated the problem on Greek handwriting on papyrus. Handwriting is extracted from the degraded images in a pre-processing steps and is divided into small patches using dense sampling. Features are extracted from handwriting patches by fine-tuning state-of-the-art ConvNets. A two-step fine-tuning is carried out by first tuning the models to contemporary hand writings and subsequently to the papyri dataset. Patch level identification decisions are combined to document level using a majority voting and, identification rates of up to 54% are reported. Considering the challenging set of writing samples, the realized identification rates are indeed very promising.

In our further study, we intend to extend the analysis to other relevant problems like classification of writing styles and dating. Furthermore, the current study revealed that pre-processing is a critical step in analyzing such documents and further investigating different pre-processing techniques could indeed be an interesting study. In addition to standard pre-trained models, relatively shallower networks can also be trained from scratch to study the performance evolution.

Acknowledgement. Authors would like to thank Dr. Isabelle Marthot-Santaniello from University of Basel, Switzerland for making the dataset available.

References

1. Baird, H.S., Govindaraju, V., Lopresti, D.P.: Document analysis systems for digital libraries: challenges and opportunities. In: Marinai, S., Dengel, A.R. (eds.) DAS 2004. LNCS, vol. 3163, pp. 1–16. Springer, Heidelberg (2004). https://doi.org/10.1007/978-3-540-28640-0_1
2. Le Bourgeois, F., Trinh, E., Allier, B., Eglin, V., Emptoz, H.: Document images analysis solutions for digital libraries. In: 2004 Proceedings of the First International Workshop on Document Image Analysis for Libraries, pp. 2–24. IEEE (2004)
3. Sankar, K.P., Ambati, V., Pratha, L., Jawahar, C.V.: Digitizing a million books: challenges for document analysis. In: Bunke, H., Spitz, A.L. (eds.) DAS 2006. LNCS, vol. 3872, pp. 425–436. Springer, Heidelberg (2006). https://doi.org/10.1007/11669487_38
4. Klemme, A.: International Dunhuang project: the silk road online. Ref. Rev. **28**(2), 51–52 (2014)
5. Van der Zant, T., Schomaker, L., Haak, K.: Handwritten-word spotting using biologically inspired features. IEEE Trans. Pattern Anal. Mach. Intell. **30**(11), 1945–1957 (2008)
6. Aiolli, F., Ciula, A.: A case study on the system for paleographic inspections (SPI): challenges and new developments. Comput. Intell. Bioeng. **196**, 53–66 (2009)
7. Hamid, A., Bibi, M., Siddiqi, I., Moetesum, M.: Historical manuscript dating using textural measures. In: 2018 International Conference on Frontiers of Information Technology (FIT), pp. 235–240. IEEE (2018)
8. Hamid, A., Bibi, M., Moetesum, M., Siddiqi, I.: Deep learning based approach for historical manuscript dating. In: 2019 International Conference on Document Analysis and Recognition (ICDAR), pp. 967–972 (2019)
9. He, S., Samara, P., Burgers, J., Schomaker, L.: Image-based historical manuscript dating using contour and stroke fragments. Pattern Recogn. **58**, 159–171 (2016)
10. Srihari, S.N., Cha, S.-H., Arora, H., Lee, S.: Individuality of handwriting. J. Forensic Sci. **47**(4), 1–17 (2002)
11. Said, H.E., Tan, T.N., Baker, K.D.: Personal identification based on handwriting. Pattern Recogn. **33**(1), 149–160 (2000)
12. He, Z., You, X., Tang, Y.Y.: Writer identification using global wavelet-based features. Neurocomputing **71**(10–12), 1832–1841 (2008)
13. He, S., Schomaker, L.: Deep adaptive learning for writer identification based on single handwritten word images. Pattern Recogn. **88**, 64–74 (2019)
14. Bulacu, M., Schomaker, L.: Text-independent writer identification and verification using textural and allographic features. IEEE Trans. Pattern Anal. Mach. Intell. **29**(4), 701–717 (2007)
15. Siddiqi, I., Vincent, N.: Text independent writer recognition using redundant writing patterns with contour-based orientation and curvature features. Pattern Recogn. **43**(11), 3853–3865 (2010)

16. Xing, L., Qiao, Y.: DeepWriter: a multi-stream deep CNN for text-independent writer identification. In: 2016 15th International Conference on Frontiers in Handwriting Recognition (ICFHR), pp. 584–589. IEEE (2016)

17. Mohammed, H., Marthot-Santaniello, I., Märgner, V.: GRK-Papyri: a dataset of Greek handwriting on papyri for the task of writer identification. In: 2019 International Conference on Document Analysis and Recognition (ICDAR), pp. 726–731 (2019)

18. Rehman, A., Naz, S., Razzak, M.I., Hameed, I.A.: Automatic visual features for writer identification: a deep learning approach. IEEE Access **7**, 17149–17157 (2019)

19. Xing, L., Qiao, Y.: DeepWriter: a multi-stream deep CNN for text-independent writer identification. In: 2016 15th International Conference on Frontiers in Handwriting Recognition (ICFHR), pp. 584–589 (2016)

20. Christlein, V., Gropp, M., Fiel, S., Maier, A.: Unsupervised feature learning for writer identification and writer retrieval. In: 2017 14th IAPR International Conference on Document Analysis and Recognition (ICDAR), vol. 01, pp. 991–997 (2017)

21. Keglevic, M., Fiel, S., Sablatnig, R.: Learning features for writer retrieval and identification using triplet CNNs. In: 2018 16th International Conference on Frontiers in Handwriting Recognition (ICFHR), pp. 211–216 (2018)

22. Awaida, S.M., Mahmoud, S.A.: State of the art in off-line writer identification of handwritten text and survey of writer identification of Arabic text. Educ. Res. Rev. **7**(20), 445–463 (2012)

23. Tan, G.J., Sulong, G., Rahim, M.S.M.: Writer identification: a comparative study across three world major languages. Forensic Sci. Int. **279**, 41–52 (2017)

24. Krizhevsky, A., Sutskever, I., Hinton, G.E.: ImageNet classification with deep convolutional neural networks. In: Advances in Neural Information Processing Systems, pp. 1097–1105 (2012)

25. Deng, J., Dong, W., Socher, R., Li, L.-J., Li, K., Fei-Fei, L.: ImageNet: a large-scale hierarchical image database. In: 2009 IEEE Conference on Computer Vision and Pattern Recognition, pp. 248–255. IEEE (2009)

26. Tang, Y., Wu, X.: Text-independent writer identification via CNN features and joint Bayesian. In: 2016 15th International Conference on Frontiers in Handwriting Recognition (ICFHR), pp. 566–571, October 2016

27. Nasuno, R., Arai, S.: Writer identification for offline Japanese handwritten character using convolutional neural network. In: Proceedings of the 5th IIAE (Institute of Industrial Applications Engineers) International Conference on Intelligent Systems and Image Processing, pp. 94–97 (2017)

28. Fiel, S., Sablatnig, R.: Writer identification and retrieval using a convolutional neural network. In: Azzopardi, G., Petkov, N. (eds.) CAIP 2015. LNCS, vol. 9257, pp. 26–37. Springer, Cham (2015). https://doi.org/10.1007/978-3-319-23117-4_3

29. Chen, S., Wang, Y., Lin, C.-T., Ding, W., Cao, Z.: Semi-supervised feature learning for improving writer identification. Inf. Sci. **482**, 156–170 (2019)

30. Islam, A.U., Khan, M.J., Khurshid, K., Shafait, F.: Hyperspectral image analysis for writer identification using deep learning. In: 2019 Digital Image Computing: Techniques and Applications (DICTA), pp. 1–7 (2019)

31. Bar-Yosef, I., Beckman, I., Kedem, K., Dinstein, I.: Binarization, character extraction, and writer identification of historical Hebrew calligraphy documents. IJDAR **9**(2–4), 89–99 (2007). https://doi.org/10.1007/s10032-007-0041-5

32. Fecker, D., Asit, A., Märgner, V., El-Sana, J., Fingscheidt, T.: Writer identification for historical Arabic documents. In: 2014 22nd International Conference on Pattern Recognition, pp. 3050–3055. IEEE (2014)

33. Schomaker, L., Franke, K., Bulacu, M.: Using codebooks of fragmented connected-component contours in forensic and historic writer identification. Pattern Recogn. Lett. **28**(6), 719–727 (2007)
34. Cilia, N., De Stefano, C., Fontanella, F., Marrocco, C., Molinara, M., Di Freca, A.S.: An end-to-end deep learning system for medieval writer identification. Pattern Recogn. Lett. **129**, 137–143 (2020)
35. Studer, L., et al.: A comprehensive study of imagenet pre-training for historical document image analysis. arXiv preprint arXiv:1905.09113 (2019)
36. Cilia, N.D., De Stefano, C., Fontanella, F., Marrocco, C., Molinara, M., Scotto Di Freca, A.: A two-step system based on deep transfer learning for writer identification in medieval books. In: Vento, M., Percannella, G. (eds.) CAIP 2019. LNCS, vol. 11679, pp. 305–316. Springer, Cham (2019). https://doi.org/10.1007/978-3-030-29891-3_27
37. Mohammed, H., Märgner, V., Stiehl, H.S.: Writer identification for historical manuscripts: analysis and optimisation of a classifier as an easy-to-use tool for scholars from the humanities. In: 2018 16th International Conference on Frontiers in Handwriting Recognition (ICFHR), pp. 534–539 (2018)
38. McCann, S., Lowe, D.G.: Local Naive Bayes nearest neighbor for image classification. In: 2012 IEEE Conference on Computer Vision and Pattern Recognition, pp. 3650–3656. IEEE (2012)
39. Pagels, P.E.: e-codices-virtual manuscript library of Switzerland (2016)
40. Sauvola, J., Pietikäinen, M.: Adaptive document image binarization. Pattern Recogn. **33**(2), 225–236 (2000)
41. He, S., Schomaker, L.: DeepOtsu: document enhancement and binarization using iterative deep learning. Pattern Recogn. **91**, 379–390 (2019)
42. Simonyan, K., Zisserman, A.: Very deep convolutional networks for large-scale image recognition. arXiv preprint arXiv:1409.1556 (2014)
43. Szegedy, C., Vanhoucke, V., Ioffe, S., Shlens, J., Wojna, Z.: Rethinking the inception architecture for computer vision. In: Proceedings of the IEEE Conference on Computer Vision and Pattern Recognition, pp. 2818–2826 (2016)
44. Targ, S., Almeida, D., Lyman, K.: Resnet in resnet: generalizing residual architectures. arXiv preprint arXiv:1603.08029 (2016)
45. Marti, U.-V., Bunke, H.: The IAM-database: an English sentence database for offline handwriting recognition. Int. J. Doc. Anal. Recogn. **5**(1), 39–46 (2002). https://doi.org/10.1007/s100320200071
46. Rong, W., Li, Z., Zhang, W., Sun, L.: An improved canny edge detection algorithm. In: 2014 IEEE International Conference on Mechatronics and Automation, pp. 577–582. IEEE (2014)

Offline Signature Verification Using Feature Learning and One-Class Classification

Safia Shabbir[1]([⊠]), Muhammad Imran Malik[2], and Imran Siddiqi[1]

[1] Bahria University, Islamabad, Pakistan
imran.siddiqi@bahria.edu.pk
[2] National University of Sciences and Technology, Islamabad, Pakistan
malik.imran@seecs.edu.pk

Abstract. Offline signature verification remains the most commonly employed authentication modality and enjoys global acceptance. From the view point of computerized verification, concluding the authenticity of a signature offers a challenging problem for the pattern classification community. A major proportion of computerized solutions treat signature verification as a two-class classification problem where both genuine and forged signatures are employed for training purposes. For most of the real world scenarios however, only genuine signatures of individuals are available. This paper presents a signature verification technique that relies only on genuine signature samples. More precisely, we employ convolutional neural networks for learning effective feature representations and a one-class support vector machine that learns the genuine signature class for each individual. Experiments are carried out in a writer-dependent as well as writer-independent mode and low error rates are reported by only employing genuine signatures in the training sets.

Keywords: Feature learning · One-class classification · Signature verification · Forgery detection

1 Introduction

Authenticating the claimed identity of an individual is a critical requirement in many practical scenarios including security systems, financial transactions and legal documents. In most cases, such systems rely on biometric technology exploiting either physical (such as face, fingerprint, iris etc.) or behavioural characteristics (such as voice, signature, handwriting, gait etc.) [13] to authenticate a person. Despite the technological advancements in DNA or finger print based authentication, signature remains the most commonly used mode of verification due to its ease of acquisition and global acceptability.

Signatures are handwritten and hence they may contain symbols, different slants and varying writing styles. In general, it is common for individuals to develop signatures which are distinct and hard to copy by others [24].

© Springer Nature Switzerland AG 2021
C. Djeddi et al. (Eds.): MedPRAI 2020, CCIS 1322, pp. 242–254, 2021.
https://doi.org/10.1007/978-3-030-71804-6_18

Forgers, however, can mimic the signature of an individual by practising it to perfection. Signature forgery refers to imitating someone else's signature in an attempt to claim their identity. Signature forgeries are typically classified into three classes namely random forgery, unskilled forgery and skilled forgery [15, 22]. Random forgery refers to the scenario in which the forger has not seen the genuine signature and produces a random signature pretending to be the authorized individual. The term unskilled forgeries refers to the situation when the forger has the knowledge of only the name not the signature of the individual. The most challenging is to identify the skilled forgery where the forger has complete knowledge of the signature of claimed identity and the signatures are practised repeatedly prior to the forgery attempt.

Depending on the mode of acquisition, signature verification techniques are classified into online and offline methods [15, 36]. Online signatures are typically captured using devices like optical pens and touch sensitive tablets. Such devices allow capturing the dynamic characteristics of a signature including attributes like pen pressure, writing speed, number and order of strokes, etc. Offline signatures, on the other hand, refer to digitized images of signatures captured using a camera or scanner [20, 23]. From the view point of verification technique, systems that rely on training a separate model for each individual to verify the signature are known as Writer-dependent (WD) systems. Writer-independent (WI) systems, on the other hand, train only one model for all individuals to differentiate between genuine and forged signatures [15].

Research in signature verification has matured progressively over decades. Deep learning has emerged as a revolutionary and state-of-the-art framework for data driven feature learning and classification [7] in the recent years. Convolutional Neural Networks (CNNs) for example, have been applied for effective feature learning in many problems including handwriting recognition [27, 32], writer identification [5, 40] and signature verification [17, 39].

In this work, we employ both WI and WD feature learning approaches using a deep CNN and validate the effectiveness of learned feature representations using WI and WD One-class Support Vector Machine (OCSVM). The CEDAR dataset and the ICDAR 2015 Competition dataset on Signature Verification and Writer Identification for On-line and Off-line Skilled Forgeries (SigWIcomp2015 Italian signatures) [21] are used for the evaluation of the proposed approaches. Three different combinations of feature learning and OCSVM are employed. These include WD feature learning with WD OCSVM, WI feature learning followed by WD OCSVM and, WI feature learning followed by WI OCSVM. The experimental study reveals low error rates despite we only used genuine signatures in the training set. This study reveals that proposed feature learning approach is robust in WI as well as WD mode.

The rest of the paper is structured as follows. An overview of significant contributions to offline signature verification is presented in Sect. 2. Section 3 introduces the datasets which have been utilized in our study while Sect. 4 details the proposed feature learning and classification technique. Experimental protocol and the reported results along with a discussion are presented in Sect. 5. In the end, we summarize the key findings in Sect. 6 and conclude the paper.

2 Related Work

Signature verification has been an active research direction for forensic experts, document examiners, and computer scientists for decades now. A number of comprehensive surveys covering both offline and online signature verification systems have also been published from time to time [30,34,36]. In general, offline signature verification is considered more demanding as compared to online signatures as only the final shape of signature image is available in case of offline images [20]. Nevertheless, offline signatures enjoy wider acceptability due to the simplicity in acquisition.

Features for verification of signature can be structural or statistical and are computed either locally (from parts of signature) or globally (from complete signature image). In some cases various features are combined to enhance the overall verification performance. In many cases, geometrical features, such as ratios of interest, information on loops and endpoints [10,15], have been effectively employed for verification of signatures. In addition to key geometric ratios, symmetry of the signature, angular displacement to a horizontal baseline and spacing etc. [29] are also considered. A number of transforms have also been investigated to characterize signatures. These include Heden transform [26], Contourlet transform [31], Discrete Radon transform [6] and Fractal transform [43]. Similarly, textural measures like Local Binary Patterns (LBP) and Histogram of Oriented Gradients (HOG) have also been employed in various studies [2,41]. From the view point of classifiers, Hidden Markov models (HMM) [19], Support vector Machine (SVM) [18], Neural networks (NN) [33] and ensemble method [3] etc. have been commonly employed.

With the advent of deep learning, the classical pipeline of hand-engineered feature extraction followed by classification is being replaced by data driven feature extraction and classification as an end-to-end learning systems. In some cases, it is also common to employ deep learning techniques as feature extractors only and employ traditional classifiers for classification. Among notable contributions exploiting deep neural networks, Nam et al. [25] present a CNN based feature representation with an autoencoder as classifier to distinguish between genuine and forged signatures. Likewise, Saffar et al. [35] employ autoencoders with one-class classifier for drawing hyper-spheres around genuine signatures (projected in the feature space) to distinguish them from the forged ones.

In a series of related studies by Hafemann et al. [11,12,14], CNN based feature learning has been thoroughly investigated. In [14] for instance, a two-step approach is presented where feature learning is first carried out in a writer-independent mode while the classification is carried out in a writer-dependent framework using binary SVM. The feature learning model was trained using GPDS-960 dataset and was used to extract features for GPDS-160. GPDS-300, MCYT, CEDAR and Brazilian PUC-PR datasets. A number of other related studies [37, 39] also demonstrate the superiority of machine learned over hand-designed features for signature verification. Dutta et al. in [9] computed Compact correlated features in WI mode and verification was performed using Euclidean distance between pairs of signatures for CEDAR and GPDS300 dataset. In another study, Dey et al. employed a WI siamese Convolutional network for verification and calculated a joined loss function. They evaluated the approach on CEDAR, GPDS300, BHSIG260 and GPDS Synthetic dataset [8]. In our study, we also investigate machine learned features to characterize the signature of an individual, details presented later in the paper. Only genuine signatures for feature learning as well as for verification are used for training which resembles the real life scenario which was not the case in above mentioned approaches. In contrast to previous studies, proposed approach is applicable to both WI and WD settings.

3   Datasets

We employ two datasets (which are publicly available) for the experimental evaluation of our proposed system. These include the CEDAR signature dataset [1] and the SigWIComp2015 Italian signature dataset (SigWIComp2015 [21]). The CEDAR dataset[1] has 24 genuine samples and 24 skilled forgeries for 55 different signers. Out of these, 12 genuine signatures of each user are used to train the CNN(s) and subsequently the feature vectors of these signatures are employed to train the OCSVM. The remaining 12 genuine signatures and 24 skilled forgeries per user are treated as the test set. The SigWIComp2015 Italian signature dataset[2] has 50 individual signers with a total of 485 genuine and 249 forged samples. The detailed distribution of signatures into training and test sets for both datasets is presented in Table 1.

4   Proposed Methodology

The proposed Methodology for verification of signatures rests on two key components, i.e., feature learning using a ConvNet and verification using a OCSVM. Feature learning and verification are carried out in WI as well as WD modes. An overview of the key processing steps is presented in Fig. 1 while the details of these steps are presented in the following section.

4.1   Feature Learning Using CNN

A typical CNN is a pile of convolutional and sampling layers with some fully connected layers at the end. Convolution operation is the core of a CNN which allows learning robust features (filters) through back propagation. The architecture of the CNN employed in our study is illustrated in Fig. 1-b while the details

---

[1] Download Dataset:http://www.cedar.buffalo.edu/NIJ/data/signatures.rar.

[2] Download Dataset: http://tc11.cvc.uab.es/datasets/SigWIcomp2015_1.

Table 1. Division of datasets into training and test set

Dataset	Authors	Dataset division	Genuine/author	Forged/author	Total
CEDAR	55	Training	12	0	660
		Test	12	24	1980
SigWiComp2015 Italian	50	Training	4 or 5	0	256
		Test	4 or 5	5	478

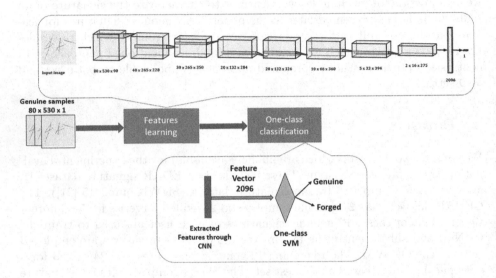

Fig. 1. Overall flow of methodology

are presented in Table 2. These details include the size and number of filters at each convolutional layer, hyper-parameters for the pooling layers and the size of feature map at each layer. All Conv layers employ the ReLu activation function while the last fully connected layer employs sigmoid activation with a single neuron. Stochastic gradient descent is used as optimizer with a decay rate of 10^{-4} and learning rate of 10^{-3}. The model is trained (until convergence) with a batch size of 4.

The model learns a function $\phi(.)$ which can project data X to a new feature space $\phi(X) \epsilon R^b$ where b is the size of feature vector. Once the CNN is trained, it is used to extract feature representation for each signature in the training and test sets. The size of feature vector in our case is 2096 which is the number of neurons in the fully connected layer before the last sigmoid layer. The training set feature vectors are used to train the OCSVM and test set feature vectors are used for evaluating OCSVM.

The CNN is trained in WI and WD modes using only genuine samples of the individuals under study. Training the CNN in each of the two modes is discussed in the following.

Table 2. Details of proposed architectural of the CNN

Layer	Type	Output shape	Kernel size	Stride	Number of filters
1	Convolution	$80 \times 530 \times 90$	7	1	90
2	MaxPooling	$40 \times 265 \times 90$	2	2	–
3	Convolution	$40 \times 265 \times 228$	5	1	228
4	MaxPooling	$20 \times 132 \times 228$	2	2	–
5	Convolution	$20 \times 132 \times 350$	3	1	350
6	Convolution	$20 \times 132 \times 284$	3	1	284
7	Convolution	$20 \times 132 \times 326$	3	1	326
8	MaxPooling	$10 \times 66 \times 326$	2	2	–
9	Convolution	$10 \times 66 \times 360$	3	1	360
10	MaxPooling	$5 \times 33 \times 360$	2	2	–
11	Convolution	$5 \times 33 \times 394$	3	1	394
12	MaxPooling	$2 \times 16 \times 394$	2	2	–
13	Convolution	$2 \times 16 \times 275$	3	1	275
14	Flatten	8800	–	–	–
15	Dense	2096	–	–	–
16	Sigmoid	1	–	–	–

Writer-Independent Feature Learning. In WI feature learning, genuine signatures of all users in the training set are fed to a single CNN for training. Once the CNN model is trained, all the test samples are fed to CNN to carry out feedforward propagation through the network and feature representation is obtained from activations at last fully connected layer before sigmoid layer. Then the extracted features for training and test set are fed to OCSVM for training and classification, respectively.

Writer-Dependent Feature Learning. WD feature learning involves training a separate model for each writer under study. A separate CNN is trained with genuine signature images of each individual in the dataset. The models are then employed to extract features for all signatures in the training and test sets from the respective CNN.

4.2 One-Class Classification Using SVM

Once features are computed using trained CNN model(s), we need to train a classifier to learn to identify the genuine signatures of an individual. As discussed previously, in real life scenarios, forged samples are not available for most of the practical signature verification applications. Instead, we may have multiple samples of an individual's genuine signatures. Signature verification problem can hence be modeled as a one-class problem where we have only positive samples for training and no negative samples. One-class classification can be viewed as an attempt to find a (hyper)sphere boundary with a specific radius around the positive samples. When a questioned sample is received, it is projected in the feature space and the distance of the sample from the origin is computed. If the sample lies within the boundary of the genuine class, it is identified as a positive sample, otherwise, it is identified as a negative sample (forged signature).

We have used OCSVM as classifier, the hyper sphere has the center a and radius $R > 0$, which is the distance from origin to the class boundary for which we will minimize R^2. The key parameters for OCSVM are kernel type, $gamma$ and nu where kernel type is either 'linear' or 'rbf', $gamma$ is the kernel coefficient for 'rbf' kernel and nu is the upper bound on the fraction of training errors and a lower bound on the fraction of support vectors. Similar to feature computation, we investigate WI and WD OCSVMs for verification.

Writer-Independent One Class Support Vector Machine. For writer-independent OCSVM, features from training images of all users are used to train a single OCSVM. During evaluation, the remaining genuine samples and skilled forgeries of all the users are used. The normalized scores for each sample are computed and used for calculating evaluation metric Equal error Rate (EER).

Writer-Dependent One Class Support Vector Machine. For writer-dependent OCSVM, features from training data of each individual are used to train a separate OCSVM for each user. Subsequently, the genuine and forged samples in the test set of each individual are employed to evaluate the respective OCSVM.

Table 3. Different experimental settings for feature learning and classification

Exp. setting	Feature learning	OCSVM
Scenario I	WD	WD
Scenario II	WI	WD
Scenario III	WI	WI

Table 4. Equal Error Rates for the three experimental scenarios, with standard deviation in parenthesis

Scenario	Dataset	
	CEDAR	SigWiComp2015
WD CNN + WD OCSVM	0.00 (±0.00)	0.27 (±1.35)
WI CNN + WD OCSVM	0.00 (±0.00)	0.27 (±1.92)
WI CNN + WI OCSVM	0.00	0.53

5   Experiments and Results

The experimental protocol and the reported results are presented in this section. We first introduce the evaluation metric followed by experimental settings and then discuss the performance of the learned features with OCSVM. Finally, a comparative overview of notable signature verification techniques is presented.

For quantization of system performance, we employ the well-known Equal Error Rate (EER) that is computed using the False Acceptance Rate (FAR) and the False Rejection Rate (FRR). The FAR is the percentage of forged signatures identified as genuine while FRR is the percentage of genuine signatures mistakenly rejected as forged. Typically, FAR and FRR are computed by varying the decision threshold and EER refers to the value when FAR equals FRR.

In SigWiComp2015, the metric of cost of log-likelihood ratio, $\widehat{Cllr}$, and its minimum value, i.e., $(\widehat{Cllr}_{min})$ were computed in order to benchmark the performance of the participating systems. $\widehat{Cllr}$ is calculated from Eq. 1:

$$\widehat{Cllr} = \frac{1}{2 * log2} \left[\frac{1}{N_0} \sum_{i=1}^{N_0} \left(1 + \frac{1}{LR_1} \right) + \frac{1}{N_1} \sum_{i=1}^{N_1} (1 + LR_1) \right] \tag{1}$$

Where N_0 are the number of genuine signatures of the reference author, N_1 are number of forged signatures of the reference author, LR is the likelihood ratio of genuine signatures and LR_1 is the likelihood ratio of forged signatures. The detail of computing $\widehat{Cllr}$ is given in [4]. $\widehat{Cllr}_{min}$ is computed by adjusting likelihood ratios (LR) using a logistic function. This metric not only computes the error rate, but it also consider the severity of errors made by a system. The severity of errors, in particular, is important in case of biometric and other forensic systems where a minor error can lead to loss of life. Please note: the smaller the value of $\widehat{Cllr}_{min}$, the better the system [21].

System evaluation is carried out using three different settings as a function of WI and WD modes for feature learning and classification. These settings are summarized in Table 3 while the EER values for each of these settings for the two datasets are presented in Table 4. It can be observed that error rates on CEDAR dataset are 0 for all three scenarios. Comparing the three scenarios on the Sig-WiComp2015 dataset, writer dependent and writer dependent feature learning reports a relatively lower error rate (0.27) when using a separate OCSVM model for classification. Using a single OCSVM for all users (WI OCSVM) reports an error rate of 0.53%. It is evident from the results, that the methodology generalizes well on both datasets.

An overview of notable signature verification techniques evaluated using the CEDAR dataset is presented in Table 5 where it can be seen that we report an EER of 0 for all three experimental scenarios and without using any forged signatures in the training set. Among other studies, Dutta et al. [9] and Dey et al. [8] also report an EER of 0 But they have used genuine and forged signatures pairs for training.

Table 6 presents the comparison of results among the system which were submitted in competition with the proposed method. The proposed system reports

Table 5. Comparison of studies on the CEDAR signature dataset

Study	Approach	Method	No. of reference signature genuine/forged	EER (%)
Hafemann et al. [14]	WI features + WD classifier	CNN + SVM	12/12	4.63
A. Hamadene and Y. Chibani [16]	Statistical features + WI classifier	Directional code co-occurrence matrix + Feature Dissimilarity measure (FDM)	3/0 4/0 5/0	3.12 2.55 2.10
Okawa and Manabu [28]	Local descriptors + WI classifier	BoVW with KAZE features + SVM	16/16	1.6
M. Sharif et al. [38]	geometrical features + WD classifier	Genetic algorithm + SVM	5/0 10/0 12/0	10.41 6.25 4.67
Zois et al. [42]	Local features + WD Classifier	Grid based features + Binary SVM	5/0 10/0	3.12 2.74
Dutta et al. [9]	Local features + WI Classifier	Compact correlated features + SVM	276 pairs of gen-gen & gen-forged each	0.00
Dey et al. [8]	WI features + Distance measure	Convolutional Siamese Network + Euclidean Distance	276 pairs of gen-gen & 276 pairs of gen-forged pairs	0.00
Proposed method	WD features + WD one-class classifier WI features + WD one-class classifier WI features + WD one-class classifier	CNN + OCSVM	12/0	0.00 0.0 0.0

Table 6. Comparison of results with the SigWiComp2015 participants

System	Participant	$\widehat{Cllr}$	$\widehat{Cllr}_{min}$
1	Proposed	**0.324723**	**0.013465**
2	Sabanci University	0.655109	0.021318
3	Tebessa University	0.993138	0.893270
4	Tebessa University	1.065696	0.952499
5	Tebessa University	1.074474	0.880930
6	Tebessa University	1.065475	0.901003
7	Tebessa University	1.041895	0.901003
8	Qatar University	8.901864	0.972708
9	Qatar University	13.111064	0.960163
10	Commercial System	1.003786	0.988845

a $\widehat{Cllr}$ value of 0.324723 and $\widehat{Cllr}_{min}$ equal to 0.013465 which outperforms all the systems which were proposed in competition.

6   Conclusion

In this study, we investigated the offline signature verification problem and employed feature learning to seek robust feature representations for signature images. Features are extracted in a writer-dependent as well as writer-independent mode. For verification, we employ one-class SVM that is trained using genuine samples only to match the real world scenarios. The technique is validated on two benchmark datasets and low error rates are reported.

In our further study on this subject, we aim to investigate the performance of one-class classification on other common datasets. Furthermore, feature learning using recurrent neural networks rather than convolutional networks is also being experimented.

References

1. Cedar signarure dataset download. www.cedar.buffalo.edu/NIJ/data/signatures. rar
2. Ahlawat, S., Goel, A., Prasad, S., Singh, P.: Offline signature verification using local binary pattern and octave pattern. In: Fifth International Conference on Graphic and Image Processing (ICGIP 2013), vol. 9069, p. 906913. International Society for Optics and Photonics (2014)
3. Batista, L., Granger, E., Sabourin, R.: Dynamic selection of generative-discriminative ensembles for off-line signature verification. Pattern Recogn. 45(4), 1326–1340 (2012)

4. Brümmer, N., du Preez, J.: Application-independent evaluation of speaker detection. Comput. Speech Lang. **20**(2), 230–275 (2006). Odyssey 2004: The Speaker and Language Recognition Workshop. https://doi.org/10.1016/j.csl.2005.08.001. http://www.sciencedirect.com/science/article/pii/S0885230805000483
5. Christlein, V., Gropp, M., Fiel, S., Maier, A.: Unsupervised feature learning for writer identification and writer retrieval. In: 2017 14th IAPR International Conference on Document Analysis and Recognition (ICDAR), vol. 1, pp. 991–997. IEEE (2017)
6. Coetzer, J.: Off-line signature verification. Ph.D. thesis, University of Stellenbosch, Stellenbosch (2005)
7. Dara, S., Tumma, P.: Feature extraction by using deep learning: a survey. In: 2018 Second International Conference on Electronics, Communication and Aerospace Technology (ICECA), pp. 1795–1801. IEEE (2018)
8. Dey, S., Dutta, A., Toledo, J.I., Ghosh, S.K., Lladós, J., Pal, U.: SigNet: convolutional siamese network for writer independent offline signature verification. arXiv preprint arXiv:1707.02131 (2017)
9. Dutta, A., Pal, U., Lladós, J.: Compact correlated features for writer independent signature verification. In: 2016 23rd International Conference on Pattern Recognition (ICPR), pp. 3422–3427. IEEE (2016)
10. El-Yacoubi, A., Justino, E., Sabourin, R., Bortolozzi, F.: Off-line signature verification using HMMs and cross-validation. In: Neural Networks for Signal Processing X. Proceedings of the 2000 IEEE Signal Processing Society Workshop (Cat. No. 00TH8501), vol. 2, pp. 859–868. IEEE (2000)
11. Hafemann, L.G., Oliveira, L.S., Sabourin, R.: Fixed-sized representation learning from offline handwritten signatures of different sizes. Int. J. Doc. Anal. Recogn. (IJDAR) **21**(3), 219–232 (2018)
12. Hafemann, L.G., Sabourin, R., Oliveira, L.S.: Analyzing features learned for offline signature verification using deep CNNs. In: 2016 23rd International Conference on Pattern Recognition (ICPR), pp. 2989–2994. IEEE (2016)
13. Hafemann, L.G., Sabourin, R., Oliveira, L.S.: Writer-independent feature learning for offline signature verification using deep convolutional neural networks. In: 2016 International Joint Conference on Neural Networks (IJCNN), pp. 2576–2583. IEEE (2016)
14. Hafemann, L.G., Sabourin, R., Oliveira, L.S.: Learning features for offline handwritten signature verification using deep convolutional neural networks. Pattern Recogn. **70**, 163–176 (2017)
15. Hafemann, L.G., Sabourin, R., Oliveira, L.S.: Offline handwritten signature verification-literature review. In: 2017 Seventh International Conference on Image Processing Theory, Tools and Applications (IPTA), pp. 1–8. IEEE (2017)
16. Hamadene, A., Chibani, Y.: One-class writer-independent offline signature verification using feature dissimilarity thresholding. IEEE Trans. Inf. Forensics Secur. **11**(6), 1226–1238 (2016)
17. Jarad, M., Al-Najdawi, N., Tedmori, S.: Offline handwritten signature verification system using a supervised neural network approach. In: 2014 6th International Conference on Computer Science and Information Technology (CSIT), pp. 189–195 (2014)
18. Justino, E.J., Bortolozzi, F., Sabourin, R.: A comparison of SVM and HMM classifiers in the off-line signature verification. Pattern Recogn. Lett. **26**(9), 1377–1385 (2005)

19. Justino, E.J., El Yacoubi, A., Bortolozzi, F., Sabourin, R.: An off-line signature verification system using hidden Markov model and cross-validation. In: Proceedings of the 13th Brazilian Symposium on Computer Graphics and Image Processing (Cat. No. PR00878), pp. 105–112. IEEE (2000)
20. Kumar, A., Bhatia, K.: A survey on offline handwritten signature verification system using writer dependent and independent approaches. In: 2016 2nd International Conference on Advances in Computing, Communication, & Automation (ICACCA)(Fall), pp. 1–6. IEEE (2016)
21. Malik, M.I., et al.: ICDAR2015 competition on signature verification and writer identification for on- and off-line skilled forgeries (SigWIcomp2015). In: 2015 13th International Conference on Document Analysis and Recognition (ICDAR), pp. 1186–1190, August 2015
22. Malik, M.I., Liwicki, M.: From terminology to evaluation: performance assessment of automatic signature verification systems. In: 2012 International Conference on Frontiers in Handwriting Recognition, pp. 613–618. IEEE (2012)
23. Malik, M.I., Liwicki, M., Dengel, A.: Part-based automatic system in comparison to human experts for forensic signature verification. In: 2013 12th International Conference on Document Analysis and Recognition, pp. 872–876. IEEE (2013)
24. Mohammed, R.A., Nabi, R.M., Sardasht, M., Mahmood, R., Nabi, R.M.: State-of-the-art in handwritten signature verification system. In: 2015 International Conference on Computational Science and Computational Intelligence (CSCI), pp. 519–525. IEEE (2015)
25. Nam, S., Park, H., Seo, C., Choi, D.: Forged signature distinction using convolutional neural network for feature extraction. Appl. Sci. 8(2), 153 (2018)
26. Nemcek, W.F., Lin, W.C.: Experimental investigation of automatic signature verification. IEEE Trans. Syst. Man Cybern. 1, 121–126 (1974)
27. Niu, X.X., Suen, C.Y.: A novel hybrid CNN-SVM classifier for recognizing handwritten digits. Pattern Recogn. 45(4), 1318–1325 (2012)
28. Okawa, M.: Offline signature verification based on bag-of-visual words model using KAZE features and weighting schemes. In: Proceedings of the IEEE Conference on Computer Vision and Pattern Recognition Workshops, pp. 184–190 (2016)
29. Oliveira, L.S., Justino, E., Freitas, C., Sabourin, R.: The graphology applied to signature verification. In: 12th Conference of the International Graphonomics Society, pp. 286–290 (2005)
30. Plamondon, R., Lorette, G.: Automatic signature verification and writer identification-the state of the art. Pattern Recogn. 22(2), 107–131 (1989)
31. Pourshahabi, M.R., Sigari, M.H., Pourreza, H.R.: Offline handwritten signature identification and verification using contourlet transform. In: 2009 International Conference of Soft Computing and Pattern Recognition, pp. 670–673. IEEE (2009)
32. Poznanski, A., Wolf, L.: CNN-N-Gram for handwriting word recognition. In: Proceedings of the IEEE Conference on Computer Vision and Pattern Recognition, pp. 2305–2314 (2016)
33. Quek, C., Zhou, R.: Antiforgery: a novel pseudo-outer product based fuzzy neural network driven signature verification system. Pattern Recogn. Lett. 23(14), 1795–1816 (2002)
34. Sabourin, R., Plamondon, R., Lorette, G.: Off-line identification with handwritten signature images: survey and perspectives. In: Baird, H.S., Bunke, H., Yamamoto, K. (eds.) Structured Document Image Analysis, pp. 219–234. Springer, Heidelberg (1992). https://doi.org/10.1007/978-3-642-77281-8_10

35. Saffar, M.H., Fayyaz, M., Sabokrou, M., Fathy, M.: Online signature verification using deep representation: a new descriptor. arXiv preprint arXiv:1806.09986 (2018)
36. Sanmorino, A., Yazid, S.: A survey for handwritten signature verification. In: 2012 2nd International Conference on Uncertainty Reasoning and Knowledge Engineering, pp. 54–57. IEEE (2012)
37. Shariatmadari, S., Emadi, S., Akbari, Y.: Patch-based offline signature verification using one-class hierarchical deep learning. Int. J. Doc. Anal. Recogn. (IJDAR) **22**(4), 375–385 (2019). https://doi.org/10.1007/s10032-019-00331-2
38. Sharif, M., Khan, M.A., Faisal, M., Yasmin, M., Fernandes, S.L.: A framework for offline signature verification system: best features selection approach. Pattern Recogn. Lett. (2018)
39. Souza, V.L., Oliveira, A.L., Sabourin, R.: A writer-independent approach for offline signature verification using deep convolutional neural networks features. In: 2018 7th Brazilian Conference on Intelligent Systems (BRACIS), pp. 212–217. IEEE (2018)
40. Tang, Y., Wu, X.: Text-independent writer identification via CNN features and joint Bayesian. In: 2016 15th International Conference on Frontiers in Handwriting Recognition (ICFHR), pp. 566–571. IEEE (2016)
41. Yilmaz, M.B., Yanikoglu, B., Tirkaz, C., Kholmatov, A.: Offline signature verification using classifier combination of HOG and LBP features. In: 2011 International Joint Conference on Biometrics (IJCB), pp. 1–7. IEEE (2011)
42. Zois, E.N., Alewijnse, L., Economou, G.: Offline signature verification and quality characterization using poset-oriented grid features. Pattern Recogn. **54**, 162–177 (2016)
43. Zouari, R., Mokni, R., Kherallah, M.: Identification and verification system of offline handwritten signature using fractal approach. In: International Image Processing, Applications and Systems Conference, pp. 1–4. IEEE (2014)

Artificial Intelligence and Intelligent Systems

Text Mining-Based Association Rule Mining for Incident Analysis: A Case Study of a Steel Plant in India

Sobhan Sarkar[1,5(✉)], Sammangi Vinay[2], Chawki Djeddi[3,4], and J. Maiti[5]

[1] Business School, University of Edinburgh,
29 Buccleuch Pl, Edinburgh EH8 9JS, UK
sobhan.sarkar@ed.ac.uk
[2] Department of Mechanical Engineering, IIT Kharagpur, Kharagpur 721302, India
[3] Department of Mathematics and Computer Science, Larbi Tebessi University,
Tebessa, Algeria
[4] LITIS Lab, University of Rouen, Rouen, France
[5] Department of Industrial and Systems Engineering, IIT Kharagpur,
Kharagpur 721302, India

Abstract. Although a large amount of accident data in terms of categorical attributes and free texts are available across large enterprises involving high-risk operations, the methodology for analyzing such mixed data is still under development. The present study proposed a new methodological approach to extract useful inherent patterns or rules for accident causation using association rule mining (ARM) of both incident narratives (unstructured texts) and categorical data. Incidents data from an integrated steel plant for a period of four years (2010–2013) are used for model building and analysis. In the first phase, the text mining approach is employed to find out the basic events that could lead to the occurrences of faults or incident events. In the second phase, text-based ARM has been used to extract the useful rules from unstructured texts as well as structured categorical attributes. A total of 23 best item-set rules are extracted. The findings help the management of the plant to augment the cause and effect analysis of accident occurrences as well as quantifying the effects of the causes, which can also be automated to minimize the human involvement.

Keywords: Text mining · Association rule mining · Occupational incidents · Steel plant

1 Introduction

Steel manufacturing sector is one of the high-risk sectors as the workers are exposed to hot, noisy, gaseous and/or dusty environment in most of the working hours [15]. From the study of [21], it is seen that metal workers take long-term sick leave which is more than double than that a normal worker takes.

© Springer Nature Switzerland AG 2021
C. Djeddi et al. (Eds.): MedPRAI 2020, CCIS 1322, pp. 257–273, 2021.
https://doi.org/10.1007/978-3-030-71804-6_19

Accidents (or undesired incidents) in such industry impose substantial burden on the stakeholders, both employers, and employees. According to the report of [11], the number of occupational accidents raise to 3 lakh mortalities, and 300 million injuries globally in every year. The cost of job related injury is more than \$27 billion annually as per the estimation by the National Safety Council in USA. Although accident data are collected, they often remain either unutilized or under-utilized. Therefore, proper analysis of accident data is essential for identification of causal factors or faults and predicting their likely occurrences.

To understand the incident causation, incident data should be utilized properly. It is found from previous studies that most of the leading organizations try to maintain their own system of investigation and reporting of accidents. It eventually helps them take precautionary measures in order to lessen its re-occurrences. However, it is very difficult to use full information within incident investigation database due to the fact that they are mix of structured and unstructured, large and manually intractable incident data [3,28,40]. Incident data comprises different data types, such as categorical, continuous, and unstructured texts of incidents. The narrative field is aimed to provide a free text description of the incidents to elaborate its causes and contributory factors that otherwise remain hidden. In most of the published literature, it is observed that association rule mining (ARM) has been used on categorical incidents data; however, very few studies have been carried out which uses incident narratives [6]. Moreover, the texts data are so unstructured that creates a high degree of difficulty in pattern extraction from them. Therefore, there exists a need of research to extract incident patterns from structured and unstructured data and analyse them properly for accident analyses and prevention.

Therefore, the aim of the study is to extract meaningful patterns from both structured categorical and unstructured texts data using association rule mining (ARM) technique. Using this technique, rules or association of factors responsible for accidents are extracted. Moreover, predictive regions is used in text mining-based ARM which helps in generation of effective rules. Results from the study reveal that the proposed approach not only helps in automation of the process, but also provides the hidden rules that might be missed by expert's knowledge. Therefore, preventive actions could be initiated in order to reduce the re-occurrence of incidents.

The rest of the paper is structured as follows: In the Sect. 2, related works are presented briefly. Dataset, data types, and the methods text-based ARM are described in Sect. 3. In Sect. 4, results are discussed. Finally, conclusions with limitations and scopes for future works are presented in Sect. 5.

2   Literature Review

Occupational incidents are serious concern for all industries. To minimize the number of incidents, investigation of causal factors is necessary. Some of the related studies also include prediction-based incident analysis and prevention, for examples, development of predictive model [34], rough set theory (RST) [29],

Bayesian Network (BN) [32], Petri nets [37], hybrid clustering [31], image processing [25], decision support system [30], optimized decision tree approach [35]. Most of these studies deploy data mining or machine learning-based techniques unlike traditional questionnaire-based analysis [33] due to their advantages over traditional ones. In addition, previous studies also indicated that the use of both categorical and text information eventually makes the analysis very difficult. Text mining (TM), in such cases, has been found to be an effective technique for analyzing such incident texts [6,26,27,39]. TM is usually used to find out the hidden patterns in the unstructured text fields which may be useful for improved information retrieval system or may be used as inputs to predictive models [6]. Overall, using TM in occupational accident analysis focuses on two broad domains: (i) auto-coding of texts [7,14,23,39], and (ii) text classification and prediction [6,9,26]. Auto-coding of incident reports reduce the human efforts to a great extent [4,14,39]. For example, [4] auto-coded compensation claims into two classes, i.e., musculoskeletal disorder (MSD), and slip-trip-fall (STF) using Naïve Bayes auto-coding classifier with 90% classification accuracy. Another work by [39] shows that Bayesian auto-coding model based on fuzzy and Naïve approaches could code near miss and injuries with considerable accuracy.

An effort is still necessary for information extraction for both unstructured text and non-text categorical data. ARM is a popular approach in this task, which has been applied in several safety studies, including construction [2,8,16], railway [18], steel [41], and roads [13,22]. The principal reason of using ARM is its capability of extracting useful patterns from huge datasets and its easier interpretation [2,17,20]. However, from the previous literature, it is found that most of the studies are conducted in construction sector. For instance, [16] tried to find associations of different factors as well as patterns of injuries in construction industry in Taiwan. [17] focused only on extraction of unapparent association rules using 'extracted probability'. Although ARM has been used in those studies on categorical data, its application on both unstructured accident texts and categorical data is rather challenging and new. The text-based ARM approach has more potential to explore the hidden patterns from both types of data in terms of associations of different factors which most of the time remain under-utilized.

2.1 Research Issues

From the review of literature, the following research issues are identified:

(i) Large amount of text data or narratives of incidents remain often under-utilized across industries as it demands a substantial amount of human efforts and time, and often manually intractable.

(ii) Extraction of rules from incident narratives has not been addressed by any previous literature. Therefore, the use of texts is expected to have potential for providing hidden incident patterns or rules.

(iii) Finally, it is mostly observed from accident studies that ARM has been deployed in construction domains. Its use in other domains still remains unexplored which demands a thorough investigation.

2.2 Contributions of the Work

The study contributes to the body of literature as follows:

(i) Both the categorical and free-text data (i.e., narratives) have been used for generation of rules

(ii) The present research encompasses both text mining-based rule-cause extraction using ARM. Predictive regions is used on text-based ARM for better rule extraction.

(iii) The proposed methodology has been validated using incident data obtained from a integrated steel plant in India.

3 Materials and Methods

In this section, a brief overview of the data set (i.e., variables and data types) obtained from an integrated steel plant and the methods used in this study are given below.

3.1 Variables and Data Types

The incident dataset for a period of 45 months (from 2010 to 2013) retrieved from the digital database system of an integrated steel plant was considered for the study. The dataset contains thirteen attributes (12 categorical, and one textual), and 998 observations. A brief description on each of the attributes is given below.

(i) *Date of incident (DOI):* This attribute implies the date when the incident was occurred.

(ii) *Department (Dept.):* This represents the location where the incident was taken place. In total, nine departments were considered, namely N1, N2, N3, N4, N5, N6, N7, N8, and N9. Here, N9 represents 'other departments' consisting of the departments having very few records of incidents during the study period.

(iii) *Incident outcome (IO):* It is the outcome variable. It has three different classes: (i) injury (I)-when someone gets injured physically from an incident; (ii) near miss (N)-when someone is narrowly escaped from an incident having full potential to cause injury or damage; and (iii) property damage (PD)-when there is damage to private or public property, due to the incident.

(iv) *Incident event (IE):* This attribute refers to the top event that qualifies the incident which has occurred. It has 23 classes. They are 'crane dashing (CD)', 'dashing/collision (DC)', 'derailment (D)', 'electric flash (EF)', 'energy isolation (EI)', 'equipment/machinery (EM)', 'fire/explosion (FE)', 'gas leakage (GL)', 'hot metals (HM)', 'hydraulic/pneumatic (HP)', 'lifting tools & tackles (LTT)', 'process incidents (PI)', 'rail (R)', 'road incidents (RI)', 'run over (RO)', 'skidding (S)', 'slip/trip/fall (STF)', 'structural integrity (SI)', 'toxic chemicals (TC)', and 'working at heights (WAH)'.

(v) *Working Condition (WC):* This attribute represents the condition of work when the incident took place. It has three categories i.e., 'group working (W1)' representing the condition where people work in groups, 'single working (W2)' representing person working alone, and 'Others (W3)' representing situations when no workers were present.

(vi) *Machine Condition (MC):* It implies the condition of machine when the accident took place; either machine is in 'idle condition (M1)' or in 'running condition (M2)', or 'others (M3)' i.e., not related to machine.

(vii) *Observation type (OT):* This attribute represents the basic causes of incident and has four categories as; (i) 'unsafe act (OT1)' representing the person himself is responsible for the cause of incident, (ii) 'unsafe act and unsafe condition (OT2)' representing the incident occurred due to presence of both the factors, person's fault and hazardous condition, (iii) 'unsafe act by other (OT3)' representing the incident occurred due to the other's fault, and (iv) 'unsafe condition (OT4)' representing a situation which is likely to cause incidents.

(viii) *Incident type (IT):* This attribute represents whether an accident happened is due to 'human behavior (IT1)', or 'process type (IT2)' which is non-human fault.

(ix) *Standard Operating Procedure (SOP) Adequacy (SOPA):* SOP implies a procedure/guideline to be followed while performing tasks by the workers/ operators. It has three categories: (i) 'SOP adequate (SOPA1)' – sufficient in quality and quantity; (ii) 'SOP inadequate (SOPA2)' – not sufficient in quality and quantity; and (iii) 'not applicable (SOPA3)'.

(x) *SOP compliance (SOPC):* This attribute indicates whether any SOP was 'followed (SOPC1)', or 'not followed (SOPC2)', or 'not applicable (SOPC3)'.

(xi) *SOP Availability (SOPAv):* This attribute implies that whether any SOP was 'available (SOPAv1)', or 'not available (SOPAv2)', or 'not applicable (SOPAv3)'.

(xii) *SOP Requirement (SOPR):* This attribute represents that whether any SOP was 'required (SOPR1)', or 'not (SOPR2)', or 'not applicable (SOPR3)'.

(xiii) *Brief description of incident (BDI):* This attribute consists of short description on how and why the incident occurred. The field contains free text logged by safety personnel after the incident was investigated.

3.2   Methods

The flowchart of the proposed methodology is depicted in Fig. 1. After data collection, text and non-text attributes are separated. Thereafter, text pre-processing techniques, namely tokenization, stemming & lemmatization, and stop words removal are performed. Finally, predictive regions are identified which finally produces pre-processed texts. Finally, rules are extracted from both pre-processed categorical and text attributes.

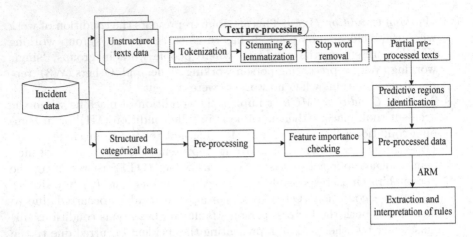

Fig. 1. Proposed methodological flowchart.

In order to find out the hidden pattern within data in terms of rules, ARM is used on both text and categorical data. The proposed text-based ARM can automatically discover association rules from text documents. The approach typically consists of three steps, which are explained as follows: (i) tokenization, filtration, stemming and indexing of the documents, (ii) determination of predictive regions in texts, and (iii) generation of association rules using ARM. All the three above-mentioned steps are briefly described below.

Step 1-Preprocessing of text: Initially, the TDM has been obtained by text mining process. It is then indexed by proper weighting scheme i.e., Term Frequency-Inverse Document Frequency (TF-IDF), which is widely used in different literature [5, 10, 42]. The term TF-IDF can be expressed in the following Eq. (1):

$$w(i,j) = tf \times idf(d_i, t_j) = \begin{cases} N_{d_i,t_j} \times log_2 \frac{|C|}{N_{t_j}} & \text{if } N_{d_i,t_j} \geq 1 \\ 0 & \text{if } N_{d_i,t_j} = 0 \end{cases} \tag{1}$$

where $w(i,j) \geq 0$, tf and idf are called the term frequency and inverse term frequency, respectively, N_{d_i,t_j} denotes the number the term t_j occurs in the document d_i (term frequency factor), N_{t_j} denotes the number of documents in collection C in which t_j occurs at least once (document frequency of the term t_j) and $|C|$ is the number of the documents in collection C. In Eq. (1), the first clause is applied for the words occurring in the document, whereas, the second clause is applied for words that do not appear (*i.e.*, $N_{d_i,t_j} = 0$), for which $w(i,j) = 0$ is set. The frequency of the document is logarithmically scaled. The formula: $log_2 \frac{|C|}{N_{t_j}} = logC - logN_{t_j}$ offers full weight to words occurring in a single document. A word occurring in entire documents would receive weight equal to zero. Using this weighting scheme, user-expected higher frequency keywords for generation of association rules were selected in this study.

Step 2-Determination of predictive regions in texts: Following the strategy adopted by [12], predictive regions in texts are identified in this step. Each region is embedded into n_f dimensional space. We have used convolution neural network (CNN) for automatic feature extraction for a given class, say injury. The regions are identified as the most predictive one towards the output class after this training. In this case, all reports are input as the training set to model in the test mode and the predictive regions are recorded. For all incident outcomes, this process is carried out. These predictive regions are helpful in building more logical rules.

Step 3-Development of association rules using ARM: After determining predictive regions in texts, ARM is used for extracting interesting relationships hidden in accident data sets. The relationships can be represented in the form of sets of frequent items or association rules. The rules are generated on the basis of the frequency of item set that exists alone or in sequence with others in database [1]. Generally, $A \rightarrow B$ is a standard representation of an association rule, where A is the antecedent and B is the consequent, which conveys that B will occur given that A has already occurred for the same item in a database with a minimum threshold value. In the present study, *Apriori* algorithm is used for ARM technique on both types of data i.e., text and categorical. Although, the algorithm being same used in two cases, the basic concept of item sets in the algorithm is different. Words are considered as items in text-based ARM and classes in each of the categorical attributes are regarded as items in categorical-based ARM.

For example, if we consider ARM used on texts, then, given a set of keywords $A = \{w_1, w_2, , ..., w_n\}$ and a collection of indexed documents $D = \{d_1, d_2., .., d_m\}$, where each document d_i is a set of keywords such that $d_i \subseteq A$. Let W_j be a set of keywords. A document d_i is said to contain W_i if and only if $W_i \subseteq d_i$. An association rule is an implication of the form $W_i \rightarrow W_j$ where $W_i \subset A$, $W_j \subset A$, and $W_i \cap W_j = \emptyset$. There are two important basic measures for association rules i.e., Support (S) and Confidence (C). The rule $W_i \rightarrow W_j$ has support S in the collection of documents D if $S\%$ of documents in D contain $W_i \cup W_j$. Then, Support is calculated by the following Eq. (2)

$$\text{Support}(W_i, W_j) = \frac{\text{Support count of } (W_i, W_j)}{\text{Total number of documents } D} \qquad (2)$$

The rule $W_i \rightarrow W_j$ holds in the collection of documents D with confidence C if among those documents that contain W_i , $C\%$ of them contain W_j also. We can compute confidence score using Eq. (3).

$$\text{Confidence}(W_i, W_j) = \frac{\text{Support}(W_i, W_j)}{\text{Support}(W_i)} \qquad (3)$$

Basically, ARM is performed in the following two steps: (i) generate all the keyword combinations or sets, called as frequency sets, whose Support values are greater than the user specified minimum Support, and (ii) use the identified frequent keyword sets to generate the rules that satisfy a user specified minimum

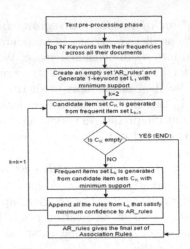

Fig. 2. The working principle of ARM on text data.

confidence. The frequent keywords generation requires more effort and the rule generation is straightforward. The *Apriori* algorithm is used on the top 25% of the keywords associated with higher *TF-IDF* matrix but only the top 25% of the keywords. The overall process of ARM on text data is depicted in Fig. 2. The extracted association rules can be visualized in textual format or tables, or in graphical format. In this study, it is designed to visualize the extracted association rules in tabular format for a incident event leading to an incident outcomes (i.e., injury, near miss, and property damage) in a particular department.

4   Results and Discussions

In this section, the rules obtained from both text and categorical data using ARM are discussed below in brief.

4.1   Extraction of the Best Item-Set Rules from Textual Data

In this stage, ARM technique has been applied on accident text data i.e., incident narratives. *Apriori* algorithm has been deployed for this approach. A set of 23 rules has been extracted for all three incident outcome cases. Of which, nine rules of injury are shown in Table 4. It can be observed that, in some cases, the rules obtained from the text-based ARM form the common basic event as obtained from fault tree analysis. For example, due to the occurrence of injury in the department N2, some of the related bag of words are identified and consequently rules using text-based ARM approach are generated like (left, operate, oven) → (STF). From this rule, it can be inferred that during the operation in oven in the department N2, STF related causes resulting injuries are often happened. In similar veins, from another rule (in Table 4), identified as (side, slip, toilet)

$\rightarrow$ (STF), it can be interpreted that number of slipping incidents causing injury are observed more near a particular region like toilet area. It is noteworthy to mention that this important factor has been identified by text-based ARM whereas text mining analysis could hardly figure this out. Therefore, considering text-based ARM with text mining process can be an effective way of analysis to utilize the complete information within the body of unstructured text. In our study, text-based rules are obtained after meeting basic three criteria: (i) minimum threshold for Support and Confidence are set to be 0.002 and 0.01, respectively; (ii) the best rules are selected based on the highest Lift value; and (iii) the best rule are considered only to be a four-item or more than four-item set rules.

4.2 Extraction of the Best Item-Set Rules from Categorical Data

After extracting rules from text data, rules are extracted from categorical data. The combination/association of the factors in the form of rules is essential, which leads to accident scenarios. In order to find out the inherent rules, ARM has been used. Minimum value or threshold for Support (S), Confidence (C) is required to be set for extracting the rules. However, by changing the threshold, number of rules can be varied as per users' requirement. Although there is no established condition mentioning the adoption of the thresholds, selection of those values depends on the data points used for the study, and usefulness of the strong rules. However, the minimum value for S and C each varies from 0.1% to 4%, and 1% to 34%, respectively [19,41]. Another important parameter in ARM is lift (L) which is usually taken as greater than 1 or 2 [19]. In the present study, for injury, near miss, and property damage, the threshold values for S, C, and L are taken as 0.1%, 1.0%, and 1.0, respectively. The rules having S, C and L values greater than threshold are selected finally, and others are discarded. Only the best rules (i.e., strong and interesting rules with higher Lift) for 3, 4, and 5-itemsets for injury, near miss, and property damage for each of the departments have been selected and shown in Tables 1, 2 and 3.

From Fig. 3(a), the most important three-item rule for injury in N1 department is found to be (incident type- IT1, observation type- OT3) $\rightarrow$ (incident category-injury) in N1 ($S = 0.60\%, C = 9.50\%, L = 3.66$) which describes that injury occurs mostly in N1 department due to behavioral related issue and unsafe acts by others. This finding supports the study of [24] in mining industry. Similarly, in case of four-item rule for the same case considered, the most important one having lift $L = 12.80$ is (working condition-W2 + machine condition-M3 + primary cause-R) $\rightarrow$ (incident category-injury) in N1 ($S = 0.10\%, C = 33.30\%$) which implies that rail is a reason for occurrence of injury in N1 department while the person is working alone and machine is running. Similarly, in case of five-item rule for the same case discussed, the most important rule having $L = 1.51$ is (SOP required-SPR3 + SOP available-SPAv1 + SOP compliance-SPC1 + SOP adequacy-SPA2) $\rightarrow$ (incident category-injury) in N1 department ($S = 0.20\%, C = 3.90\%$) which signifies that in N1 department injury has taken place for those jobs not following any SOP.

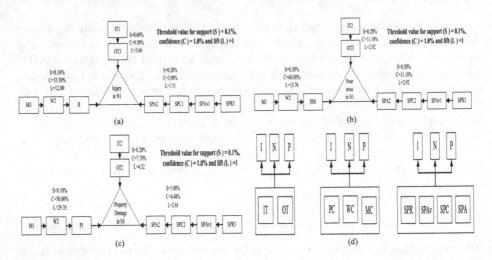

Fig. 3. Best association rules for (a) injury; (b) near-miss; (c) property damage in N1 department; and (d) attributes considered for generating three, four, and five item set rules in a department. Note: (IT = Incident types; OT = Observation types; PC = Primary causes; WC = Working conditions; MC = Machine conditions; SPR = SOP requirements; SPAv = SOP available; SOC = SOP compliance; SPA = SOP adequate).

From Fig. 3(b), the most important three-item set rule for near miss in N1 department is found to be (incident type- IT2 + observation type- OT3) → (incident category-near miss) ($S = 0.20\%, C = 11.10\%, L = 2.92$) which narrates that near miss in N1 department occurs mostly due to process related issue as well as unsafe act by others. This result also supports the study of [41] on problems related to safety in a steel plant. Similarly, in case of four-item rule for the same case considered, the most important one having lift $L = 15.76$ is (working condition-W2 + machine condition-M3 + primary cause-HM) → (incident category-near miss) in N1 ($S = 0.30\%, C = 60.00\%$) which describes that hot metal is a reason for occurrence of near miss in N1 department while the person is working alone and machine is running. This rule supports the recent study of [38] in process industry. Similarly, among five-item set rules for the near miss, the best rule having $L = 2.92$ is (SOP required-SPR3 + SOP available-SPAv1 + SOP compliance-SPC2 + SOP adequacy-SPA2) → (incident category-near miss) in N1 department ($S = 0.50\%, C = 11.10\%$) which signifies that near miss in N1 department has happened for those jobs not following any SOP. In fact, this condition has been found to be prevailed in case of derailments after discussion with safety expert. Hence, SOP should be followed for every job in the industry.

Similarly, from Fig. 3(c), the most important three-item rule for property damage is observed as (incident type- IT2 + observation type- OT2) → (incident category-property damage) in N1 ($S = 0.20\%, C = 7.70\%, L = 4.52$) which explains that property damage in N1 department occurs mostly due to process related issues and the presence of unsafe acts and unsafe conditions.

Table 1. Association rules for Injury cases in each department (8 departments, $8 \times 3 =$ 24 best rules).

Department	Association Rules (X −>Y)	Support (S %)	Confidence (C %)	Lift (L)
N1	IT1 & OT3 −>IN1	0.6	9.5	3.66
	M3 & W2 & R −>IN1	0.1	33.3	12.8
	SPR3 & SPAv1 & SPC1 & SPA2 −>IN1	0.2	3.9	1.51
N2	IT1 & OT3 −>IN2	1	15.9	2.06
	M1 & W3 & STF −>IN2	0.1	100	12.96
	SPR2 & SPAv2 & SPC3 & SPA3 −>IN2	0.8	12.7	1.65
N3	IT1 & OT3 −>IN3	0.8	12.7	5.51
	M3 & W1 & HP −>IN3	0.2	40	17.36
	SPR3 & SPAv1 & SPC2 & SPA2 −>IN3	0.2	4.4	1.93
N4	IT2 & OT1 −>IN4	0.6	8.6	1.48
	M1 & W1 & SI −>IN4	0.1	1	17.21
	SPR2 & SPAv2 & SPC3 & SPA3 −>IN4	1.3	20.6	3.55
N5	IT2 & OT3 −>IN5	0.1	5.6	2.41
	M1 & W2 & EMD −>IN5	0.1	50	21.7
	SPR2 & SPAv2 & SPC3 & SPA3 −>IN5	0.3	4.8	2.07
N9	IT1 & OT3 −>IN9	0.4	6.3	1.71
	M1 & W2 & WAH −>IN9	0.1	100	26.97
	SPR2 & SPAv2 & SPC3 & SPA3 −>IN9	0.4	6.3	1.71
N7	IT1 & OT4 −>IN7	3	11.7	1.77
	M1 & W3 & MA −>IN7	0.1	100	15.12
	SPR2 & SPAv2 & SPC3 & SPA3 −>IN7	1	15.9	2.4
N8	IT1 & OT3 −>IN8	1.3	20.6	4.58
	M1 & W2 & OI −>IN8	0.1	1	22.18
	SPR2 & SPAv2 & SPC3 & SPA3 −>IN8	0.8	12.7	2.82

This also supports the study of [41] on safety associated incidents in the steel plant. Similarly, in case of four-item rule for the same case considered, the most important one having lift $L = 29.35$ is (working condition-W2 + machine condition-M1 + primary cause-PI) $\rightarrow$ (incident category-property damage) in N1 ($S = 0.10\%, C = 50.00\%$) which reveals that process incident is also a reason for property damage in N1 department while person is working alone. The study on petroleum oil storage terminals by [36] also supports the above finding. Similarly, in case of five-item rule for the same case discussed, the most important rule having $L = 2.609$ is (SOP required-SPR3 + SOP available-SPAv1 + SOP compliance-SPC2 + SOP adequacy-SPA2) $\rightarrow$ (incident category-property damage) in N1 department ($S = 5.00\%, C = 4.40\%$) which signifies that property damage in N1 department happened for those jobs not following any SOP. Figure 3(d) shows the overall rule generation structure from the data set. Three, four, and five item set rules have been generated for I, N, PD considering the attributes including IT & OT, PC, WC & MC, and SOPA, SOPC, SOPAv & SOPR, respectively (refer to Fig. 3(d)).

Table 2. Association rules for near miss cases in each department (7 departments, $(7 \times 3 = 21$ best rules).

Department	Association Rules (X ->Y)	Support (S %)	Confidence (C %)	Lift (L)
N1	IT2 & OT3 ->NN1	0.2	11.1	2.92
	M3 & W2 & HM ->NN1	0.3	60	15.76
	SPR3 & SPAv1 & SPC2 & SPA2 ->NN1	0.5	11.1	2.92
N2	IT2 & OT1 ->NN2	1	14.3	1.62
	M2 & W3 & PI ->NN2	0.2	100	11.34
	SPR3 & SPAv1 & SPC3 & SPA3 ->NN2	0.1	100	11.34
N4	IT2 & OT3 ->NN4	0.3	16.7	7.23
	M1 & W2 & EI ->NN4	0.1	100	43.39
	SPR1 & SPAv2 & SPC3 & SPA3 ->NN4	0.7	15.2	6.6
N5	IT1 & OT1 ->NN5	2	6.1	2.02
	M2 & W1 & RO ->NN5	0.1	100	33.27
	SPR3 & SPAv1 & SPC2 & SPA1 ->NN5	2.3	10.6	3.53
N9	IT2 & OT2 ->NN9	0.3	11.5	2.13
	M2 & W3 & GL ->NN9	0.1	100	18.48
	SPR3 & SPAv1 & SPC1 & SPA2 ->NN9	0.7	13.7	2.54
N7	IT1 & OT2 ->NN7	0.9	10.3	2.07
	M2 & W1 & S ->NN7	0.1	100	20
	SPR3 & SPAv1 & SPC3 & SPA2 ->NN7	0.1	100	19.96
N8	IT2 & OT2 ->NN8	0.2	7.7	2.95
	M2 & W1 & EI ->NN8	0.1	100	38.39
	SPR3 & SPAv1 & SPC2 & SPA2 ->NN8	0.3	6.7	2.56

Table 3. Association rules for property damage cases in each department (8 departments, $(8 \times 3 = 24$ best rules).

Department	Association Rules (X ->Y)	Support (S %)	Confidence (C %)	Lift (L)
N1	IT2 & OT2 ->PN1	0.2	7.7	4.52
	M1 & W2 & PI ->PN1	0.1	50	29.35
	SPR3 & SPAv1 & SPC2 & SPA2 ->PN1	0.2	4.4	2.61
N2	IT2 & OT2 ->PN2	0.4	15.4	2.9
	M1 & W3 & EMD ->PN2	0.1	100	18.83
	SPR3 & SPAv1 & SPC1 & SPA1 ->PN2	1.6	12.6	2.37
N4	IT2 & OT4 ->PN4	0.8	5.4	3.17
	M1 & W3 & SI ->PN4	0.1	100	58.71
	SPR1 & SPAv2 & SPC3 & SPA3 ->PN4	0.4	8.7	5.11
N5	IT1 & OT1 ->PN5	2.2	6.7	1.75
	M2 & W3 & EMD ->PN5	0.1	100	26.26
	SPR3 & SPAv1 & SPC2 & SPA1 ->PN5	2.7	12.4	3.27
N9	IT2 & OT2 ->PN9	0.5	19.2	5.48
	M2 & W1 & EMD ->PN9	0.2	50	14.26
	SPR1 & SPAv2 & SPC3 & SPA3 ->PN9	0.4	8.7	2.48
N6	IT2 & OT1 ->PN6	0.1	1.4	1.43
	M1 & W1 & PI ->PN6	0.1	33.3	33.27
	SPR3 & SPAv1 & SPC1 & SPA2 ->PN6	0.1	2	1.96
N7	IT1 & OT1 ->PN7	8.8	26.7	1.99
	M2 & W2 & R ->PN7	0.1	100	7.45
	SPR3 & SPAv1 & SPC2 & SPA1 ->PN7	4.3	19.8	1.48
N8	IT2 & OT3 ->PN8	0.2	11.1	3.7
	M2 & W2 & S ->PN8	0.1	100	33.27
	SPR1 & SPAv2 & SPC3 & SPA3 ->PN8	0.5	10.9	3.62

Table 4. Key factors with corresponding rules from the proposed model for injury across all the departments.

Incident Category Frequently occurring in Department	primary cause	Relevant rule from Text based ARM (Considering only 4 or more than 4 item set rules for meaningful interpretation)	Best Rule from association rule mining (3-item rules)	Best Rule from association rule mining (4-item rules)	Best rule from association rule mining (5-item rules)
IN1	RI	{bike, come, duty} =>{IZ1_RI} {come, duty, injury} =>{IZ1_RI}	Due to unsafe act by others and behavior related problem	Rail is a reason when worker is working alone	available, inadequate SOP
IN2	STF	{side, slip, toilet} =>{IZ2_STF} {left, operate, oven} =>{IZ2_STF}	Due to unsafe act by others and behavior related problem,	STF is a reason in non-working condition	Inadequate SOP
IN3	RI	{cycle, met, ride} =>{IZ3_RI} {after, complete, duty, home} =>{IZ3_RI}	Due to unsafe act by others and behavior related problem,	Hydraulic/Pneumatic is a reason when persons are working in group	available, inadequate SOP
IN4	STF	{employee, slip, sprain} =>{IZ4_STF} {helper, proper, work} =>{IZ4_STF}	Due to unsafe act by person and process related problem	Structural integrity is a reason when people are working in group	unavailable SOP
IN5	STF	{injury} =>{IZ5_STF} **	Due to unsafe act by others and process related problem	Equipment machinery damage is a reason when person is working alone	unavailable SOP
IN7	STF	{empty, got, injury, loco} =>{IZ7_STF} {couple, got, wagon} =>{IZ7_STF}	Due to unsafe act by others and behavior related problem	Working at height is a reason when person is working alone	unavailable SOP
IN8	MH	{cover, ground, release} =>{IZ8_MH} {aid, clean, leg} =>{IZ8_MH}	Due to unsafe condition and behavior related problem	Medical alignment is a reason	unavailable SOP
IN9	STF	{granule, inhа, inspect, tank, while} =>{IZ9_STF} {inspect, tank, while} =>{IZ9_STF}	Due to unsafe act by others and behavior related problem	Occupational illness is a reason while person is working alone	unavailable SOP

5   Conclusions

In the present study, a hybrid model encompassing text mining-based ARM approach has been proposed to predict the incident outcomes i.e., injury, near miss, and property damage and to investigate the accidents through rule-based analysis in various departments in the steel plant. The main aim of this study is to use categorical and textual data together in building a prediction model which could predict the incident outcomes in different departments in the plant and finding association rules among various factors leading to incidents. In order to extract information from the unstructured text field, text-based ARM approach has been applied to uncover the hidden patterns in terms of rules or associations among the factors which might not be captured by human judgment. In addition, ARM on categorical data explores some interesting and useful findings. For examples, in N1 department, injury mostly occurs due to behavioral related issue and unsafe act. Rail is also found to be a reason for injury in the same department while person is working alone and machine is in running condition. Analyses also indicate that ignoring or not following SOP also leads to injury in the N1 department.

Like other research, the study has also some limitations. First, data pre-processing including data cleaning, standardization, consistency check could be taken care of efficiently by well-established algorithms to increase the accuracy of the model. Second, higher the data size, higher will be the generalization ability of the model. But, in this study, very limited data has been used to build the model. Another limitation of our study is that while generating association rules from text, sometimes very limited number of rules (sometimes even no rules) are generated with minimum support and confidence value which is practically very difficult for interpretation. As future aspects of this study, survey can be done for the further verification as well as validation of our proposed model by expert opinions from particular domain. Some unsupervised learning algorithms like clustering could be implemented. Moreover, other algorithms of association rule mining approaches such as predictive *Apriori*, Equivalence Class Transformation (ECLAT) algorithm could be implemented for better investigation of the problem. Decision tree modeling could also be another kind of effective approach for further investigation of occupational accident analysis in industrial domain. In addition, this paper only deals with the best rules derived from ARM, avoiding taking other rules. Future study could further investigate some high-quality item set rules finding from the data set. New algorithm for text-based ARM could be developed in order to find out more hidden interactions of factors with the reduction of human effort. Furthermore, ontology-based text mining could be incorporated at the earlier stage of the study. On top of that, though the scope of the present study is limited to steel industry, it can be implemented in other application domains also such as mining, manufacturing, construction, aviation etc.

Acknowledgment. The work is funded by UAY project, GOI (Project Code: IITKGP_022). We acknowledge the Centre of Excellence in Safety Engineering and Analytics (CoE-SEA) (www.iitkgp.ac.in/department/SE) and Safety Analytics & Virtual Reality (SAVR) Laboratory (www.savr.iitkgp.ac.in) of Department of Industrial & Systems Engineering, IIT Kharagpur for experimental/computational and research facilities for this work. We would like to thank the management of the plant for providing relevant data and their support and cooperation during the study.

References

1. Agrawal, R., Srikant, R., et al.: Fast algorithms for mining association rules. In: Proceedings of the 20th International Conference on Very Large Data Bases (VLDB), vol. 1215, pp. 487–499 (1994)
2. Amiri, M., Ardeshir, A., Fazel Zarandi, M.H., Soltanaghaei, E.: Pattern extraction for high-risk accidents in the construction industry: a data-mining approach. Int. J. Inj. Control Saf. Promot. **23**(3), 264–276 (2016)
3. Basso, B., Carpegna, C., Dibitonto, C., Gaido, G., Robotto, A., Zonato, C.: Reviewing the safety management system by incident investigation and performance indicators. J. Loss Prev. Process Ind. **17**(3), 225–231 (2004)
4. Bertke, S., Meyers, A., Wurzelbacher, S., Bell, J., Lampl, M., Robins, D.: Development and evaluation of a Naïve Bayesian model for coding causation of workers' compensation claims. J. Saf. Res. **43**(5), 327–332 (2012)

5. Blei, D.M., Ng, A.Y., Jordan, M.I.: Latent Dirichlet allocation. J. Mach. Learn. Res. **3**, 993–1022 (2003)
6. Brown, D.E.: Text mining the contributors to rail accidents. IEEE Trans. Intel. Transp. Syst. **17**(2), 346–355 (2016)
7. Bunn, T.L., Slavova, S., Hall, L.: Narrative text analysis of Kentucky tractor fatality reports. Accid. Anal. Prev. **40**(2), 419–425 (2008)
8. Cheng, C.W., Lin, C.C., Leu, S.S.: Use of association rules to explore cause-effect relationships in occupational accidents in the Taiwan construction industry. Saf. Sci. **48**(4), 436–444 (2010)
9. Chi, C.F., Lin, S.Z., Dewi, R.S.: Graphical fault tree analysis for fatal falls in the construction industry. Accid. Anal. Prev. **72**, 359–369 (2014)
10. Fu, Z., Wu, X., Wang, Q., Ren, K.: Enabling central keyword-based semantic extension search over encrypted outsourced data. IEEE Trans. Inf. Forensics Secur. **12**(12), 2986–2997 (2017)
11. ILO: Protecting Workplace Safety and Health in Difficult Economic Times. The Effect of the Financial Crisis and Economic Recession on Occupational Safety and Health. Programme on Safety and Health at Work and the Environment (Safe-Work). Seiji Machida Director. Technical Report (2013)
12. Johnson, R., Zhang, T.: Effective use of word order for text categorization with convolutional neural networks. arXiv preprint arXiv:1412.1058 (2014)
13. Kumar, S., Toshniwal, D.: A data mining framework to analyze road accident data. J. Big Data **2**(1), 26 (2015)
14. Lehto, M., Marucci-Wellman, H., Corns, H.: Bayesian methods: a useful tool for classifying injury narratives into cause groups. Inj. Prev. **15**(4), 259–265 (2009)
15. Li, C., Qin, J., Li, J., Hou, Q.: The accident early warning system for iron and steel enterprises based on combination weighting and grey prediction model GM (1, 1). Saf. Sci. **89**, 19–27 (2016)
16. Liao, C.W., Perng, Y.H.: Data mining for occupational injuries in the Taiwan construction industry. Saf. Sci. **46**(7), 1091–1102 (2008)
17. Liao, C.W., Perng, Y.H., Chiang, T.L.: Discovery of unapparent association rules based on extracted probability. Decis. Support Syst. **47**(4), 354–363 (2009)
18. Mirabadi, A., Sharifian, S.: Application of association rules in Iranian railways (rai) accident data analysis. Saf. Sci. **48**(10), 1427–1435 (2010)
19. Montella, A., Aria, M., D'Ambrosio, A., Mauriello, F.: Data-mining techniques for exploratory analysis of pedestrian crashes. Transp. Res. Rec. J. Transp. Res. Board **2237**, 107–116 (2011)
20. Nenonen, N.: Analysing factors related to slipping, stumbling, and falling accidents at work: application of data mining methods to finnish occupational accidents and diseases statistics database. Appl. Ergon. **44**(2), 215–224 (2013)
21. Nordlöf, H., Wiitavaara, B., Winblad, U., Wijk, K., Westerling, R.: Safety culture and reasons for risk-taking at a large steel-manufacturing company: investigating the worker perspective. Saf. Sci. **73**, 126–135 (2015)
22. Pande, A., Abdel-Aty, M.: A computing approach using probabilistic neural networks for instantaneous appraisal of rear-end crash risk. Comput. Aided Civ. Infrastruct. Eng. **23**(7), 549–559 (2008)
23. Patel, M.D., Rose, K.M., Owens, C.R., Bang, H., Kaufman, J.S.: Performance of automated and manual coding systems for occupational data: a case study of historical records. Am. J. Ind. Med. **55**(3), 228–231 (2012)
24. Paul, P., Maiti, J.: The role of behavioral factors on safety management in underground mines. Saf. Sci. **45**(4), 449–471 (2007)

25. Pramanik, A., Sarkar, S., Maiti, J.: Oil spill detection using image processing technique: an occupational safety perspective of a steel plant. In: Emerging Technologies in Data Mining and Information Security, vol. 814, pp. 247–257. Springer, Singapore (2019). https://doi.org/10.1007/978-981-13-1501-5_21
26. Sanchez-Pi, N., Martí, L., Garcia, A.C.B.: Text classification techniques in oil industry applications. In: International Joint Conference SOCO'13-CISIS'13-ICEUTE'13, pp. 211–220. Springer (2014). https://doi.org/10.1007/978-3-319-01854-6_22
27. Sanchez-Pi, N., Martí, L., Garcia, A.C.B.: Improving ontology-based text classification: an occupational health and security application. J. Appl. Log. **17**, 48–58 (2016)
28. Sarkar, S., Verma, A., Maiti, J.: Prediction of occupational incidents using proactive and reactive data: a data mining approach. In: Maiti, J., Ray, P.K. (eds.) Industrial Safety Management. MAC, pp. 65–79. Springer, Singapore (2018). https://doi.org/10.1007/978-981-10-6328-2_6
29. Sarkar, S., Baidya, S., Maiti, J.: Application of rough set theory in accident analysis at work: a case study. ICRCICN **2017**, 245–250 (2017)
30. Sarkar, S., Chain, M., Nayak, S., Maiti, J.: Decision support system for prediction of occupational accident: a case study from a steel plant. In: Emerging Technologies in Data Mining and Information Security, vol. 813, pp. 787–796. Springer, Singapore (2019). https://doi.org/10.1007/978-981-13-1498-8_69
31. Sarkar, S., Ejaz, N., Maiti, J.: Application of hybrid clustering technique for pattern extraction of accident at work: a case study of a steel industry. In: 2018 4th International Conference on Recent Advances in Information Technology (RAIT), pp. 1–6. IEEE, IIT Dhanbad(2018)
32. Sarkar, S., Kumar, A., Mohanpuria, S.K., Maiti, J.: Application of Bayesian network model in explaining occupational accidents in a steel industry. In: ICRCICN 2017, pp. 337–342. IEEE (2017)
33. Sarkar, S., Lakha, V., Ansari, I., Maiti, J.: Supplier selection in uncertain environment: a fuzzy MCDM approach. In: ICIC2 - 2016, pp. 257–266. Springer (2017)
34. Sarkar, S., Pateshwari, V., Maiti, J.: Predictive model for incident occurrences in steel plant in India. ICCCNT **2017**, 1–5 (2017)
35. Sarkar, S., Raj, R., Sammangi, V., Maiti, J., Pratihar, D.: An optimization-based decision tree approach for predicting slip-trip-fall accidents at work. Saf. Sci. **118**, 57–69 (2019)
36. Sharma, R.K., Gurjar, B.R., Singhal, A.V., Wate, S.R., Ghuge, S.P., Agrawal, R.: Automation of emergency response for petroleum oil storage terminals. Saf. Sci. **72**, 262–273 (2015)
37. Singh, K., Raj, N., Sahu, S., Behera, R., Sarkar, S., Maiti, J.: Modelling safety of gantry crane operations using petri nets. Int. J. Inj. Control Saf. Promot. 24(1), 32-43 (2015)
38. Stefana, E., Marciano, F., Alberti, M.: Qualitative risk assessment of a dual fuel (LNG-diesel) system for heavy-duty trucks. J. Loss Prev. Process Ind. **39**, 39–58 (2016)
39. Taylor, J.A., Lacovara, A.V., Smith, G.S., Pandian, R., Lehto, M.: Near-miss narratives from the fire service: a Bayesian analysis. Accid. Anal. Prev. **62**, 119–129 (2014)
40. Verma, A., Chatterjee, S., Sarkar, S., Maiti, J.: Data-driven mapping between proactive and reactive measures of occupational safety performance. In: Maiti, J., Ray, P.K. (eds.) Industrial Safety Management. MAC, pp. 53–63. Springer, Singapore (2018). https://doi.org/10.1007/978-981-10-6328-2_5

41. Verma, A., Khan, S.D., Maiti, J., Krishna, O.: Identifying patterns of safety related incidents in a steel plant using association rule mining of incident investigation reports. Saf. Sci. **70**, 89–98 (2014)
42. Zheng, W., Shuai, J., Shan, K.: The energy source based job safety analysis and application in the project. Saf. Sci. **93**, 9–15 (2017)

Mining Interesting Association Rules with a Modified Genetic Algorithm

Abir Derouiche[1]([✉]), Abdesslem Layeb[2], and Zineb Habbas[3]

[1] MISC Laboratory, Abdelhamid Mehri, Constantine 2 University,
Constantine, Algeria
abir.derouiche@univ-constantine2.dz
[2] Abdelhamid Mehri, Constantine 2 University, Constantine, Algeria
abdesslem.layeb@univ-constantine2.dz
[3] University of Lorraine, Metz, France
zineb.habbas@univ-lorraine.fr

Abstract. Association Rules Mining is an important data mining task that has many applications. Association rules mining is considered as an optimization problem; thus several metaheuristics have been developed to solve it since they have been proven to be faster than the exact algorithms. However, most of them generates a lot of redundant rules. In this work, we proposed a modified genetic algorithm for mining interesting non-redundant association rules. Different experiments have been carried out on several well-known benchmarks. Moreover, the algorithm was compared with those of other published works and the results found proved the efficiency of our proposal.

Keywords: Data mining · Association rules mining · Multi-objective association rules mining · Metaheuristics · Genetic algorithm · Quality measures · Redundancy

1 Introduction

Association Rules Mining (ARM) has become one of the main topics in data mining. It attracts a lot of attention because of its wide applicability in different area such as in web mining [24], document analysis [17], telecommunication alarm diagnosis[19], network intrusion detection [5], and bioinformatics applications [27].

Most of the classical association rules mining algorithms, such as the Apriori algorithm [2] and the FP-growth algorithm [13] work in two phases, the first phase is the frequent itemsets generation and the second phase is the rules generation.

Generating the frequent itemsets might be considered as a straightforward task. However, it is a time-consuming task when the number of items is large. For example a dataset comprising n items contains $2^n - 1$ different itemsets,

C. Djeddi et al. (Eds.): MedPRAI 2020, CCIS 1322, pp. 274–285, 2021.
https://doi.org/10.1007/978-3-030-71804-6_20

whereas the number of itemsets of size k is equal to $\binom{n}{k}$ for any $k \leqslant n$. Thus, given the amount of computations needed for each candidate rule is O(k) the overall complexity is $O(\sum_{k=1}^{n} k \times \binom{n}{k}) = O(2^{n-1} \times n)$.

So the complexity of finding itemsets is in exponential order, and this complexity is even higher when the frequency of each itemset is calculated[10].

For any dataset comprising n items and m different transactions, the complexity to compute the frequencies of all the itemsets within the dataset is equal to $O(2^{n-1} \times n \times m)$ [28].

On the other hand, metaheuristics are increasingly considered as a more promising alternative approach. They have been proven beneficial as they directly generate association rules, skipping the frequent itemsets generation phase by maximizing the support and the confidence of the rules. The quality of an association rule is not limited to its support and confidence, there are many other metrics available to measure the quality of an association rule such as coverage, comprehensibility, leverage, interestingness, lift and conviction. Therefore, the problem of ARM can be considered also as a multi-objective optimization problem [11] .

Although ARM metaheuristics are proved to be faster than ARM exact algorithms, most of them suffer from accuracy. They do not generate all the rules and not necessarily those of good quality. Besides, a large number of association rules returned to the user are redundant, so it is time-consuming to analyses the results, the user has to handle a large proportion of redundant rules, most of these rules are not interesting for the application at hand.

This article proposed a Modified Genetic Algorithm for Mining interesting Association Rule (MGA-ARM), different contributions have been embedded in the proposed algorithm. First, the random initial population is replaced by a special initial population to enhance both the CPU time and the solution quality. Secondly, we consider different measures beside support and confidence in the objective function in order to extract better association rules and finally, we propose a method to handle and prune the non-significant redundant rules. Different experiments have been carried out on several well-known benchmarks. The results were compared with those of other published methods and proved the efficiency of the proposal.

2   Association Rules Mining

2.1   Definitions

The formal definition of an association rule was initiated by Agrawal in [1]. Let $I = \{i_1, i_2, \ldots, i_n\}$ be a set of n items, $T = \{t_1, t_2, \ldots t_m\}$ a set of m transactions where each transaction t_i is a set of items such that $t_i \subseteq I$. An association rule is a pattern of the form $X \rightarrow Y$ meaning that there is an association between the presence of the itemsets X and Y in transactions. X is called antecedent or left-hand side of the rule, Y is called consequence or right-hand side of the rule. The association rules have two significant basic measures: support and confidence. Given an association rule $(X \rightarrow Y)$:

- The support denoted support $(X \rightarrow Y)$ is the ratio between the number of transactions containing $X \cup Y$ and the number of transactions in the database. It determines how often the rule is applicable to a given dataset.

$$\text{Support}(X \rightarrow Y) = \frac{\text{Support}(X \cup Y)}{\text{Total number of transactions}} \quad (1)$$

- The Confidence denoted confidence $(X \longrightarrow Y)$ is the ratio between the number of transactions containing $X \cup Y$ and the number of transactions containing X. It determines how frequently items in Y appear in transactions that contain X.

$$\text{Confidence}(X \rightarrow Y) = \frac{\text{Support}(X \cup Y)}{\text{Support}(X)} \quad (2)$$

Association rules mining task is formally stated as follows: given a set of transactions T= $\{T_1, T_2, ..., T_m\}$, the objective is to find all valid rules i.e. rules having support and confidence greater than the user-specified minimum support (minsup) and minimum confidence (minconf).

2.2   Association Rules Mining as an Optimization Problem

Association rules mining task is not limited to the previous definition, it is considered as an optimization problem that consists to find the best rules $r \in R$ where R is the set of all possible rules, while maximizing the values of the support and confidence [8].

There are many other metrics available to measure the quality of an association rule such as coverage, comprehensibility, leverage, interestingness, lift and conviction [11]. Therefore, the problem of ARM can be considered also as a multi-objective optimization problem rather than a single objective one, where the goal is to find association rules while optimizing several objective measures simultaneously.

Whether we use just support and confidence or we use more measures, metaheuristic always generate duplicated and redundant rules and this effects the quality of the results presented to the user.

2.3   Redundant Rules

Definition 1. *Let* $X \longrightarrow Y$ *and* $X' \longrightarrow Y'$ *be two rules with confidence cf and cf', respectively.* $X \longrightarrow Y$ *is said a redundant rule to* $X' \longrightarrow Y'$ *if X belongs to X'; Y belongs to Y' and cf $\leq$ cf' [29].*

Definition 2. *Let R1 be the rule* $X \longrightarrow Y$ *and R2 the rule* $X' \longrightarrow Y'$*. We say that the rule R1 is more general than the rule R2 , denoted R1 $\leq\leq$ R2, if R2 can be generated by adding additional items to either the antecedent or consequent of R1 [30].*

Formally let $R = R_1, ..., R_n$ be a set of rules, such that all their supports and confidences are equal. For all i, $1 \leq i \leq n$ if $X \subseteq X'$ and $Y \subseteq Y'$, then we say that a rule R_j is redundant if there exists some rule R_i, such that $R_i \leq\leq R_j$.

In other words, since all the rules in the collection R have the same support and confidence, the simplest rules in the collection should suffice to represent the whole set. Thus the non-redundant rules in the collection R are those that are most general, i.e., those having minimal antecedents and consequent, in terms of subset relation [30]. This second definition is considered in our work.

3   Related Works

Most metaheuristics were investigated to solve the ARM problem, whether evolutionary or swarm intelligence algorithms. Saggar et al. [25] were the first authors to propose the use of evolutionary algorithms for ARM, their idea consisted in optimizing association rules extracted with the Apriori algorithm by using a genetic algorithm, after that genetic programming was also used for ARM in [23]. An interesting survey about the use of evolutionary computation for frequent pattern mining with particular emphasis on genetic algorithms can be found in [28]. Particle swarm optimization was largely used to mine association rules a survey of its applications is proposed in [4], we can cite for example the work published in [20] and the work proposed by Sarath and Ravi in [26], after that in [21] a Modified Binary Cuckoo search (MBCS-ARM) was proposed. In [14] the authors present an adaptation of bat algorithm to ARM issue known as BAT-ARM. Later, they proposed a multi-population bat algorithm in [15].

In [22], the authors used Ant Colony Optimization for continuous domains (ACO_R), this algorithm mines numeric association rules without any need to specify minimum support and minimum confidence. Another recent works propose an algorithm based on animal migration optimization [6] and chemical reaction optimization metaheuristic [7].

Hybrid approaches was also proposed such as the work in [9] where the authors proposed an algorithm based on bees swarm algorithms and tabu-search and in the work [18] where the authors combine both genetic algorithm and particle swarm optimisation in an algorithm called (GPSO).

The following works considered the association rules mining as a multi-objective problem rather than a single-objective one, in [12] the authors proposed a pareto based genetic algorithm where they used three measures: comprehensibility, interestingness and confidence as objective functions.

Alatas et al. [3] proposed pareto-based multi-objective differential evolution (DE) for extracting association rules. They formulated the association rule mining problem as a four-objective optimization problem, where, support, confidence and comprehensibility of rules are maximized, while the amplitude of the intervals, which conforms the item set and rule is minimized.

In [11], the Multi-objective Binary Particle Swarm Optimization (MO-BPSO), the Multi-objective Binary Firefly optimization and Threshold Accepting (MO-BFFO-TA), and the Multi-objective Binary Particle Swarm optimization and Threshold Accepting (MO-BPSO-TA) were used to extract association rules without specifying support and confident threshold's. Recently a multi-objective bat algorithm known as MOB-ARM is proposed in [16].

4   The Proposed Modified Genetic Algorithm for ARM

To use metaheuristics, the objective function, the representation of the solution and the different operators need to be defined and adapted to the problem in hand.

4.1   Objective Function and Rule Representation

For the rule encoding, the solution S is represented by an integer vector defined as follows:

- $S[i] = 0$ if the item i is not present in the rule S.

- $S[i] = 1$ if the item i belongs to the antecedent part of the rule S.

- $S[i] = 2$ if the item i belongs to the consequent part of the rule S.

Example: Given a set of five items $\{1, 2, 3, 4, 5\}$, the rule $\{1, 4 \rightarrow 2, 5\}$ is represented by $S = \{1, 2, 0, 1, 2\}$.

The Objective Function: Four quality measures of the rule was maximized in the objective function, we used the comprehensibility and the interestingness measure in addition to the support and the confidence.

$$F(S) = Max(Support(S)*Confidence(S)*Comprehensibility(S)*Interestingness(S)) \quad (3)$$

where according to [12]

- The Comprehensibility of an association rule quantify how much the rule is comprehensible

$$Comprehensibility(X \rightarrow Y) = \frac{\log(1 + |X|)}{\log(1 + |X \cup Y|)} \quad (4)$$

- Interestingness: a rule is interesting when the individual support count values are greater than the collective support $(X \rightarrow Y)$ values

$$Interestingness(X \rightarrow Y) = \frac{support(X \cup Y)}{support(X)} \times \frac{support(X \cup Y)}{support(Y)} \times \frac{1 - support(X \cup Y)}{|N|} \quad (5)$$

4.2   Algorithm and Operators

In this section we present the Modified Genetic Algorithm for ARM (MGA-ARM), we explain the different steps of the algorithm and the proposed method to prune the non-significant redundant rules.

– Search space: we believe that the search space can be easily pruned using the Apriori principle and some other propriety. The following example shows that the infrequent items are useless because they always lead to infrequent rules. Let $ab \rightarrow c$ be a given frequent rule and d an infrequent item, that means $sup(d) < minsup$. Consequently $sup(abcd) < minsup$, therefore, all rules generated from the itemset {abcd} will be infrequent. In our proposal, the search space contains a set of frequent items instead of considering all the items [8].
– Initial population: most the metaheuristic use a random initialization and exploit all the set of items to create the population where infrequent items generate infrequent rules and this is useless for the search procedure and it is a waste of time as explained previously. For MGA-ARM, the random population is replaced by a set of valid rules of size two. Algorithm 1 resumes the different steps of the procedure **InitPop** used for the generation of the initial population.

Algorithm 1. InitPop(T, $ValidAR\_2$)

Input: T a transactional dataset
Ouputs: $ValidAR\_2$ a set of valid Association Rules of size 2,
Begin
1: $FIS\_1 \leftarrow$ **BestFrequentItemset_1(T)**
2: $AR\_2 \leftarrow$ **GenerateRules** (FIS_1, T)
3: $ValidAR\_2 \leftarrow$ **SelectValidRules** (AR_2)
End

InitPop starts by extracting a set of frequent items FIS_1 from the dataset T, then based on this set, it generates a set of rules that contains two frequent items one at the antecedent and the other one at the consequence of the rule. Finally, it selects the best rules within the generated rules and saves it as $ValidAR\_2$ to be the special initial population exploited by our algorithm [8].
– Crossover: in our algorithm, the proposed crossover takes an item that does not exist in parent1 and add it to parent2 , and add a new item to parent1 from parent2 that does not exist beforehand. This operator ensures that the new solutions are feasible since the parents were feasible solutions. Figure 1 shows an example of the crossover operator. First, we copy parent1 to child1 and parent2 to child2, then we move an item that does not exists in parent2 and exists in parent1 to child2 and vice versa respectively.

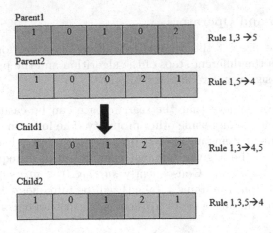

Fig. 1. Example of the crossover operator

- Mutation: the exchange operator is applied between two items one at the antecedent and one at the consequent of the rule. Figure 2 shows an example of applying the mutation operator on the rule $1, 5 \longrightarrow 2$.
- Selection: the elitism selection is used.

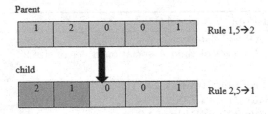

Fig. 2. Example of the mutation operator

- Stopping criteria: it can be reached if the objective function value is less than a predefined threshold, or a maximum number of iterations performed without improvements. In our case, we use the maximum number of iterations.
- Filter_rules procedure introduced at the final step of MGA-ARM is used to eliminates three types of useless rules. First, it eliminates the duplicated rules. The second type of discarded rules are the rules constructed from the same itemset thus they have the same support however their confidence and fitness are different since they have different antecedent and consequence. The third type is the redundant rules, defined in Sect. 2.3, they are eliminated by grouping the rules that have the same values of support and confidence and their itemsets are included in each other. We keep then the general rule that has the smallest number of items and we delete the other ones.

The details of the proposed algorithm are given by Algorithm 2.

Algorithm 2. MGA-ARM

Input: T a transactional database
Ouput: IR a set of interesting Association Rules
1: Initialize the parameters $pop\_size, iter$, max_iter, $cross\_rate, mutate\_rate$;
2: $pop \leftarrow InitPop()$
3: Evaluate_fitness(pop)
4: **while** $iter \leq max\_iter$ **do**
5:    **for** $i \leftarrow 1$ to pop_size **do**
6:       Select(parent1,parent2)
7:       **if** $rand(0,1) \leq cross\_rate$ **then**
8:          Child $\leftarrow$ Crossover(parent1,parent2)
9:       **end if**
10:      **if** $rand(0,1) \leq mutate\_rate$ **then**
11:         Child $\leftarrow$ Mutation()
12:      **end if**
13:   **end for**
14:   iter$\leftarrow$iter+1
15:   Update pop
16: **end while**
17: S $\leftarrow$ best chromosomes
18: IR $\leftarrow$ Filter_rules(S)

---

5   Experiments and Results

The experiments were done in two steps, in the first step a study that compares the proposed approach to other approaches in terms of quality of solutions and CPU run time is presented. Then in the second step, a study about the effect of pruning redundancy on the final solution is explained.

5.1   Experimental Environment and Datasets

The experiments were done under Windows 8 using a desktop computer with Intel Core-i3 processor, 1.8 GHz and 6 GB memory, all the implementations have been achieved using Matlab. The tests have been conducted on well-known scientific datasets, frequently used by the data mining community: Chess database that contains 3196 transactions and 75 items. Mushroom dataset which has much more transactions 8124 and 119 items. IBM Quest Standard dataset with 1000 transaction and 40 items. Finally, two small data set Book and Food with also 1000 transaction and 11 items.

The dataset can be found found in (http://fimi.uantwerpen.be/data/) and (http://funapp.cs.bilkent.edu.tr/DataSets/) and (https://www.solver.com/xlminer) and (www.ibm.com/software/analytics/spss/) respectively.

5.2   A Comparative Study with Other Approaches

In this section, we compared our proposed MGA-ARM to single and multi-objective algorithms. We used three different versions of the bat algorithm designed for mining association rules BAT-ARM [14], MPB-ARM [15], MOB-ARM [16]. The experiment was carried out on three datasets within the dataset stated before. The size of the population was fixed to 50 and the maximum number of iteration to 100.

Tables 1 and 2 presents the average results of support and confidence respectively in thirty executions.

Table 1. Comparing our approaches with other works in terms of support

Dataset	Algorithm			
	MGA-ARM	MOB-ARM	BAT-ARM	MPB-ARM
IBM-Quest	0.275	0.26	0.25	0.23
Chess	0.935	0.51	0.38	0.46
Mushroom	0.371	0.34	0.23	0.23

Table 2. Comparing our approaches with other works in terms of confidence

Dataset	Algorithm			
	MGA-ARM	MOB-ARM	BAT-ARM	MPB-ARM
IBM-Quest	0.594	0.54	0.52	0.59
Chess	0.970	0.83	0.72	0.79
Mushroom	0.653	0.87	0.54	78.5

In terms of support and confidence, the results show that our proposed algorithm MGA-ARM outperforms MOB-ARM, BAT-ARM and MPB-ARM in most cases.

Table 3 presents the CPU run times for the different algorithms in 100 runs the result are given in seconds.

Table 3. Comparing our approaches with other works in terms of CPU run time

Dataset	Algorithm		
	MGA-ARM	BAT-ARM	MPB-ARM
IBM-Quest	9.1	10	7
Chess	47	67	70
Mushroom	119	141	130

Our proposed algorithm is faster than the other algorithms in most cases thanks to the special population proposed that avoid a lot of useless exploitation of the search space.

5.3   Study on the Effect of Pruning Redundancy

In this section, we will see the effect of applying Filter_rules procedure on the results to eliminates the duplicated and redundant rules.

Table 4. Effect of pruning redundancy

Measures	Rules pruned	Support		Confidence	
Dataset	%	Before	After	Before	After
Book	[40 44]	0.1641	0.157	0.5432	0.525
Food	[40 50]	0.1053	0.1036	0.3571	0.3545
IBM-Quest	[10 16]	0.2778	0.2768	0.5366	0.5335
Chess	[06 14]	0.9008	0.8842	0.9537	0.9517
Mushroom	[04 10]	0.4520	0.4382	0.7437	0.7289

Table 4 shows the changes in support and confidence values before and after applying the Filter_rules procedure. The interval in the first columns presents the percentage of rule deleted, it is different from dataset to another. It is clear that for the small datasets book and food, the percentage of rule pruned is large, in the best cases 40% of rules are deleted in the worst-case half of the rules are duplicated and redundant. For the larger data set, we notice that the percentage of rule deleted is smaller 16% in worst cases and 4% in best cases.

On the other hand, for the quality measures, we noticed that there is not a big difference in the average of the support and confidence in different runs. For the different data sets, the values in the worst-case decrease with 0.02 and in the best cases with 0.001 this is not important compared to the number of useless rules pruned.

The Filter_rules procedure indeed decreases considerably the number of rules but it ensures to present to the user a set of interesting non-redundant association rules. It should be noted that when applying the filter procedure, it is recommended to select a large number of valid rules because after applying the Filter_rules procedure the number of rules will decrease.

6   Conclusion

In this work, we proposed a modified genetic algorithm for mining interesting association rules by considering four different quality measures: support, confidence, comprehensibility, and interestingness. Moreover, we propose a new technique to build the initial population of GA, and we handle duplicated and redundant rules by proposing the Filter_rules procedure. Different experiments have been carried out on several well-known benchmarks. The results compared with those of other published methods proved the efficiency of the proposal. We emphasize to optimize our algorithm by testing different crossover and mutation, and to test it on larger datasets. Moreover, we can use more quality measurements to define which are really better for ARM problem.

References

1. Agrawal, R., Imieliński, T., Swami, A.: Mining association rules between sets of items in large databases. In: ACM SIGMOD RECORD, vol. 22, pp. 207–216. ACM (1993)
2. Agrawal, R., Srikant, R., et al.: Fast algorithms for mining association rules. In: Proceedings of the 20th International Conference on Very Large Data Bases, VLDB, vol. 1215, pp. 487–499 (1994)
3. Alatas, B., Akin, E., Karci, A.: MODENAR: multi-objective differential evolution algorithm for mining numeric association rules. Appl. Soft Comput. **8**(1), 646–656 (2008)
4. Ankita, S., Shikha, A., Jitendra, A., Sanjeev, S.: A review on application of particle swarm optimization in association rule mining. In: Satapathy, S.C., Udgata, S.K., Biswal, B.N. (eds.) Proceedings of the International Conference on Frontiers of Intelligent Computing: Theory and Applications (FICTA). AISC, vol. 199, pp. 405–414. Springer, Heidelberg (2013). https://doi.org/10.1007/978-3-642-35314-7_46
5. Barbará, D., Couto, J., Jajodia, S., Wu, N.: ADAM: a testbed for exploring the use of data mining in intrusion detection. ACM SIGMOD Rec. **30**(4), 15–24 (2001)
6. Chiclana, F., et al.: ARM-AMO: an efficient association rule mining algorithm based on animal migration optimization. Knowl.-Based Syst. **154**, 68–80 (2018)
7. Derouiche, A., Layeb, A., Habbas, Z.: Chemical reaction optimization metaheuristic for solving association rule mining problem. In: 2017 IEEE/ACS 14th International Conference on Computer Systems and Applications (AICCSA), pp. 1011–1018, October 2017
8. Derouiche, A., Layeb, A., Habbas, Z.: Metaheuristics guided by the apriori principle for association rule mining: Case study-CRO metaheuristic. Int. J. Organ. Collective Intell. (IJOCI) **10**(3), 14–37 (2020)
9. Djenouri, Y., Drias, H., Chemchem, A.: A hybrid bees swarm optimization and tabu search algorithm for association rule mining. In: 2013 World Congress on Nature and Biologically Inspired Computing (NaBIC), pp. 120–125. IEEE (2013)
10. Freitas, A.A.: Data Mining and Knowledge Discovery with Evolutionary Algorithms. Springer, Heidelberg (2013). https://doi.org/10.1007/978-3-662-04923-5
11. Ganghishetti, P., Vadlamani, R.: Association rule mining via evolutionary multi-objective optimization. In: Murty, M.N., He, X., Chillarige, R.R., Weng, P. (eds.) MIWAI 2014. LNCS (LNAI), vol. 8875, pp. 35–46. Springer, Cham (2014). https://doi.org/10.1007/978-3-319-13365-2_4
12. Ghosh, A., Nath, B.: Multi-objective rule mining using genetic algorithms. Inf. Sci. **163**(1), 123–133 (2004)
13. Han, J., Pei, J., Yin, Y., Mao, R.: Mining frequent patterns without candidate generation: a frequent-pattern tree approach. Data Min. Knowl. Disc. **8**(1), 53–87 (2004)
14. Heraguemi, K.E., Kamel, N., Drias, H.: Association rule mining based on bat algorithm. In: Pan, L., Păun, G., Pérez-Jiménez, M.J., Song, T. (eds.) BIC-TA 2014. CCIS, vol. 472, pp. 182–186. Springer, Heidelberg (2014). https://doi.org/10.1007/978-3-662-45049-9_29
15. Heraguemi, K.E., Kamel, N., Drias, H.: Multi-population cooperative bat algorithm for association rule mining. In: Núñez, M., Nguyen, N.T., Camacho, D., Trawiński, B. (eds.) ICCCI 2015. LNCS (LNAI), vol. 9329, pp. 265–274. Springer, Cham (2015). https://doi.org/10.1007/978-3-319-24069-5_25

16. Heraguemi, K.E., Kamel, N., Drias, H.: Multi-objective bat algorithm for mining interesting association rules. In: Prasath, R., Gelbukh, A. (eds.) MIKE 2016. LNCS (LNAI), vol. 10089, pp. 13–23. Springer, Cham (2017). https://doi.org/10.1007/978-3-319-58130-9_2

17. Holt, J.D., Chung, S.M.: Efficient mining of association rules in text databases. In: Proceedings of the Eighth International Conference on Information and Knowledge Management, pp. 234–242. ACM (1999)

18. Indira, K., Kanmani, S.: Mining association rules using hybrid genetic algorithm and particle swarm optimisation algorithm. Int. J. Data Anal. Tech. Strat. 7(1), 59–76 (2015)

19. Klemettinen, M.: A knowledge discovery methodology for telecommunication network alarm databases (1999)

20. Kuo, R.J., Chao, C.M., Chiu, Y.: Application of particle swarm optimization to association rule mining. Appl. Soft Comput. 11(1), 326–336 (2011)

21. Mlakar, U., Zorman, M., Fister Jr., I., Fister, I.: Modified binary cuckoo search for association rule mining. J. Intell. Fuzzy Syst. 32(6), 4319–4330 (2017)

22. Moslehi, P., Bidgoli, B.M., Nasiri, M., Salajegheh, A.: Multi-objective numeric association rules mining via ant colony optimization for continuous domains without specifying minimum support and minimum confidence. Int. J. Comput. Sci. Iss. (IJCSI) 8(5), 34–41 (2011)

23. Olmo, J.L., Luna, J.M., Romero, J.R., Ventura, S.: Association rule mining using a multi-objective grammar-based ant programming algorithm. In: 11th International Conference on Intelligent Systems Design and Applications (ISDA), pp. 971–977. IEEE (2011)

24. Pei, J., Han, J., Mortazavi-asl, B., Zhu, H.: Mining access patterns efficiently from web logs. In: Terano, T., Liu, H., Chen, A.L.P. (eds.) PAKDD 2000. LNCS (LNAI), vol. 1805, pp. 396–407. Springer, Heidelberg (2000). https://doi.org/10.1007/3-540-45571-X_47

25. Saggar, M., Agrawal, A.K., Lad, A.: Optimization of association rule mining using improved genetic algorithms. In: 2004 IEEE International Conference on Systems, Man and Cybernetics, vol. 4, pp. 3725–3729. IEEE (2004)

26. Sarath, K., Ravi, V.: Association rule mining using binary particle swarm optimization. Eng. Appl. Artif. Intell. 26(8), 1832–1840 (2013)

27. Satou, K., et al.: Finding association rules on heterogeneous genome data. In: Proceedings of Pacific Symposium on Biocomputing, pp. 397–480. Citeseer (1997)

28. Ventura, S., Luna, J.M.: Pattern Mining with Evolutionary Algorithms. Springer, Cham (2016). https://doi.org/10.1007/978-3-319-33858-3

29. Zaki, M.J.: Generating non-redundant association rules. In: Proceedings of the Sixth ACM SIGKDD International Conference on Knowledge Discovery and Data Mining, pp. 34–43 (2000)

30. Zaki, M.J.: Mining non-redundant association rules. Data Min. Knowl. Disc. 9(3), 223–248 (2004)

ASCII Embedding: An Efficient Deep Learning Method for Web Attacks Detection

Ines Jemal[1(✉)], Mohamed Amine Haddar[2,3], Omar Cheikhrouhou[1,3], and Adel Mahfoudhi[1,3]

[1] ENIS, CES, LR11ES49, University of Sfax, 3038, Sfax, Tunisia
`ines.jemal@stud.enis.tn`
[2] ReDCAD Laboratory, University of Sfax, Sfax, Tunisia
[3] College of Computer and Information Technology, Taif University, Taif, Saudi Arabia

Abstract. Web security is a homogeneous mixture of modern machinery and software technologies designed to protect the personal and confidential data of all Internet users. After many decades of hard work in web security, the protection of personal data remains an obsession for legitimate internet users. Nowadays, artificial intelligence techniques are overcoming classical signature-based and anomaly-based techniques, which unable to detect zero-day attacks. To help reduce fraud and electronic theft at the server-side, we propose in this paper a novel deep learning method to preprocess the input of neural networks. This technique, called ASCII Embedding, aims to efficiently detect web server attacks. Using an online real dataset CSIC 2010, we evaluated and compared our technique to existing ones as word, and character embedding approaches. The experimental results prove that our technique outperforms the existing works accuracy and reaches 98.2434%.

Keywords: Web security · Web attacks · Convolutional neural network · Word embedding · Character embedding · ASCII code

1 Introduction

The World Wide Web has made our daily life easier. We can buy our needs, pay our bills and consult the news using the Internet. This technology is responsible for electronic fraud. Web Attacks persist even with the more sophisticated security policies and standards. Skilled hackers can overtake security controls and steals sensitive data. To enhance the web application security, the cyber world endows several prevention software tools ready-made such as Web Application Firewalls (WAF) [1], Intrusion Detection Systems (IDS) [2]. The majority of these products use anomaly based and signature-based techniques. These techniques that are developed to secure the server, are unable to stop zero-day attacks. Nowadays, Artificial Intelligence (AI) [3] shows a significant aptness in many domains

© Springer Nature Switzerland AG 2021
C. Djeddi et al. (Eds.): MedPRAI 2020, CCIS 1322, pp. 286–297, 2021.
https://doi.org/10.1007/978-3-030-71804-6_21

and particularly web security. Among the very popular techniques of AI comes the machine learning [4]. The key concept of this technique is making the machine learns from the existing data. After a while, the machine becomes able to get the right decision. The learning phase is based on a huge amount of data that helps the machine learns how to react to each existing situation. After this phase, the machine makes for new situations a decision with an accuracy concurrent to the human one. The more adequate technique in machine learning is the Neural Network. This technique mimics the human brain and makes somehow the machine reacts intelligently to unknown circumstances. For web security purposes, the neural network learns from a huge number of Http requests stored in a chosen dataset. To reach a higher attack detection accuracy rate, the neural network input data must be carefully preprocessed from the rough dataset requests. The most used techniques in the literature to process the Http request are the word embedding [5] and the character embedding [6]. The first transform word by word the Http request to a vector of numbers. The second approach does the same task at the character level. However, the main problem of these techniques is the unpredictable behavior of the neural network for new characters or words.

To tackle this problem, in this paper, we propose a new technique of Http request preprocessing called ASCII Embedding. This technique outperforms existing techniques by increasing neural network performances. A set of experiments are conducted to measure the performance of the new method. Our technique proved experimentally that it performs better than the existing approaches, it fulfills 98.2434% of accuracy.

The remainder of this paper is organized as follows: The second section presents the state of the art of neural networks preprocessing techniques. Our method is presented in Sect. 3. The evaluation of our method together with the existing techniques is conducted via an experimental test and exposed in Sect. 4. This section lays the results and compares our technique to the existing ones. The last section concludes this paper and briefly explains our future work.

2   Related Works

Studying machine learning and especially deep learning techniques have realized enormous attraction after the success proved in the image processing domain. To get benefit from this success, many domains have applied these techniques such as web security. To detect the web attacks, more strictly, detect the attacks at the server-side, many works proposed the use of deep learning techniques. Mickiaki et al. [7] investigated on Character Level Convolution Neural Network (CLCNN) to detect web application attacks. Each character included in the Http request was represented by 8 bits numeric string and converted into 128-dimensional vector expressions. The authors used the CSIC 2010 [8] dataset to train their model and test their approach. They compared two different architecture using different kernel sizes. The accuracy varied between 95% and 98%. The same dataset was used by Zhang et al. [9], they dissected the Http request into words and deleted the non-alphanumeric characters. Their CNN model achieved 96.49% of accuracy. The authors believed that the embedding vectors generated by word embedding approach are more helpful to detect web attacks, while Hung et al. [10] considered that using word embedding has some limits because the Http request contains too many unique words that deal with memory constraints, and in many cases, it cannot obtain the embedding vector for each new words at the test time. For this reason, Hung et al. [10] proposed an advanced word embedding approach to solving the problem of many words observed. They applied the CNN to both characters and words approaches to process the URL String. The authors used the AUC ROC curve [11] to show the performance of their approach, it achieved 98%. Jane et al. [12] used two neural networks multilayer Feed Forward networks, the first neural network checking by trained web application data, while the second neural network checking by trained the behavior user. The input of the first neural network (ANN1) is defined by a set of collected information from several sections of Http request: Post Parameters, Get Parameters, Cookie-Parameters, database operations, file system operations, errors, warning. The second neural network (ANN2) stores data about user behavior as an input: address IP, country, name, version of the browser, version of the operating system, language system, screen resolution, color depth, and browser home page. The two neural networks ANN1 and ANN2 achieved 92% and 95% of accuracy, respectively. Joshua et al. [13] used the eXpose neural network based on character embedding approach to detect malicious URL, they investigated the automatic extraction of features for a short string. Their model achieved a 92% detection rate.

Erxue et al. [14] used CNN to improve IDS systems. The authors used the word embedding approach to detect malicious payloads, whereas our study is on detecting attacks on the server-side. Their model achieved 95.75% of accuracy.

The previously presented work has used either the word embedding or the character embedding approaches to process the Http requests. Trying to enhance the attack detection rate, we propose a new embedding approach called ASCII Embedding, which is presented in the next section.

3   ASCII Embedding Method

The works presented in the literature review use word or character embedding techniques to Http request preprocessing. These two approaches are widely used for text processing. The word embedding approach starts by cleaning the Http request from the non-alphanumeric symbols. Then, it maps each word to a vector of real values. The character embedding is an interpolation of word embedding to the character level. The works that used these techniques and especially word embedding show acceptable accuracy. Nevertheless, when the Http request contains too many words or new words, the decision made is very likely to be incorrect.

We present in this section our new method called ASCII Embedding. The new approach is an interpolation of character embedding to integers. A replacement of characters by their machine value code (like ASCII) is considered. The idea of using ASCII code comes from the successful results showed when using the CNN models for image classification, where the features engineering are the pixels. Every pixel has a value between 0 and 255. The Http request is then transformed into a sequence of numbers. Each number represents the ASCII code of the corresponding character. We choose the Convolutional neural network to test our technique because it has a special architecture and it can learn important features from a big scale. Our new preprocessing method aims to help the neural network to detect efficiently the malicious Http requests even with new words not learned during the training phase. In our case, we are interested in the request sent from the client computer and received by the webserver. Figure 1 describes the different parts of the Http request. Each part contains eventually a set of words, characters, and symbols.

To not lose any information and to ensure a high detection rate, our method is applied to the whole Http request without deleting any word, character, or even symbol. The preprocessing of the Http request consists of two successive steps. First, we split the Http request into a sequence of characters and symbols. Then, we replace each character or symbol with its integer value (the ASCII code). The result of these steps is a vector V of integer (see Fig. 2).

The output V of the Http request preprocessing is the input of the CNN.

GET http://localhost:8080/tienda1/publico/productos.jsp HTTP/1.1
User-Agent: Mozilla/5.0 (compatible; Konqueror/3.5; Linux) KHTML/3.5.8 (like Gecko)
Pragma: no-cache
Cache-control: no-cache
Accept: text/xml,application/xml,application/xhtml+xml,text/html;q=0.9,text/plain;q=0.8,image/png,*/*;q=0.5
Accept-Encoding: x-gzip, x-deflate, gzip, deflate
Accept-Charset: utf-8, utf-8;q=0.5, *;q=0.5
Accept-Language: en
Host: localhost:8080
Cookie: JSESSIONID=6075D9A19F97EDC825A2385A8DA9867C
Connection: close

Fig. 1. A real example of Http request

GEThttp://localhost:8080/tienda1/publico/productos.jspHTTP/1.1User-A
gent:Mozilla/5.0(compatible;Konqueror/3.5;Linux)KHTML/3.5.8(likeGeck
o)Pragma:no-cacheCache-control:no-cacheAccept:text/xml,application/x
ml,application/xhtml+xml,text/html;q=0.9,text/plain;q=0.8,image/png,*/
*;q=0.5Accept-Encoding:x-gzip,x-deflate,gzip,deflateAccept-Charset:utf-
8,utf-8;q=0.5,*;q=0.5Accept-Language:enHost:localhost:8080Cookie:JSES
SIONID=6075D9A19F97EDC825A2385A8DA9867CConnection:close

103 32 101 32 116 32 104 32 116 32 112 32 58 32 47 32 47 32 108 32 111 32 99 32 97 32 108 32 104 32 111 32 115 32 116 32 58 32
56 32 48 32 56 32 48 32 47 32 116 32 105 32 101 32 110 32 100 32 97 32 49 32 47 32 112 32 117 32 98 32 108 32 105 32 99 32 111 32 47
32 112 32 114 32 111 32 100 32 117 32 99 32 116 32 111 32 115 32 46 32 106 32 115 32 112 32 104 32 116 32 116 32 112 32 47 32 49 32
46 32 49 32 49 32 117 32 115 32 101 32 114 32 45 32 97 32 103 32 101 32 110 32 116 32 58 32 109 32 111 32 122 32 105 32 108 32 108 32 97 32
47 32 53 32 46 32 48 32 40 32 99 32 111 32 109 32 112 32 97 32 116 32 105 32 98 32 108 32 101 32 59 32 107 32 111 32 110 32 113 32 117
32 101 32 114 32 111 32 114 32 47 32 51 32 46 32 53 32 59 32 108 32 105 32 110 32 117 32 120 32 41 32 107 32 104 32 116 32 109 32 108
32 47 32 51 32 46 32 53 32 46 32 56 32 40 32 108 32 105 32 107 32 101 32 103 32 101 32 99 32 107 32 111 32 41 32 112 32 114 32 97 32
103 32 109 32 97 32 58 32 110 32 111 32 45 32 99 32 97 32 99 32 104 32 101 32 99 32 97 32 99 32 104 32 101 32 45 32 99 32 111 32 110
32 116 32 114 32 111 32 108 32 58 32 110 32 111 32 45 32 99 32 97 32 99 32 104 32 101 32 97 32 99 32 99 32 101 32 112 32 116 32 58 32
116 32 101 32 120 32 116 32 47 32 120 32 109 32 108 32 44 32 97 32 112 32 112 32 108 32 105 32 99 32 97 32 116 32 105 32 111 32 110
32 47 32 120 32 109 32 108 32 44 32 97 32 112 32 112 32 108 32 105 32 99 32 97 32 116 32 105 32 111 32 110 32 47 32 120 32 104 32 116
32 109 32 108 32 43 32 120 32 109 32 108 32 44 32 116 32 101 32 120 32 116 32 47 32 104 32 116 32 109 32 108 32 59 32 113 32 61 32 48
32 46 32 57 32 44 32 116 32 101 32 120 32 116 32 47 32 112 32 108 32 97 32 105 32 110 32 59 32 113 32 61 32 48 32 46 32 56 32 44 32
105 32 109 32 97 32 103 32 101 32 47 32 112 32 110 32 103 32 44 32 42 32 47 32 42 32 59 32 113 32 61 32 48 32 46 32 53 32 97 32 99 32
99 32 101 32 112 32 116 32 45 32 101 32 110 32 99 32 111 32 100 32 105 32 110 32 103 32 58 32 120 32 45 32 103 32 122 32 105 32 112 32
32 44 32 120 32 45 32 100 32 101 32 102 32 108 32 97 32 116 32 101 32 44 32 103 32 122 32 105 32 112 32 44 32 100 32 101 32 102 32 108
32 97 32 116 32 101 32 97 32 99 32 99 32 101 32 112 32 116 32 45 32 99 32 104 32 97 32 114 32 115 32 101 32 116 32 58 32 117 32 116 32
102 32 45 32 56 32 44 32 117 32 116 32 102 32 45 32 56 32 59 32 113 32 61 32 48 32 46 32 53 32 44 32 42 32 59 32 113 32 61 32 48 32 46
32 53 32 97 32 99 32 99 32 101 32 112 32 116 32 45 32 108 32 97 32 110 32 103 32 117 32 97 32 103 32 101 32 58 32 101 32 110 32 104 32
111 32 115 32 116 32 58 32 108 32 111 32 99 32 97 32 108 32 104 32 111 32 115 32 116 32 58 32 56 32 48 32 56 32 48 32 99 32 111 32 111
32 107 32 105 32 101 32 58 32 106 32 115 32 101 32 115 32 115 32 105 32 111 32 110 32 105 32 100 32 61 32 54 32 48 32 55 32 53 32 100 32
57 32 97 32 49 32 57 32 102 32 57 32 55 32 101 32 100 32 99 32 56 32 50 32 53 32 97 32 50 32 51 32 56 32 53 32 97 32 56 32 100 32 97 32 57
32 56 32 54 32 55 32 99 32 99 32 111 32 110 32 110 32 101 32 99 32 116 32 105 32 111 32 110 32 58 32 99 32 108 32 111 32 115 32 101

Fig. 2. Http request preprocessing.

Figure 3 presents the different layers and the hyper-parameters that shape our CNN model. The embedding layer of the CNN transforms V to a digital matrix. The height of the digital matrix l equals to the length of V, and its width d defines the size of the embedding vector ($d = 128$). Based on the choice of the kernel size (3, 4, 5, 6), the convolutional layer extracts the features that it considers important. The max-pooling layer selects the features based on an activation function (Relu). These layers reduce the matrix dimension and speed up the computation. Finally, the Softmax layer takes the binary decision and classifies the Http request into two classes. We use 1 to designate the benign requests and 0 to designate the malicious ones.

The neural network architecture presented in Fig. 3 is implemented in order to evaluate our method.

In the next section, we present the evaluation results and compare our technique to the existing works.

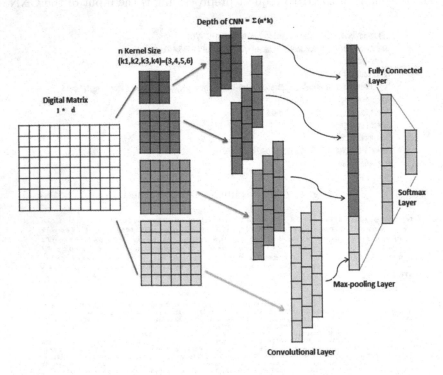

Fig. 3. Implementation of ASCII Embedding technique using CNN.

4   Performance Evaluation of ASCII Embedding

In this section, we evaluate our technique using the two famous splitting methods train/test and k fold cross-validation. We carried out the experiments with the online Http CSIC 2010 dataset [8].

4.1 Dataset Pre-processing

We used the open-access dataset CSIC 2010. It was developed at the "Information Security Institute" of CSIC (Spanish Research National Council) [8]. It was generated to test web attacks protection systems. It contains thousands of Http requests automatically generated: 36000 normal traffic Http requests and 25065 malicious traffic Http requests. This dataset is close to reality as it considers several types of anomalous requests such as SQL injection, buffer overflow, information gathering, files disclosure, CRLF injection, Cross-Site Scripting (XSS), Server-side include, parameter tampering, and Unintentional illegal requests. We split the dataset with the train/test method, we divide the entire dataset into three parts: the training set, the validation set, and the test set. The training and validation set present 80% of the complete CSIC 2010 dataset, and the remaining 20% is for the test. Table 1 shows the distribution of the CSIC 2010 dataset to train, validate, and test the CNN. 63288 requests are used in the training phase and 19413 requests are used to test the efficiency of our method.

Table 1. Experimental dataset distribution.

Http requests	Training & validation phase	Testing phase
Normal	43236	14400
Abnormal	20052	5013
Total number	63288	19413

The second experiment used the k fold cross-validation method. The goal of this method is to avoid under-fitting and over-fitting problems that can arise with the first method. This experiment aims to validate the results found using the first splitting method. We choose two cases k = 5 and k = 10. The whole dataset is then divided into k parts. The experiments are repeated k times. In each time, k − 1 parts are used for training and one part for testing.

4.2 CNN Hyper-Parameters and Evaluation Metrics

To start the experiments, we choose first the convolutional neural network hyper-parameters. For the depth of the CNN, we choose four different kernel size (k1, k2, k3, k4) = (3, 4, 5, 6) and n = 128 filters per kernel size. We choose Adam as the optimizer, cross-entropy as the loss function, the Relu is the activation function, the batch size is equal to 64, the dropout equal to 0.5, and the embedding vector d equals to 128. To evaluate the effectiveness of our technique, we used accuracy, recall, precision and F1-Score as metrics. These metrics are based on the confusion matrix that determines the value of TP, TN, FP, and FN.

- TP: The True Positive rate designates the correct prediction of malicious requests
- TN: The True Negative rate designates the number of correct prediction for benign requests
- FP: The False Positive rate designates the incorrect prediction of malicious requests
- FN: The False Negative rate designates the number of incorrect prediction for benign requests

The metrics mentioned above are presented using TP, TN, FP, and FN as follow.

$Accuracy = \frac{TP+TN}{TP+TN+FN+FP}$

$Sensitivity = Recall = True\,Positive\,Rate(TPR) = \frac{TP}{FN+TP}$

$Specificity = False\,Positive\,Rate\,(FPR) = \frac{TN}{TN+FP}$

$Precision = \frac{TP}{TP+FP}$

$F1 - Score = 2 * \frac{Precision*Recall}{Precision+Recall}$

Ready to start the experiments, we will present in the next subsection the results.

4.3 Experimental Study and Results

Our experiments are conducted using the free cloud Google Collaboratory [15] as platform and software services. It provides an excellent GPU and free deep learning software. Our experiments are conducted using the two different methods of data splitting explained above. The train/test results are presented in the next subsection. The k fold cross-validation results will be presented later.

Train/Test Split Method. With 80% of the whole CSIC 2010 dataset, we trained our model CNN using the ASCII embedding method about 6000 steps (about 7 epochs). We recorded the training loss and accuracy rates after every 100 steps. In Fig. 4, we can remark that after 4500 steps of training, the training accuracy rate exceeds 98% while the training losses decrease rapidly towards zero. These trends of accuracy and loss reveal the good performance of our CNN model in the training phase using our new method.

After 6000 steps of training and with 20% of the whole CSIC 2010 dataset, we tested the newly trained CNN using our new method. Table 2 presents the confusion matrix for the binary classification. It presents the different rates TP, TN, FP, and FN. It demonstrates that the ASCII Embedding performs well in the detection of malicious Http requests. Our model CNN based on the ASCII embedding correctly predicts 14282 from 14400 benign requests and 4767 from 5013 malicious requests.

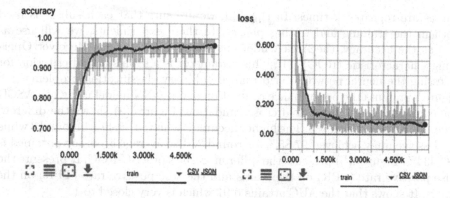

Fig. 4. The Loss and Accuracy rates in the training phase.

Table 2. Confusion matrix of the binary classification task.

	Predicted as malicious	Predicted as normal
Malicious requests	4767	246
Benign requests	118	14 282

Table 3 presents the value of the different metrics obtained from the confusion matrix. Using our model CNN with the new method, the attack detection rate reached: 98.125% of accuracy rate, the precision rate is 99.1805%, the Recall rate is 98.306% and the F1-Score is 96,284%.

Table 3. Performance of ASCII Embedding.

Metrics	Rate
Accuracy	98.125%
Recall	97,779%
Precision	94,833%
F1-Score	96,284%

Table 3 reveals that with a convenient amount of training data, our new CNN model based on ASCII Embedding achieved very satisfactory results in detecting web attacks.

The next subsection will present the experiments that used the k fold cross-validation data splitting method.

k-Fold Cross-validation Method. Using the Training/Test method for data splitting has some drawbacks. In some cases, either under-fitting or over-fitting can be observed. To avoid these problems, we use the K-fold cross-validation method. This method splits the dataset to k subsets, trains the model with k-1 subsets, and holds the last subset for the test. Consequently, the train/test phases are repeated k times. In the end, we are sure that each subset is used both in the training and testing phases. In these experiments, we will use as well as the accuracy, the Area Under the Curve (AUC) of the Receiver Operating Characteristic (ROC) [11]. This parameter is a sophisticated criterion for assessing the neural network performance in binary classification problems.

Figure 5 presents the performance evaluation of our CNN model using the ASCII embedding method with 5 fold cross-validation. Figure 5(a) shows the different accuracy obtained for k = 5. The higher accuracy achieved 98.49% in round 3 while the less accuracy achieved 97.85% for round 2. The average accuracy obtained is 98.2434%. Figure 5(b) presents the different results of AUC-ROC. It presents the false positive rate (FPR) on the x-axis and the true positive rate (TPR) on the y-axis. It shows that the AUC attains 0.97 which is very closed to 1.

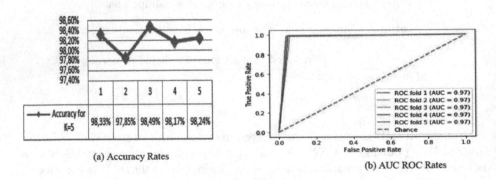

(a) Accuracy Rates

(b) AUC ROC Rates

Fig. 5. Performance evaluation of ASCII embedding using 5-Fold cross-validation.

Figure 6 shows the obtained results using a 10 fold cross-validation method. Figure 6(a) presents the different accuracy found during the experimental tests. The best accuracy equals to 98.44% reached in round 8 while the less accuracy is 97.95% attained in round 7 and 9. The average accuracy reached to 98.2073%. As shown in Fig. 6(b), the Auc reaches 0.97. This value near one proves the considerable performance of the CNN model in detecting web attacks.

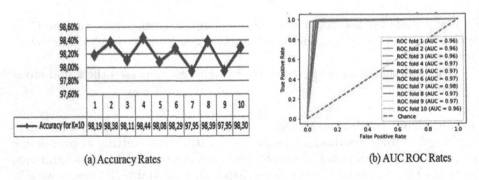

(a) Accuracy Rates

(b) AUC ROC Rates

Fig. 6. Performance evaluation of ASCII Embedding using 10-Fold cross-validation.

The experiments we did in this section have two purposes. First, they confirm the efficiency of our technique in preprocessing the input of the model CNN. Second, it outputs the results that will help us compare our technique to the existing ones.

The next subsection will be the scene of the second purpose.

4.4   Comparative Study and Discussion

In the previous subsection, we compared the discrimination ability of our new technique called ASCII Embedding. Table 4 summarizes the results achieved when testing the designed CNN using the new method ASCII Embedding. It shows that the new model CNN performs well in detection web application attacks, the accuracy exceeds 98%.

Table 4. Performance evaluation of ASCII Embedding

Data splitting method	Accuracy rate
Train/Test	98.125%
5 Fold cross validation	98.2434%
10 Fold cross validation	98.2073%

Under the same experimental conditions (dataset, hardware, software) and using the same CNN model (same hyper-parameters values), we implemented and compared the word, and character embedding techniques together with our proposed ASCII embedding. The word and character techniques did not overtake 97.6% and 96.12%, respectively while our approach exceeds 98%. Table 5 presents the obtained results based on the attack detection accuracy criterion. Using the same CNN, we proved by experiments that our CNN based on the ASCII embedding approach achieved better accuracy, it reached 98.2434%.

Table 5. Comparison of embedding approaches using the same experimental conditions and the same CNN model.

Embedding approach	Accuracy
Word Embedding	97.6%
Character Embedding	96.12%
ASCII Embedding	98.2434%

Using the CSIC 2010 dataset, we reveal by all the experiments described above that the ASCII Embedding was successfully used in the web attacks detection. It has a good performance in Http request classification (benign or malicious class). It achieved a high web attack detection rate with a low number of false alarms. Our technique uses a simple way to preprocess the neural network input and leads to an improvement of the accuracy rate better than the works using the word or character embedding approaches.

5 Conclusion

In this paper, we pushed a step further the accuracy of neural networks for web attacks detection. We come up with a new method called ASCII Embedding to improve the detection of server-side web application attacks. Using an especially designed convolutional neural network model, our technique outperforms the existing ones and reached 98.2434%. When experimenting with ASCII Embedding, we note an extra waiting time to get the results compared to the character and word embedding techniques.

In future work, we will try to decrease the time overhead. Semantic processing of the Http request can be a possible solution for this problem.

References

1. Prokhorenko, V., Choo, K.-K.R., Ashman, H.: Web application protection techniques: a taxonomy. J. Netw. Comput. Appl. **60**, 95–112 (2016)
2. Kumar, K.N., Sukumaran, S.: A survey on network intrusion detection system techniques. Int. J. Adv. Technol. Eng. Explor. **5**(47), 385–393 (2018)
3. Russell, S.J., Norvig, P.: Artificial Intelligence: A Modern Approach. Pearson Education Limited, Malaysia (2016)
4. Xin, Y., et al.: Machine learning and deep learning methods for cybersecurity. IEEE Access **6**, 35365–35381 (2018)
5. Lebret, R.P.: Word embeddings for natural language processing. Technical report EPFL (2016)
6. Kim, Y., Jernite, Y., Sontag, D., Rush, A.M.: Character-aware neural language models. In: Thirtieth AAAI Conference on Artificial Intelligence (2016)
7. Ito, M., Iyatomi, H.: Web application firewall using character-level convolutional neural network. In: 2018 IEEE 14th International Colloquium on Signal Processing and Its Applications (CSPA), pp. 103–106. IEEE (2018)
8. Dataset CSIC-2010. http://www.isi.csic.es/dataset/
9. Zhang, M., Xu, B., Bai, S., Lu, S., Lin, Z.: A deep learning method to detect web attacks using a specially designed CNN. In: Liu, D., Xie, S., Li, Y., Zhao, D., El-Alfy, E.-S.M. (eds.) ICONIP 2017, Part V. LNCS, vol. 10638, pp. 828–836. Springer, Cham (2017). https://doi.org/10.1007/978-3-319-70139-4_84
10. Le, H., Pham, Q., Sahoo, D., Hoi, S.C.: URLNet: Learning a URL representation with deep learning for malicious URL detection. arXiv preprint arXiv:1802.03162 (2018)
11. Yang, S., Berdine, G.: The receiver operating characteristic (ROC) curve. Southwest Respir. Crit. Care Chron. **5**(19), 34–36 (2017)
12. Stephan, J.J., Mohammed, S.D., Abbas, M.K.: Neural network approach to web application protection. Int. J. Inf. Educ. Technol. **5**(2), 150 (2015)

13. Saxe, J., Berlin, K.: Expose: a character-level convolutional neural network with embeddings for detecting malicious URLs, file paths and registry keys. arXiv preprint arXiv:1702.08568 (2017)
14. Min, E., Long, J., Liu, Q., Cui, J., Chen, W.: TR-IDS: anomaly-based intrusion detection through text-convolutional neural network and random forest. Secur. Commun. Netw. **2018** (2018)
15. Carneiro, T., Da Nóbrega, R.V.M., Nepomuceno, T., Bian, G., De Albuquerqu, V.H.C., Reboucas Filho, P.P.: Performance analysis of Google colaboratory as a tool for accelerating deep learning applications. IEEE Access **6**, 61677–61685 (2018)

Conditional Graph Pattern Matching with a Basic Static Analysis

Houari Mahfoud[(⊠)] [iD]

LRIT Laboratory, Abou-Bekr Belkaid University, Tlemcen, Algeria
houari.mahfoud@univ-tlemcen.dz

Abstract. We propose conditional graph patterns (*CGPs*) that extend conventional ones with simple counting quantifiers on edges, attributes on nodes, positive and negative predicates. In emerging applications such as social network marketing, *CGPs* allow to express complex search conditions and to find more sensible information than their traditional counterparts. We show that the *CGPs* expressivity does not come with a much higher price. Indeed, we propose a matching algorithm that is based on a revised notion of graph simulation and allows to match *CGPs* over any data graphs in quadratic time, as opposed to the prohibitive solutions based on subgraph isomorphism. We discuss a parallel version of our algorithm that makes it very efficient over real-life data. We investigate the satisfiability and containment problems of *CGPs* and we show that they are in quadratic time by providing a non-trivial checking algorithm for each one. This paper is the first effort that investigates static analysis of non-conventional graph patterns containing important features that are widely used in practice. An extensive experimental study has been conducted to show effectiveness and efficiency of our results.

Keywords: Isomorphism · Graph simulation · Predicates · Conditional patterns · Parallel matching · Static analysis · Satisfiability · Containment

1 Introduction

Given a data graph G and a graph pattern Q, graph pattern matching is to find all subgraphs of G that match Q. Matching here is typically expressed in terms of subgraph isomorphism which consists to find all subgraphs of G that are *isomorphic* to Q. However, subgraph isomorphism is an NP-COMPLETE problem [4]. Moreover, the number of matches via subgraph isomorphism may be exponential in the size of the data graph. To reduce this cost, graph simulation [18] and its extensions [5,6,15] have been proposed that allow graph pattern matching to be conducted in polynomial time. Unlike subgraph isomorphism that defines a one-to-one mapping, these extensions map a node of a graph pattern to many nodes of a data graph, which allows overcoming the *NP-Completeness* aspect. However, many complex graph patterns are needed in practice and which

© Springer Nature Switzerland AG 2021
C. Djeddi et al. (Eds.): MedPRAI 2020, CCIS 1322, pp. 298–313, 2021.
https://doi.org/10.1007/978-3-030-71804-6_22

are not expressible by existing simulation-based models, notably patterns with counting quantifiers (*CQs*), *predicates* and *negation* as we illustrate by the next example.

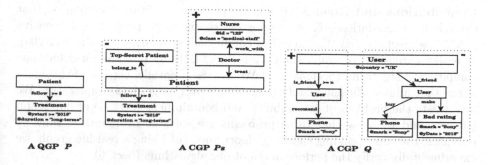

Fig. 1. Example of expressive graph patterns.

Example 1. I) Consider the patterns of Fig. 1 where node labels represent type of entities (e.g. *Patient, User*); edge labels represent type of the relationships that exist between these entities (e.g. *is_friend*); a label of the form "$\geq k$" specifies quantification on edges (e.g. number of treatments prescribed for a patient). Moreover, dotted-line blocks with "+" (resp. "−") represent positive (resp. negative) predicates that must be satisfied (resp. unsatisfied) by some nodes. P depicts a request that is defined by a nurse identified by "*123*" in order to return information of all patients that have at least five *long-term* treatments. Suppose that the hospital wants to impose an access control policy as follows: *1*) only nurses of *medical staff* can access information of patients; *2*) a nurse can access only information of patients which are treated by a doctor working with her; and *3*) information of *top-secret* patients (e.g. diplomat patients) cannot be shown to the nurses. To enforce this policy, one may easily rewrite P into a safe one by adding some parts that guarantee (resp. prevent) access to accessible (resp. inaccessible) patient information. The safe version of P is given by the pattern P_s that defines a positive and negative predicate over the node *Patient* to enforce respectively conditions 1–2 and condition 3. In other words, a patient must not be returned to the nurse if he belongs to the *Top-Secret* category or is being treated by a doctor which does work with the underlying nurse. The result of P_s over any data graph must be composed by only the entities *Patient* and *Treatment* along with their edge, while the remaining parts of P_s are used only to refine (make safe) this result. II) The pattern Q is useful in social media marketing. It looks for each user x in UK which has at least n friends whose recommend a *Sony* product; and no friend of x gave a bad rating since 2018 for a *Sony* product after buying one. The result of Q will be composed by single nodes representing profile of the users satisfying predicates of Q. □

To the best of our knowledge, no existing graph pattern matching model can express the queries Ps and Q of the previous example. Thus, we revised the notion of graph simulation to strike a balance between its computational complexity and its ability to deal with more expressive graph patterns.

Contributions and Road-Map. (*i*) we propose conditional simulation that extends dual simulation [15] by supporting simple CQs, positive and negative predicates (Sect. 3). (*ii*) We show that conditional simulation remains in PTIME as earlier extensions of graph simulation [5,6,14,15] by providing a cubic-time computation algorithm (Sect. 4). (*iii*) We discuss a parallel version of this algorithm that allows efficient matching of $CGPs$ over large data graphs. (*iv*) We investigate the problem of satisfiability and containment (Sect. 5) of our graph patterns and we show that these problems are solvable in quadratic time by providing the corresponding checking algorithms. (*v*) Using a real-life graph, we experimentally verify the performances of our algorithms (Sect. 6).

Related Work. We classify previous work as follows.

Graph Pattern Matching. Graph pattern matching (GPM) is typically defined in terms of subgraph isomorphism which is an NP-COMPLETE problem [19]. Moreover, it is often too restrictive to capture sensible matches [6] as it requires matches from a data graph to have the same topology as a graph pattern, which hinders its applicability in real-life applications such as social network marketing. To overcome these limits, *graph simulation* [18] has been first adopted for graph pattern matching due to its low computational complexity. GPM via graph simulation has been useful for various applications (e.g. social position detection [1]). However, it preserves only downward mappings which raised a need to extend it in order to find more sensible matches in emerging applications. There has been a host of work on improving the notion of graph simulation (e.g. bounded simulation [6], regular simulation [5], dual simulation [15]). Unfortunately, all existing extensions remain limited in emerging applications that need patterns with complex features, notably *counting quantifiers* (*CQs*), *predicates* and *negation*. Among these features, only CQs have received some attention. The visual tool $QGraph$ [12] allows annotating edges of a graph pattern with CQS of the form $[min, max]$ that can express different semantics (e.g. negated ($[0,0]$) and optional ($[0,1]$) edges). The formal matching algorithm of $QGraph$ (whose complexity is undefined) is a heavy extension of subgraph isomorphism which makes it probably more higher than NP-COMPLETE[1]. Authors of [8] proposed CQs that can express numeric and ratio aggregates of the forms: "$=p(\%)$", "$\geq p(\%)$", and "$=0$" for negation. Their matching algorithm is based on subgraph isomorphism and has been proved to be DP-COMPLETE.

In contrast, our first motivation was to use simple CQs that are less expressive than those of [8,12] but make quantified matching in PTIME. Moreover, we allow negation of any part of a graph pattern which is more useful then negation of

---

[1] As observed in [8].

simple edges. At the time of writing this paper, we do not know any approach that allows definition and matching of predicates within graph patterns.

Static Analysis of Graph Patterns. The satisfiability and containment problems are classical and fundamental problems for any query language. They have been well studied for XPath (e.g., [10,11]). For graph patterns however, it is striking how little attention has been paid for these problems. The containment problem has been studied in [5] for graph patterns without neither predicates nor negation. The satisfiability problem has been studied in [16] for child relationships only, which raised for a trivial solution. Apart from these works, we are not aware of other ones that investigate static analysis of graph pattern queries.

2 Background

2.1 Data Graphs and Graph Patterns

A ***Data Graph*** is a directed graph $G = (V, E, \mathcal{L}, \mathcal{A})$ where: 1) V is a finite set of nodes; 2) $E \subseteq V \times V$ is a finite set of edges in which (v, v') denotes an edge from node v to v'; 3) $\mathcal{L}$ is a function that assigns a label $\mathcal{L}(v)$ (resp. $\mathcal{L}(e)$) to each node $v \in V$ (resp. edge $e \in E$); and 4) for each node $v \in V$, $\mathcal{A}(v)$ is a tuple $(A_1 = c_1, \ldots, A_n = c_n)$ where: A_i is an attribute of v, c_i is a constant value, $n \geq 0$, and $A_i \neq A_j$ if $i \neq j$.

Intuitively, for any data node v, the label $\mathcal{L}(v)$ represents the type of v (e.g. *Movie*) while the tuple $\mathcal{A}(v)$ defines its properties (e.g. *title, release date, running time*). Moreover, since an edge relies two entities (e.g. *Movie* and *Person*), then its label may represent a relationship between them (e.g. *produced by, edited by*). Notice that the attributes defined over a node $v \in V$ may be different for those defined over another node $w \in V$, even if $\mathcal{L}(v) = \mathcal{L}(w)$.

A ***Subgraph*** $G_s = (V_s, E_s, \mathcal{L}_s, \mathcal{A}_s)$ of $G = (V, E, \mathcal{L}, \mathcal{A})$ must satisfy: 1) $V_s \subseteq V$; 2) $E_s \subseteq E$; 3) $\mathcal{L}_s(x) = \mathcal{L}(x)$ for each $x \in E_s \cup V_s$; and 4) $\mathcal{A}_s(v) = \mathcal{A}(v)$ for each $v \in V_s$.

A ***Ball*** in G with center v and radius r is a subgraph of G, denoted by $\mathcal{B}(G, v, r)$, s.t.: 1) all nodes v' are in $\mathcal{B}(G, v, r)$ if the number of hops between v' and v is at most r; and 2) it has exactly the edges appearing in G over the same node set.

A ***Graph Pattern***[2] is a directed connected graph $Q = (V, E, \mathcal{L}, \mathcal{A})$ where: 1) V, E, and $\mathcal{L}$ are defined as for data graphs; and 2) for each node $u \in V$, $\mathcal{A}(u)$ is a predicate defined as a conjunction of atomic formulas of the form "A *op* c" where: A is an attribute of u, c is a constant, and $op \in \{\geq, \leq, =, \neq\}$.

For any pattern node u, we call $\mathcal{A}(u)$ the ***attributes constraints*** of u which specify a search condition: e.g. a movie released in *US* after *2017* (i.e. $\mathcal{A}(u)$ = "*country=US $\wedge$ year > 2017*"). If $\mathcal{A}(u) = \emptyset$ then $\mathcal{L}(u)$ is the only search condition for u as in [8,15]. Notice that conflicting constraints over u (e.g. $\mathcal{A}(u)$ = "*Age$\geq$ 25 $\wedge$ Age < 20*") should be considered by the satisfiability checking.

---

[2] Inspired from [5,6].

The **_Diameter_** of Q, written d_Q, is the longest distance between all pairs of nodes in Q. That is, $d_Q = max(dist(v,v'))$ for all pairs (v,v') in Q where: $dist(v,v')$ is the length of the shortest undirected path from v to v'.

2.2   Conventional Graph Pattern Matching Revisited

We slightly revise subgraph isomorphism [9], graph simulation [18] and dual simulation [15] to take in account labels on edges and attributes on vertices. We refer next to the data graph $G = (V, E, \mathcal{L}, \mathcal{A})$ and the graph pattern $Q = (V_Q, E_Q, \mathcal{L}_Q, \mathcal{A}_Q)$.

Subgraph Isomorphism. A subgraph $G_s = (V_s, E_s, \mathcal{L}_s, \mathcal{A}_s)$ of G matches Q via *subgraph isomorphism* if there exists a *bijective function* $f{:}V_Q \rightarrow V_s$ s.t.: *1)* for each $u \in V_Q$, $\mathcal{L}_Q(u) = \mathcal{L}_s(f(u))$; *2)* for each $e = (u, u')$ in E_Q, there exists an edge $e' = (f(u), f(u'))$ in G_s with $\mathcal{L}_Q(e) = \mathcal{L}_s(e')$; and *3)* for each atomic formula "$A\ op\ c$" in $\mathcal{A}_Q(u)$, there exists $A = c'$ in $\mathcal{A}_s(f(u))$ where $c'\ op\ c$ holds.

Graph Simulation. G matches Q via *graph simulation* if there exists a *binary match relation* $S \subseteq V_Q \times V$ s.t.: *1)* for each $(u, v) \in S$, $\mathcal{L}_Q(u) = \mathcal{L}(v)$; *2)* for each $(u, v) \in S$ and each atomic formula "$A\ op\ c$" in $\mathcal{A}_Q(u)$, there exists $A = c'$ in $\mathcal{A}(v)$ where $c'\ op\ c$ holds; *3)* for each $(u, v) \in S$ and each edge $e_u = (u, u')$ in E_Q, there exists an edge $e_v = (v, v')$ in E with: $(u', v') \in S$ and $\mathcal{L}_Q(e_u) = \mathcal{L}(e_v)$; *4)* for each node $u \in V_Q$, there exists at least one node $v \in V$ with $(u, v) \in S$.

By condition (3), graph simulation preserves only child relationships.

Dual Simulation. G matches Q via *dual simulation* if there exists a *binary match relation* $S_D \subseteq V_Q \times V$ s.t.: *1)* for each $(u, v) \in S$, $\mathcal{L}_Q(u) = \mathcal{L}(v)$; *2)* for each $(u, v) \in S$ and each atomic formula "$A\ op\ c$" in $\mathcal{A}_Q(u)$, there exists $A = c'$ in $\mathcal{A}(v)$ where $c'\ op\ c$ holds; *3)* for each $(u, v) \in S$ and each edge $e_u = (u, u')$ (resp. $e_u = (u', u)$) in E_P, there exists an edge $e_v = (v, v')$ (resp. $e_v = (v', v)$) in E with $(u', v') \in S$ and $\mathcal{L}_Q(e_u) = \mathcal{L}(e_v)$; *4)* for each node $u \in V_Q$, there exists at least one node $v \in V$ with $(u, v) \in S$.

Dual simulation enhances graph simulation by preserving parent relationships.

Match Result. When G matches Q via subgraph isomorphism, the match result is the set of all subgraphs of G that are isomorphic to Q. Moreover, the match result w.r.t. a binary match relation $S \subseteq V_P \times V$ (i.e. produced by dual simulation or its extensions) is a subgraph G_s of G s.t.: 1) a node $v \in V_s$ if it matches some node of Q via S; and 2) an edge $e = (v, v')$ is in E_s if there exists an edge $(u, u') \in E_Q$ s.t. $\{(u, v), (u', v')\} \in S$.

3 Conditional Graph Patterns

3.1 Definition of *CGPs*

Contrary to complex *CQs* proposed in [12] that lead for a prohibitive cost, we use simple but useful *CQs* in order to strike a balance between the expressivity and matching cost.

Definition 1. *A* QGP *is a connected directed graph* $Q = (V, E, \mathcal{L}, \mathcal{A}, \mathcal{C})$ *where: 1)* V, E, $\mathcal{L}$, $\mathcal{A}$ *are defined as for conventional graph patterns; 2) for each edge* $e \in E$, $\mathcal{C}(e)$ *is a* CQ *given by an integer* p $(p \geq 1)$. □

Intuitively, for any data graph G and any edge $e = (u, u')$ in E with $\mathcal{C}(e) = p$, a node v from G matches u if it has at least p children that match u', and moreover, these children must be reached from v via an edge labeled $\mathcal{L}(e)$. As a special case, $\mathcal{C}(e) = 1$ expresses *existential quantification*. Contrary to [8], we do not allow *CQ* of the form $\mathcal{C}(e) = 0$ since its semantic would be ambiguous with negation. Using *QGPs* as building blocks, we next define *CGPs*.

Definition 2. *A* CGP *is a connected directed graph* $Q = (V, E, \mathcal{L}, \mathcal{A}, \mathcal{C}, \mathcal{P})$ *where:*

1. $(V, E, \mathcal{L}, \mathcal{A}, \mathcal{C})$ *is a* QGP *called the* core *of* Q *and denoted by* Q^c; *and*
2. *For each node* $u \in V$, $\mathcal{P}(u)$ *is given by* $l_1 \wedge \dots \wedge l_k$ *s.t.: a)* $k \geq 0$; *b) each* l_i *is given by* q_i *(positive predicate) or* $not(q_i)$ *(negative predicate); c)* $q_i = (V_i, E_i)$ *is a* QGP *satisfying* $V_i \cap V = \{u\}$. □

Remark that *CGPs* extend *QGPs* with the function $\mathcal{P}$ that allow definition of positive and negative predicates. Intuitively, $\mathcal{P}(u)$ assigns a (possibly empty) conjunction of *positive* and/or *negative* predicates to the vertex u of Q^c. Each positive (resp. negative) predicate specifies a *quantified and attributed graph-based condition*[3] that must be satisfied (resp. unsatisfied) by each match of u in a data graph. This kind of predicates give our matching model some expressivity that is not covered by existing approaches [5,6,8,12,15].

The whole semantic of Q can be stated naturally with the friendly syntax "***match** Q^c$ **where** $\mathcal{P}(u_1) \wedge \dots \wedge \mathcal{P}(u_k)$" ($u_i \in V$, $1 \leq i \leq |V|$). This means that a data graph G matches Q if it has a subgraph G_s that satisfies all constraints expressed by Q^c (child and parent relationships, attribute constraints, and *CQs*). Moreover, for any node $u \in Q^c$, each match of u in G_s must satisfy (resp. unsatisfy) all positive (resp. negative) predicates given by $\mathcal{P}(u)$. Inspired by well-known conditional languages (e.g. SQL, XPath), the core Q^c of Q represents the structure of the match result that will be returned to the user, predicates of Q are used only during the matching process to refine this match result.

The size of a *QGP* $q' = (V', E')$ is given by $|V'| + |E'|$, while the size of a *CGP* $Q = (V, E, \mathcal{L}, \mathcal{A}, \mathcal{C}, \mathcal{P})$ is given by $|V| + |E| + \sum_{u \in V}(\sum_{q' \in \mathcal{P}(u)} |q'| +$

---

[3] This is why we call them *conditional graph patterns*.

$\sum_{not(q') \in \mathcal{P}(u)} |q'|$). In other words, the size of Q is given by the number of vertices and edges that belong to the core Q^c, positive and/or negative predicates of Q.

We simply denote the *CGP* Q as (V, E) when it is clear from the context.

Example 2. Consider the *CGPs* of Fig. 2. According to Definition 2 (condition c), remark that each predicate intersects with the core of the original *CGP* in only one node[4]. The *QGP* Q_1 returns all professors (Pr), their PhD students (PhD), and the articles $(Article)$ published by these latter. The *QGP* Q_2 is a special case of Q_1 since it requires: 1) each PhD student to have at least two published articles; and 2) each professor to be from *UK* and between 38 to 45 years old. The *CGP* Q_3 returns pairs of nodes composed by professors and their PhD students providing that each of these student have exactly two published articles. This restriction is imposed by the conjunction of a positive and negative predicate defined over the node *PhD* of Q_3. This means that each PhD node from a data graph is returned by Q_3 only if it has a parent node labeled *Pr* and satisfies each predicate of Q_3 (has exactly two children labeled *Article*).   □

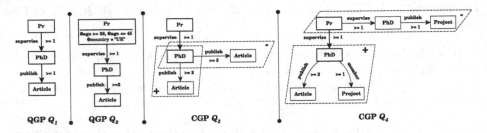

Fig. 2. Examples of *CGPs*.

Definition 3. *The* positive version *of a CGP Q, denoted by Q^+, is a QGP that contains nodes and edges belonging to the core and/or positive predicates of Q; by keeping their labels and attributes constraints unchanged.*   □

3.2   Conditional Simulation

We introduce *conditional simulation* that extends dual simulation of Ma et al. [15] with attribute constraints, *CQs*, positive and negative predicates. Our extension allows matching of large data graphs in PTIME via more expressive patterns.

Definition 4. *A data graph $G = (V, E, \mathcal{L}, \mathcal{A})$ matches a CGP $Q = (V_Q, E_Q, \mathcal{L}_Q, \mathcal{A}_Q, \mathcal{C}_Q, \mathcal{P}_Q)$ via conditional simulation, denoted by $Q \prec_c G$, if there exists a binary match relation $S_Q^G \subseteq V_Q \times V$ s.t.:*

---

[4] This may not reduce the practicability of our approach since many query languages (e.g. XPath, SQL) adopt this syntax of predicates.

1. *For each* $(u, v) \in S_Q^G$, $\mathcal{L}_Q(u) = \mathcal{L}(v)$.
2. *For each* $(u, v) \in S_Q^G$ *and each atomic formula "A op m" in* $\mathcal{A}_Q(u)$, *there exists a tuple "A = n" in* $\mathcal{A}(v)$ *where "n op m" holds.*
3. *For each* $(u, v) \in S_Q^G$ *and each* $\mathcal{C}_Q(u, u') = n$, v *has at least* $v_1, \ldots, v_n$ *children in* G *where:* $\mathcal{L}(v, v_i) = \mathcal{L}_Q(u, u')$ *and* $(u', v_i) \in S_Q^G$ *for* $i \in [1, n]$.
4. *For each* $(u, v) \in S_Q^G$ *and each edge* $e = (u', u)$ *in* E_Q, *there exists an edge* (v', v) *in* E *where:* $\mathcal{L}(v', v) = \mathcal{L}_Q(u', u)$ *and* $(u', v') \in S_Q^G$.
5. *For each* $(u, v) \in S_Q^G$ *and each* q *(resp. not(q)) in* $\mathcal{P}_Q(u)$, *there is a ball (resp. no ball)* $\mathcal{B}(G, v, d_q)$ *s.t.:* $q \prec_c \mathcal{B}(G, v, d_q)$ *with a match relation* S, $(u, v) \in S$.
6. *There is at least one couple* $(u, v) \in S_Q^G$ *for each* $u \in V_Q$. □

Conditions (1–2) concern node properties: a pattern node u can be matched by any data node v that has its label and whose attribute values satisfy attribute constraints of u. Conditions (3) and (4) check respectively the satisfaction of *CQs* and parent relationships. Condition (5) specifies that for each match v of u, the ball centered at v in G satisfies (resp. does not satisfy) each positive (resp. negative) predicate defined over u. Finally, condition (6) states that there are matches in G for any node in Q.

As graph simulation and its counterparts, conditional simulation aims to find the maximum version of S_Q^G, that is all subgraphs of G that satisfy topology and constraints of Q. Based on this notion, we make the following result[5].

Proposition 1. *For any CGP Q and data graph G with $Q \prec_c G$, there is a unique maximum match relation S_Q^G for G and Q.* □

We denote by $\mathcal{M}_c(Q, G)$ the match result that corresponds to this maximum match relation S_Q^G. It can be constructed as explained in Sect. 2.2.

Proposition 2. *For any CGP $Q = (V_Q, E_Q)$ and data graph $G = (V, E, \mathcal{A})$ with $Q \prec_c G$, $\mathcal{M}_c(Q, G)$ is constructed w.r.t the maximum match relation S_Q^G in $O(|V_Q||V| + |E_Q||E|)$ time.* □

4   An Algorithm for *CGPs* Matching

4.1   Description and Complexity Analysis

Figure 3 shows our *CGPs* matching algorithm, referred to as MATCH^C, that inputs a *CGP* Q and a data graph G, and returns $\emptyset$ if $Q \not\prec_c G$ or the corresponding maximum matching relation S_Q^G otherwise. Firstly, the match relation S_Q^G is initialized by matching each node in Q with all nodes of G that have its label (line 1). Since $Q^c \not\prec_c G$ implies $Q \not\prec_c G$, then MATCH^C starts by refining the initial version of S_Q^G w.r.t Q^c constraints only (lines 2–3). This step is ensured by the algorithm MATCH^Q that is explained below. If the call of

---
[5] One can prove this result by leveraging that of dual simulation [15].

Algorithm MATCH$^C(Q, G)$
Input: A CGP $Q=(V_Q, E_Q, \mathcal{L}_Q, \mathcal{A}_Q, \mathcal{C}_Q, \mathcal{P}_Q)$ and a data graph $G=(V, E, \mathcal{L}, \mathcal{A})$.
Output: The maximum match relation S_Q^G if $Q \prec_C G$, and $\emptyset$ otherwise.

1: $S_Q^G := \{(u, v) \setminus u \in V_Q, v \in V, \mathcal{L}_Q(u) = \mathcal{L}(v)\}$;   /* *Initialize the match relation* S_Q^G */
2: $S_Q^G := $ MATCH$^Q(Q^c, G, S_Q^G)$;   /* *Refine* S_Q^G *w.r.t the core of* Q */
3: **if** $(S_Q^G = \emptyset)$ **then return** $\emptyset$;   /* $Q^c \nprec_C G$ */
4: **for each** $(u, v) \in S_Q^G$ **and each** $q \in \mathcal{P}_Q(u)$ **do**   /* *Whether* v *satisfies* q */
5:     **if** (not($q \prec_C \mathcal{B}(G, v, d_q)$ with S and $(u, v) \in S$)) **then** $S_Q^G := S_Q^G \setminus \{(u, v)\}$; **end if;**
6: **end for**
7: **for each** $(u, v) \in S_Q^G$ **and each** $not(q) \in \mathcal{P}_Q(u)$ **do**   /* *Whether* v *does not satisfy* q */
8:     **if** ($q \prec_C \mathcal{B}(G, v, d_q)$ with S and $(u, v) \in S$) **then** $S_Q^G := S_Q^G \setminus \{(u, v)\}$; **end if;**
9: **end for**
10: $S_Q^G := $ MATCH$^Q(Q^c, G, S_Q^G)$;
11: **return** S_Q^G;

Algorithm MATCH$^Q(Q^c, G, S)$
Input: A QGP $Q=(V^c, E^c, \mathcal{L}^c, \mathcal{A}^c, \mathcal{C}^c)$, a data graph $G=(V, E, \mathcal{L}, \mathcal{A})$, and an initial match relation S to refine.
Output: A refined version of S that ensures $Q^c \prec_C G$, and $\emptyset$ if this is not possible.

1: **for each** $(u, v) \in S$ **and each** "A op n" $\in \mathcal{A}^c(u)$ **do**
2:     **if** ($\nexists$ "$A = m$" $\in \mathcal{A}(v)$ s.t (m op n) holds) **then** $S := S \setminus \{(u, v)\}$; **end if;**
3: **end for**
4: **do**
5:     **for each** $(u, v) \in S$ **and each** $e_u = (u', u)$ in E^c **do**
6:         **if** ($\nexists e_v = (v', v) \in E : \mathcal{L}^c(e_u) = \mathcal{L}(e_v), (u', v') \in S$) **then** $S := S \setminus \{(u, v)\}$; **end if;**
7:     **end for**
8:     **for each** $(u, v) \in S$ **and each** (u, u') in E^c **do**
9:         $C(v, u, u') := \{v' \in V \setminus (v, v') \in E, \mathcal{L}(v, v') = \mathcal{L}^c(u, u'), (u', v') \in S\}$;
10:        **if** ($|C(v, u, u')| < \mathcal{C}^c(u, u')$) **then** $S := S \setminus \{(u, v)\}$; **end if;**
11:    **end for**
12: **while** there are changes in S;
13: **if** ($\forall u \in V^c, \exists v \in V : (u, v) \in S$) **then return** S; **else return** $\emptyset$;

Fig. 3. Algorithm for *CGPs* matching.

MATCH^Q returns an empty version of S_Q^G then $Q^c \nprec_C G$ and the principal algorithm MATCH^C ends up. Otherwise, the new version of S_Q^G reflects all matches of Q^c in G, and it must be refined w.r.t each predicate of Q as follows. A couple (u, v) is deleted from S_Q^G if there exists a predicate q defined over u in Q where: q is positive but the ball centered at v in G, $\mathcal{B}(G, v, d_q)$, does not match it (lines 4–6); or q is negative but it is matched by the ball $\mathcal{B}(G, v, d_q)$ (lines 7–9). As remarked in [17], when a couple (u, v) is deleted from S_Q^G (lines 5 + 8), other couples in S_Q^G may become incorrect w.r.t Q^c constraints. For this reason, after deleting all couples of S_Q^G that are incorrect w.r.t predicates of Q (lines 4–9), we refine again the match relation S_Q^G to keep only matches that are correct w.r.t Q^c constraints (line 10). The last version of S_Q^G that yields from this refinement is finally returned.

The algorithm MATCH^Q of Fig. 3 extends dual simulation of Ma et al. [15] by attribute constraints, labeled edges, and specially by CQs. The algorithm checks whether $Q^c \prec_C G$ for any data graph G and QGP Q^c in input. This is done by checking conditions $(1 - 4 + 6)$ of Definition 2. Given a match relation S (defined by algorithm MATCH^C) that maps nodes of Q^c to nodes of G, the goal is to eliminate all incorrect matches from S as follows. A couple (u, v) is deleted from S if: i) an atomic formulas "A op m" (e.g. "$age > 35$") is defined over u in Q^c but there is no tuple "$A = n$" over v in G that holds this formulas (e.g. "$age = n$" with $n < 35$) [lines 1–5]; ii) there exists an edge (u', u) in E^c with label l but v has no parent node v' in G that matches u' and reaches v with an edge labeled l (lines 7–9); iii) u must have at least n instances of the child u' in Q^c (i.e. $C^c(u, u') = n$) but the number of children of v in G that match u' (i.e. size of the set $C(v, u, u')$) is lesser than n (lines 10–13). The two latter cases are repeated (lines 6–14) until there is no incorrect match in S. Finally, if each node in Q^c gets some matches from S then $Q^c \prec_C G$ and the refined version of S that ensures this matching is returned; otherwise $Q^c \not\prec_C G$ and $\emptyset$ is returned.

Lemma 1. *For any QGP Q, any data graph G and any match relation $S \subseteq V_Q \times V$, algorithm MATCH^Q takes at most $O(|Q||G|)$ time to refine S.* $\square$

Theorem 1. *For any CGP Q and any data graph G, it takes $O(|Q||G|)$ time to determine whether $Q \prec_C G$ and to compute the maximum match relation S_Q^G.* $\square$

4.2   Parallel Version

To allow efficient matching of $CGPs$ over large data graphs, we discuss here a parallel version of our algorithm MATCH^C, referred to as PMATCH^C (not shown here due to page limit). The intuition behind this version is as follows: rather to evaluate the core and predicates of a given CGP C in a sequential manner, the goal is to match each of them over the underlying data graph G via separated threads. If the data graph does not match the core and/or at least one positive predicate of C then we return *null*. Otherwise, we combine the match relations produced by the different threads to compute the final match result.

As stated in [15], the *parallel scalability* is an important property that each parallel algorithm must verify. This guarantees that the more processors are used, the less time is taken by the parallel algorithm. We practically prove this property over large data graph in Sect. 6. Even thought PMATCH^C is quite simple, its allows to improve sequential matching time on average 39.48%–60.74%.

5   Static Analysis

We introduce first the notion of matching between $QGPs$ that plays an important role in static analysis tasks as satisfiability and containment checking.

5.1   Pattern-Only Matching

The notion of *Pattern-only Matching* (*PoM*) is to check for two graph patterns Q and R, whether Q matches R. This means that there is at least one sub-pattern of Q that satisfies all constraints of R.

Definition 5. *Given two QGPs* $Q = (V_Q, E_Q, \mathcal{L}_Q, \mathcal{A}_Q, \mathcal{C}_Q)$ *and* $R = (V_R, E_R, \mathcal{L}_R, \mathcal{A}_R, \mathcal{C}_R)$. *For any nodes* $u \in V_R$ *and* $w \in V_Q$, *we say that* $\mathcal{A}_Q(w)$ *matches* $\mathcal{A}_R(u)$, *written* $\mathcal{A}_Q(w) \sim \mathcal{A}_R(u)$, *if the constraints defined over any attribute A in* $\mathcal{A}_R(u)$ *are satisfied by those defined over A in* $\mathcal{A}_Q(w)$. $\square$

Intuitively, $\mathcal{A}_Q(w) \sim \mathcal{A}_R(u)$ if for any data graph G and any node v in G, if v satisfies $\mathcal{A}_Q(w)$ then it also satisfies $\mathcal{A}_R(u)$. For instance, the constraint "*age > 25*" satisfies the constraint "*age $\neq$ 20*", but the inverse does not hold.

Definition 6. *Consider the QGPs* $Q = (V_Q, E_Q, \mathcal{L}_Q, \mathcal{A}_Q, \mathcal{C}_Q)$ *and* $R = (V_R, E_R, \mathcal{L}_R, \mathcal{A}_R, \mathcal{C}_R)$. *We say that* Q *matches* R, *denoted by* $R \lhd Q$, *if there exists a binary match relation* $S \subseteq V_R \times V_Q$ *s.t.:*

1. *for each* $(u, w) \in S$: $\mathcal{L}_Q(w) = \mathcal{L}_R(u)$ *and* $\mathcal{A}_Q(w) \sim \mathcal{A}_R(u)$.
2. *for each* $(u, w) \in S$ *and each edge* $e_u = (u', u)$ *in* E_R, *there exists an edge* $e_w = (w', w))$ *in* E_Q *with:* $(u', w') \in S$ *and* $\mathcal{L}_Q(e_w) = \mathcal{L}_R(e_w)$.
3. *for each* $(u, w) \in S$ *and each edge* $e_u = (u, u') \in E_R$, *there is an edge* $e_w = (w, w') \in E_Q$ *s.t.:* $(u', w') \in S$, $\mathcal{L}_R(e_u) = \mathcal{L}_Q(e_w)$, $\mathcal{C}_Q(e_w) \geq \mathcal{C}_R(e_u)$.
4. *For each node* $u \in V_R$, *there exists a node* $w \in V_Q$ *with* $(u, w) \in S$. $\square$

Intuitively, $R \lhd Q$ if for any data graph G that matches Q, G matches R too.

Definition 7. *Given two QGPs* $Q = (V_Q, E_Q, \mathcal{L}_Q, \mathcal{A}_Q, \mathcal{C}_Q)$ *and* $R = (V_R, E_R, \mathcal{L}_R, \mathcal{A}_R, \mathcal{C}_R)$ *s.t.* $R \lhd Q$ *with the maximum match relation* S. *We say that an edge* $e_w = (w, w')$ *in* Q *is* covered *by* S *if there exists an edge* $e_u = (u, u')$ *in* R *s.t.:* (u, w) *and* (u', w') *are in* S, *and* $\mathcal{L}_Q(e_w) = \mathcal{L}_R(e_u)$. *Moreover, we denote by* S^Q *the set of all edges of* Q *that are covered by* S. $\square$

Example 3. Consider Q_1 and Q_2 of Fig. 2. As Q_2 makes more restrictions over nodes and edges of Q_1, any data graph G that matches Q_2 will match Q_1 too, i.e. $Q_1 \lhd Q_2$. We can see that $Q_2 \not\lhd Q_1$ since there exists a data graph G that matches Q_1 but not Q_2. Consider a *QGP* Q_5 given by $Team \xleftarrow[\geq 1]{member} Pr \xrightarrow[\geq 2]{supervise} PhD \xrightarrow[\geq 2]{publish} Article$. Remark that $Q_1 \lhd Q_5$ even if Q_5 has nodes (resp. edges) that match no nodes (resp. edges) in Q_1. If S is the maximum match relation that ensures $Q_1 \lhd Q_5$, then S^{Q_5} is given by $\{Pr \xrightarrow[\geq 2]{supervise} PhD_2, PhD \xrightarrow[\geq 2]{publish} Article\}$ while $Pr \xrightarrow[\geq 1]{member} Team$ is not covered by S. $\square$

Lemma 2. *For any QGPs* Q *and* R, *it takes at most* $O(|Q||R|)$ *time to check whether* $R \lhd Q$ *and to determine the corresponding maximum match relation.* $\square$

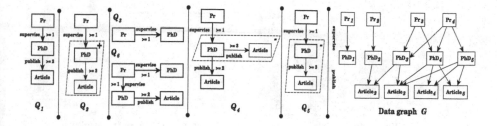

Fig. 4. Examples of *CGPs* containment.

5.2   Satisfiability of *CGPs*

The satisfiability problem discussed in this section is to determine, given a *CGP* Q, whether or not there exists a data graph G that matches Q via conditional simulation, i.e. $Q \prec_c G$. Contrary to existing graph pattern models [2,5,6,15], the problem is more intriguing in our case due to the presence of predicates.

Example 4. Given the *CGP* Q_4 of Fig. 2, it is clear that no data graph G can match Q_4 since each subgraph of G that matches the positive predicate of Q_4 mismatches its negative predicate and vice versa.   □

Theorem 2. *The satisfiability of any CGP Q can be checked in $O(|Q|^2)$ time.* □

Given a *CGP* $Q = (V, E, \mathcal{L}, \mathcal{A}, \mathcal{C}, \mathcal{P})$. One of the unsatisfiability cases is due to the presence of conflicting attribute constraints over the vertices of Q (e.g. "$Age > 25$ & $Age < 20$"). Moreover, Q is unsatisfiable if there exist conflicts between a negative predicate $not(q) \in \mathcal{P}(u)$ and the constraints defined over u in Q^+. This can be checked in quadratic time thanks to the notion of *PoM* (Lemma 2).

5.3   Containment of *CGPs*

As widely defined in the literature [11,13], the containment problem is to determine whether all nodes and edges returned by a query Q are also returned by the query R. We revisit this traditional definition via conditional simulation as follows.

Definition 8. *A CGP Q is contained in a CGP R via conditional simulation, written $Q \subseteq_c R$, if for any data graph G: $\mathcal{M}_c(Q, G) \subseteq \mathcal{M}_c(R, G)$.*   □

The static checking of $Q \subseteq_c R$ may help decreasing matching time over a large data graph G as follows. If $R \not\prec_c G$ then we deduce statically that $Q \not\prec_c G$, and if $Q \prec_c G$ then we do not need to test R anymore since $R \prec_c G$ holds automatically. In general, if $Q \subseteq_c R$ then we can consider $\mathcal{M}_c(Q, G)$ as an *upper-evaluation* of R over G; and $\mathcal{M}_c(R, G)$ as an *over-evaluation* of Q over G.

We give next necessary and sufficient conditions for the containment of *CGPs*.

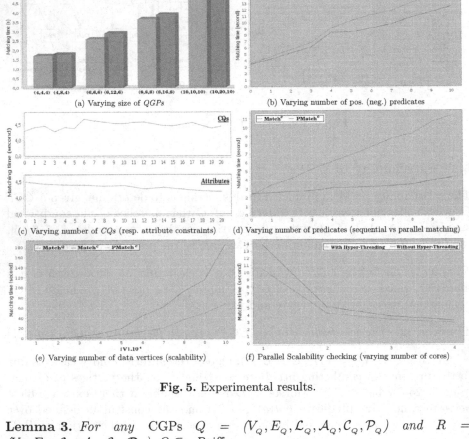

(a) Varying size of *QGPs*

(b) Varying number of pos. (neg.) predicates

(c) Varying number of *CQs* (resp. attribute constraints)

(d) Varying number of predicates (sequential vs parallel matching)

(e) Varying number of data vertices (scalability)

(f) Parallel Scalability checking (varying number of cores)

Fig. 5. Experimental results.

Lemma 3. *For any* CGPs $Q = (V_Q, E_Q, \mathcal{L}_Q, \mathcal{A}_Q, \mathcal{C}_Q, \mathcal{P}_Q)$ *and* $R = (V_R, E_R, \mathcal{L}_R, \mathcal{A}_R, \mathcal{C}_R, \mathcal{P}_R)$, $Q \subseteq_c R$ *iff:*

1. $R^+ \lhd Q^+$ *with a match relation* $S_R^Q \subseteq V_R^+ \times V_Q^+$;
2. *For each* $(u, w) \in S_R^Q$ *and* $not(q_u) \in \mathcal{P}_R(u)$, *there exists* $not(q_w) \in \mathcal{P}_Q(w)$: $q_w \lhd q_u$ *with the match relation* S *and* $(u, w) \in S$.
3. *Each edge in* Q^c *matches at least one edge in* R^c *via* S_R^Q. □

Example 5. Consider the data graph G and the *CGPs* Q_i of Fig. 4 ($i \in [1, 5]$). Based on Lemma 3, one can deduce that: $Q_2 \subseteq_c Q_1$ (*all conditions satisfied*), $Q_4 \subseteq_c Q_1$ (*all conditions satisfied*), $Q_5 \not\subseteq_c Q_1$ (*condition 1 unsatisfied*), $Q_3 \not\subseteq_c Q_5$ (*condition 2 unsatisfied*), $Q_1 \not\subseteq_c Q_3$ (*condition 3 unsatisfied*). □

Theorem 3. *For CGPs* Q *and* R, $Q \subseteq_c R$ *is checked in* $O(|Q||R|)$ *time.* □

6   Experimental Study

We conducted extensive experiments to evaluate the (1) effectiveness of *QGPM* and *CGPM*; (2) effectiveness of parallel *CGPM*; (3) scalability of algorithms MATCH^Q, MATCH^C and PMATCH^C, and (4) parallel scalability of PMATCH^C.

Experimental Settings. We used the *Amazon* real-life network dataset[6], that is a product co-purchasing graph with *548K* nodes and *1.78M* edges. Each node has attributes such as *ID*, *Title*, *Rating*, and *Group*, and an edge from product u to w indicates that people who buy u would also buy w with a high probability.

Using Java language, we implemented the algorithms (1) MATCH^Q; (2) MATCH^C; and (3) PMATCH^C, the parallel version of MATCH^C that detects the number of processors and dispatches core and predicates of the *CGP* over them. Moreover, a data graph extractor has been implemented to extract an *Amazon* subgraph data with a fixed number of vertices.

All the experiments were run on a Ubuntu desktop machine with an Intel Core i5-8250u CPU, 8GB memory, and 256GB SSD storage. Each experiment was run 5 times and the average is reported.

Experimental Results. We present next our findings.

Experiment 1. We first evaluated the performances of *quantified* and *conditional GPM* using an *Amazon* data graph that has *10000* nodes and *37854* edges.

Varying $|V_Q|$ and $|E_Q|$ (MATCH^Q): we generated 8 *QGPs* with sizes ($|V_Q|$, $|E_Q|$, $|\mathcal{C}_Q|$) ranging from $(4, 4, 4)$ to $(10, 10, 20)$. As shown in Fig. 5 (a), we remark that: (i) the larger $|V_Q|$ is, the longer time is taken by algorithm MATCH^Q, as expected; (ii) $|V_Q|$ influences on matching time more than $|E_Q|$.

Varying $|\mathcal{C}_Q|$ (MATCH^Q): fixing $|V_Q| = 10$ and $|E_Q| = 20$ (a very large *QGP*), we varied the number of *CQs* from 0 (query with only existential quantifications) to 20. As shown in Fig. 5(c), the number of *CQs* influences slightly in matching time which is consistent with the fact that our quantified simulation does not increase cost of dual simulation (Lemma 1).

Varying $|\mathcal{A}_Q|$ (MATCH^Q): using the same *QGP* of size $(10, 20)$, we varied the number of attribute constraints from 0 to 20 by adding incrementally two attribute constraints (e.g. "*Group = Book*", "*Rating $\geq$ 3*") to each vertex of the pattern. As remarked in Fig. 5(c), attribute constraints may reduce slightly the matching time taken by MATCH^Q. This is due to the fact that attribute constraints reduce the size of the initial match relation (lines 1–5 of Fig. 3) which leads for slight (considerable) reduction of matching time. For instance, the average of vertex matches ranges from 2946 ($|\mathcal{A}_Q| = 0$) to 1814 ($|\mathcal{A}_Q| = 20$).

Varying $|\mathcal{P}_Q^+|$ and $|\mathcal{P}_Q^-|$ (MATCH^C): we defined two *CGPs* C_1 and C_2 with cores of size $(|V_Q|, |E_Q|, |\mathcal{C}_Q|, |\mathcal{A}_Q|){=}(5, 10, 10, 5)$. We varied the number of positive (resp. negative) predicates from 0 to 10 in C_1 (resp. C_2) by adding incrementally two predicates of sizes $(3, 2, 2, 2)$ to each vertex of C_1 (resp. C_2). The results are reported in Fig. 5(b). As expected, each predicate requires to be evaluated over the underlying data graph which increases the matching time of the whole *CGPs*. MATCH^C gives good performance for a reasonable number of predicates: it takes around 7 seconds for three positive (resp. negative) predicates since the whole

---

[6] http://snap.stanford.edu/data/index.html..

size[7] of C_1 (resp. C_2) becomes $(11, 16, 16)$, which is a little bit large compared to real-life patterns. Contrary to what one may deduce from the figure, positive and negative predicates require theoretically the same computational time.

Experiment 2. This set of experiments evaluated the performances of PMATCH^C compared to MATCH^C. Using the same data set as *Experiment 1*, we generated a *CGP* with a core of size $(|V_Q|, |E_Q|, |\mathcal{C}_Q|, |\mathcal{A}_Q|) = (3, 6, 6, 3)$. We varied the number of predicates from 0 to 10 by incorporating fairly 5 positive predicates and 5 negative predicates to different vertices of the core. As shown in Fig. 5(d), the running time of PMATCH^C increases very slightly contrary to MATCH^C. This is due to the fact that our machine has 4 cores with hyper-threading technology that allows to execute 8 threads at the same time, hence, the increasing number of predicates influences slightly at the matching time. Remark that PMATCH^C outperforms MATCH^C by 2.7 times, a significant improvement.

Experiment 3. We evaluated the scalability of algorithms MATCH^Q, MATCH^C and PMATCH^C. We generated a *CGP* C with a core of size $(3, 4)$, a positive and a negative predicates of size $(3, 4)$ too. This gives a whole graph pattern of a large size, $(7, 16)$. We generated ten data graphs whose sizes varied from $(10^4, 37854)$ to $(10^5, 391545)$. For algorithm MATCH^Q, we compute only the time needed to evaluate the core of C. As shown in Fig. 5(e), (1) time of PMATCH^C is close to that of MATCH^Q since the core and predicates of C have the same size and are matched in parallel; (2) PMATCH^C scales well with large data graph and is on average 39.48%–60.74% times faster than MATCH^C.

Experiment 4. We evaluated the parallel scalability of algorithm PMATCH^C. We generated a *CGP* C with a core of size $(3, 6)$, three positive and three negative predicates of size $(3, 2)$. This gives a whole graph pattern of size $(15, 18)$. Next, we computed the running times of PMATCH^C by varying the number of CPU cores from 1 to 4. In the second part of this experiment, we disabled the hyper-threading technology to see its impact in matching time. As shown in Fig. 5(f): (1) PMATCH^C is parallel scalable since the more cores are used, the less time it takes to match C over the data graph, (2) enabling hyper-threading allows to increase slightly matching time of *CGPs*. This suggests to use more CPU cores in order to efficiently match *CGPs* over large data graphs.

7   Conclusion

We have proposed *conditional graph patterns* (*CGPs*) that extend traditional graph patterns with edge quantifications of the form "$\geq k$", attribute constraints on nodes, positive and negative predicates. Despite their increased expressivity, *CGPs* do not make our lives much harder which is proved by our matching algorithm that runs in quadratic time. In the second part of this paper, we have studied satisfiability and containment of *CGPs* that are fundamental problems

---

[7] Number of vertices and edges that belong to the core and/or predicates.

of any query language. We have shown that these problems are decidable in low PTIME by providing two checking algorithms. Our experimental results have verified the effectiveness, efficiency and scalability of our algorithms, using real-life data. As future work, we will investigate some strategies to speed up matching of *CGPs* such *data graphs distribution* [3] and *incremental matching* [7].

References

1. Brynielsson, J., Högberg, J., Kaati, L., Mårtenson, C., Svenson, P.: Detecting social positions using simulation. In: ASONAM
2. Cao, Y., Fan, W., Huai, J., Huang, R.: Making pattern queries bounded in big graphs. In: ICDE
3. Cong, G., Fan, W., Kementsietsidis, A.: Distributed query evaluation with performance guarantees. In: SIGMOD
4. Cordella, L.P., Foggia, P., Sansone, C., Vento, M.: A (sub)graph isomorphism algorithm for matching large graphs. IEEE Trans. Pattern Anal. Mach. Intell., 1367–1372 (2004)
5. Fan, W., Li, J., Ma, S., Tang, N., Wu, Y.: Adding regular expressions to graph reachability and pattern queries. In: ICDE (2011)
6. Fan, W., Li, J., Ma, S., Tang, N., Yinghui, W., Yunpeng, W.: From intractable to polynomial time. In: VLDB Endowment, Graph Pattern Matching (2010)
7. Fan, W., Wang, X., Wu, Y.: Incremental graph pattern matching. ACM Trans. Database Syst., 18:1–18:47 (2013)
8. Fan, W., Wu, Y., Xu, J.: Adding counting quantifiers to graph patterns. In: SIGMOD (2016)
9. Gallagher, B.: Matching structure and semantics: a survey on graph-based pattern matching. In: The AAAI Fall Symposium Series
10. Geerts, F., Fan, W.: Satisfiability of X path queries with sibling axes. In: DBPL
11. Genevès, P., Layaïda, N.: A system for the static analysis of X path. ACM Trans. Inf. Syst. **24**(4), 475–502 (2006)
12. Blau, D.J.H., Immerman, N.: A visual language for querying and updating graphs. University of Massachusetts, Technical report (2002)
13. Kostylev, E.V., Reutter, J.L., Vrgoc, D.: Containment of queries for graphs with data. J. Comput. Syst. Sci. **92**, 65–91 (2018)
14. Liu, G., et al.: Multi-constrained graph pattern matching in large-scale contextual social graphs. In: ICDE (2015)
15. Ma, S., Cao, Y., Fan, W., Huai, J., Wo, T.: Strong simulation: capturing topology in graph pattern matching. ACM Trans. Database Syst. **39**(1), 1–46 (2014)
16. Ma, S., Li, J., Hu, C., Liu, X., Huai, J.: Graph pattern matching for dynamic team formation. CoRR, abs/1801.01012 (2018)
17. Mahfoud, H.: Graph pattern matching with counting quantifiers and label-repetition constraints. Clust. Comput. **23**(3), 1529–1553 (2019). https://doi.org/10.1007/s10586-019-02977-3
18. Milner, R.: Communication and Concurrency. Prentice-Hall Inc., Upper Saddle River (1989)
19. Ullmann, J.R.: An algorithm for subgraph isomorphism. J. ACM **23**(1), 31–42 (1976)

An Effective Framework for Secure and Reliable Biometric Systems Based on Chaotic Maps

Lakhdar Laimeche[1(✉)], Abdallah Meraoumia[1(✉)], Lotfi Houam[1(✉)],
and Amel Bouchemha[2(✉)]

[1] LAboratory of Mathematics, Informatics and Systems (LAMIS),
University of Larbi Tebessi, 12002 Tebessa, Algeria
{lakhdar.laimeche,ameraoumia,lotfi.houam}@univ-tebessa.dz
[2] Laboratory of Electrical Engineering (LABGET), University of Larbi Tebessi,
12002 Tebessa, Algeria
amel.bouchemha@univ-tebessa.dz

Abstract. The last few years have plunged us at high speed into a
new means of communication, namely the Internet, which has set a new
trend for the next millennium. So, the rapid growth of online applications
reflects the speed with which most countries can develop. An essential
aspect of online communication is related to the trust of users and is a
very necessary element to ensure the success of an online application.
One of the main elements underlying this trust is the remote authentication of the user through its biometric features while of course protecting
these features in different storage media. In this paper, we propose a
new palmprint/palm-vein recognition framework based on a hand-craft
image feature learning method is suggested. Furthermore, to increase the
anti-spoof capability of the system, an effective biometric templates protection method based on chaotic systems was proposed. Experimental
results have shown that high accuracy can be obtained with a very high
level of template protection, which implies that the proposed cancelable
biometric system can operate in highly secure applications.

Keywords: Feature extraction · Feature learning · Cancelable
biometric · Chaos system · Template protection · Palmprint ·
Palm-vein

1 Introduction

For security purposes, most offline/online electronic applications are usually
afforded with physical/logical access authorization request procedures. In such
applications, the persons identity needs to be authenticated to know if the person is the one claiming it. It is a procedure that involves claiming a persons
identity and then providing evidence to prove this. In recent years, the use of
biometrics has been increasingly used as an alternative to traditional means in

© Springer Nature Switzerland AG 2021
C. Djeddi et al. (Eds.): MedPRAI 2020, CCIS 1322, pp. 314–328, 2021.
https://doi.org/10.1007/978-3-030-71804-6_23

the procedure of a persons identity authentication [1]. Biometrics addresses the physiological and/or behavioral characteristics that make each person unique for authentication purposes and encompasses any personal characteristic that can be used to uniquely verify the identity of a person [2]. Most noteworthy, in order to optimize the use of biometrics, systems have been developed to incorporate automated methods, generally performed by a computer, to verify the person's identity based on physiological characteristics such as faces, fingerprints and palmprints, and/or behavioral characteristics such as signatures, voices, and keystroke dynamics. Basically, a biometric system can involve [3] *i)* an acquisition module to capture biological data from a person, *ii)* a processing module to extract the unique identifiable features of this data (biometric template), *iii)* a matching module to compare the registered template with a template processed from a sample provided at the authentication time, and *iv)* a decision module for determining the final classification of the person using a similarity score obtained from the matching module. Indeed, the processing module (which essentially represents the feature extraction task) is one of the most important modules which has received a lot of work from researchers, due to its importance and its strong impact on the system accuracy.

Many applications in image processing and computational vision, including biometrics, rely upon the efficient representation of image features. Consequently, accurate estimates of this representation are of vital importance for higher levels of visual processing [4]. Nowadays, there are many hand-crafted methods that can be well used to extract the distinctive features of an image. However, most of them cannot work well on all types of applications (*e.g.* all biometric modalities). For example, unlike the deep learning methods which can be used to analyze the image at several levels, the hand-crafted methods are applied at one level and due to its limits, it is not possible to access the depth of the image to extract the distinctive features even when there are very high-resolution biometric images [5]. However, deep learning is not always effective, especially in large databases, due to its need for powerful devices to overcome their main limitations, which are memory capacity and processor speed [6]. For this, in recent times, most research efforts related to hand-crafted feature extraction methods have focused on improving their results by adapting it to images of the whole context. In general, this idea, which aims to provide the hand-crafted feature extraction method with a priori knowledge on the context, has proved remarkably effective because of its very impressive results compared to those which operate without learning [7]. In our new method, learning takes place once and for all during the first use of the system to extract specific information in the form of a projection matrix and a codebook which will then be used in the enrollment and classification phases. This information makes it possible to adapt the hand-crafted feature extraction method to the images processed to extract a distinct vector of discrimination and therefore improve the system performance (for more details, see Sect. 2).

The majority of previous research in biometric recognition has focused on improving system accuracy (most often using an efficient feature extraction method), but attack resistance is also a central and important characteristic of any biometric system. Indeed, although biometrics effectively outperforms the traditional token-based authentication methods, such as a passport or ID cards, and knowledge-based authentication methods, such as a password or PIN code, they also raise many security concerns that can affect user confidence [8]. So far, cancelable biometric technologies have attracted increasing attention and interest among researchers, in the hope that the possibility of canceled of the biometric template will improve the security performance of biometric systems and thereby overcome security concerns and privacy which, in turn, would increase users' confidence in the system [9]. Therefore, to strengthen the proposed system against attack on the biometric template, we adopted the revocability technique so that the template can be canceled if it is stolen or spoofed. Of course, our scalable approach may not solve all system security issues, but it does reduce incidents of a security breach because not doing so can lead to insufficient security, which will undoubtedly make the system vulnerable to attack. In this study, a new biometric template protection scheme based on chaotic maps systems to guarantee both high performance and enhanced security is also proposed (for more details, see Sect. 2).

The rest of this paper is organized as follows: In Sect. 2, we detail the proposed cancelable biometric system architecture. This section describes the two main steps, which are feature learning and feature extraction. Experimental results relating to the biometric system performance and security analysis are presented and commented in Sect. 3. Finally, the conclusion and some future work are presented in Sect. 4.

2   System Description

The subject of this paper concerns the biometric system security. Indeed, a biometric system must be available to work correctly and reliably in all circumstances and therefore be resistant to abuse due to any spoofing. To achieve this objective, we decided to protect the biometric template by building a system capable of changing it in the event of spoofing. Thus, our proposed system includes three main phases, namely the training phase, the extraction phase, and the classification phase. Figure 1 shows the block diagram of the training (learning) phase which includes four stages.

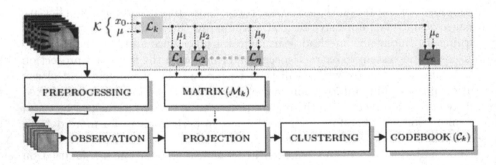

Fig. 1. Block diagram for learning the cancelable palmprint features

2.1   Training Phase

As mentioned earlier, the hand-crafted feature extraction method can be improved by incorporating the concept of learning. This learning can provide prior knowledge (information) to extract the most precise feature vectors. Indeed, the knowledge provided is represented in the form of a codebook.

1) Observation vector: In our method, the image is analyzed block by block, and the observation vector of each block is extracted by the Histogram of Oriented Gradients (HOG) technique. Thus, the input $H \times W$-sized image is divided into square and overlapped blocks, each of which is then mapped into a observation vector $\nu \in \mathbb{R}^{\rho \times 1}$ via the HOG technique. The length of this vector (ρ) is a function of the number of HOG windows (n_w) and the number of histogram bins (n_b), $\rho = f(n_w, n_b)$. In addition, the number of observation vectors extracted from each image (n_ν) is identical to the number of blocks and is equal to:

$$n_\nu = \lfloor \frac{H-o}{b-o} \rfloor \cdot \lfloor \frac{W-o}{b-o} \rfloor \tag{1}$$

where o denotes the horizontal/vertical overlap between two adjacent blocks and $\lfloor \alpha \rfloor$ is the integer part of the value α. Finally, the observation vectors extracted from all the blocks are concatenated into a single vector (ν) in order to represent the preliminary feature of the entire image:

$$v_i = [\nu_{i1}, \nu_{i2}, \nu_{i3}, \cdots, \nu_{in_\nu}]^T \in \mathbb{R}^{n_\nu \times \rho} \tag{2}$$

In order to determine the projection matrix and the codebook, we use N images to extract $n_\nu \cdot N$ observation vectors.

$$\begin{aligned} \mathcal{V} &= [v_1, v_2, v_3, \cdots, v_N] \\ &= [\nu_{11}, \nu_{12}, \cdots, \nu_{21}, \nu_{22}, \cdots, \nu_{N1}, \nu_{N2}, \cdots, \nu_{N \cdot n_\nu}] \in \mathbb{R}^{(N \cdot n_\nu) \times \rho} \end{aligned} \tag{3}$$

The vector $\mathcal{V}$ contains, after transformation (projection), the training base for generating the codebook. Of course, the higher the value of N, the more effective the learning.

2) Vectors transformation: In this step, the projection matrix $\mathcal{M}_k$ is created. By using this matrix, the biometric template can be protected by changing the secret key $(\mathcal{K})$, which in turn modifies this matrix. This change allows us to extract different vectors for the same person. In our scheme, the matrix $\mathcal{M}_k$ was generated using 1D logistics maps [10] (see Eq. 4) due to its simplicity and efficiency.

$$x_{n+1} = \mathcal{L}(x_n) = \mu x_n (1 - x_n), \quad \mu \in [3.57, 4], \quad x_n \in [0, 1] \tag{4}$$

where x_n is the state of the system (for $n = 0, 1, 2, \cdots$) and μ is the control parameter. This system generates pseudo-random sequences by means of an initial state x_0 and a fixed control parameter μ. Thus, the two parameters (x_0 and μ) can be used as a secret key ($\mathcal{K}$).

The role of this matrix is to transform each vector ($\nu_{ij} \in \mathcal{V}$) of dimension $\rho \times 1$ into a vector $\tilde{\nu}_{ij}$ of dimension $\eta \times 1$. To create this matrix, each column is generated with a chaotic system. Therefore, we used ($\eta + 1$) logistics maps, one of which is the main system ($\mathcal{L}_k$), and the rest (η) are secondary systems ($\mathcal{L}_i|_{i=1,2,3,\cdots,\eta}$). The initial state of each secondary system ($\mathcal{L}_i$) is determined as:

$$x_{0i} = \mathcal{S}_k(L_i), \quad i = 1, 2, \cdots, \eta, \quad \text{and} \quad \mathcal{S}_k = \{x_j\}_{j=1}^{\max(L_i)} \tag{5}$$

where $\mathcal{S}_k$ is a sequence generated with $\mathcal{L}_k$ and L_i are predefined integer values. In addition, the control parameters of the secondary systems ($\mu_i|_{i=1}^{\eta}$) are determined by an optimization method (in our work, we used the Bat Algorithm (BA) optimization [11]) in order to maximize the biometric identification rate. Finally, for a given secret key ($\mathcal{K}$) and after optimization of the recognition rate, we obtain the final projection matrix ($\mathcal{M}_k$) which takes the following form:

$$\mathcal{M}_k = [w_1, w_2, w_3, \cdots, w_\eta] \in \mathbb{R}^{\rho \times \eta} \tag{6}$$

The values of L_i and η can be modified in order to achieve better performance.

3) Codebook learning: Indeed, the observation vectors extracted from all the training images represent the different features that can be found in the work context. Intuitively, all of these features (for example, features in the palmprint for several persons) have a finite dimension. Consequently, many vectors (features) in the training base after the transformation ($\tilde{\mathcal{V}}$) can be very close. For this, an unsupervised clustering process was carried out to select only the most discriminating vectors (features) of the work context. After clustering, the resulting vectors form a so-called codebook ($\mathcal{C}_k$), which represents prior knowledge which is presented to the hand-crafted feature extraction method to effectively represent the feature of the image.

In our study, we used the Linde-Buzo-Gray (LBG) [12] as a clustering technique. This algorithm takes a set of feature vectors $\tilde{\mathcal{V}} \in \mathbb{R}^{\eta \times (N \cdot n_\nu)}$ as input and generates a representative subset of feature vectors (codebook $\mathcal{C}_k$) with a $\ell \ll N \cdot n_\nu$ specified by the user at the output according to the similarity measure.

$$\mathcal{C}_k = \mathcal{F}_{\text{LBG}}(\tilde{\mathcal{V}}) \in \mathbb{R}^{\eta \times \ell} \quad \text{and} \quad \tilde{\mathcal{V}} = \mathcal{V} \cdot \mathcal{M}_k \in \mathbb{R}^{\eta \times (N \cdot n_\nu)} \tag{7}$$

The initial codebook, the distortion, and the threshold are the parameters that control the convergence of the algorithm, which generally requires a maximum number of iterations to ensure this convergence.

In addition, to further improve the protection of the template, we shuffle (redistribute) the vectors in the codebook. Thus, let $\mathcal{S}_c$ the sequence, with integer components, generated by the chaotic system $\mathcal{L}_c$:

$$\mathcal{S}_c = \{y_i\}_{i=1}^{\ell} \quad y_i = \lfloor (10^4 \cdot x_i) \bmod (\ell) \rfloor \tag{8}$$

We divide this sequence into two subsequences ($\mathcal{S}_c^1$ and $\mathcal{S}_c^2$) as:

$$\mathcal{S}_c^1 = \{y_i^1\}_{i=1,3,5,\cdots\ell-1} \qquad \mathcal{S}_c^2 = \{y_i^2\}_{i=2,4,6,\cdots\ell} \tag{9}$$

Then a simple permutation between the components of $\mathcal{C}_k$ is applied:

$$\mathcal{C}_k(\mathcal{S}_c^1(i)) \leftrightarrows \mathcal{C}_k(\mathcal{S}_c^2(i)) \Leftrightarrow \mathcal{C}_k(y_i^1) \leftrightarrows \mathcal{C}_k(y_i^2), \quad i = 1, 2, 3, \cdots, \frac{\ell}{2} \tag{10}$$

In the case of spoofing, it is possible either to redistribute only the vectors of the codebook ($\mathcal{C}_k$) or to re-estimate the projection matrix ($\mathcal{M}_k$), in which a new codebook is created.

2.2 Feature Extraction

The role of this phase is to represent the feature of the image using the projection matrix ($\mathcal{M}_k$) and the codebook ($\mathcal{C}_k$) previously obtained in the learning phase. Thus, the sequence diagram for this phase is illustrated in Fig. 2. In this phase, the observation vectors are extracted from the input image in the same way as the training phase (using the HOG technique). After having projected these vectors, a coding process is applied. Let v_i be the extracted observation vectors from the input image i:

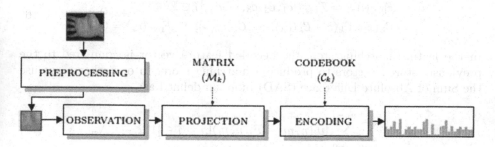

Fig. 2. Block diagram for cancelable palmprint features representation

$$v_i = [\nu_{i1}, \nu_{i2}, \nu_{i3}, \cdots, \nu_{in_\nu}]^T \in \mathbb{R}^{n_\nu \times \rho} \tag{11}$$

The vector v_i is then transformed (projected) using the matrix $\mathcal{M}_k$:

$$\tilde{v}_i = \mathcal{F}_{\text{PROJ}}(v_i) = v_i \cdot \mathcal{M}_k \in \mathbb{R}^{\eta \times n_\nu} \tag{12}$$

To obtain the final feature representation of the image, the vector obtained ($\tilde{v}_i$) must be encoded. In this case, each column on the vector $\tilde{v}_i$ is replaced by the coordinate of the nearest vector in the codebook. Thus, for each column, the system calculates the similarity between it and all the vectors in the codebook.

$$D_i = [d_1, d_2, d_3, \cdots d_\ell] \in \mathbb{R}^{1 \times \ell}, \quad i \in [1 \cdots n_\nu] \tag{13}$$

After that, the system determines the coordinates based on the lowest similarity score as follows:

$$c_i = \arg \min_{c_i \in [1 \cdots \ell]} (D_i) \tag{14}$$

Encode all the columns of the vector $\widetilde{v}_i$, we obtain the final feature representation of the image ($\mathcal{X}_i$):

$$\mathcal{X}_i = \mathcal{F}_{\text{COD}}(\widetilde{v}_i) = [c_1, c_2, c_3, \cdots c_{n_v}] \in \mathbb{R}^{1 \times n_v}, \quad c_i \in [1 \cdots \ell] \tag{15}$$

This representation makes it possible to hide the feature of the image in a compact form, it plays the role of pooling.

2.3 Classification Phase

In all biometric systems, before the classification phase (identification or verification), the person must be enrolled in the system database. In the two phases (enrollment and classification), the image feature is represented as we described in Subsect. 2.2. Thus, in the classification phase and before the matching step, the feature vector must be decoded using the same codebook ($\mathcal{C}_k$) as is used in the enrollment phase. Let $\mathcal{X}_i$ be the feature vector of the person to be classified, where $\mathcal{X}_i$ is defined as in Eq. 15. This vector is decoded as follows:

$$\begin{aligned} \widetilde{v}_i = \mathcal{F}_{\text{DEC}}(\mathcal{X}_i) &= \mathcal{F}_{\text{DEC}}([c_1, c_2, c_3, \cdots c_{n_v}]) \in \mathbb{R}^{\eta \times n_v} \\ &= [\mathcal{C}_k(c_1), \mathcal{C}_k(c_2), \mathcal{C}_k(c_3), \cdots, \mathcal{C}_k(c_{n_v})], \quad \mathcal{F}_{\text{DEC}}(c_i) = \mathcal{C}_k(c_i) \end{aligned} \tag{16}$$

In the feature matching step, the decoded feature vector is compared to the previously stored vectors to produce a matching score. In our scheme, we use the Sum of Absolute Difference (SAD) function defined as:

$$d_{ij} = \sum_{n=0}^{\eta-1} \sum_{m=0}^{n_v-1} |\widetilde{v}_i(n, m) - \widetilde{v}_j(n, m)|, \quad j \in [1, 2, \cdots, \mathcal{N}_p] \tag{17}$$

where d_{ij} indicates the similarity score between the examined feature vector $\widetilde{v}_i$ and the stored feature vectors $\widetilde{v}_j|_{j=1,2,3,\cdots,\mathcal{N}_p}$ and $\mathcal{N}_p$ is the number of persons in the system database.

3   Experimental Results an Discussion

The purpose of this section is to discuss in detail the experimental results obtained in this study for user identification via palmprint/palm-vein recognition. Therefore, experiments were conducted on an accessible and public Multispectral palmprint dataset provided by the Hong Kong Polytechnic University (PolyU) [13]. In our experiments, we used a database of 300 persons, which is similar to the number of employees in a small to medium-sized enterprise. In this dataset, each person has twelve samples for each biometric modality. In the

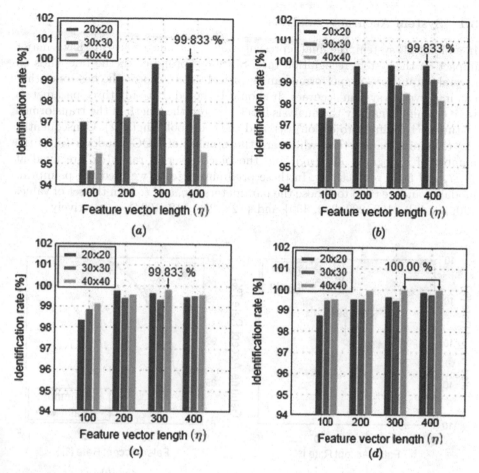

Fig. 3. Selection of parameters for our learned hand-crafted feature extraction method for better biometric system performance $\{\mathcal{K} \equiv (x_0, \mu) = (0.4191, 3.8841)\}$. *(a)* 128-sized codebook, *(b)* 256-sized codebook, *(c)* 512-sized codebook and *(d)* 1024-sized codebook

enrollment phase, we randomly used three samples from each person's biometric modality to register them, while the other nine samples of the person were used to evaluate the system performance. By comparing the nine test samples with all those enrolled in the database, we can obtain 282375 matching scores divided into 2250 scores for client experiments and 280125 scores for impostor experiments. The set of experiences of our work is divided into two sub-parts. In the first one, we present the palmprint/palm-vein based system performance. In this sub-part, we perform several tests in order to best choose the parameters of the proposed method. The second sub-part focuses on the biometric system security, in which their performance against attacks is examined.

3.1   System Accuracy Analysis

In a biometric system, the final representation of the images' feature has a major impact on the system recognition rate. Since our proposed method depends on several parameters, we performed an empirical test to choose the best ones that can improve the system accuracy. It should be noted that only three parameters were examined, namely the analysis block size (b), the length of the transformed feature vector (after projection) (η), and the codebook length (ℓ). Consequently, the remaining parameters, which are the number of HOG windows (n_w), the number of histogram bins (n_b), and the blocks overlap ratio (o), are fixed at 11, 7, and 50%, respectively. In these preliminary tests, we used the palmprint modality and we tried to choose the parameters b, η, and ℓ, from the set of values {20, 30, 40}, {100, 200, 300, 400} and {128, 256, 512, 1024}, respectively.

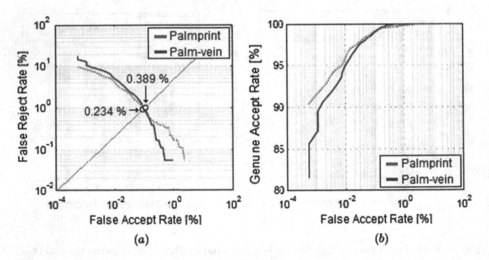

Fig. 4. Palmprint/palm-vein based open-set biometric identification system performance. *(a)* DET curves, and *(b)* ROC curves

Since varying these parameters can produce many feature representations, we can experimentally select a combination (b, η, ℓ) that can effectively improve the system accuracy by changing one of them each time and by choosing the best that gives the best performance. Thus, in order to see the effect of these parameters (b, η, ℓ) on the biometric system performance, we clearly illustrate, in Fig. 3, the results of the closed-set identification system (Rank-One Recognition (ROR)) operating with a secret key ($\mathcal{K}$) equal to $\equiv (x_0, \mu) = (0.4191, 3.8841)$. From these curves, we can find four important cases: *i)* Acceptable performances can be obtained with all possible combinations since an actual identification rate (ROR) higher than 94% has already been obtained. *ii)* Generally, the smaller the analysis block, the higher the identification rate. The average RORs obtained by a block size of 20 × 20 is better than those obtained by a block size of

40×40, particularly in the lower codebook sizes. *iii)* System performance can be improved by using long codebook lengths. Thus, the average RORs obtained by a codebook length of 1024 is better than those obtained by codebook lengths of 128, 256, and 512. *iv)* Finally, increasing the feature vector length (η) effectively improves system performance. From Fig. 3, it is clear that the combinations (b, η, ℓ) equal to (40×40, 400, 1024) and (40×40, 300, 1024) offer better results in terms of ROR (100% with a Rank of Perfect Recognition (RPR) equal to 1), see Fig. 3. *(d)*. But when the identification system works in open-set mode, the first combination (40×40, 400, 1024) gives the best performance (Equal Error Rate (EER) equal to 0.2334% ($T_o = 0.5357$) instead of 0.2721% ($T_o = 0.5492$)).

Henceforth, we have considered the best parameters ($b \times b = 40 \times 40, \eta = 400$ an $\ell = 1024$) in order to conduct several experiments to compare the effectiveness of the biometric system using palmprint/palm-vein biometric modalities. As these modalities give a perfect closed-set identification performance (ROR = 100% with RPR = 1), we only represent in Fig. 4 the open-set identification performance. From the curves in Fig. 4. *(a)* (DET curves), it is clear that the palmprint modality offers better results than the palm-vein modality in terms of EER (0.234% ($T_o = 0.5541$) instead of 0.389% ($T_o = 0, 5761$)). In this case, a performance improvement of 39,846% is obtained. Finally, to summarize this series of tests, graphs showing the Receiver Operating Characteristic (ROC) curves using the two biometric modalities were generated in Fig. 4. *(b)*.

Since the emergence of biometric systems, interest in the use of several biometric modalities has increased due to their potential to overcome certain important limitations of unimodal systems, in particular the low identification rate [14]. Thus, the aim of this part is to examine whether the performance of the open-set identification system can be improved by integrating complementary information which comes mainly from different modalities (palmprint and palm-vein). In our work, we use a rule-based technique to fuse the matching scores produced by the different unimodal identification systems. Thus, the sum rule (SUM) and the product rule (MUL) are used. The experimental results for the open-set/closed-set identification mode, respecting the two fusion rules, are presented, as EER and ROR, in Table 1. The results in this table show that, generally, the use of fusion allows effectively improve open-set biometric identification system performance with an improvement of 68,974% and 81,331% (using MUL rule)

Table 1. Open-set/closed-set biometric identification test result

	OPEN-SET		CLOSED-SET	
	T_o	EER	RPR	ROR
PALMPRINT	0.5541	0.2340	1	100.00
PALM-VEIN	0.6030	0.3889	1	100.00
FUSION (SUM)	0.5837	0.0798	1	100.00
FUSION (MUL)	0.3381	0.0726	1	100.00

compared to palmprint and palm-vein, respectively. In conclusion, the obtained identification rates are identical to those obtained in several previous works in literature and make our proposed method sufficient for several applications.

3.2 System Security Analysis

Given the encouraging results obtained with our proposed system in identifying persons, in this section we will try to assess the security level against potential attacks (templates protection level). In this security analysis, we will take into account that the system structure is already known to attackers and we will try to evaluate attempts to retrieve the biometric template. In general, the high-security level is obtained when: $i)$ Impossibility of retrieving the biometric template by exhaustive searches (so the key space must be sufficiently large) and $ii)$ a slight change in the secret key gives completely different templates.

$i)$ **Key space analysis:** According to Fig. 1, the security of our system is guaranteed by $(\eta+2)$ chaotic systems, one of which is main $(\mathcal{L}_k)$ and $(\eta+1)$ secondary $(\mathcal{L}_i|_{i=1}^{\eta}$ and $\mathcal{L}_c)$. The role of the main chaotic system is to vary the initial state of the $(\eta+1)$ secondary chaotic systems, while the role of the $(\eta+1)$ chaotic systems is to change the projection matrix and to mix the extracted template. In a chaotic system, the secret-key space is calculated using all the mean absolute errors $(\mathcal{E})$ between two sequences generated by two close secret keys [15]. So let S^x and $\widetilde{S}^x$ (or S^μ and $\widetilde{S}^\mu$) two sequences generated by the same system under x_0 and $x_0 + d^x$ (or μ and $\mu + d^\mu$): The $\mathcal{E}^x$ (or $\mathcal{E}^\mu$) is defined as:

$$\mathcal{E}^x(S^x, \widetilde{S}^x) = \frac{1}{L} \sum_{i=1}^{L} |S^x(i) - \widetilde{S}^x(i)| \tag{18}$$

where L denotes the sequence length which is different from one system to another. Thus, the key space for x_0 called s_x (or s_μ for μ) is equal to $1/d_x$ (or $1/d_u$), where d_x (or d_μ) is the value of d^x (or d^μ) when $\mathcal{E}^x$ (or $\mathcal{E}^\mu$) becomes 0. So, the total key space in our system is equal to:

$$S = \underbrace{(s_{x_k} \cdot s_{\mu_k})}_{\mathcal{L}_k} \cdot \underbrace{(s_{x_c} \cdot s_{\mu_c})}_{\mathcal{L}_c} \cdot \underbrace{\left(\prod_{i=1}^{\eta} s_{x_i} \cdot s_{\mu_i}\right)}_{\mathcal{L}_i|_{i=1}^{\eta}} \tag{19}$$

For the $\mathcal{L}_k$ system, the pair (s_x, s_μ) is equal to $(1.1420 \cdot 10^{16}, 0.5248 \cdot 10^{16})$. This pair is equal to $(1.2541 \cdot 10^{16}, 0.8542 \cdot 10^{16})$ for $\mathcal{L}_c$. Finally, for any $L_i|_{i=1}^{\eta}$ system, (s_x, s_μ) becomes $(2.0248 \cdot 10^{16}, 1.3125 \cdot 10^{16})$. Therefore, the total key space of our system becomes:

$$S = (0.6420 \cdot 10^{64}) \cdot (2.6576^\eta \cdot 10^{32\eta}) = (0.6420) \cdot (2.6576^\eta) \cdot 10^{32(\eta+2)} \tag{20}$$

In our proposed biometric identification system, the value of η must be high enough to obtain high accuracy for the identification of persons, and therefore the security level is guaranteed ($\eta = 400 \Rightarrow$ key space is too high).

ii) **Key sensitivity analysis:** In order to test the system sensitivity to slight variations of the key, we test in this subpart the system behavior resulting from many closest secret keys. Therefore, we used three different keys: $\mathcal{K}_c$: correct key $(x_0, \mu) = (0.4191, 3.8841)$, $\mathcal{K}_1$: wrong key $(0.4140, 3.8511)$, and $\mathcal{K}_2$: wrong key $(0.4191 + 10^{-16}, 3.8841)$. In order to assess the security level, we enrolled all persons with the correct key $(\mathcal{K}_c)$, and then we tested the open-set/closed-set identification, using palmprint and palm-vein, with the three keys $(\mathcal{K}_c, \mathcal{K}_1$ and $\mathcal{K}_2)$. The system performance under the three keys is illustrated in Fig. 5 for the two biometric modalities.

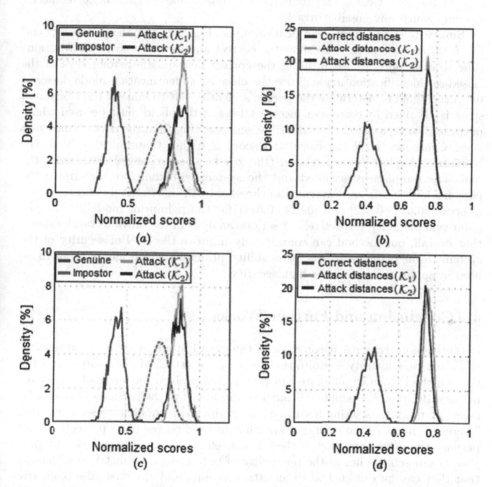

Fig. 5. Biometric system performance during an attack (theft of the biometric template for a spoofing attempt). *(a)* Palmprint based open-set identification system, *(b)* Palmprint based closed-set identification system, *(c)* Palm-vein based open-set identification system and *(d)* Palm-vein based biometric system

For open-set identification systems, Fig. 5. *(a)* (for the palmprint) and Fig. 5. *(c)* (for the palm-vein) presents the distribution of genuine and impostor scores obtained using the correct key ($\mathcal{K}_c$) as well as the distribution of genuine scores when the changing the key due to an attack (scores obtained by keys other than the correct secret key, therefore wrong keys ($\mathcal{K}_1$ and $\mathcal{K}_2$)). In these figures, it is clear that all the attack scores are completely displaced above the security threshold ($\gg T_o$), and thus have become impostor scores for the system. In addition, a greater confidence interval between genuine and attack scores was obtained ([0.567−0.648] for palmprint and [0.621−0.648] for palm-vein), which reflects the effectiveness and robustness of our proposed cancelable biometric system against any possible attack.

Similar to the open-set identification mode, Fig. 5. *(b)* (for the palmprint) and Fig. 5. *(d)* (for the palm-vein) show the correct and incorrect score distributions (due to attacks) obtained in using the correct key and the wrong keys in the closed-set identification mode. Since the closed-set identification mode does not use a threshold to determine the person's identity but to know if the calculated score is obtained by correct or incorrect keys, a threshold must be used whose purpose is to separate the two distributions resulting from the correct/incorrect keys. Consequently, if the calculated score is higher than the threshold, the biometric template is then refused (the key has been changed), otherwise the biometric template is accepted and the system will, therefore, determine the person's identity. In our system, the threshold can be effectively chosen in the intervals [0.572−0.652] and [0.614−0.611] for the palmprint modality and the palm-vein modality, respectively. A serious analysis of the previous results shows that overall, our method can considerably improve the level of security of the system through the use of the revocability principle, which allows them to be used in applications requiring high security.

4   Conclusion and Further Works

Recently, biometrics has become one of the most important means used to identify a person's identity. Despite this success, the attack on the system and the theft of the biometric template can pose a real problem in terms of a person's privacy. Because this template is intrinsically linked to the person and cannot be changed, the fear of losing it can be one of the most important users' distrust. Therefore, many of the emerging work has focused on template protection, and perhaps the most important of these is cancelable biometric systems. The purpose of our scheme lies in the possibility of extracting a biometric template so that they can be canceled when an attack occurs, and of course, the biometric system performance must be preserved. Therefore, this study is mainly related to the biometric feature extraction task. In this paper, we have established two main objectives. The first consists in proposing a new feature extraction method based on the learning principle to increase their efficiency in extracting the distinctive template. While the second concerns the template protection by canceling it in any attack. By decomposing the image on several blocks, we used the HOG technique to extract the observation vector from each block. Using observation vectors of several images, a codebook was created, which aims to provide a priori knowledge of the working context in order to effectively represent the image in the two phases of the system (enrollment and identification). To protect the template, we used the transformation method by projecting the template into a matrix created by chaotic systems and optimized by the genetic algorithm. The experimental results show the robustness against template theft with a high identification rate, which can also be improved by combining the two biometric methods. As future work, we plan to change the HOG technique used to extract the feature vector of the blocks with the DCT and oBIF techniques. We will also try to test some hyperchaotic systems.

References

1. Wei, J., Zhang, B., Lu, J., Zhu, Y., Yang, Z., Zuo, W., et al.: Palmprint recognition based on complete direction representation. IEEE Trans. Image Process. **26**(9), 4483–4498 (2017)
2. Fang, Y., Wu, Q., Kang, W.: A novel finger vein verification system based on two-stream convolutional network learning. Neurocomputing **290**(17), 100–107 (2018)
3. Unar, J., Seng, W., Abbasi, A.: A review of biometric technology along with trends and prospects. Pattern Recognit **47**(8), 2673–2688 (2014)
4. Wang, Q., Li, B., Chen, X., Luo, J., Hou, Y.: Random sampling local binary pattern encoding based on Gaussian distribution. IEEE Signal Process. Lett. **24**(9), 1358–1362 (2017)
5. Genovese, A., Piuri, V., Scotti, F.: Palmprint biometrics. Touchless Palmprint Recognition Systems. AIS, vol. 60, pp. 49–109. Springer, Cham (2014). https://doi.org/10.1007/978-3-319-10365-5_4
6. Sundararajan, K., Woodard, D.L.: Deep learning for biometrics: a survey. J. ACM Comput. Surv. (CSUR) **51**(3), 1–34 (2018)
7. Feng, Z., et al.: DLANet: a manifold-learning-based discriminative feature learning network for scene classification. Neurocomputing **157**, 11–21 (2015)
8. Yu, J., Zhang, B., Kuang, Z., Lin, D., Fan, J.: iPrivacy: image privacy protection by identifying sensitive objects via deep multi-task learning. IEEE Trans. Inf. Forensics Secur. **12**(5), 1005–1016 (2017)
9. Nandakumar, K., Jain, A.: Biometric template protection: bridging the performance gap between theory and practice. IEEE Signal Process. Mag **32**(5), 88–100 (2015)
10. Farsana, F.J., Gopakumar, K.: Private key encryption of speech signal based on three dimensional chaotic map. In: International Conference on Communication and Signal Processing, pp. 2197–2201 (2017)
11. Laimeche, L., Meraoumia, A., Bendjenna, H.: Enhancing LSB embedding schemes using chaotic maps systems. Neural Comput. Appl. **32**(21), 16605–16623 (2019). https://doi.org/10.1007/s00521-019-04523-z
12. Li, Z., Li, X., Liu, Y., Cai, Z. (eds.): ISICA 2012. CCIS. Springer, Heidelberg (2012). https://doi.org/10.1007/978-3-642-34289-9
13. Hong Kong Polytechnic University (PolyU) multispectral palmprint database (2011). http://www.comp.polyu.edu.hk/~biometrics

14. Sunil Khandelwal, C., Maheshewari, R., Shindec, U.B.: Review paper on applications of principal component analysis in multimodal biometrics system. Procedia Comput. Sci. **92**, 481–486 (2016)
15. Bhatnagar, G., Wu, Q.M.J.: Chaos-based security solution for fingerprint data during communication and transmission. IEEE Trans. Instrum. Meas. **61**(4), 876–887 (2012)

Learning Word Representations for Tunisian Sentiment Analysis

Abir Messaoudi(✉), Hatem Haddad(✉), Moez Ben HajHmida(✉),
Chayma Fourati(✉), and Abderrazak Ben Hamida(✉)

iCompass, Tunis, Tunisia
{abir,hatem,moez,chayma,razzak}@icompass.digital
https://www.icompass.tn

Abstract. Tunisians on social media tend to express themselves in their local dialect using Latin script (TUNIZI). This raises an additional challenge to the process of exploring and recognizing online opinions. To date, very little work has addressed TUNIZI sentiment analysis due to scarce resources for training an automated system. In this paper, we focus on the Tunisian dialect sentiment analysis used on social media. Most of the previous work used machine learning techniques combined with handcrafted features. More recently, Deep Neural Networks were widely used for this task, especially for the English language. In this paper, we explore the importance of various unsupervised word representations (word2vec, BERT) and we investigate the use of Convolutional Neural Networks and Bidirectional Long Short-Term Memory. Without using any kind of handcrafted features, our experimental results on two publicly available datasets [18,19] showed comparable performances to other languages.

Keywords: Tunisian dialect · TUNIZI · Sentiment analysis · Deep learning · Neural networks · Natural language analysis

1 Introduction

Since the end of the twentieth century and the spread of mobile communication technologies in the Arab world, youth, in particular, have developed a new chat alphabet to communicate more efficiently in informal Arabic. Because most media and applications initially did not enable chatting in Arabic, these Arab speakers resorted to what is now commonly known as "Arabizi". In [1], Arabizi was defined as the newly-emerged Arabic variant written using the Arabic numeral system and Roman script characters. With the widespread use of social media worldwide in more recent years, Arabizi emerged as an established Arabic writing system for mobile communication and social media in the Arab world.

Compared to the increasing studies of sentiment analysis in Indo-European languages, similar research for Arabic dialects is still very limited. This is

Supported by iCompass.

mainly attributed to the lack of the needed good quality Modern Standard Arabic (MSA) publicly-available sentiment analysis resources in general [2], and more specifically dialectical Arabic publicly-available resources. Building such resources involves several difficulties in terms of data collection and annotation, especially for underrepresented Arabic dialects such as the Tunisian dialect. Nevertheless, existing Tunisian annotated datasets [3] focused on code-switching datasets written using the Arabic or the Romanized Alphabet. The studies on these datasets applied off-the-shelf models that have been built for MSA on a dataset of Tunisian Arabic. An intuitive solution is to translate Tunisian Romanized Alphabet into Arabic Script [4]. This approach suffers from the need for a parallel Tunisian-Arabic text corpus, the low average precision performances achieved and the irregularity of the words written.

Using a model trained on Modern Standard Arabic sentiment analysis data and then applying the same model on dialectal sentiment analysis data, does not produce good performances as shown in [5]. This suggests that MSA models cannot be effective when applied to dialectical Arabic. There is, thus, a growing need for the creation of computational resources, not only for MSA but also for dialectical Arabic. The same situation holds when one tries to use computational resources used for a specific dialect of Arabic with another one.

To the best of our knowledge, this is the first study on sentiment analysis TUNIZI Romanized Alphabet. This could be deduced in the next sections where we will present TUNIZI and the state-of-the-art of Tunisian sentiment analysis followed by our proposed approach, results and discussion before conclusion and future work.

2   TUNIZI

Tunisian dialect, also known as "Tounsi" or "Derja", is different from Modern Standard Arabic. In fact, Tunisian dialect features Arabic vocabulary spiced with words and phrases from Tamazight, French, Turkish, Italian and other languages [6].

Tunisia is recognized as a high contact culture where online social networks play a key role in facilitating social communication [7]. In [8], TUNIZI was referred to as "the Romanized alphabet used to transcribe informal Arabic for communication by the Tunisian Social Media community". To illustrate more, some examples of TUNIZI words translated to MSA and English are presented in Table 1.

Since some Arabic characters do not exist in the Latin alphabet, numerals, and multigraphs instead of diacritics for letters, are used by Tunisians when they write on social media. For instance, "ch" is used to represent the character ش. An example is the word شرير[1] represented as "cherrir" in TUNIZI characters.

After a few observations from the collected datasets, we noticed that Arabizi used by Tunisians is slightly different from other informal Arabic dialects such

---

[1] Wicked.

Table 1. Examples of TUNIZI common words translated to MSA and English.

TUNIZI	MSA translation	English translation
3asslema	مرحبا	Hello
chna7welek	كيف حالك	How are you
sou2el	سؤال	Question
5dhit	أخذت	I took

as Egyptian Arabizi. This may be due to the linguistic situation specific to each country. In fact, Tunisians generally use the french background when writing in Arabizi, whereas, Egyptians would use English. For example, the word مشيت would be written as "misheet" in Egyptian Arabizi, the second language being English. However, because the Tunisian's second language is French, the same word would be written as "mchit".

In Table 2, numerals and multigraphs are used to transcribe TUNIZI characters that compensate the absence of equivalent Latin characters for exclusively Arabic sounds. They are represented with their corresponding Arabic characters and Arabizi characters in other countries. For instance, the number 5 is used to represent the character ح in the same way as the multigraph "kh". For example, the word "5dhit" is the representation of the word أخذت as shown in Table 1. Numerals and multigraphs used to represent TUNIZI are different from those used to represent Arabizi. As an example, the word غالية[2] written as "ghalia" or "8alia" in TUNIZI corresponds to "4'alia" in Arabizi.

Table 2. Special Tunizi characters and their corresponding Arabic and Arabizi characters.

Arabic	Arabizi	TUNIZI
ح	7	7
خ	5 or 7'	5 or kh
ذ	d' or dh	dh
ش	$ or sh	ch
ث	t' or th or 4	th
غ	4'	gh or 8
ع	3	3
ق	8	9

[9] mentioned that 81% of the Tunisian comments on Facebook used Romanized alphabet. In [10], a study was conducted on 1, 2 M social media Tunisian comments (16M words and 1M unique words) showed that 53% of the comments used Romanized alphabet while 34% used Arabic alphabet and 13% used

---

[2] Expensive.

script-switching. The study mentioned also that 87% of the comments based on Romanized alphabet are TUNIZI, while the rest are French and English. In [11], a survey was conducted to address the availability of Tunisian Dialect datasets. The authors concluded that all existing Tunisian datasets are using the Arabic alphabet or a code-switching script and that there is a lack of Tunisian Romanized alphabet annotated datasets, especially datasets to address the sentiment analysis task.

[12] presented a multidialectal parallel corpus of five Arabic dialects: Egyptian, Tunisian, Jordanian, Palestinian and Syrian to identify similarities and possible differences among them. The overlap coefficient results, representing the percentage of lexical overlap between the dialects, revealed that the Tunisian dialect has the least overlap with all other Arabic dialects. On the other hand, because of the specific characteristics of the Tunisian dialect, it shows phonological, morphological, lexical, and syntactic differences from other Arabic dialects such that Tunisian words might infer different syntactic information across different dialects; and consequently different meaning and sentiment polarity than Arabic words.

These results highlight the problem that the Tunisian Dialect is a low resource language and there is a need to create Tunisian Romanized alphabet datasets for analytical studies. Therefore, the existence of such a dataset would fill the gap for research purposes, especially in the sentiment analysis domain.

3 Tunisian Sentiment Analysis

In [13], a lexicon-based sentiment analysis system was used to classify the sentiment of Tunisian tweets. The author developed a Tunisian morphological analyzer to produce linguistic features and achieved an accuracy of 72.1% using the small-sized TAC dataset (800 Arabic script tweets).

[14] presented a supervised sentiment analysis system for Tunisian Arabic script tweets. With different bag-of-word schemes used as features, binary and multiclass classifications were conducted on a Tunisian Election dataset (TEC) of 3,043 positive/negative tweets combining MSA and Tunisian dialect. The support vector machine was found of the best results for binary classification with an accuracy of 71.09% and an F-measure of 63%.

In [3], the doc2vec algorithm was used to produce document embeddings of Tunisian Arabic and Tunisian Romanized alphabet comments. The generated embeddings were fed to train a Multi-Layer Perceptron (MLP) classifier where both the achieved accuracy and F-measure values were 78% on the TSAC (Tunisian Sentiment Analysis Corpus) dataset. This dataset combines 7,366 positive/negative Tunisian Arabic and Tunisian Romanized alphabet Facebook comments. The same dataset was used to evaluate Tunisian code-switching sentiment analysis in [15] using the LSTM-based RNNs model reaching an accuracy of 90%.

In [16], authors conducted a study on the impact on the Tunisian sentiment classification performance when it is combined with other Arabic based preprocessing tasks (Named Entities tagging, stopwords removal, common emoji recognition, etc.). A lexicon-based approach and the support vector machine model were used to evaluate the performances on the above-mentioned datasets (TEC and TSAC datasets).

In order to avoid the hand-crafted features labor-intensive task, syntax-ignorant n-gram embeddings representation composed and learned using an unordered composition function and a shallow neural model was proposed in [17]. The proposed model, called Tw-StAR, was evaluated to predict the sentiment on five Arabic dialect datasets including the TSAC dataset [3].

We observe that none of the existing Tunisian sentiment analysis studies focused on the Tunisian Romanized alphabet which is the aim of this paper.

Recently, a sentiment analysis Tunisian Romanized alphabet dataset was introduced in [18] as "TUNIZI". The dataset includes more than 9k Tunisian social media comments written only using Latin script was introduced in [8]. The dataset was annotated by Tunisian native speakers who described the comments as positive or negative. The dataset is balanced, containing 47% of positive comments and 53% negative comments.

Table 3. Positive and negative TUNIZI comments translated to English.

TUNIZI	English	Polarity
enti ghalia benesba liya	You are precious to me	Positive
nakrhek 5atrek cherrir	I hate you because you are wicked	Negative

Table 3 presents examples of TUNIZI dataset comments with the translation to English where the first comment was annotated as positive and the second as negative.

TUNIZI dataset statistics, including the total number of comments, number of positive comments, number of negative comments, number of words, and number of unique words are stated in Table 4.

Table 4. TUNIZI and TSAC-TUNIZI datasets statistics.

Dataset	#Words	#Uniq Words	#Comments	#Negative	#Positive	#Train	#Test
TUNIZI	82384	30635	9911	4679	5232	8616	1295
TSAC-TUNIZI	43189	17376	9196	3856	5340	7379	1817

For the purpose of this study, we filtered the TSAC dataset [3] to keep only Tunisian Romanized comments. The new dataset that we called TSAC-TUNIZI includes 9196 comments. The dataset is not balanced as the majority of the comments are positive (5340 comments). TSAC-TUNIZI dataset statistics are presented in Table 4.

4 Proposed Approach

In this section, we describe the different initial representations used, the hyper-parameters' values and the classifiers' architectures.

4.1 Initial Representations

In order to evaluate Tunisian Romanized sentiment analysis, three initial representation were used: word2vec, frWaC and multilingual BERT (M-BERT).

- Word2vec [20]: Word-level embeddings were used in order to represent words in a high dimensional space. We trained a word2vec 300-vector on the TUNIZI dataset.
- frWaC [21]: Word2vec pretrained on 1.6 billion French word dataset constructed from the Web. The use of the French pretrained word embedding is justified by the fact that most of the Tunizi comments present either French words or words that are inspired by French but in the Tunisian dialect. Examples of TUNIZI comments containing code switching are shown in Table 5.

Table 5. Examples of Tunizi comments switching-code.

Comment	Languages
je suis d'accord avec vous fi hkeyet ennou si 3andha da5l fel hkeya bouh	Tun, **Fr**
good houma déjà 9alou fih 11 7al9a	Tun, **Eng**
t5afou mnha **vamos** el curva sud y3ayech weldi bara a9ra	Tun, **Spa**

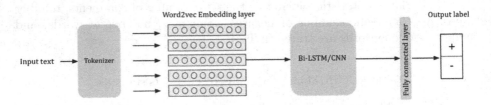

Fig. 1. Global architecture of the first proposed model

- Multilingual BERT (M-BERT) [22]: We decided to use the Bidirectional Encoder Representations from Transformers (BERT) as a contextual language model in its multilingual version as an embedding technique, that contains more than 10 languages including English, French and Arabic. Using the BERT tokenizer, we map words to their indexes and representations in the BERT embedding matrix. These representations are used to feed the classification models.

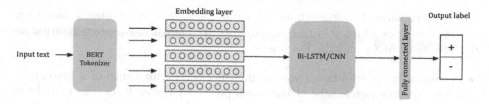

Fig. 2. Global architecture of the second proposed model

4.2 Classifiers

Based on the state of the art, RNNs and CNNs are considered to be more efficient for the sentiment analysis (SA) task. In this work, we experimented two classifiers, a Convolutional Neural Network (CNN) with different sizes of filters and a Bidirectional Long Short-Term Memory (Bi-LSTM), a variant of RNNs. As a consequence, we ended up with two different models. The first model uses word2vec or frWac as initial representations followed by Bi-LSTM or CNN classifier and a fully connected layer with a softmax activation function for prediction as shown in Fig. 1. The second model uses M-BERT as initial representation followed by Bi-LSTM or CNN classifier and a fully connected layer with a softmax activation function for prediction as shown in Fig. 2. The different hyper-parameters including number of filters, number of epochs and batch size for each embedding and classifier achieving the best performances are shown in Table 6. The number of epochs and the Batch size are equal to 3 and 16, respectively. The number of filters is equal to 200 for Word2vec representation. The best performances of frWac representation and M-BERT embeddings combined with CNN are achieved when the number of filters is equal to 100.

Table 6. Hyper-parameters used during the training phase.

Embedding	Classifier	Number of filters	Number of epochs	Batch size
Word2vec	CNN	200	3	16
frWaC	CNN	100	3	16
M-BERT	CNN	100	3	16
M-BERT	Bi-LSTM	-	3	16

5 Results and Discussion

All experiments were trained and tested on the two datasets presented in Table 4. Datasets were divided randomly for train and test without using any kind of data pre-processing technique. Models are trained according to the hyper-parameters in Table 6.

The performance of sentiment analysis models is usually evaluated based on standard metrics adopted in the state-of-the-art. They are: Accuracy referred in our results as ACC. and the F-score.

- Accuracy is the traditional way to measure the performance of a system. It represents the percentage of instances predicted correctly by the model for all class categories.
- F-score provides a measure of the overall quality of a classification model as it combines the precision and recall through a weighted harmonic mean.
  For our experiments two variants of F-score were used: the micro-averaging biased by class frequency (F1. micro) and macro-averaging taking all classes as equally important (F1. macro). This is important in the case of the TSAC-TUNIZI where classes are unbalanced.

5.1   TUNIZI Dataset Results

Table 7 reviews the sentiment classification performances for TUNIZI dataset. The word2vec representation trained on the TUNIZI dataset did not achieve better performances than frWaC representation trained on a French dataset. Indeed frWac representation achieved a 70,2% accuracy performance when word2vec representation was only 67,2%. This could be explained by the limited size of the TUNIZI dataset (82384 words) used to train word2vec representation compared to the French dataset (1.6 billion words) used to train frWac representation. Training word2vec on the limited size of the TUNIZI dataset does not include all the Tunisian words, hence the out of vocabulary (OOV) phenomenon. The pretrained French word2vec did not solve the problem of OOV, but since it was trained on a very large corpus it handled most of French words that are frequent in Tunizi comments.

Table 7 results suggest the outperformance of the M-BERT embeddings over those generated by word2vec and frWac. Indeed, M-BERT embeddings combined with CNN or Bi-LSTM performed better than word2vec embeddings for all performance measures. This could be explained by the ability of Multilingual BERT to overcome the problem of switch-coding comments presented previously in Table 5 since it includes more than 10 languages like English, French, and Spanish.

BERT tokenizer was created with a WordPiece model. First, it will check if the whole word exists in the vocabulary, if not, then it will break down the word into sub-words and repeat the process until it becomes divided into individual characters. Because of this, a word will always have its representation in the BERT embedding matrix, and the OOV phenomenon is partially overcome.

5.2   TSAC-TUNIZI Dataset Results

To confirm TUNIZI classification results, experiments were also performed on the TSAC-TUNIZI dataset with CNN and Bi-LSTM since they showed better

Table 7. Tunizi classification results.

Embedding	Classifier	Dataset	ACC	F1. micro	F1. macro
Word2vec	CNN	TUNIZI	67,2%	67,2%	67,1%
frWaC	CNN	TUNIZI	70,2%	70,2%	69%
M-BERT	Bi-LSTM	TUNIZI	76,3%	76,3%	74,3%
M-BERT	CNN	TUNIZI	**78,3%**	**78,3%**	**78,1%**

performances than word2vec embeddings. Table 8 shows the results of the proposed models on the TSAC-TUNIZI dataset. We can notice that the BERT embedding combined with the CNN leads to the best performance with a 93,2% of accuracy compared to 92,6% scored by Bi-LSTM. This is also the case for the F1.micro and F1. macro performances with values 93,2% and 93%, respectively.

F1. micro and F1. macro performances for CNN and Bi-LSTM are close even though the TSAC-TUNIZI dataset is unbalanced having dominant positive polarity.

Table 8. TSAC-TUNIZI classification results.

Embedding	Classifier	Dataset	Acc	F1. micro	F1. macro
M-BERT	Bi-LSTM	TSAC-TUNIZI	92,6%	92,6%	92,5%
M-BERT	CNN	TSAC-TUNIZI	**93,2%**	**93,2%**	**93%**

5.3 Discussion

Experiments on TUNIZI and TSAC-TUNIZI datasets showed that the bidirectional encoder representations from transformers (BERT) as a contextual language model in its multilingual version as an embedding technique outperforms word2vec representations. This could be explained by the code switching characteristic of the Tunisian dialect used on social media. Results suggest that M-BERT can overcome the out of vocabulary and code switch phenoma. This defines the M-BERT embeddings as expressive features of Tunisian dialectal content more than word2vec embeddings and without need to translate Tunisian Romanized alphabet into Arabic alphabet.

The CNN classifier performed better than the Bi-LSTM suggesting representation based Bi-LSTM did not benefit from the double exploration of the preceding and following contexts. This confirms the conclusion in [15] where LSTM representation outperformed Bi-LSTM representation.

Due to the non-existent work on Tunisian Romanized sentiment analysis, it wasn't possible to perform a comparison state of the art study. Nevertheless, the obtained performances of our proposed approach was further compared against the baseline systems that tackled the TSAC dataset as shown in Table 9.

Table 9. Compared classification results.

Model	Dataset	ACC	F-measure (%)
[3]	TSAC	78%	78%
[17]	TSAC	86.5%	86.2%
[15]	TSAC	90%	-
M-BERT+CNN	TSAC-TUNIZI	93.2%	93%
M-BERT+CNN	TSAC	**93.8%**	**93.8%**

Compared to the state-of-the-art applied on the tackled dataset, our results showed that CNN trained with M-BERT improved the performance over the baselines. As we can see in Table 9, with the proposed approach, the performed accuracy and F-measures outperformed the baselines performances.

6   Conclusion and Future Work

In this work, we have tackled the Tunisian Romanized alphabet sentiment analysis task. We have experimented two different word-level representations (word2vec and frWaC) and two deep neural networks (CNN and Bi-LSTM), without the use of any pre-processing step. Results showed that CNN trained with M-BERT achieved the best results compared to the word2vec, frWac and Bi-LSTM. This model could improve the performance over the baselines. Experiments and promising results achieved on the TUNIZI and TSAC-TUNIZI datasets helped us to better understand the nature of the Tunisian dialect and its specificities. This will help the Tunisian NLP community in further research activities not limited to the sentiment analysis task, but also in more complex NLP tasks.

A natural future step would involve releasing TunaBERT, a Tunisian version of the Bi-directional Encoders for Transformers (BERT) that should be learned on a very large and heterogeneous Tunisia dataset. The Tunisian language model can be applied to complex NLP tasks (natural language inference, parsing, word sense disambiguation). To demonstrate the value of building a dedicated version of BERT for Tunisian, we also plan to compare TunaBERT to the multilingual cased version of BERT.

References

1. Mulki, H., Haddad, H., Babaoglu, I.: Modern trends in Arabic sentiment analysis: a survey. Traitement Automatique des Langues **58**(3), 15–39 (2018)
2. Guellil, I. and Azouaou, F. and Valitutti, A.: English vs Arabic sentiment analysis: a survey presenting 100 work studies, resources and tools. In: 16th International Conference on Computer Systems and Applications, pp. 1–8. IEEE Computer Society Conference Publishing Services, Abu Dhabi (2019)

3. Medhaffar, S., Bougares, F., Estève, Y. and Hadrich-Belguith, L.: Sentiment analysis of Tunisian dialects: linguistic resources and experiments. In: 3rd Arabic Natural Language Processing Workshop, pp. 55–61. Association for Computational Linguistics, Valencia (2017)
4. Masmoudi, A., Khmekhem, M., Khrouf, M., Hadrich-Belguith, L.: Transliteration of Arabizi into Arabic script for Tunisian dialect. ACM Trans. Asian Low-Resour. Lang. Inf. Process. **19**(2), 1–21 (2019)
5. Qwaider, C., Chatzikyriakidis, S., Dobnik, S.: Can modern standard Arabic approaches be used for Arabic dialects? Sentiment analysis as a case study. In: 3rd Workshop on Arabic Corpus Linguistics, pp. 40–50. Association for Computational Linguistics, Cardiff (2019)
6. Stevens, P.B.: Ambivalence, modernisation and language attitudes: French and Arabic in Tunisia. J. Multiling. Multicult. Dev. **4**(2–3), 101–114 (1983)
7. Skandrani, H., Triki, A.: Trust in supply chains, meanings, determinants and demonstrations: a qualitative study in an emerging market context. Qual. Mark. Res. **14**(4), 391–409 (2011)
8. Fourati, C. and Messaoudi, A. and Haddad, H.: TUNIZI: a Tunisian Arabizi sentiment analysis Dataset. arXiv preprint arXiv:2004.14303
9. Younes, J., Achour, H., Souissi, E.: Constructing linguistic resources for the Tunisian dialect using textual user-generated contents on the social web. ICWE 2015. LNCS, vol. 9396, pp. 3–14. Springer, Cham (2015). https://doi.org/10.1007/978-3-319-24800-4_1
10. Abidi, K.: Automatic Building of Multilingual Resources from Social Networks: Application to Maghrebi Dialects (Doctoral Dissertation). Université de Lorraine, France (2019)
11. Younes, J., Achour, H., Souissi, E., Ferchichi, A.: Survey on corpora availability for the Tunisian dialect automatic processing. In: JCCO Joint International Conference on ICT in Education and Training, International Conference on Computing in Arabic, and International Conference on Geocomputing (JCCO: TICET-ICCA-GECO), pp. 1–7. IEEE, Tunis, Piscataway (2018)
12. Bouamor, H., Oflazer, K., Habash, N.: A multidialectal parallel corpus of Arabic. In: 9th International Conference on Language Resources and Evaluation (LREC-2014), pp. 1240–1245. European Language Resources Association (ELRA), Reykjavik (2014)
13. Karmani, N.: Tunisian Arabic Customer's Reviews Processing and Analysis for an Internet Supervision System (Doctoral dissertation). Sfax University, Sfax (2017)
14. Sayadi, K., Liwicki, M., Ingold, R., Bui, M.: Tunisian dialect and modern standard Arabic dataset for sentiment analysis: Tunisian election context. In: 2nd International Conference on Arabic Computational Linguistics, Konya (2016)
15. Jerbi, M., Achour, H., Souissi, E.: Sentiment analysis of code-switched tunisian dialect: Exploring RNN-based techniques. In: International Conference on Arabic Language Processing, pp. 122–131 (2019)
16. Mulki, H., Haddad, H., Bechikh Ali, C., Babaoglu, I.: Tunisian dialect sentiment analysis: a natural language processing-based approach. Computación y Sistemas **22**(4), 1223–1232 (2018)
17. Mulki, H., Haddad, H., Gridach, M., Babaoglu, I.: Syntax-ignorant N-gram embeddings for sentiment analysis of Arabic dialects. In: 4th Arabic Natural Language Processing Workshop, pp. 30–39. Association for Computational Linguistics, Florence (2019)
18. TUNIZI   dataset.   https://github.com/chaymafourati/TUNIZI-Sentiment-Analysis-Tunisian-Arabizi-Dataset

19. TSAC dataset. https://github.com/fbougares/TSAC
20. Mikolov, T., Sutskever, I., Chen, K., Corrado, G., Dean, J.: distributed representations of words and phrases and their compositionality. In: Advances in Neural Information Processing Systems, vol. 26, pp. 3111–3119. Curran Associates Inc., Lake Tahoe (2013)
21. French Word Embeddings. http://fauconnier.github.io
22. Devlin, J., Chang, M., Lee, K., Toutanova, K.: BERT: pre-training of deep bidirectional transformers for language understanding. In: Proceedings of the 2019 Conference of the North American Chapter of the Association for Computational Linguistics: Human Language Technologies, Volume 1 (Long and Short Papers, pp. 4171–4186. Association for Computational Linguistics, Minneapolis (2019)

Correction to: Pattern Recognition and Artificial Intelligence

Chawki Djeddi⬤, Yousri Kessentini⬤, Imran Siddiqi,
and Mohamed Jmaiel

Correction to:
C. Djeddi et al. (Eds.): *Pattern Recognition and Artificial*
Intelligence, **CCIS 1322,**
https://doi.org/10.1007/978-3-030-71804-6

The affiliations of the first two volume editors were incorrect. They were corrected to:

Chawki Djeddi
Larbi Tebessi University
Tebessa, Algeria

Yousri Kessentini
Digital Research Center of Sfax
Sfax, Tunisia

The updated version of the book can be found at
https://doi.org/10.1007/978-3-030-71804-6

Author Index

Printed in the United States
by Baker & Taylor Publisher Services